Religion and superstition
in Reformation Europe

D0145186

STUDIES IN EARLY MODERN EUROPEAN HISTORY

This exciting new series aims to publish
challenging and innovative research in all areas
of early modern continental history.
The editors are committed to encouraging work that
engages with current historiographical
debates, adopts an interdisciplinary
approach, or makes an original contribution
to our understanding of the period.

SERIES EDITORS
Professor Joseph Bergin, William G. Naphy and
Penny Roberts

Religion and superstition in Reformation Europe

EDITED BY HELEN PARISH
AND WILLIAM G. NAPHY

Manchester University Press

Manchester and New York

distributed exclusively in the USA by Palgrave

Copyright © Manchester University Press 2002

While copyright in the volume as a whole is vested in Manchester University Press, copyright in individual chapters belongs to their respective authors, and no chapter may be reproduced wholly or in part without the express permission in writing of both author and publisher.

Published by Manchester University Press
Oxford Road, Manchester M13 9NR, UK
and Room 400, 175 Fifth Avenue, New York, NY10010, USA
www.manchesteruniversitypress.co.uk

Distributed exclusively in the USA by
Palgrave, 175 Fifth Avenue, New York,
NY10010, USA

Distributed exclusively in Canada by
UBC Press, University of British Columbia, 2029 West Mall,
Vancouver, BC, Canada V6T 1Z2

British Library Cataloguing-in-Publication Data
A catalogue record is available from the British Library

Library of Congress Cataloging-in-Publication Data applied for

ISBN 0 7190 6157 1 *hardback*
       0 7190 6158 X *paperback*

First published 2002

10   09   08   07   06   05   04   03   02   10   9   8   7   6   5   4   3   2   1

BR 307
.R45
2002

ο 50183335

Typeset in Monotype Perpetua with Albertus
by Northern Phototypesetting Co Ltd, Bolton
Printed in Great Britain
by Bookcraft (Bath) Ltd, Midsomer Norton

Contents

Illustrations

Tables

Contributors

Maria Crăciun is Senior Lecturer in the Department of History at the Babes-Bolyai University of Cluj (Romania). She has written *Protestantism si ortodoxie in Moldova secolului al XVI-lea* (1996), several articles on the development of piety in Transylvania and Moldavia prior to and during the Reformation as well as editing (with Ovidiu Ghitta) *Ethnicity and Religion in Central and Eastern Europe* (1995), *Church and Society in Central and Eastern Europe* (1998), and (with Ovidiu Ghitta and Graeme Murdock) *Confessional Identity in East Central Europe* (2001).

Dr Bridget Heal is a research fellow at Newnham College (Cambridge). She recently completed her doctorate at the University of London, and is currently working on a book on Marian imagery and devotion in early modern Germany.

Dr Dale Walden Johnson served in the Department of History at Southern Wesleyan University for fourteen years. He joined the theological faculty at Erskine Theological Seminary in Due West, South Carolina in the autumn of 2001 as Professor of Church History. He is a contributor to *The Encyclopedia of North American History, the Calvin Theological Journal, the Sixteenth Century Journal* and *Church History*.

Dr Ute Lotz-Heumann is *wissenschaftliche Assistentin* in History at the Humboldt University in Berlin. She is the author of *Die doppelte Konfessionalisierung in Irland: Konflikt und Koexistenz im 16. und in der ersten Hälfte des 17. Jahrhunderts* (2000) and of several articles on the religious history of early modern Ireland and Europe. She is currently working on the social and cultural history of spas in early modern Germany.

Dr Peter Marshall is Senior Lecturer in History at the University of Warwick. His books include *The Catholic Priesthood and the English Reformation* (1994) *The Impact of the English Reformation* (1997) and *The Place of the Dead: Death and Remembrance in Late Medieval and Early Modern Europe* (2000).

Dr Maxwell-Stuart is an Honorary Lecturer in the School of History at St Andrews. His books include: *The Occult in Early Modern Europe; Witchcraft: A History; Witchcraft in Europe and the New World, 1400-1800; Martin Del Rio: Investigations into Magic*; and *Satan's Conspiracy, Magic and Witchcraft in Sixteenth-Century Scotland*.

Dr William G. Naphy is Senior Lecturer in History at the University of Aberdeen. He is the author of *Calvin and the Consolidation of the Genevan Reformation* (1994), *Plagues, Poisons, and Potions: Plague-Spreading Conspiracies in the Western Alps* (2001) as well as co-author of *The Black Death and the History of Plagues* (2000) and co-editor of *Fear in Early Modern Society* (1997).

Dr Eric W. Nelson is Assistant Professor in History at the University of Southern Mississippi. He is the author of 'Defining the Fundamental Laws of France: The Proposed First Article of the Third Estate at the French Estates General of 1614' (*EHR*, November 2000) and is currently completing a monograph on the Society of Jesus in France.

Dr Jason Nye completed his doctorate at the University of St Andrews in 2000 and is now an independent scholar.

Dr Helen Parish is Lecturer in History at the University of Reading. She is the author of *Clerical Marriage and the English Reformation. Precedent, Policy and Practice* (2000), and a number of articles on early modern religious and cultural history.

Dr Luc Racaut is Lecturer in History at the Crichton Campus of the University of Glasgow. He is the author of the forthcoming *Hatred in Print: Catholic Propaganda and Protestant Identity during the French Wars of Religion*.

Introduction

HELEN PARISH AND WILLIAM G. NAPHY

> It is superstitious to expect any effect from anything, when such an effect cannot be produced by natural causes, by divine institution, or by the ordination or approval of the Church. (Council of Malines, 1607)

A comparable modern definition describes superstition as either a 'belief that events can be influenced by certain acts and circumstances that have no demonstrable connection with them' or 'an idea or practice based on this [belief]' or 'a belief that is held by a number of people but without foundation'.[1] Such beliefs, it has been suggested, are of their very nature irrational, mere 'fragmentary remains of forgotten faiths, rituals, and systems of thought, left behind when these faded from human minds'.[2] These fragments of past faith, ritual and thought, it seems, are always with us, testimony to the enduring capacity of popular beliefs and practices to survive in a developing and changing intellectual and cultural climate. While today many may still prefer to walk around a ladder rather than beneath it, or bemoan the breaking of a mirror, fewer perhaps affirm with any conviction the existence of a sacred or supernatural power inherent in these objects or actions. A passive remnant of times past, superstitions are (for most) harmless and ineffectual activities or beliefs, constructed around the fundamentally flawed premise that natural objects and human actions have, of themselves, the capacity to affect the lives and surroundings of individuals and communities.

Yet historically the term 'superstition' has carried a less benign meaning. Used either to denounce the beliefs of others, or retrospectively to condemn ignorance and falsehood in past cultures, 'superstition' entered the historical and particularly the religious discourse as a pejorative and all-inclusive description of the beliefs and values of one's opponents. Classical writers used the term *superstitio* to denounce what seemed to be worthless or barbarous religious practices.[3] Likewise, Christian missionaries either adopted a similar stance when representing the beliefs of the pagan societies, or permitted popular pagan customs to survive in order that the new faith might be more readily planted.[4] Fifteenth-century writers saw in contemporary ritual evidence that the 'pristine' worship of the past had become tarnished, in the corrosion of orthodoxy by popular practice.[5] In the turmoil of the Protestant and Catholic Reformations, 'superstition' came to be the embodiment of the 'other', of the despised, the defective, the diabolical and the deluded, with which there could be no compromise, and no room for debate.

In traditional theological understandings of 'superstition', the error had a twofold meaning. First, any unauthorised, erroneous or excessive devotions to God were deemed to be superstitious. Second, any religious observance which did not have God as its object was superstitious. Keeping these definitions in mind, there is a very real sense in which the Catholic denunciation of Protestant beliefs as heresy was an illustration of the term 'superstition' interpreted in the broadest sense. 'Heresy' was perhaps the more damning term, implying a conscious deviation from the truth, while 'superstition' might include error through ignorance. However, there was valuable polemical capital to be made from the equation of superstition with heretical doctrine, not least because 'heresy' focused the polemical attack much more squarely on the beliefs and doctrines of the Protestants, while superstition was more closely focused on actions and modes of worship.

The term 'superstition' rapidly found its way into the evangelical armoury. From the first stirrings of the Protestant Reformation, evangelicals were convinced that 'superstition' existed and that it threatened the very foundations of Christianity. The sheer volume of polemic devoted to the topic has encouraged historians to look more closely at what might conveniently be termed 'popular religion', and consider more carefully the conclusion that the Reformation was an enterprise devoted to the education of the laity and the eradication of deviant or ill-informed belief.[6] The Protestant assault on superstition had as its targets some of the most visible and tangible components of late medieval Catholic theology and devotion, sacraments and sacramentals. Evangelical theologians and polemicists saw superstition in the 'externals' of Catholic piety, in the multiplication of rituals in the church, in the repetition of a set number of masses, and especially masses for the dead. Belief in transubstantiation was 'superstitious', and Heinrich Bullinger argued that the basic belief that words and utterances might have any practical or material effect was superstition.[7] The lighting of candles, the recitation of a fixed number of prayers, the consecration of physical objects and their use inside and outside the church was 'superstitious'. Divine power was exercised by God alone, and the church, its priests, and its holy objects and places were no more *loci* of the sacred or supernatural than any other. All this amounted to a potent critique of the 'magic of the medieval church', which, in Keith Thomas's enduring account, fell prey to the Protestant Reformation, with its determination to dispense with superstition and ecclesiastical magic, and undermine the notion that the church and its priesthood acted as a repository of supernatural power.[8]

However none of these applications of the label come close to offering a definition of superstition as rigid as that from the Oxford American Dictionary set out above. In many cases, it would appear that 'superstition' was no more than a polemical word that broadly meant 'the practices and beliefs of others with which we disagree'. Used in this manner, 'superstition' has a meaning alien to modern usage and, indeed, to thoughtful usage at the time. Moreover, there is also the danger that the constant application of the word by early modern Protestant polemicists to Catholicism may have led later historians to use the word as a type of shorthand for pre-Reformation Catholic practices or late medieval and early modern popular religion. Again, if the word is being used with these definitions in mind then its usage is, at best, misleading and negative and, at worst, inaccurate and polemical. If one takes as a modern starting point the idea that superstition refers to 'an irrational, non-causal and non-demonstrable connection between certain events, words, and actions and certain results', then one can begin to examine Protestant belief and practice, to ascertain to what extent they were as likely to engage in 'superstition' as their opponents. However, the more important question is to discern to what extent the use of so critical and subjective a term as superstition has a place in modern historiographical discourse. Many modern atheists and secular humanists might be inclined to label all religious belief and practice, in every age, a type of superstition and, thereby, render the word almost meaningless for historical discourse.

This final point highlights the real problem in discussing superstition. The term, by its very nature and meaning, can only really be applied by an external viewer. No group believing or doing something is likely to admit that there is no reason for its actions or beliefs. Hence, instead of dismissing the beliefs and practices of earlier ages, opposing denominations, or even our own times with the simple and simplistic vocabulary of superstition, it might be more useful and honest to admit that people usually have a reason for their actions and beliefs. Once the practices and beliefs of pre-Reformation Catholicism, late medieval / early modern popular religion, Tridentine Catholicism, and Protestantism are freed from the label of superstition, an attempt can be made to understand the motivations and preoccupations that encouraged individuals and communities to believe or behave in a certain way. However, behind the question of what is or is not superstition lies a more interesting issue. The recognition that the term superstition was essentially judgemental and pejorative need not preclude any attempt to identify the beliefs and practices that were deemed superstitious by polemical writers in the era of the Reformation, but it must also require a more detailed analysis of attempts to rationalise and defend the very devotional activities that were under attack. It is not the intention in this volume simply to present a list of 'superstitious' activities, culled from the works of writers across the spectrum of early modern religious practice, but rather to focus upon the multiple uses and abuses of the term superstition, and the circumstances of its employment by Catholic and Protestant alike in religious debate. The essays that follow consider not only the polemical value of accusations of superstition, but also the efforts of individuals and institutions to justify the continued presence of controversial beliefs and practices, either by directly confronting their critics, and indeed promoting such beliefs more vigorously by ignoring the issue entirely, or by deflecting discussion into the realms of heresy and doctrinal error. In the hands of Catholic and Protestant writers, the question of superstition was not a minor debate over inconsequential matters, but rather an opportunity to engage in a penetrating attack on fundamental matters of faith and doctrine, truth and error.

Yet despite the diametric opposition between true and false religion set out in the propaganda of the Reformation, recent scholarship reminds us that it would be wrong to suggest that the battle-lines of the debate were as firmly drawn. Stuart Clark's authoritative study of the supernatural encourages us to take heed of harmony among the voices of Catholic and Protestant writers on magic and demonology, and Euan Cameron has questioned the underlying assumption that even the churchmen knew where to draw the line between religion and superstition.[9] The continued practice of exorcism among Reformed congregations, for example, proved problematic, given assertions both before and during the Reformation that the practice was implicitly demonic, and the abolition of the theology of purgatory left evangelicals with the very real problem of explaining post-Reformation apparitions.[10] Catholic writers, well aware of ambiguity over the meaning and definition of superstition, reasserted the validity and the efficacy of sanctioned ecclesiastical rites, while condemning their critics by alleging that there was scant difference between the medieval cult of the saints and the reverence with which Protestant martyrs and leaders were treated by their followers, between the miracles of the saints and the providential acts of God wrought for the benefit of his people and to the detriment of his enemies.[11] The reluctance to concede to evangelicals that the medieval heritage of the church was in any way magical or superstitious constrained Catholic writers by encouraging a defence of ecclesiastical remedies and continuity of faith and practice across the centuries, alongside an attack on unorthodox or unsanctioned practices within the church.

However, in theory it was desirable, even possible, to draw a line between religion and superstition, or at least to set out which popular practices might be proscribed and which prescribed.[12] Catholic polemicists generally fell back upon the twofold definition formulated by St Thomas Aquinas, which identified both excessive and inappropriate worship of the true God, and the giving of correct service to a false god as superstitious.[13] Within the boundaries of 'excessive worship', however, lay any number of practices that embodied the adaptive capacity of popular religion and the readiness of the faithful to divert the rites of the church towards the fulfilment of necessary practical needs in the community. Hence the category of 'vain observances' could include the general expectation of supernatural effects from natural objects or signs, but also the belief that certain saints' days might be either propitious or inauspicious, that holy water removed from church might help to secure a bountiful harvest, or that prayers recited backwards could be used as a potent weapon against an enemy. Pedro Ciruelo set out a basic definition; if the actions or words intended to bring about an event lacked the natural or supernatural capacity to produce the desired result, then such acts were superstitious, vain and diabolical.[14] Misplaced trust in quasi-liturgical formulae, the use of consecrated objects for purposes other than that which was intended, and the popular appropriation of ecclesiastical ritual threatened the internal consistency of the authoritative definition of 'superstitions' offered at Malines, as those practices of which the church disapproved.[15] In practical terms, 'superstition' was an elastic concept, which could be at once narrowly defined to exclude individual practice and stretched to capacity to include a wide spectrum of beliefs and actions.

Bridget Heal's essay, which opens this volume, reminds us that 'vain observances' were, like 'superstitious practices', in the eye of the beholder. To critics of the cult of the saints, and especially Marian devotion, the retention of any prominent role for the Virgin smacked of superstition. However, the preservation of familiar imagery was seen to be justified not by reference to tradition, or by pragmatism, but rather by a radical adjustment in the rationale for such representations, which should remind us how easily a practice or belief can be retained if a new meaning is supplied. Reinterpretation was just as valid a 'conversion' methodology as replacement. This syncretic approach would have made sense to St Augustine and the missionaries of post-Conquest Latin America. However, as with 'vain' and 'superstition', 'syncretic' tends most often to be a dismissive and disparaging word. Despite its connotations, it is also often very successful.

These word games remind the reader of the ease with which this generic term 'superstition' slipped into Reformation debate and dialogue, belying the complexity of its meaning, and the virtual impossibility of reaching a watertight definition of what was (or was not) a superstitious act. However, 'superstition' was still condemned with vigour, and the energy expended in the obliteration of superstitious practice from religion was justified by the apparent conjunction between the superstitious, the magical, and the diabolic. The medieval church had encouraged the perception that misfortune could be attributed to the powers of the devil, and writers on both sides of the religious divide during the Reformation were prepared to concede that the devil did indeed have the capacity to work wonders. Thus where superstition attributed a power or efficacy to natural objects and words that they did not of themselves possess, or that God did not provide, the effect expected was not miraculous, but demonic. Such a stance would justify the nature of the clerical assault on lay religious practice suggested by Jean Delumeau, yet even where the ultimate authority to condemn or condone rested with the church, it would be erroneous to assume that the assault on superstition was led by a militant clergy against an intransigent and ignorant laity.[16] The authors of the *Malleus Malefi-carum*, for example, assumed that it was impossible for a natural object to have a supernatural effect, yet still condoned the practice of processing with the host to secure preservation from a storm.[17] As Euan Cameron suggests of the late medieval church, 'to the endless frustration of the theologians, "religion" and "superstition" stubbornly refused to remain clearly separate, despite the intellectual effort expended in forcing them into different compartments'.[18]

The best examples in this volume of the confusion of religion (*religio*) and superstition (*superstitio*) are to be found in the essays of Dale Johnson and Ute Lotz-Heumann. In both cases, they show the tension in Protestantism around revelation (*revelatio*) and authority (*magisterium*). Who spoke for God and how? Was the Bible (*sola scriptura*) really the final word of God to man? The revelatory nature of Old Testament prophecy was problematic for many Protestant preachers, and the distinctively Protestant appropriation of the image of the prophet is discussed by Johnson and Lotz-Heumann. Knox, like his fellow Protestant reformers, argued against post-biblical revelation, yet cast himself in the role of God's prophet in Scotland, speaking the word of God, and endowed with the ability to interpret the word of God in nature and in history. Supporters of Knox accepted his position as a prophet cast in the biblical mould, and as Johnson demonstrates, Knox's Catholic opponents were also willing to concede a prophetic gift to the reformer, but only a gift which had its origins in witchcraft, and not in divine approbation for the Reformation. The possibility of prophecy was not questioned but rather the source of inspiration called into question. In claiming such divinely inspired powers, Johnson argues, Knox was out of line with other Protestant reformers, but theory and practice in the era of the reformation were not always commensurate, and the understanding of the place of Protestant preachers in the prophetic and revelatory tradition was complex.

Despite the apparent contradiction between the rejection of post-biblical revelation and the continued presence of prophets in the church, it is clear that even the leaders of the Protestant Reformation were not always able to control the interpretations that were placed on their utterances. Lotz-Heumann's essay demonstrates the malleability and utility of 'prophecy' in social and political situations supposedly far removed from the pulpit. Popular belief in prophecy had the potential to shape the reputation of the heroes of the Reformation, and Archbishop Ussher was no exception. Although Ussher never claimed prophetic power, the most influential biography of the archbishop, published in 1656, cast him firmly in the mould of a Protestant prophet. Later pamphlets made this image more explicit still and subsequent editions, rather than questioning the validity of prophecy, made the predictions attributed to Ussher more specific, and tied to demonstrable historical events. Ussher's words were manipulated to meet the political and religious needs of the age, and defenders of prophecy by Protestant divines argued that the fact that Old Testament prophets and 'holy men' in the Bible were able to predict the future made it entirely reasonable for people to expect that God's servants in their day would also be able to warn God's people of future events. The repeated publication of extracts from Bernard's work certainly suggests a popular enthusiasm for vernacular literature on prophecy, and a reluctance on the part of church leaders to attribute such popular interest to superstition or error. Bernard and his successors were clearly aware of contemporary debates within Protestantism over the nature of prophecy, and the deliberate portrayal of Ussher as prophet and preacher certainly owed much to earlier representations of Luther. Recent work on early modern popular prophecy has largely ignored ecclesiastical figures such as Ussher, but Lotz-Heumann's essay here not only reveals the extent to which the changing reputation of Ussher was indicative of diverse of attitudes towards prophets and prophecy but also highlights the variety of forms of prophetic discourse in post-Reformation Ireland.[19]

The continued presence of prophets in the Reformed churches provides a useful corrective to the assumption that the Reformation precipitated a seismic shift in attitudes to revelation and the supernatural. Early modern Protestants, along with all their contemporaries, lived in a world intimately connected with super-, supra- and preter-natural realms. Witches, demons and angels were real and peopled the natural world; magic was possible and was employed by various people for good or ill. Yet evangelicals faced a dilemma when confronted by the nature of the reality into which they had been born but about which they now believed radically different things. Ghosts, apparitions and poltergeists made sense in the traditional world-view and yet Protestant theology and theory rejected them. Peter Marshall's essay on post-Reformation ghosts highlights the potential conflict between what Protestants thought they knew about reality from their experiences (and those of others) and what their theology told them about that same reality. P. G. Maxwell-Stuart advances this discussion by examining exorcism, poltergeists, and the role of ill-will in affecting nature. His essay shows that despite the best theology, Protestants were constantly forced to rely upon a more 'Catholic' world-view when facing such forces, and in dealing with practices that appeared either magical or superstitious.

This simply serves to reinforce the point that one of the most significant and contested terms in the history of early modern popular culture, especially religious culture, is also one of the most difficult to define. What, in the sixteenth and seventeenth century, was 'superstition'; where might it be found, what should be done when 'superstition' was encountered, and indeed, how might the individual know if he was, inadvertently or deliberately, supporting it? As the dividing lines of the Reformation were drawn and redrawn, so definitions of what was and was not acceptable in the field of popular religious practice became more rigid, although this need not mean that they were necessarily more consistent. In part, this is perhaps because it was easier to criticise an opponent, to level accusations of doctrinal error and ill-informed credulity, than it was to come up with a popular, effective and watertight definition of what was proper and acceptable. It is always easier to shout what one rejects than to dare to declare what one supports. In the polemical world of the Reformation, where debates were dictated by sharp dichotomies, and where the language of discourse could be violently accusatory, it is easy to see why such definitions would rapidly be made and, just as rapidly changed. Faced with the full panoply of traditional Catholic practice and theology, evangelical reformers were quick to point the finger at those things that they liked and those that they did not. Building upon the foundations of religious vocabulary laid in Reformation debate, historians have often been all too willing to use the same kind of terminology to describe the beliefs and, particularly, the practices of the medieval church, to caricature the conduct and piety of the laity in particular, and to argue that elements of magic within medieval Christianity suggest that the main function of the church was to offer access not to heaven but to the mysterious supernatural powers that might affect material life.

But how can the historian begin to describe or categorise the beliefs of the laity, and mark out those features of popular religion that deserve to be seen as superstitious? The best part of a century ago, James Frazer attempted to set out the relationship between the supernatural and religion, as part of what became a twelve-volume survey of the progression of man from magic, through religious belief, to scientific thought.[20] As Frazer indicated, any attempt to separate magic from religion, and compare or contrast the two, must be contingent upon a set of assumptions over the nature of religion itself. Frazer concluded that all a writer can do is to state what he means by the term 'religion' and then use that term consistently throughout his work. The picture of early modern religious practice in The Golden Bough is less than positive, characterised by the assumption that popular piety was based around ignorance rather than intellectual understanding, creating a faith that was informed more by the charm than by the catechism. Although trends in historical scholarship have served to modify this assessment in recent decades, there is still an element of Frazer in some approaches to the study of popular religion, not least where local variations in practice are seen to be coterminous with the survival and passive acceptance of superstition.

Thus the question of the relationship, or conflict, between magic and religion in the early modern period is still a challenging one. The purpose of this collection is to examine the representation and redefinition of 'superstition' during the Reformation through the eyes of historians, but more particularly through the eyes of those who participated in religious practices on both sides of the confessional divide, those who called for change, those who sought to define and identify true religion, and those who attempted by propaganda and persuasion to change the beliefs and practices of the peoples of Europe. Contributions from scholars with very different geographical, chronological and conceptual approaches to the topic make a substantial contribution to the ongoing debate over the nature and character of the Protestant and Catholic Reformations in Britain and Europe, and open up the possibility of a wide-ranging discussion of the consequences of religious division across the breadth of early modern European culture.

Keith Thomas's magisterial work on *Religion and the Decline of Magic* continues to exert a powerful influence over the way in which the relationship between religion, popular belief and magic has been discussed and debated by scholars and students. Thomas concluded that in medieval England, as much as in the primitive societies studied by modern anthropologists and sociologists, the dividing line between magic and religion cannot be firmly delineated.[21] Jean Delumeau's *Catholicism between Luther and Voltaire* suggests that there was something unavoidable about this intermingling of magic and religion among the beliefs of the laity, given the overall lack of informed knowledge of the dogma of the church, and the ever present fear of harm, illness, misfortune and death that seemed to characterise early modern lay culture.[22] When confronted by popular religious practice in early modern Europe, particularly its functional aspects, this kind of clear-cut distinction is more problematic, and the subtle nuances of the vocabulary of debate are not always reflected in the intermingling of magic, religion and superstition at a local level. There is often a tendency to assume that orthodoxy lay in the hands of the church, and that the laity, for whatever reason, either passively accepted or distorted this to fit their needs, often material rather than spiritual. Yet Bernd Moeller's work on pre-Reformation piety in Germany suggests that it was the religious practice of the laity rather than the clergy that was the most vibrant, while Robert Swanson has pointed to the importance of diversity within the overall unity of late medieval piety.[23] The church was not a rigid monolithic institution before the

Reformation, and local variations are often more instructive than doctrinal assertions in a study of religious practice across Christendom.

The early modern cosmos was governed by often unpredictable super-natural forces, and in the drive to control, understand, and influence this mag-ical universe, the genesis of popular rituals lay in the realms of magic, religion and superstition.[24] When lay-folk attempted to remove the consecrated host from the church after mass, in order to bless their house or secure a better har-vest, were they engaging in an over-enthusiastic act of basically orthodox piety, or were they turning the central rite of the church into an essentially magical, wonder-working act? We might be tempted to conclude that it was the latter: that any activity predicated upon the assumption that a material object might act as a repository of supernatural power betrays a flawed understanding of reli-gion and a tendency to treat the church simply as a means of gaining access to the world of the supernatural. But the fourteenth-century sermon collection and instruction for parish priests, John Mirc's *Festial*, reminded its pious audi-ence that anyone who saw a priest carrying the consecrated host would be well provided for that day, and would be in no danger of sudden death or blindness, claiming none other than St Augustine as its authority.[25]

Recent debate over success and failure in the Reformation, and the capac-ity of churchmen to change the beliefs of their flock, has raised the issue of the extent to which the conflicts of the sixteenth century opened up a fracture between the piety of past generations and that of the present.[26] Considerable effort has been made to assess the influence of 'orthodox' or official religion upon the beliefs of the majority, and to measure the spread of religious change in terms of success and failure – from the debate over 'Reformation from above'/'Reformation from below' among historians of the English church, to theories of acculturation advanced by historians of early modern popular culture in France. The work of David Cressy and Ronald Hutton has enhanced our understanding of the process by which the rituals and calendars of the pre-Reformation church were challenged and adapted in the search for a new Pro-testant culture, yet often preserved locally, despite the best efforts of the proponents of the Reformation.[27] Bob Scribner's study of the 'incombustible Luther' has become the touchstone for studies of the common ground on which the pre-Reformation cult of the saints and the post-Reformation veneration of Protestant heroes might stand.[28] Similar themes have been explored by Scribner and Trevor Johnson, in a recent collection of essays on popular religion in Germany and Central Europe. Scribner and Johnson highlight the importance of a better understanding of the extent to which popular religious practice was adopted and adapted by the Protestant Reformation, and of the interaction between official doctrine and magic, witchcraft and lay religion. Their appeal to scholars to be sensitive to context and local experience in the study of early modern religion has been heeded by contributors to this volume, extended across a broader geography, and augmented by more obvious emphasis upon the vocabulary of polemical debate alongside popular religious observances.[29]

It is clear that traditional piety and observances did not disappear overnight, and even the most rigorous evangelical assault on popular 'superstition' could not guarantee that these beliefs and practices would not resurface in an altered form, either spontaneously, or even as part of the effort to ground the new reformed faith in the minds of the people. This tension between survival and revival should encourage a reassessment of the process by which popular religion interacted with the official faith of the church(es), as well as a greater appreciation of the willingness of post-Reformation writers and preachers to use a common vocabulary to disseminate their message, and even to develop a similar repertoire of activities to propagate and inculcate a new sense of cultural identity. Given the centrality of the assault on superstition to the ideology and the implementation of the Protestant and Catholic Reformations, the extent to which such 'superstitions' were obliterated from the religious and cultural cosmos of the people of early modern Europe is clearly pivotal to such an analysis. Equally enlightening is an analysis of the degree to which both traditional practices, and new mythologies generated by the heat of religious conflict, were simply interpreted or represented anew in order that they might be more palatable and acceptable. In other words, did the reformers, whether Catholic or Protestant, succeed in banishing 'superstition', or did they simply redefine the term, in order that it might be used as a simple and efficient shorthand for the beliefs and practices of opponents which were deemed abhorrent or repugnant? The diversity of responses to the question of superstition from contributors to this collection suggests that the search for continuities as well as discontinuities between traditional and reformed practice is vital to a full understanding of the processes of religious conflict and change in the early modern period, especially in the context of the distinctive chronology and geography of the challenges posed by polemical debate and division. Evidence of a shared vocabulary of superstition is indicative of the extent to which Protestantism and post-Tridentine Catholicism can be seen to be in pursuit of the same quarry, albeit in a different guise, and of the value of a consideration of mutation and exploitation, rather than a concentration on destruction and innovation.

These themes are explored in more depth in this volume by P. G. Maxwell-Stuart, Luc Racaut and Eric Nelson. Maxwell-Stuart and Racaut's contributions challenge the reader to jettison any easy association of Protestantism with rationalism and Catholicism with superstition. In his essay on astrology and eschatology, Racaut shows that both Protestants and Catholics used charges of superstitious use of the supernatural against their opponents.

Both accepted a range of practices and 'sciences' which would today be dismissed as superstitious. In addition, both were able to differentiate between types of astrology and eschatological belief that were acceptable and unacceptable. Neither was more or less inclined to use these tools in practice or to employ them polemically to hurt their opponents. Finally, echoing the essays of Lotz-Heumann and Johnson, he discusses the complex and ambivalent attitude that most confessions had towards prophecy and the prophetic tradition.

Maxwell-Stuart's survey of early modern demonology identifies significant parallels in Catholic and Protestant attitudes to magic. Natural events, climatic abnormalities, and monstrous births continued to be debated and interpreted in the aftermath of the Reformation, and the correct understanding of demonic possession and exorcism was continually contested by individuals seeking to draw the line between sanctioned practice and popular misconceptions. Despite the fact that demonological writing was very much part of heated doctrinal and pastoral controversy, an examination of the works of François Perreaud and Lambert Daneau suggests that below the surface level of propaganda there was still a shared worldview evident in Protestant and Catholic writing. In light of these debates, it would be wrong, he suggests, to assume that Protestant and Catholic were fundamentally different 'religions' in the aftermath of the Reformation, or to exclude the possibility that even where the dividing lines were drawn – such as over the issue of superstition – there might be no 'seepage' across the borders.

Echoing these examinations of the parallels between Catholic and Protestant language on demonology and astrology, Nelson's analysis of the growth of the 'Black Legend' sheds light upon the formation of new myths, legends and superstitions as communities re-evaluated their relationship with their surroundings during periods of upheaval and transformation. The 'Black Legend' emerged as Protestant writers sought to explain the apparent failures of the Reformation by reference to a Catholic enemy, described in the language of popular myth and legend. The traditional attribution of disorder and disruption to forces of evil allowed evangelical polemicists to cast the Jesuits as the most modern and menacing manifestation of such powers in the life of the church, drawing upon tales of witches and fairies that would have a resonance in the popular imagination. However, the dependence of the Protestant mythologising of the Jesuits upon a vocabulary that was shared and exploited by the Jesuits' Catholic opponents was reinforced by the degree of interaction between critics of the Jesuits on both sides of the confessional divide. The myth of the Jesuits built upon the conviction that demons and devils were a real and potent force, suggesting that just as the devil and his minions could create deceptive illusions, so could those other servants of Satan, the Jesuits. Protestant communities found a way to use the imagery and terminology of witchcraft and demonology to new and great effect just as these concepts were being questioned in their older forms. While their fears of the Jesuits may have had some basis in reality, the interpretation placed on Jesuit successes was largely derived from a cultural lexicon shared with Catholics. Thus, although their polemic was targeted towards the centre of post-Tridentine Catholic renewal, the terminology that was used suggests that the two churches could, if nothing else, interact in the creation of a new myth.

Maria Crăciun's essay serves as an interesting corrective to the Jesuit legend. She presents an image of a Jesuit mission which was confused and confined in its relationship with Protestants. Rather than being omnipotent, all-pervasive and deceitfully effective, the Jesuits were only really successful – or inclined to work – in areas where Catholicism had a measure of noble protection and support. She shows the confusion in the Jesuit mind about the status of Protestants. Were they simply deluded 'lost sheep' or were they heretics? The Jesuits were obviously able to engage and attack Protestantism at a theoretical and theological level but it is insightful that they also chose to use ritual to shore up Catholicism. For many early modern Protestants, 'superstitious practice' was a polemical shorthand for 'traditional Catholic practice', yet the Jesuit response in these Hungarian lands was to rely heavily on these practices. Crăciun's study explores, in a different context, the issues raised by Heal's analysis of the status of the cult of the Virgin in post-Reformation Nuremberg. Just as the Nuremberg council perceived in the imagery of the Virgin not superstition but a powerful pedagogic tool, so the Jesuit missions saw the traditional rites and rituals of the church, grounded in scriptural teaching and ecclesiastical tradition, not as a superstitious weakness, but as the most solid defence against the opponents of Catholicism. The behaviour of the Jesuits amounted to a determined rejection of the Protestant polemic and an endorsement of traditional practice as the best bulwark against innovation. Although this was a strong and, as Crăciun shows, a successful defensive strategy it did not amount to an effective assault on Protestantism. Clearly, in Hungarian lands, the Jesuits rejected the idea that 'the best defence is a strong offence' and, instead, worked on the principle that, in the face of the near collapse of Catholicism, 'the Faith of our Fathers' and 'Holy Mother Church' were rallying cries that would sustain the faithful until a more propitious opportunity for an assault on Protestantism might present itself.

The Jesuits were not alone in perceiving the rituals and the sacraments of the Catholic church as the best defence against new Protestant worship and theologies. Indeed, despite the fact that many traditional beliefs and practices, including prayer for the dead in purgatory, auricular confession, the veneration of the saints and the adoration of the consecrated host, were the prime targets for the evangelical assault on superstition, it was these aspects of piety and devotion that Catholic propagandists and clergy regarded as the most effective bulwark against Protestantism. As Jason Nye demonstrates in his study of post-Reformation Catholicism in Rottweil, the formation of a strong sense of Catholic identity, built from the very materials discarded and condemned by evangelicals, was regarded by both secular and ecclesiastical authority as the most effective defence against the infiltration of Protestant ideas into the city. The preservation of religious unity in the city was accomplished in part by the vilification of Protestantism, but in the main by the promotion of traditional theology and practice from the pulpit. Participation in the sacraments and rites of the church was argued to be necessary not only for the individual soul but for the welfare of the civic community, encouraging the laity to engage in an active piety that reinforced a strongly Catholic identity for the city. The Protestant polemical application of the label 'superstition' to key elements in this Catholic identity had failed to persuade the city and its people that traditional practices were dangerous or erroneous, and the use of ritual as a pedagogic tool in Rottweil was no less successful than evangelical attempts to use the written word of the Bible or catechism to educate the faithful. Nye is more positive in his assessment of the effectiveness of this strategy than Crăciun: in Rottweil at least, the active promotion of Catholic theology and ritual in the second half of the sixteenth century may well have discouraged further evangelical efforts in the area.

The essays by Nye and Crăciun provide a salutary reminder of the potential for stark contrast between Catholics and Protestants on the issue of superstition. For Protestants, the term had little substance beyond providing a polemical shorthand for Catholic faith and practice. As the bulk of the essays in this volume demonstrate, it was certainly not a concept that allowed for introspective analysis of one's own faith and practice. However, despite its apparent convenience as an all-encompassing term of reference, 'superstition' does seem to have been a relatively toothless weapon of attack. The Catholic response, as seen in Rottweil and in Transylvania, was to ignore the accusation entirely. The priests, Jesuits, and lay authorities made no attempt to refute the charges of superstition. Nor did they shy away from the beliefs and practices singled out by Protestant polemic as predominately superstitious. Rather, these very elements of Catholicism are accentuated by the church's officials and become the litmus test of the faith. Post-Tridentine Catholicism upheld the saints and their miracles, and in Rottweil and in Transylvania a Catholic was defined by his or her belief in transubstantiation and Purgatory. This would seem to suggest that the Catholic church was unperturbed by the accusation of superstition, had little faith in its ability to persuade, and felt that the most effective response was simply to educate its laity in the veracity and validity of Catholic doctrine.

Since Protestants continued to levy the accusation, and spectacularly failed to turn the analysis on their own practices, one must wonder what function 'superstition' as a polemical device fulfilled for them. It might be argued that rather acting as an offensive weapon, the word was more effective as a defensive tool to reinforce Protestant belief in the truth of Protestant practice. Evangelical writers might well have hoped that by dismissing Catholic practices as superstitious, the Protestant faithful would be less likely to give them serious consideration, thus contributing to the widening of the confessional divide. Catholics, on the other hand, settled upon what was to them was a more effective weapon in the defence of orthodoxy: they stressed the unique truth of their own doctrines. Protestants were kept from Catholic practices by a campaign of proselytisation that marked them out as irrational and potentially demonic, while Catholics avoided Protestant activities which they were convinced were in error and ungodly. Under attack from polemical allegations of 'superstition', Catholic propagandists adopted 'heresy' and 'heretical' as their all-inclusive equivalent. In their respective confessions, the terms served the same defensive, confessionalising, purpose. This divergent approach to polemic surely highlights the nature of the relationship between the two confessions. Protestantism came out of Catholicism. Catholics were thus inclined to stress the error and novelty of the Protestant action, rather than imply that Protestant doctrine was 'irrational' or 'without any foundation'. It was neither, it was simply 'wrong' and 'distorted'. Protestants, for their part, could not claim that the whole panoply of Catholicism was erroneous or 'heretical' since that would have suggested that no link existed to connect them with Apostolic times. Thus, for evangelicals, the best polemical attack was to suggest that Catholicism suffered from pointless, misleading accretions and needed purification from superstition. For Protestants, Catholicism held the kernel of truth but it was overlaid with error; for Catholics, Protestantism had sprung from the truth but was a distortion of it.

The relationship between new theologies and traditional practices, and between 'official' and 'popular' beliefs is therefore clearly central to our understanding of early modern attitudes to 'superstition'. Sara Schechner's recent study of early modern cosmology and attitudes to comets highlights the importance of cultural interchange between popular and elite attitudes, and the dangers inherent in assuming that at the parish level the belief and worldview of the clergy were tangibly different from those of their flock.[30] There are also clear dangers in assuming that the Reformation arrived 'fully formed', either in thought or in practice.[31] The age of miracles might have passed (at least according to the propagandists of the Reformation) but dreams, portents, prodigies and providences seemed to satisfy the continued expectations of the people that God had communicated with his people and would continue to do so through material objects and in the natural world. 'The religious supernatural', Hans-Christoph Rublack writes, 'was tangible and immanent rather than intangible and transcendent', and any attempt to break down the foundations of popular magic and superstition was unlikely to succeed, given the propensity of the faithful to assume that there was no conflict between their traditional observances and proper religious practice.[32] The drive to remove the supernatural from religious practice often created as many problems as it resolved; indeed Bob Scribner has gone as far as to suggest that the Reformation was as much a part of the problem as it was an overall solution to it.[33] Faced with a new liturgy or set of religious instructions, the laity tended to assimilate sections piecemeal into local practice, building stock phrases into popular culture, while maintaining a firm grasp of the traditional observances of the past.[34] Where Protestantism attempted to take the magic out of religion, by deriding the miracles of the saints, dismissing the mass as idolatry and attacking both sacraments and sacramentals, there is evidence that the laity sought alternative sources of supernatural power, or took the disputed practices of the church under their own control and adapted them to meet their needs. When English Protestant reformers in the mid-sixteenth century unpicked the doctrine of purgatory and dismissed common practices such as the ringing of church bells and the lighting of bonfires on All Souls' Night as 'superstitious', popular adherence to such activities was slow to wear down. Ronald Hutton notes that some reform-minded clerics found themselves forced by violence to ring the bells of their church, to provide comfort and consolation for the souls of the dead in purgatory. By comparison, in areas where the local parson was less amenable, families continued to commemorate and console the dead outside the church, by meeting together and lighting bonfires in fields, and praying for the departed until the fires died out.[35]

The apparent ease with which individuals and even whole communities found alternatives to the established church after the Reformation was a frequent cause for ecclesiastical concern. The Council of Ansbach in 1569 claimed to be startled that even with the 'pure preaching of the efficacious and salvation-inducing word of God' the people remained preoccupied with so-called 'magic and superstitious things'. This was not purely a problem for evangelicals: in his study of local religion in sixteenth-century Spain, William Christian has pointed to the despair of enthusiasts for Catholic reformation, who found that although the doctrines of the church seemed to be accepted and observed, there lay beyond these certainties 'an extensive religion as practiced by the people, which from the clerical heights seemed nothing less than deformed, superstitious, even idolatrous'.[36] Striking a similar note, Delumeau's study of the post-Tridentine Catholic clergy characterises popular piety, as a collection of 'polytheistic pagan rites' that had at best been only superficially Christianised.[37]

For William Monter, this reflected a clash between what the church offered and what the people required – religion was functional, not devotional, and in the search for remedies, cures and survival, it was precisely in these functional areas that religion and magic were most prone to coincide. Many local practices were pruned and suppressed on the basis that they were fraudulent, impious, or superstitious, but miraculous images and cults of individual saints had to be given their proper place within the devotional life of the church. The appropriation or abuse of sacramentals was criticised, but the *Rituale Romanum* of 1614 still set out the rites that were to be used to bless crops and to ward off thunder. Yet Philip Soergel's recent study of the Catholic Reformation in Bavaria suggests that lay and clerical leaders were well aware of the persuasive powers of the traditional vocabulary of images and actions, and indeed exploited popular rituals and beliefs to inculcate a stronger loyalty to, and enthusiasm for, the institutional church. A similar attempt to reform and appropriate traditional devotional activity in the popular German reformation has been identified by Scott Dixon, demonstrating the extent to which deep-rooted opinions and practices could be divested of their original meaning and used to promote a reformed faith.[38]

Heal's essay highlights a clear example of the potential for the exploitation of traditional images and models in Lutheran churches to provide the message of the Gospel with solid local cultural roots. The cult of the Virgin had flourished at Nuremberg in the late fifteenth and early sixteenth centuries, and the imagery of the Virgin and the Marian feast days appeared to have survived the Lutheran Reformation in the city. However this survival concealed a radical transformation in the meaning and function of the cult of the Virgin, domesticated and secularised as a reflection of Christian motherhood. Purged of 'superstition and idolatry', the image of the Virgin had a powerful didactic purpose. The survival of the imagery, accepted even by the ruling council, was not simply evidence of the enduring significance of remnants of a past that had been forgotten or rejected, or of continuity in belief or practice. Rather the Nuremberg Virgin symbolised the potential to adapt traditional images to fit the needs of the Reformation, as part of the endeavour to convince the inhabitants of the city to exchange idolatry and superstition for legitimate devotion.

As Marshall's contribution to this collection suggests, discussions of the relationship between religion and superstition in Reformation Europe that polarise practice into official and unofficial often paint a distorted picture, based on the language of polemic and not the logistics of practice. Marshall highlights the continued presence of ghosts as a problematic feature of early modern English Protestantism. Ghosts, and belief in ghosts, appeared to be the most obvious manifestation of the link between false doctrine and superstition; in the eyes of critics, the promotion of the doctrine of purgatory by the medieval church had encouraged the faithful to accept the existence and appearance of ghosts. The abolition of purgatory should, almost literally, have closed the door on ghosts, yet apparitions continued to be seen, and the enduring presence of ghosts created a pressing pastoral problem for the reformers. The evangelical response to the problem not only revealed tensions within Protestantism, but also the existence of a substantial expanse of common ground between Catholic and Protestant writers. The resulting Protestant construction of the ghost owed much to the apparent interaction and dialogue between popular and elite culture, leading Marshall to conclude that belief (or unbelief) in ghosts should not be regarded as a clear marker of the divide between two cultures.

However, at all levels, the availability of alternative sources of supernatural power was a perpetual problem, and the frequent enquiries into popular attitudes to the supernatural suggest that this issue continued to be a cause of concern to ecclesiastical authorities throughout the sixteenth and seventeenth centuries. Some common threads emerge, not least in tracing the history of the popular prophet, from visions of the saints which spoke to the pious or berated the idle, through upsurges of popular fervour around particular individuals like the fifteenth-century drummer of Niklashausen, to a post-Reformation interest in prophets and prophecy, including Puritan child-prophets and Lutheran apparitions that gave the church and people what amounted to a divine assessment of progress towards true religion. A recent study of popular prophecy suggests that such apparitions were indeed a Lutheran adaptation of the traditional Catholic vision, preaching impeccably Lutheran theology but within the context of a popular world view that expected or even required the intrusion of supernatural power into the affairs of the material world.[39] Johnson, Lotz-Heumann, and Marshall's essays in this volume all indicate the extent to which the presence of 'reformed' prophets and apparitions reopened the traditional channels of communication with the sacred that the Reformation had attempted to close up, against the demands and claims of both Catholic and radical reformers.

It is thus vital that historians of early modern religion should give consideration to evidence not merely of the survival of traditional and deeply held mentalities, but also of the formation of a new and distinctive 'Protestant superstition'. In the essays that follow, contributors have addressed the question of the extent to which the Reformed churches might be seen to have accommodated practices that had once been termed 'superstition' both in thought and in practice, in attitudes to miracles, wonders, or providences. Attempts to defend or rationalise these beliefs, or to soften the impact of religious change by accommodation with popular 'superstition' have been analysed. The crucial issue in this context is surely the relationship between survival and revival, toleration and representation. Did the sixteenth century witness the eradication of ritual through the suppression of superstition, or a reformation of ritual, in which traditional (and occasionally controversial practices) were redefined and reshaped in order that their popular meaning might be used as an instrument for religious change?[40] As Susan Karant-Nunn has commented, the leaders of the Reformation were presented with a clear opportunity to reform and 'reorder cultic observances', but the degree to which post-Reformation religious culture deserves to be seen as a distinct departure from its late medieval antecedents is worthy of further consideration, not least in relation to attitudes to superstition and superstitious practices.[41] The appeal to 'pure' biblical and apostolic models that dominated evangelical demands for the reform of the church carried with it the assumption that the Reformation would indeed 'purify' doctrine and practice, and suppress novelty, error and superstition. True faith was defined in relation to false, and godly practice in relation to superstition, creating a series of delineations that were contingent upon an awareness, understanding and recognition (however grudging or hostile) of the existence of the other.

It is apparent that many of the beliefs that early modern reformers and later historians would like to dismiss as superstitious and relegate to the dusty corner of popular religion were in fact part of a broad religious consensus that was socially inclusive. Local reverence for the relics of the saints was matched, if not exceeded, by those among the wealthy and powerful who accumulated vast relic collections for themselves, Luther's protector among them. Popular obsession with the afterlife and indulgences was matched, if not exceeded by the wealthy indulgence collector. The presence of ghosts on the seventeenth century English stage and the promotion of Protestant leaders as prophetic heroes are suggestive of the existence of an audience across society for such cultural norms, even after a century of religious change. If we start to take down the edifice of early modern religious practice brick by brick, it is possible to look at each piece and see it as pagan, as magical, as superstitious, as popular distortion of true religion. But looking at the whole, it is easier to see a coherent structure and religious culture. Ritual and popular religion were not the consequence of a deficient world-view, but rather they were the world-view, not just of the peasant but also of the clergy and educated. Is it possible, then, to uncover and appreciate the real meaning of 'superstition' during the Reformation, and appreciate the reasons behind the persistent opposition to all that seemed 'superstitious' in religious practice?

The concept of superstition, hatred of superstition and the identification of superstition were of more concern in the sixteenth century than at almost any other point in the past. Polemical debate and the propaganda of the Reformation relied upon the ability to draw a stark division between two opposites: true and godly religion on one hand, and the false and idolatrous religion on the other. The presence of 'superstition' signified the presence of feigned religion and diabolic influence, either in ecclesiastical and para-liturgical practice, or in the search for access to the supernatural outside the church, in magic, in divination and in witchcraft. Yet even with this categorisation of superstition in theory, contributions to this volume suggest that it is less than transparent that these ideas were followed through in reality, especially in the reality of religious debate and activity in which superstition could often be a generic term of abuse as much as a theological concept. The investigation of the meaning of a single yet multifaceted term ensures that conclusions are unlikely to be concrete, and the more historians plough one furrow, the more difficult the ground becomes. However, the centrality of superstition to Reformation debate should encourage us to give heed to Francis Bacon's assertion that 'there is a superstition in avoiding superstition', and delve more deeply into this fascinating topic.

NOTES

1 E. Ehrlich et al., eds, Oxford American Dictionary (Oxford, 1980), 688. The first two modern definitions accord almost exactly with that of the Council of Malines, while the third could, depending on one's views, embrace all religious belief.

2 A comment by Christina Hole as found in E. and M. A. Bradford, eds, Encyclopedia of Superstitions (London, 1961), 7.

3 For example, pagan Roman legislation referred to Judaism as both religio (that is, religion in a neutral sense comparable to the belief systems practised by the Romans themselves) and superstitio, a pejorative term reserved for non-Roman, barbaric religions. By the fifth century, Romano-Christian law had reserved the term religio for the Christian faith and Judaism (along with other religions) became solely a superstitio. See M. R. Cohen, Under Crescent and Cross. The Jews in the Middle Ages (Princeton, 1994), 30–6.

4 William Monter, Ritual, Myth and Magic in Early Modern Europe (Brighton, 1993), 1; Valerie Flint, The Rise of Magic in Early Medieval Europe (Princeton, 1991).

5 Euan Cameron, 'For Reasoned Faith or Embattled Creed? Religion for the People in Early Modern Europe', Transactions of the Royal Historical Society (1988), 165–87, especially 166; Joannes Nider, Preceptorium Divine Legis (Basle, n. pr., c.1470).

6 R. W. Scribner, 'Elements of Popular Belief', in Thomas A. Brady, Heiko Oberman and James D. Tracey, eds, Handbook of European History (Leiden, 1995), 231–62; Scribner, 'The Reformation, Popular Magic and the "Disenchantment of the World"', Journal of Interdisciplinary History 23 (1993), 475–94; Gerald Strauss, Luther's House of Learning. Indoctrination of the Young in the German Reformation (Baltimore, 1978); R. Po-Chia Hsia, Social Discipline in the Reformation. Central Europe 1550–1750 (London, 1989); S. L. Kaplan, Understanding Popular Culture. Europe from the Middle Ages to the Nineteenth Century (New York, 1984); C. Scott Dixon, The Reformation and Rural Society: The Parishes of Brandenburg-Ansbach-Kulmbach, 1525–1603 (Cambridge, 1996); R. W. Scribner and Trevor Johnson, eds, Popular Religion in Germany and Central Europe 1400–1800 (Basingstoke, 1996).

7 Thomas Harding, ed., The Decades of Heinrich Bullinger (Cambridge, 1848–52), 4 vols, 4: 253–5.

8 Keith Thomas, Religion and the Decline of Magic (London, 1971), chapters 1–3.

9 Stuart Clark, Thinking with Demons. The Idea of Witchcraft in Early Modern Europe (Oxford, 1997), Cameron, 'Reasoned Faith', 178.

10 See Peter Marshall, chapter 9 in this volume; Cameron, 'Reasoned Faith', 176; Clark, Thinking with Demons, 417–18, 533.

11 On the Calvinist doctrine of providence see, especially, Alexandra Walsham, Providence in Early Modern England (Oxford, 1999). See also R. W. Scribner, 'Incombustible Luther. The Image of the Reformer in Early Modern Germany', Past and Present 110 (1986), 38–68.

12 David Gentilcore, *From Bishop to Witch. The System of the Sacred in Early Modern Terra d'Otranto* (Manchester, 1992).

13 St Thomas Aquinas, *Summa Theologica*, translated by the Fathers of the English Dominican Province (London, 1920), 22 vols, 11: 169–78 (2: 92, 93); H. J. Schroeder, *Canon and Decrees of the Council of Trent. Original Text with English Translation* (St Louis, 1941), Session 22; Clark, *Thinking with Demons*, 475.

14 Pedro Ciruelo, *A Treatise Reproving all Superstitions and Forms of Witchcraft*, quoted in Clark, *Thinking with Demons*, 482.

15 Thomas, *Religion*, 55.

16 Jean Delumeau, *Catholicism between Luther and Voltaire. A New View of the Counter Reformation* (London, 1977).

17 Thomas, *Religion*, 55; Cameron, 'Reasoned Faith', 165, Kramer and Sprenger, *Malleus Maleficarum*, ed. M. Summers (New York, 1971), 189–90 (2: 2. 7).

18 Cameron, 'Reasoned Faith', 165.

19 R. W. Scribner, 'Luther Myth. A Popular Historiography of the Reformer', in R. W. Scribner, ed., *Popular Culture and Popular Movements in Reformation Germany* (London, 1987), 301–22; Michael Wilks, ed., *Prophecy and Eschatology* (Oxford, 1994); Jürgen Beyer, 'A Lübeck Prophet in Local and Lutheran Context', in Scribner and Johnson, *Popular Religion*, 166–82.

20 James Frazer, *The Golden Bough* (Basingstoke, 1914).

21 Thomas, *Religion*, chapter 1; Flint, *Rise of Magic*.

22 Delumeau, *Catholicism between Luther and Voltaire*.

23 Bernd Moeller, 'Piety in Germany around 1500', in S. Ozment, ed., *The Reformation in Medieval Perspective* (Chicago, 1971), 50–75; Robert Swanson, 'The Pre-Reformation Church', in A. Pettegree, ed., *The Reformation World* (Routledge, 2000), 9–30; Natalie Zemon Davis, 'Towards Mixtures and Margins', *American Historical Review* 97 (1992), 1400–9; Hsia, *Social Discipline*.

24 Stephen Wilson, *The Magical Universe. Everyday Ritual and Magic in Pre-Modern Europe* (London, 2000), xvii–xviii; Gabor Klaniczay, *The Uses of Supernatural Power* (Princeton, 1990).

25 Thomas, *Religion*, 39.

26 Ronald Hutton, 'The English Reformation and the Evidence of Folklore', *Past and Present* 148 (1995), 89–116; J. J. Scarisbrick, *The Reformation and the English People* (Oxford, 1984); Eamon Duffy, *The Stripping of the Altars: Traditional Religion in England c.1400–c.1580* (New Haven, 1993); Tessa Watt, *Cheap Print and Popular Piety 1550–1640* (Cambridge, 1991); Georgina Boyes, 'Cultural Survivals Theory and Traditional Customs', *Folk Life* (1987–88), 5–11; Walsham, *Providence*; Susan Karant-Nunn, *The Reformation of Ritual. An Interpretation of Early Modern Germany* (London, 1997); R. W. Scribner, *Popular Culture and Popular Movements in Reformation Germany* (London, 1987); Scribner 'The Impact of the Reformation on Daily Life', in *Mensch und Objekt in Mittelalter und in der frühen Neuzeit. Leben, Alltag, Kultur* (Vienna, 1990); Scribner, 'The Reformation and the "Disenchantment of the World"', in C. Scott Dixon, ed., *The German Reformation: The Essential Readings* (London, 1999), 262–79; Gerald Strauss, 'Success and Failure in the German Reformation', *Past and Present* 67 (1975), 30–63; Strauss, 'The Reformation and Its Public in an Age of Orthodoxy', in R. Po-Chia Hsia, ed., *The German People and the Reformation* (Ithaca, 1988), 194–214.

27 David Cressy, *Bonfires and Bells. National Memory and the Protestant Calendar in Elizabethan and Stuart England* (London, 1989); Hutton, 'Folklore'; Ronald Hutton, *The Rise and Fall of Merry England: The Ritual Year 1400–1700* (Oxford, 1994).

28 Scribner, 'Incombustible Luther'; Scribner, 'The Reformation and the "Disenchantment of the World"'.

29 Scribner and Johnson, *Popular Religion*, 15.

30 Sara J. Schechner, *Comets, Popular Culture and the Birth of Modern Cosmology* (Princeton, 1999), 8.

31 R. W. Scribner, 'Introduction', in Scribner and Johnson, *Popular Religion*, 1–15, especially 5.

32 Hans-Christoph Rublack, 'New Patterns of Christian Life', in Brady *et al.*, *Handbook of European History*, 585–605, especially 586; Scribner, 'Cosmic Order and Daily Life', in,

Scribner, *Popular Culture*, 1–16; Scribner, 'Ritual and Popular Religion in Catholic Germany at the time of the Reformation', in Scribner, *Popular Culture*, 17–48; Thomas, *Religion*.

33 R. W. Scribner, 'Ritual and Reformation', in Scribner, *Popular Culture*, 103–23.

34 Rublack, 'New Patterns', 594.

35 Hutton, 'Folklore'.

36 William Christin, *Local Religion in Sixteenth-Century Spain* (Princeton, 1981).

37 Delumeau, *Catholicism between Luther and Voltaire*.

38 P. Soergel, *Wondrous in His Saints: Counter Reformation Propaganda in Bavaria* (Berkeley, London, 1993); Dixon, *The Reformation and Rural Society*.

39 Jurgen Beyer, 'A Lubeck Prophet in Local and Lutheran Context', in Scribner and Johnson, *Popular Religion*, 166–82; R. L. Kagan, *Lucrecia's Dreams. Politics and Prophecy in 16th Century Spain* (London, 1995); O. Niccoli, *Prophecy and People in Renaissance Italy* (Princeton, 1990); Alexandra Walsham, '"Frantic Hackett": Prophecy, Sorcery, Insanity, and the Elizabethan Puritan Movement', *Historical Journal* 41: 1 (1998), 27–66; Walsham, '"Out of the Mouths of Babes and Sucklings": Prophecy, Puritanism and Childhood in Elizabethan Suffolk', *Studies in Church History* 31 (1994), 285–99; Richard M. Wunderli, *Peasant Fires: The Drummer of Niklashausen* (Bloomington, 1992).

40 For recent comments on this theme see R. W. Scribner, 'Ritual and Reformation', in Scribner, ed., *Popular Culture*, 103–23; Susan C. Karant-Nunn, *The Reformation of Ritual. An Interpretation of Early Modern Germany* (London, 1997).

41 Karant-Nunn, *Reformation of Ritual*, 4.

PART I

Superstition, tradition and this world

1

Images of the Virgin Mary and Marian devotion in Protestant Nuremberg

BRIDGET HEAL

The cult of the Virgin flourished in the imperial city of Nuremberg on the eve of the Reformation. Prayer to Mary offered the promise of consolation in this world – of miraculous intervention during times of crisis – and of salvation in the next. She was the embodiment of mercy, and would shelter all those who had recourse to her from the wrathful judgement of God. Each of Nuremberg's churches contained an altar dedicated to the Virgin as well as numerous paintings, sculptures and stained-glass windows bearing her image. *Hausmadonnen* adorned many of the city's secular buildings. Seven feast-days were celebrated in Mary's honour. The antiphon *Salve regina*, which invoked the merciful Mother of God as 'our life, sweetness and hope', was part of the currency of lay piety, and rosary devotion was also widespread, fostered by representatives of the Dominican order, in particular the nuns of the convent of St Katharina.[1] Local citizens even travelled as far afield as Loreto to invoke the Virgin's favour through pilgrimage.[2]

Such manifestations of Marian devotion inevitably attracted the scorn of Protestant reformers. Luther believed that Christians, inspired by the pope and his monks, had wrongly made a god out of Mary and had accorded her all power in heaven and earth. They had sought grace and favour from her, a 'poor vessel' who had merely showed obedience to God's will, rather than from the true source of all salvation, God himself. There was only one mediator, Christ, and to address Mary as such was a horrifying blasphemy.[3] Reflecting on the traditional image of the Virgin of Mercy, safeguarding supplicants beneath her mantle, Luther wrote: 'to invoke the Virgin Mary and the saints may make a beautiful show of holiness; but we must stay together under the head, or we are eternally damned. What will become of those . . . who crawl for shelter under Mary's cloak?'[4]

The rites that had served to secure Mary's aid in the past were now condemned as idolatrous and superstitious. Luther spoke scathingly of the mindless repetition of the Hail Mary, rejecting as useless what he described as the 'babbling of lips and the rattling of rosaries'.[5] Antiphons such as the *Salve regina* and *Regina caeli* were abolished because they dishonoured Christ, contravening his assertion that he himself was the way, the truth and the light.[6] Pilgrimages were ridiculed as fools' works, the products of diabolic and monastic manipulation. The Protestant position was summed up most succinctly by the Rostock reformer Nicholas Gryse in his *Spegel des Antichristischen Pawestdoms vnd Luttherischen Christendoms* (1593). Gryse dismissed the cult of saints, consecrated images, candles, and herbs blessed at the festivals of Purification and Assumption, the recitation of the Hail Mary and the use of rosary beads as 'superstitious, vain and powerless things'.[7]

The reformers' abrupt and apparently unequivocal condemnation of the cult of the Virgin raises certain questions about the nature of Protestant belief and practice. Marian prayer and pilgrimage had offered the possibility of direct divine intervention. Could men and women be persuaded to renounce this, and if so how did they cope once it was gone? Moreover, Christians were now required to seek salvation directly from God rather than from a compassionate, maternal figure who promised unquestioning protection to all her supplicants. Mary had played a key role in the lay piety of the late medieval church. Could the reformers possibly have succeeded in eliminating this role, in convincing men and women that they need no longer have recourse to the merciful Mother of God in their prayers?

In the case of Nuremberg it looks, at first glance, as if local pastors and preachers failed to persuade their congregations to relinquish the consolations of the Virgin's cult. Almost all of the city's pre-Reformation Marian imagery, both ecclesiastical and domestic, remained intact and *in situ*. Prayers could still be addressed to any one of a great number of statues and paintings of the Virgin. Several of Mary's feast-days also continued to be celebrated. In fact, however, beneath this façade of Marian moderation a radical transformation occurred. In the writings and sermons of the Protestant reformers Mary was stripped of her maternal authority, denuded of the divine power that had determined her appeal in the pre-Reformation church. Images and festivals were permitted to survive only because they were reinterpreted to fit with a new, specifically Lutheran vision of the Virgin. At an official level Mary came to be valued merely as an example of right belief and conduct, though the reformers' success in changing the nature of popular devotion to the Virgin cannot, of course, be taken for granted.

Patterns of Marian devotion

Nuremberg was the first imperial free city to adopt the Lutheran faith. The religious colloquy held in March 1525 marked the official beginning of the city's

Reformation and the Church Order produced in 1533 in conjunction with the Margrave of Brandenburg-Ansbach codified the liturgical and administrative procedures of the newly established Lutheran Church.[8] Nuremberg's Reformation was moderate in tone: the city consistently refused, for example, to join the Schmalkaldic League and to take up arms against its political overlord, the emperor. Yet thanks to its influential circle of humanist patricians, its Lutheran provosts and preachers and its evangelical printing presses it played a leading role in the events of the early Reformation years. Indeed in 1530 Martin Luther wrote from the Coburg: 'Nuremberg verily shines on the whole German land, like a sun among moon and stars, strongly moving other cities by what is going on there.'[9]

Given Nuremberg's impeccable Protestant credentials, the extent of the survival of Marian imagery and liturgy within the city is remarkable.[10] Two engravings produced by the local printmaker Johann Ulrich Krauss in the late seventeenth century provide eloquent testimony to this survival. The first (Figure 1) shows the interior of the Lorenzkirche, one of Nuremberg's two parish churches. The second (Figure 2) shows the interior of the Frauenkirche, the imperial chapel built at the behest of Charles IV on the city's main market square. Were it not for the alignment of pews in the foreground, facing towards the pulpit rather than towards the high altar, the viewer could be forgiven for assuming that these churches still served as Catholic places of worship. In fact, of course, they had long since been consigned to Protestant use. Andreas Osiander, one of the leading Lutheran theologians of his generation, had been appointed preacher at the Lorenzkirche in 1522 and from that time onwards the church had been continually at the forefront of Nuremberg's reform movement. The Frauenkirche functioned as a Protestant preaching hall from 1525 until 1810.[11]

As Krauss's engravings demonstrate, both churches retained many remnants of medieval Mariolatry.[12] The drapery suspended behind the triumphal cross in Figure 1 concealed Veit Stoß's magnificent polychrome sculpture of the Angelic Salutation, set within two rosaries (Figure 3).[13] The retable visible behind the high altar in Figure 2 had been donated around 1522 by the local merchant Jakob Welser and his wife. This elaborate evocation of the pre-Reformation cult of the Virgin remained intact and *in situ* until 1815: ironically it was dismantled only after the Frauenkirche had been returned to Catholic use. Its central shrine contained a particularly venerated statue of the Virgin and Child dating from the mid-fifteenth century and its painted wings showed scenes from the lives of Christ and the Virgin.[14] The survival of depictions of apocryphal episodes from the life of the Virgin – the meeting of Joachim and Anne at the Golden Gate, the Birth and Presentation of the Virgin, and Mary's Coronation by the Trinity – is particularly surprising, given the reformers' determination to eliminate what Osiander described as 'fabricated legends', stories that were without scriptural basis.[15] Amongst the other Marian images preserved in the Frauenkirche were a rosary panel, a sculpture of St Anne with the Virgin and Child, a depiction of the *Mater dolorosa* and a stained-glass

1 Johann Ulrich Krauss (after Johann Andreas Graff),
Interior of the Lorenzkirche, engraving, 1685,
Germanisches Nationalmuseum, Nuremberg

window showing the Virgin of Mercy (Mary sheltering diminutive supplicants beneath her cloak).[16]

Mary's continued prominence in the visual culture of post-Reformation Nuremberg was not confined to the ecclesiastical sphere. When, in the mid-nineteenth century, a Nuremberg librarian drew up a list describing the city's medieval sculpted house signs there were forty of the Virgin Mary still surviving.[17] Depictions of the Virgin also occupied a prominent place in the art collections established by members of Nuremberg's patrician elite.[18] Over the course of the sixteenth century the city's Lutheran council, for example, assembled a collection of paintings and other art objects that was displayed in the town hall. The council had no qualms about incorporating Marian images into this collection: a Virgin and Child from the Cranach workshop that had been given to the city in 1522 was added to the town-hall display during the first half of the sixteenth century. Amongst the other works that entered the collection at some point during the later sixteenth or seventeenth century was Martin von

Proſpectiva Ædis, ad Divum B. MARIÆ Virginis, NORIBERGÆ. Proſpect der MARIÆ-Kirche, zu vnſer Lieben Frauen genannt in NÜRNBERG

2 Johann Ulrich Krauss (after Johann Andreas Graff),
Interior of the Frauenkirche, engraving, 1696,
Germanisches Nationalmuseum, Nuremberg

3 Veit Stoß, *Angelic Salutation*, limewood and polychrome, 1517–18, Lorenzkirche, Nuremberg

Heemskerck's *St Luke Painting the Virgin*. And amongst the silverware belonging to the council that was inventoried in 1613 was a table ornament in the form of the Virgin Mary.[19]

The preservation of visual manifestations of pre-Reformation Marian devotion was accompanied by the perpetuation of certain aspects of Marian liturgy. In April 1525 the council asked its preachers and provosts to discuss which pre-Reformation feast-days should be retained.[20] In their response the preachers and provosts argued that since feast-days had, in the past, led to 'nothing other than all evil, vice, disgrace, drinking [and] murder' their number should be severely curtailed. In addition to Sunday, the day of rest instituted by the Lord, only Easter, Ascension, Pentecost, Christmas and the Circumcision should be allowed to remain. On all other traditional feast-days Nuremberg's citizens should be free to work or not work, as they pleased. Not satisfied with this answer the council asked whether the Annunciation and the feast-days of the Twelve Apostles might not also be retained. With some reluctance the preachers and provosts eventually conceded these festivals, along with the Purification, the Visitation, St John the Baptist and St Stephen.[21]

These were the festivals that were named in a mandate issued by the council on 24 May 1525 and prescribed in the 1533 Church Order.[22] The belated addition of two extra Marian festivals – the Purification and the Visitation – is of particular interest: Nuremberg's religious authorities were apparently compelled to adopt a more moderate position with regard to Marian liturgy than they would, of their own volition, have chosen. Nuremberg's decision to retain the feasts of the Annunciation, the Visitation and the Purification was not, in fact, unusual: almost all Lutheran church orders decreed the continued celebration of these three festivals.[23] Its attitude towards the feast of the Assumption, which was without scriptural basis and was therefore usually abolished, was, however, unconventional. Nuremberg's council was advised in May 1525 that although the Visitation was more firmly grounded in scripture than the Assumption, the feast of the Assumption 'has had . . . much standing amongst the common folk'. Its day, 15 August, which was an important holiday, should therefore be appropriated for the celebration of the Visitation.[24]

Given the continued prominence of the Virgin Mary in the visual and liturgical culture of Nuremberg's post-Reformation church it comes as little surprise to find that local magistrates persisted in designating blasphemy against the Virgin as a punishable crime. Verbal attacks on the Virgin, which had become part of the standard repertoire of offences condemned by civic authorities during the fifteenth century, were sometimes omitted from edicts drawn up by Protestant city councils.[25] In Nuremberg, however, decrees issued in 1526, 1529 and 1560 stated that

> where someone speaks malevolently of the Virgin Mary and Mother of Christ our Saviour, as though she had not borne Christ the Son of the most high (that is God) as a pure virgin . . . thus immediately harming the Virgin Mary in abuse or damage of the honour with which she is endowed by God, according to Holy Scripture, he should be punished in body, life, members or possessions.[26]

Nuremberg's decision to continue to threaten those who infringed Mary's honour with punishment must be seen as another manifestation of its deliberate moderation.

There may, of course, have been a significant gap between prescription and practice. Nuremberg's citizens heard from their preachers that they were not to impugn God's virginal mother, but were they in fact punished if they did so? The nature of Nuremberg's criminal sources makes it difficult to answer this question: no comprehensive series of interrogation records survives from the sixteenth century. The council minutes (*Ratsverlässe*) record, however, that in January 1525 (i.e. three months before the official introduction of the Reformation) Marx Plickner, a knife-maker who had 'blasphemed much against the Virgin Mary', was imprisoned. Plickner's fellow knife-makers petitioned for his punishment to be moderated, but their case was dismissed until after carnival and Plickner was expelled from the city. At the end of March, as a result of the knife-makers' 'fluent plea', Plickner was sentenced to four weeks imprisonment after which he was pardoned by the city.[27] Despite the fact that Nuremberg's council was already, by this time, firmly committed to the Protestant cause its members were still determined to castigate those who spoke ill of the Virgin.

The reinterpretation of imagery and liturgy

Is this remarkable preservation of Marian imagery and devotion, so much at odds with evangelical rhetoric, a case of Protestant superstition? Does it reflect a willingness to tolerate the perpetuation of certain aspects of pre-Reformation belief and practice? It certainly looks, at first sight, like another example of what Gerald Strauss, Scott Dixon and others have documented for various Protestant territories: a failure to eradicate traditional attitudes and to instil in their place a truly Lutheran belief system.[28] Yet on closer analysis it becomes apparent that there were fundamental transformations in Marian doctrine. In the writings and sermons of the reformers Mary was still accorded considerable importance. She was presented, however, not as a divine figure, one who could render material assistance to her devotees and intercede for them in matters of salvation, but rather as an exemplary recipient of God's grace and a model of humble domestic virtue.

Cultural artefacts do not, as both historians and art historians have long been aware, have fixed meanings: the significance of images and texts is defined only through a process of appropriation on the part of the audience.[29] As David Sabean observed in his study of village discourse in early modern Württemberg, 'inherited items of culture continually changed shape as they were situated in new contexts'.[30] It was this possibility for transformation in meaning that validated the survival of pre-Reformation imagery and liturgy from a Lutheran perspective. Parishioners could be taught, through the power of the word, to abandon the 'superstitious' elements of Marian veneration and to regard the Virgin not as an intercessor and protector but as a model of right belief and conduct.

In order for this process of appropriation to proceed, images and festivals first had to be cleansed of their traditional abuses. The practices that had, in the pre-Reformation period, served to honour certain images and indicate their significance as *loci* of sacred power were discontinued: altarpieces and statues were no longer illuminated by numerous lamps and candles; statues were no longer clothed and adorned with precious textiles and jewels.[31] A description of Nuremberg's reformed liturgy dating from 1527 records that 'public processions, in which the saints were made into intercessors and called upon' (i.e. processions during which images and relics had been carried) were abolished.[32] The benediction rituals that had accompanied the feast-days of the Purification and the Assumption were also discarded. Consecrated candles and herbs had, in the past, been taken away by members of the congregation, ostensibly for devotional purposes. These objects had been used for protective magic, to ward off bad weather, evil spirits and other dangers.[33] The Order introduced in both parish churches in 1524 stated that wax was no longer blessed at the Purification and that all other benedictions were held to be 'fools' works', and the feast-day ordinance issued in 1525 referred to the Assumption as the feast that 'we *until now* have called herb dedication'.[34] This cessation of benedictions necessarily prevented the apotropaic misuse of blessed objects.

Once Marian images and liturgy had been shorn of their superstitious significations they could be reinterpreted. Lutheran reformers were well aware of the didactic value of images and exemplars. In a report submitted to Nuremberg's council in 1526 Osiander wrote, for example, that images could serve as 'writing and reminders for the peasants'. In a sermon published in 1543 he emphasised the pastoral importance of providing simple Christians with concrete models of right belief and conduct, acknowledging to his congregation that 'although God's word in Holy Scripture teaches us sufficiently and plentifully what we should do and not do . . . we also need, because of our weak will, good examples and patterns'. It was from this need, he added, that the 'ancient and long custom' of commemorating saints whose holiness was beyond dispute – for example the Virgin, John the Baptist and the Twelve Apostles – and of preaching about their lives and works on specified days of the year had arisen. When cleansed of the 'great corrupting abuse' into which it had fallen, the custom of commemorating saints could, Osiander believed, bring positive spiritual benefits.[35]

Mary was the Mother of God and was therefore, as Lazarus Spengler, the lay leader of Nuremberg's Reformation put it, 'deserving of all honour and praise'.[36] Yet she was to be revered not, as Catholics believed, because of her own surpassing merit, but rather because of God's supreme goodness towards her. An unworthy mortal, she had been chosen to bear God's only son 'despite her insignificance, lowliness, poverty, and inferiority'. Her story therefore provided a message of hope for all Christians, a message that should, Luther believed, be reflected in Marian imagery. In his commentary on the Magnificat, begun in 1521, he criticised 'the masters who so depict and portray the blessed Virgin that there is found in her nothing to be despised, but only great and lofty things'.

> What are they doing but contrasting us with her instead of her with God? Thus they make us timid and afraid and hide the Virgin's comfortable picture, as the images are covered over in Lent. For they deprive us of her example, from which we might take comfort; they make an exception of her and set her above all examples. But she should be, and herself gladly would be, the foremost example of the grace of God, to incite all the world to trust in this grace and to love and praise it.[37]

In describing Mary as 'the foremost example of the grace of God' Luther placed her firmly on the human side of the human–divine divide. Her 'comfortable picture' may have inspired confidence in God's mercy, but she was entirely stripped of the salvific power that had, in the past, been attributed to her. Her motherhood no longer conferred on her authority over Christ. In a publication purporting to repeat a sermon preached by Osiander in 1523, an anonymous Lutheran author discussed the account given in John's Gospel of the marriage at Cana. He maintained that when Jesus turned down Mary's request for help supplying wine he called her woman and not mother because she 'had asked for heavenly, godly works; over those she was no mother, only over the humanity of Christ'.[38] With her maternal power removed she was left secularised and domesticated. No Catholic author could possibly have described Mary as Luther did:

> She seeks not any glory, but goes about her meals and her usual household duties, milking the cows, cooking the meals, washing pots and kettles, sweeping out the rooms, and performing the work of a maidservant or housemother in lowly and despised tasks.[39]

Mary, as Luther's description suggests, also derived significance from the discourse of domesticity that accompanied the institution of the Protestant Reformation. In Lutheran writings for the first time the virtues for which she was singled out corresponded exactly with the virtues for which real women were praised: maternal devotion, competence in the home, and humble submission to male authority. As has frequently been remarked, reformers placed great emphasis on the 'glory of motherhood' and on women's household duties. For Luther femaleness and maternity were synonymous. He famously remarked, for example, that 'women ought to stay at home; the way they were created indicates this, for they have broad hips and a wide fundament to sit upon, keep house, and bear and raise children'.[40] Such prescriptions were not just theoretical, as Lyndal Roper's work on sixteenth-century Augsburg has demonstrated: 'the institutionalised Reformation was most successful when it most insisted on a vision of women's incorporation within the household under the leadership of their husbands'.[41] In this climate of heightened domestic awareness Mary's familial relationships could be used as a paradigm for the relationships within a Lutheran 'holy household'.

Part, at least, of the visual shift that might have accompanied this transformation in Marian doctrine, from Mary as divine ruler to Mary as human mother, had been accomplished well before the Reformation. By the early sixteenth century Mary's motherhood was a dominant theme in both ecclesiastical and household imagery. Touchingly maternal images of the Virgin and Child such as those produced by Albrecht Dürer were by no means incompatible with Lutheran sentiment, even though in their original contexts they had referred more to divine intercession than to right belief and parenthood. The actual process by which Marian imagery was appropriated is, however, difficult to trace, except in a few unusual cases. The reuse of a woodcut produced by Lucas Cranach in 1509 to illustrate the Wittenberg *Heiligtumsbuch* (relic book) is one such case (Figure 4). This woodcut showed a statue of the Virgin and Child that, according to the *Heiligtumsbuch*, contained fifty-six Marian relics. Yet in Georg Rhau's *Hortulus Animae, Lustgarten der Seelen*, a Lutheran educational text produced in Wittenberg in 1558, it appeared alongside a text condemning the invocation of the saints, beginning 'one should not call on the Virgin Mary'. The text went on to explain that Mary was blessed above all other women and that she had found grace with God, although she, like every other saint, had done nothing to merit this grace.[42]

Visual emphasis on Mary's humanity may have been acceptable in Lutheran terms and even pre-Reformation notions of her regality could be accommodated. Luther himself wrote that 'it is necessary . . . to keep within the bounds and not make too much of calling her "Queen of Heaven", which is a true enough name and yet does not make her a goddess'.[43] Yet in their original, pre-Reformation contexts many images had alluded to more than Mary's humanity and queenship. Depictions of the Apocalyptic Woman and of St Anne with the Virgin and Child had, for example, been used to illustrate the contested doctrine of the Immaculate Conception.[44] In the absence of accompanying texts or inscriptions such depictions did not, however, have autonomous meanings. Their association with specific Marian doctrines became clear only through context: the presence of an Apocalyptic Woman in a miniature at the beginning of a mass in honour of the Immaculate Conception or the juxtaposition of St Anne and the Virgin and Child with prayers in honour of Mary's purity. In a Protestant environment the specific meaning of these Marian iconographies was no longer signposted through verbal and visual context and they were therefore open to reinterpretation.

Vom anruffen

Die Jungfraw=
en Mariam/sol
man nicht an
ruffen.

S. Lucas der E=
uangelist schrei
bet am j. Cap. sei=
nes Euangelij / da
der Ertzengel Ga=
briel MARIÆ
den Grus bracht /
Sprach Er vnter
andern. Fürchte
dich nicht Maria /
Du hast Gnad
bey Gott fundē.
Dis wort sollen wir
ja wol merckē/Deñ
es hat nicht allein
dazu gedienet/das
das Megdlin / die
Jungfraw Maria
damit getröstet wür

4 Lucas Cranach the Elder, *Virgin and Child*, woodcut,
1509, reused in Georg Rhau's *Hortulus Animae:
Lustgarten der Seelen* (Wittenberg, 1558)

A woodcut of the Holy Kindred (St Anne with Mary and Christ, her other
two daughters and their husbands and children) produced by Lucas Cranach
around 1510 became, in the hands of the reformers, a statement about parental
duty, despite the fact that its iconography derived from apocryphal sources
(Figure 5). The woodcut was probably produced in connection with the cult of
St Anne that flourished in Wittenberg on the eve of the Reformation. It was

**5 Lucas Cranach the Elder, *Holy Kindred*, c.1510,
Kupferstichkabinett, Staatliche Museen zu Berlin,
Preußischer Kulturbesitz**

reissued twice in 1518 or shortly thereafter with verses by Philip Melanchthon added beneath. These verses explained the central importance of education to a Christian upbringing. They thus served to reinterpret the woodcut in a Lutheran context, focusing the attention of its audience on the educational obligations of parents, exemplified by the figure of Alpheus teaching his two sons to read in the lower left-hand corner of the image.[45] If, in the heart of Lutheran Saxony, a woodcut that had been produced to promote devotion and pilgrimage to the relics of St Anne could be reinterpreted as a depiction of an exemplary family gathering, Nuremberg's *Holy Kindred* paintings could surely have been viewed in the same light.

One caveat should, however, be added. The determination of Nuremberg's magistrates to keep ecclesiastical images in the public domain, to preserve as many elements as possible of pre-Reformation liturgy and to perpetuate decrees against Marian blasphemy was not a result of exclusively religious concerns. Indeed the council's decisions regarding imagery and liturgy some-times contravened the recommendations of its leading theologians. Osiander, for example, initially had serious reservations about the use of religious imagery and was also (as we have seen above) opposed to the continued celebration of Marian feast-days.[46] In disregarding his views the council was privileging political circumspection above religious resolution. Nuremberg had no desire to disasso-ciate itself more than was necessary from its glorious Catholic past and imperial present: historic memories, economic interests, and fresh political experience combined to make the city loyal to its imperial overlord, despite its religious transgression.[47] The council therefore sought to demonstrate for the benefit of outside observers its religious and political moderation. Leniency with regard to certain elements of pre-Reformation devotion was one manifestation of this moderation. The preservation of Marian imagery and liturgy within the city may have depended ultimately upon the reformers' conviction that they could change the nature of devotion to the Virgin, but tactical considerations facilitated the survival of images that could not possibly have been assimilated into Lutheran teaching, for example Veit Stoß's *Angelic Salutation* (Figure 3) and the *Virgin of Mercy* window in the Frauenkirche.

Popular belief

It is relatively easy to prove that at the level of theological debate the meaning of Marian imagery and liturgy was transformed. But did Nuremberg's reformers actually succeed in convincing the majority of the city's population to stop praying to the paintings and statues that continued to fill local churches and to regard Mary as no more than an example of right faith and good conduct? In attempting to convince people to attach new meanings to old images the reformers were playing a dangerous game: they were privileging the art of intel-lectual persuasion over custom with all its tenacity. The assumptions that had characterised popular devotion to images of the saints in the pre-Reformation period – that they could, in Bob Scribner's words, 'exemplify an indwelling per-sonality' and enter into an affective relationship with the viewer – had to be abandoned.[48] People were required to believe that images were no more than blocks of stone or wood, but there was no iconoclasm to provide proof for this belief. From the mid-1970s, when Gerald Strauss argued, on the basis of visita-tion records, that the Lutheran Reformation had limited impact on the popu-lace, historical literature has tended to emphasise continuity in pre-Reformation belief and practice.[49] Is there any reason to suppose that Nuremberg's experience was exceptional, that the transition from Mary as powerful inter-cessor to Mary as subservient *Hausmutter* was successfully achieved?

At least within the city of Nuremberg itself Protestant reformers do indeed seem to have transformed popular belief with regard to Marian devotion. In 1529 the city council was forced to remove one statue of the Virgin from the Frauenkirche because of idolatry but after the initial stages of the Reformation the subject was rarely mentioned.[50] During and after the 1543 Imperial Diet, which was held in Nuremberg, Veit Dietrich, preacher at the parish church of St Sebald, felt obliged to report some abuses to the city council, but idolatry did not feature amongst them. In a sermon preached later the same year during a severe outbreak of plague Dietrich did remind his congregation of the dangers of turning to the saints, but he located this abuse firmly in the past: 'We all know what idolatry there *was* in the time of the papacy.'[51] Evidence from artisan household inventories also suggests that 'Mariolatry' was essentially dead by the mid-sixteenth century. Although about half of the householders whose possessions were inventoried in 1530 still owned rosaries a sample of seventy inventories for the period 1550–60 revealed only one solitary set of prayer beads.[52] Local patricians may have kept Marian paintings in their private collections but by the mid-century the majority of Nuremberg's citizens had abandoned their 'papist playthings'.

In Nuremberg's rural hinterland the situation was less clear-cut, as the city's earliest surviving visitation records from 1560 and 1561 reveal. The commissioners in charge of this visitation toured fifty-four rural parishes and examined local pastors and members of their congregations for knowledge of the catechism, frequency of attendance at communion, and morality of lifestyle in general.[53] They uncovered a number of individual cases of the misuse of Marian formulae and of image worship. Stefan Rummer's wife, from the village of Rasch near Altdorf, was accused, for example, of having repeatedly participated in a pilgrimage to the parish church in Trautmannshofen in the Upper Palatinate that took place annually on the feast-day of Mary's birth. She was said to have offered veils to the image of the Virgin that formed the focal point of this pilgrimage and, according to the commissioners, she believed that that she had successfully brought up a daughter through doing this. Although the woman denied having offered veils she admitted that she had twice pledged her seven-year old daughter before the miraculous image.[54]

The commissioners also found evidence of four image cults within Nuremberg's own territory. The statues of the Virgin and St Martin that stood in the church at Hüll near Betzenstein were, according to the local pastor, the subjects of 'very horrifying, terrible, idolatrous abuses' involving pilgrimage, processions and offerings of money, votive candles and human hair. A local resident, the wife of Fritz Linberger, had, for example, made an offering to the Madonna at Hüll: 'She took a wax [candle], as thick as she is, and offered it to Our Lady in the name of the Father, Jesus and the Holy Ghost, so that our God would confer grace on her birth.' In the village of Rasch near Altdorf rural women burnt candles and genuflected before an image of the Virgin located behind the church, before going into the church to sing psalms. In Tennelohe a richly clothed image of the Virgin formed the focus of parishioners' idolatry. And in the neighbouring village of Eltersdorf, where the parish folk were apparently still obsessed with idolatry, another Madonna, decorated with (amongst other things) a veil, occupied a privileged place on the church's altar.[55]

In the case of Hüll the commissioners decreed that the image of the Virgin should be removed and replaced with a crucifix.[56] This decree was apparently not put into effect. Right up to the beginning of the twentieth century, when the Madonna was forcibly transferred to the church of St Aposteln in Viernheim (*Landkreis* Heppenheim/Bergstraße) against the wishes of Hüll's residents, it continued to form a focal point for pilgrimage and prayer. The cult was maintained in part by visiting Catholics, yet there can be little doubt that the grace-giving image also continued to command the devotion of local Lutherans. Indeed, even in 1978, the evangelical pastor at Hüll travelled with his congregation to Viernheim to visit their beloved statue in its new home![57] In Rasch the Madonna image itself was allowed to remain in place but the commissioners in charge of the visitation decreed that the veils that had adorned it were to be removed early in the morning, while the congregation was absent.[58] It is unclear whether this action was sufficient to break the Lutheran congregation's idolatrous habits: parish records reveal that until the 1820s the evangelical church retained a Marian image that was visited by Catholics from the neighbouring Upper Palatinate.[59] In Tennelohe the commissioners apparently took possession of the Marian image whilst in Eltersdorf they oversaw its removal from altar to sacristy (i.e. from a prominent and privileged position to a place accessible only to church officials).[60] It seems that in both of these communities the image cults were successfully eradicated.

What are we to make of these cases? It is inevitably problematic to base conclusions solely upon records of prosecutions. The cases that were prosecuted were the cases that reached the attention of the authorities. There may have been other cults that went unnoticed. Bearing in mind this proviso, four localised cults and a few individual idolaters constitute a relatively small total in a rural hinterland the size of Nuremberg's.[61] Various extenuating circumstances may also be invoked to account for the persistence of these particular cults. Hüll and Tennelohe were filial churches – churches without their own pastors to hold weekly services and direct the sustained efforts necessary to eradicate deeply held beliefs. Hüll and Rasch were also on the very edge of Nuremberg's territory, Hüll next to the Catholic bishopric of Bamberg and Rasch next to the only relatively recently Protestantised Upper Palatinate. The testimony of local residents concerning the cult at Hüll indicates that it was maintained partly through contact with neighbouring communities. One parishioner reported to the visitors that the local pastor no longer wished to hold services in Hüll because 'the bishop's [people] and other people make pilgrimages there and . . . do idolatry'.[62] Nineteenth-century evidence from Hüll and Rasch confirms that both cults survived partly because of the peregrinations of nearby Catholics.[63]

Within the evangelical community various groups seem to have been particularly susceptible to the charge of idolatry. Firstly, and most conspicuously, women: almost all of the individuals accused were female and several of the cults were, according to the men conducting the visitation, maintained only by women. In Tennelohe and Eltersdorf it was women who visited the 'idolatrous statues' and 'held them in higher esteem than God' and in Rasch it was 'old wives from the countryside' who made offerings before the Madonna behind the church.[64] The notion that superstition was a female prerogative was deeply ingrained in the reformers' consciousnesses. Alongside women the elderly were singled out. Elisabeth Roth argues that 'the main caesura for the gradual stopping of pilgrimage to evangelical churches is the second half of the sixteenth century, when the generation died out, for whom this practice had since childhood been a matter of course'.[65] This is confirmed by the commissioners' report on Tennelohe, where it was especially the elderly parishioners who persisted in their idolatry.[66] Finally, accusations were levelled at the ignorant, the 'simple people' as the pastor at Hüll described those who had been seduced into idolatry there. In Eltersdorf too, the authorities believed that ignorance was the root of the problem: 'In this parish . . . the parishioners did not do well in the general questioning; moreover they still do all kinds of idolatry and are obsessed with this.' [67]

Whether or not the nature of Marian devotion was successfully transformed within a particular community appears to have depended upon the extent of educational provision and upon geographical location. In areas that were under the supervision of a competent Lutheran pastor and that were effectively isolated from the subversive influence of Catholicism the superstitious practices that had characterised popular devotion to the Virgin in the late medieval period died out. Reform was not immediate: it did not take full effect until the demise of the generation that had been brought up in the traditions of the pre-Reformation church. Moreover the gradual cessation of superstitious practices cannot be taken as conclusive evidence of a transformation in belief. The fact that people stopped going on pilgrimage and making offerings to Marian images does not necessarily mean that they no longer had recourse to the Virgin in their prayers. Given, however, that for the vast majority of the population behaviour is the only indication we have of belief it behoves us at least to consider the possibility that changes in practice may genuinely reflect changes in attitude.

If this is indeed the case then we need to return to the question articulated at the beginning of this chapter: how did Protestants manage without the magical solutions offered by the medieval church, without the kind of direct divine intervention sought by Stefan Rummer's wife when she pledged her daughter before a miraculous Madonna and by Fritz Linberger's wife when she asked Mary to ease her childbirth? Protestant teaching was characterised, as Keith Thomas pointed out in *Religion and the Decline of Magic*, by an increased emphasis on God's sovereignty. The belief that day-to-day events reflected the working-out of God's purpose perhaps compensated in some way for the loss of the medieval church's 'apparatus of supernatural assistance'.[68] In condemning the superstitious prayers and rituals that often accompanied childbirth Luther argued, for example, that women should be comforted and encouraged not by the repetition of 'St Margaret legends and other silly old wives' tales', but with the following words:

> Dear Grete, remember that you are a woman, and that this work of God in you is pleasing to him. Trust joyfully in his will, and let him have his way with you. Work with all your might to bring forth the child. Should it mean your death, then depart happily, for you will die in a noble deed and in subservience to God.[69]

It seems possible that the knowledge that they were doing God's work, that events were firmly under divine direction, consoled those who might otherwise have turned to the Virgin Mary for succour.

In pre-Reformation devotion Mary had offered not only consolation in this world but also the promise of salvation in the next. What substitute was there for the spiritual solace that had, in the past, been supplied by knowledge of the unquestioning and undiscriminating protection that she offered to all sinners? According to Luther the perceived need for this protection was a mere papist construct:

> Christ was depicted as a grim tyrant, a furious and stern judge who demanded much of us and imposed good works as payment for our sins. There is a shameful and blasphemous picture . . . of Judgment Day in which we see the Son on His knees before the Father, showing Him His wounds, and St John and Mary interceding for us . . . Such paintings should be put aside; for they have been used to frighten people's consciences and to make them think that they must fear and flee from the dear Saviour, as though He wanted to drive us from Him and avenge our sins.[70]

In Lutheran teaching the need for Mary's intercessory role vanished. A Christian who truly repented of his sins and approached God directly with a good conscience need have no fear: he would be forgiven.

This transition to an unmediated relationship with God may perhaps have been eased by the fact that the Father was no longer described and depicted as a 'grim tyrant', but rather assumed some of the female functions of nurturing and consoling that had formerly been attributed to Mary. The early Protestant Church assimilated the religious rhetoric of motherhood only with caution; there was certainly nothing to parallel the 'feminisation of religious language' that had characterised late medieval piety.[71] Yet Luther did use some images of motherhood to describe the Godhead. God 'wants to gather us under this Clucking Hen [i.e. Christ], lest we go astray and fall prey to the hawk'. Similarly:

> The love of a mother's heart cannot forget its child. This is unnatural. A mother would be ready to go through fire for her children. So you see how hard women labour in cherishing, feeding, and watching. To this emotion God compares Himself, as if to say, 'I will not forsake you, because I am your mother. I cannot desert you'.[72]

Some Lutheran iconography, especially Christ amongst the children, picked up on this theme of the approachable and maternal Godhead. In around 1600, for example, a Nuremberg printmaker, Georg Scheurer, produced a woodcut entitled *Jesus der Kinder Freund* (Jesus the Friend of Children). Christ embraces and blesses the infants that are brought to him and the verses beneath the image invoke his gentle, loving nature in very physical terms: 'it is good to sit in his lap and to be embraced. Blessed are the little children who are so well cared for'.[73] In a drawing attributed to Lucas Cranach, Christ is even shown sheltering supplicants beneath his cloak, just as the Virgin of Mercy had once done.[74] It is possible that the existence of such maternal images, both verbal and visual, of the Godhead compensated to a certain extent for the loss of Mary's nurturing and consoling functions.

The cult of the Virgin was associated with many practices that were, according to the Protestant reformers, papist abominations. The word 'superstition' appeared frequently alongside the word 'idolatry' in their condemnations of intercessory prayer, image worship, pilgrimage and rosary devotion. It is tempting, given this Protestant polemic, to interpret the persistence of pre-Reformation imagery and liturgy in Nuremberg as evidence of local reformers' failure to eradicate traditional attitudes and to instil in their stead a new, Lutheran belief system. But, as this chapter has demonstrated, the survival of such externals does not necessarily indicate continuity in belief and practice. Marian paintings, sculptures and feast-days may have remained, but they were cleansed of their pre-Reformation abuses and reinterpreted to suit the devotional and social concerns of the reformers. Mary was stripped of her salvific power and was reduced to the status of a humble *Hausmutter*, a mere model of right belief and conduct. It is, of course, difficult to determine the extent to which this process of re-presentation actually transformed the Marian beliefs of the majority of the populace. Yet the evidence that can be assembled concerning popular piety suggests that in all except a handful of marginal cases Nuremberg's inhabitants, perhaps consoled by an increased emphasis on divine providence and on Christ's maternal nature, did indeed exchange their 'superstitious and idolatrous veneration' for 'legitimate' devotion.

NOTES

1 On Marian devotion in pre-Reformation Nuremberg see K. Schlemmer, *Gottesdienst und Frömmigkeit in der Reichsstadt Nürnberg am Vorabend der Reformation* (Würzburg, 1980), 295–9 and 339–40.

2 G. Pfeiffer, ed., *Quellen zur Nürnberger Reformationsgeschichte. Von der Duldung liturgischer Änderungen bis zur Ausübung des Kirchenregiments durch den Rat (Juni 1524–Juni 1525)* (Nuremberg, 1968), no. 144.

3 See, for example, M. Luther, *D. Martin Luthers Werke. Kritische Gesamtausgabe* (Weimar, 1883–1983), 61 vols, 10 (pt 3): 321–2; 21: 62–5; 52: 627.

4 J. Pelikan, ed., *Luther's Works* (Philadelphia, 1958–67), 55 vols, 22: 490.

5 Luther, *Luthers Werke*, 7: 596.

6 See for example G. Müller and G. Seebass, eds, *Andreas Osiander d. Ä: Gesamtausgabe* (Gütersloh, 1975–97), 10 vols, 1: 242.

7 N. Gryse, *Spegel des Antichrstlichen Pawestdoms Vnd Lutterischen Christendoms/Na Ordenung der V. Höetstücke vnsers H. Catechismi vnderscheiden* (Rostock, Steffen Muellman, 1593), fol. B.iv.

8 For a general introduction to the history of Nuremberg's Reformation see G. Strauss, *Nuremberg in the Sixteenth Century: City Politics and Life between Middle Ages and Modern Times* (London, 1976). The 1533 Church Order is published in E. Sehling, ed., *Die evangelischen Kirchenordnungen des XVI. Jahrhunderts* (Leipzig and Tübingen, 1902–77), 16 vols, 11 (Bayern I, Franken): 126–283.

9 Quoted in G. Seebass, 'The Importance of the Imperial City of Nuremberg in the Reformation', in J. Kirk, ed., *Humanism and Reform: The Church in Europe, England, and Scotland 1400–1643. Essays in Honour of James K. Cameron* (Oxford, 1991), 113–27, especially 113.

10 For general discussions of the fate of ecclesiastical imagery within the city see C. Christensen, 'Iconoclasm and the Preservation of Ecclesiastical Art in Reformation Nuremberg', *Archiv für Reformationsgeschichte* 61 (1970), 205–21 and G. Seebass, 'Mittelalterliche Kunstwerke in evangelisch gewordenen Kirchen Nürnbergs', in J. M. Fritz, ed., *Die bewahrende Kraft des Luthertums: mittelalterliche Kunstwerke in evangelischen Kirchen* (Regensburg, 1997), 34–53.

11 A. Würfel, *Diptycha Cappellae B. Mariae* (Nuremberg, Roth, 1761), 20–3; M. Herold, *Alt-Nürnberg in seinen Gottesdiensten. Ein Beitrag zur Geschichte der Sitte und des Kultus* (Gütersloh, 1890), 253–72.

12 The evidence provided by these engravings is confirmed by written sources: in the mid-eighteenth century Andreas Würfel and Christoph Gottlieb von Murr published guidebook-like accounts of the interiors of Nuremberg's churches, which describe in detail almost all of the items visible in Krauss's engravings. See A. Würfel, *Diptycha Ecclesiæ Laurentianæ* (Nuremberg, Roth, 1756); A. Würfel, *Cappellae* and C. Gottlieb von Murr, *Beschreibung der vornehmsten Merkwürdigkeiten in des H. R. Reichs Freyen Stadt Nürnberg und auf der hohen Schule zu Altdorf* (Nuremberg, 1778).

13 Stoß's sculpture was apparently kept covered even on feast-days after 1529 but was revealed on various occasions during the seventeenth century for the benefit of visiting dignitaries. Gemanisches Nationalmuseum publication, *Veit Stoss in Nürnberg: Werke des Meisters und seiner Schule in Nürnberg und Umgebung* (Munich, 1983), 203.

14 The statue is displayed today in front of the east window in the Frauenkirche; the wings entered the collection of the Germanisches Nationalmuseum. For illustrations of the wings see P. Strieder, *Tafelmalerei in Nürnberg 1350–1550* (Königstein im Taunus, 1993), 154, 278–9.

15 Müller and Seebass, eds, *Gesamtausgabe*, 3: 164.

16 The rosary panel entered the collection of the Germanisches Nationalmuseum (Plo 229) and the sculpture of St Anne is displayed today in the church of St Jakob. On the Virgin of Mercy window see the publication of the Metropolitan Museum of Art and Germanisches National-museum, *Gothic and Renaissance Art in Nuremberg, 1300–1550* (New York, 1986), 92.

17 G. W. K. Lochner, *Die noch vorhandenen Abzeichen Nürnberger Häuser* (Nuremberg, 1855).

18 See, for example, H. Pohl, ed., *Willibald Imhoff, Enkel und Erbe Willibald Pirckheimers* (Nuremberg, 1992), 279–339.

19 W. Schwemmer, 'Aus der Geschichte der Kunstsammlungen der Stadt Nürnberg', *Mitteilungen des Vereins für Geschichte der Stadt Nürnberg* 40 (1949), 97–133, especially 97–9, 110.

20 G. Seebass, *Das reformatorische Werk des Andreas Osiander* (Nuremberg, 1967), 179–80.

21 For a record of the debate see Pfeiffer, *Quellen*, 230–9.

22 Stadtarchiv Nürnberg (StadtAN), Rep. A6, Sammlung der (gedruckten) Mandate, Urkunden und Verordnungen der Reichsstadt und Stadtverwaltung Nürnberg, 1219 bis Gegenwart, 1525 Mai 24; Sehling, ed., *Die evangelischen Kirchenordnungen*, 11 (Bayern I, Franken): 204.

23 E. W. Zeeden, *Katholische Überlieferungen in den lutherischen Kirchenordnungen des 16. Jahrhunderts* (Münster, 1959), 47–8.

24 Pfeiffer, *Quellen*, 239.

25 The blasphemy decree contained in the Discipline Ordinance issued by Augsburg's Protestant magistrates in 1537, for example, omits all mention of the Virgin and saints. Stadtarchiv Augsburg, Reichsstadt, Ratserlasse (1507–99), 14/8, fol. 3 (1537).

26 StadtAN, Rep. A6, Sammlung der (gedruckten) Mandate, Urkunden und Verordnungen der Reichsstadt und Stadtverwaltung Nürnberg 1219 bis Gegenwart, fol. 2 (1526 März 3); fol. 3v (1527); B 31/1, fol. 100.

27 Pfeiffer, *Quellen*, 289, 311, 445.

28 G. Strauss, 'Success and Failure in the German Reformation', *Past and Present* 67 (1975), 30–63; C. Scott Dixon, *The Reformation and Rural Society: The Parishes of Brandenburg-Ansbach-Kulmbach, 1528–1603* (Cambridge, 1996), 143–93.

29 See, for example, R. Chartier, *Cultural History: Between Practices and Representations*, trans. Lydia G. Cochrane (Cambridge, 1988), 40–1 and E. H. Gombrich, *Art and Illusion: A Study in the Psychology of Pictorial Representation* (London, 1960), 154–244.

30 D. Sabean, *Power in the Blood: Popular Culture and Village Discourse in Early Modern Germany* (Cambridge, 1984), 4.

31 On candles see G. Hirschmann, *Die Kirchenvisitation im Landgebiet der Reichstadt Nürnberg 1560 und 1561: Quellenedition* (Neustadt a. d. Aisch, 1994), 258. Post-Reformation church inventories no longer listed robes and jewels for statues of the Virgin. See, for example, Staatsarchiv Nürnberg, Rep. 44e, Losungsamt, Akten, SIL 131, no. 14.

32 Pfeiffer, *Quellen*, 444.

33 R. W. Scribner, 'Ritual and Popular Religion in Catholic Germany at the Time of the Reformation', *Journal of Ecclesiastical History* 35: 1 (1984), 47–77, especially 62–3.

34 My italics. StadtAN, Rep. E1, Familienarchiv Spengler, no. 47, fol. 2–2v; Rep. A6, Sammlung der (gedruckten) Mandate, Urkunden und Verordnungen der Reichsstadt und Stadtverwaltung Nürnberg, 1219 bis Gegenwart, 1525 Mai 24.

35 Müller and Seebass, *Gesamtausgabe*, 2: 287; 7: 884–7.

36 StadtAN, Rep. E1 (Familienarchive Spengler), no. 4, fol. 4v.

37 Pelikan, *Luther's Works*, 21: 299, 323.

38 Müller and Seebass, *Gesamtausgabe*, 1: 80–1.

39 Pelikan, *Luther's Works*, 21: 329.

40 Luther, *D. Martin Luthers Werke. Tischreden* (Weimar, 1912–21), 6 vols, 1: 19 (no. 55) quoted in L. Roper, *Oedipus and the Devil: Witchcraft, Sexuality and Religion in Early Modern Europe* (London, 1994), 19.

41 L. Roper, *The Holy Household: Women and Morals in Reformation Augsburg* (Oxford, 1991), 2.

42 See Hamburger Kunsthalle, *Luther und die Folgen für die Kunst*, ed. W. Hofmann (Munich and Hamburg, 1983), 227.

43 Pelikan, *Luther's Works*, 21: 327.

44 G. Schiller, *Ikonographie der christlichen Kunst* (Gütersloh, 1966–90), 8 vols, 4.2: 157–9 and 169–72. For Luther's position on the Immaculate Conception see H. Graef, *Mary: A History of Doctrine and Devotion* (London, 1985), 2: 11.

45 C. Andersson, 'Religiöse Bilder Cranachs im Dienste der Reformation', in L. W. Spitz, ed., *Humanismus und Reformation als kulturelle Kräfte in der deutschen Geschichte* (Berlin, 1980), 43–79, especially 45–9.

46 Seebass, 'Mittelalterliche Kunstwerke', 40.

47 On Nuremberg's relationship with its emperor see Strauss, *Nuremberg*, 163; H. Baron, 'Religion and Politics in the German Imperial Cities during the Reformation', *English Historical Review* 52 (1937), 405–27, 614–33 and E. Franz, *Nürnberg, Kaiser und Reich: Studien zur Reichsstädtischen Aussenpolitik* (Munich, 1930).

48 R. W. Scribner, 'Ways of Seeing in the Age of Dürer', in D. Eichberger and C. Zike, eds, *Dürer and His Culture* (Cambridge, 1998), 93–117, especially 101–2.

49 Strauss, 'Success and Failure'. See also, for example, Dixon, *The Reformation and Rural Society*, 143–93.

50 T. Hampe ed., *Nürnberger Ratsverlässe über Kunst und Künstler im Zeitalter der Spätgotik und Renaissance* (Vienna and Leipzig, 1904), 2 vols, 1: no. 1729.

51 My italics. B. Klaus, *Veit Dietrich. Leben und Werk* (Nuremberg, 1958), 221–2.

52 StadtAN, Rep. B14/III (Inventarbücher), nos. 8 and 12 (fol. 87).

53 G. Hirschmann, 'The Second Nürnberg Church Visitation', in L. P. Buck and J. W. Zophy, eds, *The Social History of the Reformation* (Columbus, 1972), 355–80, especially 375.

54 Hirschmann, *Die Kirchenvisitation*, 183, 190–1.

55 On these four cults see Hirschmann, *Die Kirchenvisitation*, 131–2, 141 (Hüll); 182 (Rasch); and 245, 256, 258–9 (Tennenlohe and Eltersdorf). On the Hüll cult see also E. Roth, *Volkskultur in Franken. Band I: Kult und Kunst* (Bamberg and Würzburg, 1990), 257, and on the Hüll and Rasch cults, 256–8.

56 Hirschmann, *Die Kirchenvisitation*, 144.

57 Roth, *Volkskultur in Franken*, 256–7.

58 Hirschmann, *Die Kirchenvisitation*, 197.

59 Roth, *Volkskultur in Franken*, 257–8.

60 Hirschmann, *Die Kirchenvisitation*, 256, 258–9.

61 Nuremberg's territory comprised approximately 1200 km^2; Hirschmann, *Die Kirchenvisitation*, 6.

62 Hirschmann, *Die Kirchenvisitation*, 139.

63 Roth, *Volkskultur in Franken*, 256–8.

64 Hirschmann, *Die Kirchenvisitation*, 245, 182, respectively.

65 Roth, *Volkskultur in Franken*, 269.

66 Hirschmann, *Die Kirchenvisitation*, 256.

67 Hirschmann, *Die Kirchenvisitation*, 134, 305–6.

68 Thomas, *Religion*, 89, 91.

69 Pelikan, *Luther's Works*, 45: 40.

70 Pelikan, *Luther's Works*, 23: 57. For examples of this iconography see Schiller, *Ikonographie*, 2: 239–40 (ills. 798–802).

71 C. Walker Bynum, *Jesus as Mother: Studies in the Spirituality of the High Middle Ages* (London, 1984), 129.

72 Pelikan, *Luther's Works*, 22: 490; 17: 183.

73 See Hamburger Kunsthalle, *Luther*, no. 117.

74 See O. Thulin, *Cranach-Altäre der Reformation* (Berlin, 1955), 133.

2

Not like us:
Catholic identity as a defence against
Protestantism in Rottweil, 1560–1618

JASON K. NYE

The sisters have also allowed the erection of a pulpit in the parish church in Hausen without our previous knowledge. Because this village is half Württembergish and half under our lordship, this would serve to promote Lutheran preaching in the village. We have earnestly set out against this. (The city council and mayor of Rottweil in a letter to the Bishop of Constance, 28 December 1593)[1]

This chapter focuses on the German Catholic city of Rottweil and how it viewed Protestantism during the late sixteenth and early seventeenth centuries. During this time, Rottweil felt threatened by Protestant belief and worship and took steps to stop the infiltration of ideas. Protestant thought was treated as dangerous, even mysterious. Protestant ideas themselves could receive serious punishment such as the ritual burning of books as 'arch-heretical' objects. Religious festivals presented additional danger, because Rottweilers could venture into neighbouring Protestant lands either to observe or engage in activities of worship other than Catholic. As a defence against the potential of Protestant infiltration into Rottweil, the city's church and secular leaders chose to concentrate their efforts on strengthening Catholicism in Rottweil by instilling a strong sense of Catholic identity and therefore, it was hoped, a Catholic society more resistant to the introduction of Protestantism.

Rottweilers were afraid of the effects of Protestant preaching and books, beginning with a failed attempt by some of the city's priests to introduce Evangelical ideas and practices of worship in 1526–29. From this point onwards, the city allied itself closely with the confessionally charged interests of the Habsburgs and maintained unwavering support for Catholicism. Secular and ecclesiastical leaders endeavoured to instil a sense of Catholic identity as part of their continuing patronage of Catholicism. The greatest perceived threat to Catholicism in Rottweil was the exchange of ideas and practice with neighbouring Protestants. Both church and state took steps to stop the 'heretical' and 'mysterious' customs of the Protestants from entering Rottweil. Efforts to protect the city from Protestantism can be classified into two main areas: 1) spreading the message to Rottweilers about the dangers of Protestant thinking and the benefits of Catholicism in comparison with the 'heretics'; and 2) ensuring participation in distinctly Catholic rituals. Priests were directed to point out the differences between Protestants and Catholics in their sermons, portraying the Protestants as 'poor souls' who had made many mistakes regarding religion.[2] The goal of their efforts was to create a Catholic identity. They believed that by encouraging and regulating participation in distinctive Catholic rituals and worship while pointing out the differences with, and the failures of, their Protestant counterparts, that the populace would assume a distinct Catholic identity and, therefore, be stronger Catholics and resistant to a potential introduction of Protestant ideas. The city government attempted to regulate the behaviour of the populace, ensuring compliance with the Catholic liturgical calendar as well as the confiscation of Protestant literature and the punishment of individuals who attempted to arouse support for the Evangelical cause. Priests were also sanctioned by the city council, which could dismiss them from office if it suspected them of harbouring Evangelical sympathies. This chapter illuminates these anti-Protestant protectionist schemes designed to create a Catholic identity in Rottweil and its territory.

The censorship of ideas and behaviour that were incompatible with the prevailing confession in an early modern state or territory has been the topic of much research and has resulted in a number of overarching theories on the subject. This research has concentrated primarily on the relationship between church, state and the people, where the churches and states concentrated their power over subjects through the enforcement of religious discipline. Gerhard Oestreich first promoted the term 'social discipline' in the late 1960s to describe the contributions that post-Reformation religious discipline made towards the formation of the early modern absolutist state in Europe by providing princes with subjects who were conditioned for obedience, piety and diligence.[3] Also in the 1960s, Ernst Walter Zeeden advanced the theory of confession formation, which emphasised similarities between Lutheranism, Calvinism and Catholicism as they codified and ordered their respective doctrines, rituals and institutional structures for an intense struggle for believers.[4] In the 1980s, Wolfgang Reinhard and Heinz Schilling synthesised many of the principles of social discipline and confession formation to form their thesis of confessionalisation, which stresses the strengthening of the early modern state through the efforts of ecclesiastical and secular officials, working together to discipline society from above towards a common goal of establishing order and religious uniformity.[5] The confessionalisation thesis therefore provides a sound explanation for social discipline in the larger states of the Empire with strong centralised control institutions in both state and church. The confessionalisation thesis is much less applicable for the numerous smaller states where control institutions were weaker. Rottweil can be counted among this group and, although a few attempts at social discipline were made, clergy and church institutions were not employed to strengthen the authority of the state in its own territory. Rottweil rarely levied disciplinary penalties on its clergy and people, choosing instead to censor information in the city by monitoring the message presented by its own church and by resisting the influx of foreign ideas from abroad. I choose, therefore, to use the term social censorship as an alternative descriptor to social discipline and confessionalisation in order to portray more accurately the situation in Rottweil.

The thesis of confessionalisation attributes the combination of church attempts to rejuvenate and define religious practices with secular enforcement as an important function in the emergence of the modern state.[6] The Rottweil church received strong support from the *Rat* (town council) in an attempt to preserve the stability of the state, rather than a consolidation of secular power. The goals of the church and *Rat* were unified, but for different reasons. Rottweil's ecclesiastical leadership perceived a potential threat from the influences of neighbouring Protestant areas and wished to strengthen Catholic identity and religious belief in order to check an influx of Protestant ideas and practices. The *Rat* continued to protect its status as a Catholic state, a measure which standardised the religious belief of the community. The *Rat* also felt that strong Catholicity ensured much of the city's status and economic well-being by maintaining favourable relations with the Habsburgs and thus securing the future of the *Hofgericht* (the Imperial High Court which sat in Rottweil) which served as a great source of income and prestige for the city and especially its elites. The *Rat* did not take the lead nor did it interfere with local church initiatives to strengthen Catholic belief and practice among the populace. From the 1560s, the structure and implementation of the programme to forge a greater Catholic identity in Rottweil was initiated and carried out by Rottweil's church leadership, which received support from the *Rat* when required.

Beginning in the 1560s, Rottweil's church leaders chose a programme of reform starting with church institutions. Lay participation in religious feasts and festivals was increasingly encouraged by the city's chief lay confraternity and the *Rat* from the failed Reformation in 1529 to 1563, but the content of daily religious life for the laity went largely unchanged up to this point. Greater emphasis was placed on lay participation in religious activities by the 1560s, especially catechetical instruction and the reception of sacraments. Expectations of lay religious participation increased and were more widely enforced along with expansion in spiritual education and the availability of activities. Rejuvenation of lay spirituality was central to the programme of forging a Catholic identity among the populace. The laity appear to have joined willingly in a resurgence of piety. Threats of enforcement by the *Rat* appeared only once: improved religious educational structures were implemented, but punishments were rarely invoked. These endeavours resulted in a marked difference in lay behaviour and expectations between the early sixteenth and seventeenth centuries; the laity became more aware of its obligations, popular religious activities were more readily available, and people came to expect better performance from their priests in providing them with spiritual leadership.

Sermons and catechisation

The Council of Trent placed new emphasis on catechesis in an attempt to promulgate Catholic teaching and to illuminate differences between Protestant and Catholic doctrines for the Catholic populace.[7] New catechisms were prepared and presented to the laity through the freshly emphasised mediums of preaching and scholastic instruction.[8] Trent hoped that this strategy would result in the creation of a Catholic consciousness for the population and ward off the influence of Protestantism.[9] Competent preaching, catechisms and schoolteachers were key elements to the success of this programme. In effect, Catholicism responded to charges by Protestants of superstitious practices and beliefs by ensuring that its adherents were better educated in the theological and confessional basis for these very practices and beliefs. As Crăciun shows in chapter 3, the Catholic Church did not attempt to downplay controversial aspects of the Catholic faith, rather it made these very elements the touchstones of true belief.

Trent underscored the importance of episcopal visitation for the supervision of preaching, *catechesis* and scholastic instruction.[10] Visitations concentrated largely on the clergy and, when diligently maintained, could serve as an effective means of monitoring the proficiency of religious instruction of the laity. The bishops of Constance, who held religious authority over the Church in Rottweil, did not directly administer visitations until the early seventeenth century, drawing instead on rural deans to perform visitations on their behalf. Tridentine style legislation concerning preaching, catechesis, and religious instruction in schools was echoed in the diocese of Constance's synodal statutes of 1567, which provided a base for the deans' work.[11] The diocese, however, provided little regulation until the early seventeenth century. Thus, the onus for governing lay religious instruction in Rottweil fell on the dean of Rottweil.

Johannes Uhl served as city priest for Rottweil from 1559 and dean of Rottweil from 1574 until his death in 1606 and paid considerable attention to preaching and *catechesis* in the deanery of Rottweil during his tenure. Himself a prolific preacher, he took steps to guarantee that other priests under his guidance were at least competent preachers, and demanded that his priests took the opportunity to catechise also from the pulpit. Supervision of catechetical instruction in the city's Latin School was aided by his revision of the school ordinance in 1567. Orchestrated by Uhl, the ordinance shifted the supervision of the school from a panel of three city council members to a panel consisting of a guild master, a member of the Imperial High Court and the city priest, so giving the local church direct involvement in supervising curriculum at the school.[12] All these measures made it certain that the laity would have much exposure to Catholic doctrine during the later sixteenth century and be fully instructed in the bases of Catholic practice as the best defence against Protestant accusations of superstition.

Johannes Uhl placed a strong emphasis on the role of preaching because he believed that this was the main function of priests when caring for souls in their parishes, and that sermons were the most effective medium for promulgating doctrine to the people.[13] In 1588 he wrote a preaching manual for priests in the deanery to use, which outlined basic teachings that should be communicated in every sermon and points of emphasis to be made on certain festivals.[14] Uhl also tried to ensure that priests in the deanery were giving frequent and competent sermons through his active use of visitations. Priests with difficulties were given instruction on how to improve their abilities, and were re-evaluated soon thereafter.[15]

Johannes Uhl established himself as a capable and prolific preacher. He prepared sermons for every Sunday and feast-day; if he was not preaching in the city of Rottweil, he was delivering a sermon in one of the other parishes in the deanery. A large collection of his sermons (thirty volumes) remains behind as testimony to his diligence in preaching. Each volume covers one year between 1569 and 1605, and contains notes for over a hundred sermons.[16] Unfortunately, Uhl wrote this series of notes only for his own use, and his tiny, scrawling hand prohibits access to these rich sources. He did, however, leave behind a further two volumes which are more accessible.[17] They consist of a selection of hand-written exhortations dating from between 1579 and 1602, all of which were attempts to help people deal with crop failures and epidemics in the period. Chosen by Uhl as his best examples of exhortation from the pulpit, they were intended for use as reference by other priests in the deanery.[18]

Catechesis was an integral part of preaching according to Uhl. The importance he attached to catechesis is apparent in his 1588 preaching manual and its section on basic instruction which should be presented to parishes with each sermon.[19] According to Uhl, sermons ought to be followed by a prayer for those who died in sin.

> And now let us pray for those souls who departed from these times in imperfection and were not completely without sin: that God will look upon them

kindly, because they stand before the punishment of God. This petition is made now for them so that they are taken out of worldly punishment and placed in eternal peace. Remember them, and everyone also their fathers and mothers and also all of my and their beloved souls, for them and all other Christian souls health and prosperity.[20]

This was Uhl's way of catechising the doctrine of Purgatory to the parish. Purgatory was the destination of the souls which died in sin, where they would remain for a period of purification before entering heaven. It explained how sinners could atone for their sins before advancing to the last judgement. The process could be accelerated with the help of the living who prayed and commissioned masses to be said on behalf of the deceased, an option which was particularly popular in Spain.[21] Emphasising Purgatory was also an opportunity to underscore differences between Catholic and Protestant belief, Protestants having eliminated the doctrine of Purgatory altogether.[22] Throughout the Empire, stressing points of doctrine which contrasted with Protestants was seen as an effective method of creating a Catholic identity for the populace.[23]

Uhl took advantage of the opportunity to inject as much confessional contrast as he could into sermons. A *Pater Noster* and an *Ave*, the latter being a prayer unique to Catholicism amongst German Christians, followed prayers for the dead.[24] He then added the qualification that God would hear the prayers of true Christians only and asked them to recite the Creed: 'Because prayer is not valid for those who are not prepared in proper belief, and without belief one cannot be pleasing to God, we also recite the twelve parts of our Christian Catholic beliefs.'[25] Although Protestants also maintained the Creed, Uhl called it a statement of Catholic belief, thereby implying that Protestants did not adhere to it. His reference to the validity of prayer being dependent on the person being in 'proper belief' makes the assertion even more significant. In essence, Uhl declared Protestants outside the protection of God, who accordingly turned a deaf ear to their requests. By contrast, his parishioners were told they were God's children and that their prayers would be heard if they remained in 'proper belief'. This liturgical exercise also taught the Creed, providing a greater impetus to learn and follow it, so parishioners would continue in God's favour. Parishioners were then told that reciting the Creed alone was not enough: 'Those are the Christian Catholic beliefs, but that is not enough. One must also abide by God's will, so also hear and follow the Holy Ten Commandments.'[26] Hearing the Ten Commandments was one of the central points of catechesis and Uhl believed it should be part of each and every sermon.[27] A final opportunity to teach catechism to the parish came at the end of the service at the reading of marriage banns, as well as the marriage statutes.[28]

Teaching catechism during Sunday worship was an effective way of reaching the entire population. By the sixteenth century, Catholics began teaching catechism in formalised classes on Sundays and feast-days.[29] Classes were directed at the young, but parents and householders were expected to accompany their children and servants.[30] Parents and householders, however, were reluctant to attend because they felt that it was too embarrassing.[31] Records do not indicate if a 'Sunday School' existed, but all citizens of Rottweil would have been exposed to the catechism when taught from the pulpit on Sundays. Uhl was not the first to come up with the idea; the Mainz Agenda from 1551 had previously encouraged priests to teach the catechism in their sermons.[32] It is not known if Uhl was familiar with the Mainz Agenda. Regardless of his inspiration, what was important for Uhl was that Rottweil parishioners be taught at least once each week the Creed, the Ten Commandments, the prayers (*Pater Noster* and *Ave*), as well as the doctrine of Purgatory and the statutes against clandestine marriage. Johannes Uhl's plan, as witnessed in his preaching manual, wished to extend this practice to all parishes in the deanery as well. The subtle nature in which he underscored differences between Protestant and Catholic belief were designed to create a distinct identification with Catholicism among the laity in Rottweil, and this would have been relayed to each parish in the deanery once his sermon formula was adopted. Clearly, rather than taking the Protestant approach which sought to paint one's opponent's practices as superstitious (irrational, wrong), Uhl sought to show that his opponents (i.e. Protestants) were wrong by stressing the validity of his (i.e. Catholicism's) beliefs. This echoes the response of the Jesuits in Transylvania (see Crăciun's essay) which responded to Protestant attacks by entrenching the very beliefs and practices being labelled superstitious.

Rottweil's Latin School also provided catechetical instruction to the city's youth. The catechism of Peter Canisius was used from 1554, and provided the basis for religious instruction at the school.[33] Clergy in the deanery changed to the *Catechismus Romanus* in 1567, but it is likely that the Latin School continued to use Canisius' work.[34] The *Catechismus Romanus* was not intended for the laity but for use by priests as guidance for preaching and the administration of sacraments.[35] Canisius' catechism, however, remained the most popular for lay instruction such as that found in Rottweil's Latin School.[36] Canisius' catechism was used on a daily basis to instruct students in the Catholic faith. Only students with the goal of joining the priesthood were instructed in more specific theology, when they would have been exposed to the *Catechismus Romanus*.[37] Further spiritual training occurred on Saturday mornings when the Gospels and Epistles were explained to them.[38] Learning the catechism normally placed heavy emphasis on memorisation but, unfortunately, the examination process in Rottweil's Latin School is unknown.[39]

Catechism instruction extended beyond the prayers and doctrines emphasised by Uhl in his sermon manual for each Sunday. He also stressed the need to explain two other occasions in the liturgical year: the beginning of Lent and Good Friday.[40] Uhl felt it necessary for all priests in the deanery to underscore the importance and content of the forty days of fasting during Lent. Carnival was more than a religious occasion in Rottweil; it was the city's largest social event of the year and drew people from all over the region to its festivities.[41] Uhl did not discourage the entertainment, but wanted to stress the duty to fast for Lent immediately following the festival.

> You ought to feast and seek your mischief, because after this Wednesday the fasting begins according to the authority of the Holy Church of God. What follows is forty consecutive days until Easter without eating meat . . . Christ himself fasted for forty days after his baptism. We are all but members of Christ and we ought to follow him in this example as our head and fast and suffer with Christ so that we are prepared to take part in the fruits of his suffering, which will be in view after the fast.[42]

With this sermon, Uhl was interested in more than just teaching the laity about the merits of Lenten fasting, although this was a very important part of the Catholic liturgical cycle.[43] Another reason he concerned himself with its emphasis was the need to underscore the parity between the Catholic practice of Lenten fasting and the Protestant rejection of the custom.[44] German Protestants had dismissed the efficacy of Lenten fasting, instead calling it the invention of 'greedy clergy' and a 'false way to heaven'.[45] Once again, Uhl fostered a Catholic consciousness by pointing out differences with other confessions and implying that the Protestant view was disobedient to Christ's example and, by extension, irreligious.

This creation of Catholic identity may have been even more important to Uhl than the regulation of Lenten fasting, an argument supported by the reports of visitors from Constance in 1608, who noted,

> There is a serious complaint about the eating of meat on prohibited days, which is a cause of scandal to many people, especially the peasants who, either through deliberate wrong-headedness or through naivety, generally imitate the corrupt morals and example of the townspeople.[46]

This evidence comes two years after Uhl's death and suggests that he did not enforce Lenten fasting vigorously and that it was not the main point of his message. The *Rat* lent support for the enforcement of Lent only once between 1525 and 1618, and that occasion came after Uhl's death. In 1614, Rottweilers were prohibited from attending carnival in Württemberg.[47] The reason given was that due to the different calendars used in Lutheran Württemberg and Catholic Rottweil, Carnival in Württemberg fell during Holy Week that year.[48] Although there was no apparent attempt to enforce Lenten fasting during Uhl's tenure, his preaching directives were not misguided. Uhl believed that an understanding of Catholic belief and its variation from Protestant belief was sometimes more important than the enforcement of its practice.

Visitations performed on the deanery concerned themselves solely with clerical performance and neglected the role of the laity in religious instruction until 1608, two years after Uhl's death. The visitations concerned themselves greatly with the preaching ability of priests.[49] Building upon the premise stated in Uhl's 1588 preaching manual that priests ought to take the opportunity to teach the catechism with each Sunday sermon, one can assume that proper catechetical instruction was gauged along with preaching aptitude. Beginning in 1574 and ending in 1597, Uhl made numerous observations about priests' preaching abilities, admonishing those who needed to improve as well as praising those who excelled.[50] Priests with difficulties were given the opportunity to increase their effectiveness, presumably with Uhl's advice and any assistance they might find in literature such as his preaching manual. If priests followed Uhl's preaching strategies, they would also have been teaching the catechism on a regular basis.

The earliest extant and in-depth examination of the effects of catechetical teaching and preaching was made in 1608, when the first post-Tridentine visitation made by diocesan officials was conducted.[51] The findings of the visitors from Constance provide testimony to the effectiveness of Uhl's approach.[52] They remarked on most priests' diligence in catechetical instruction.[53] Only the priest in Dauchingen was noted as needing improvement with teaching the catechism.[54] The new dean, Joannes Brenneissen, admonished him to improve on his catechesis: the same method employed by his predecessor Uhl, who had warned his priests to ameliorate their preaching. There was little difference between these two warnings because Uhl instructed his priests always to include the catechism in their sermons. Unfortunately little is known about lay knowledge of the catechism prior to Uhl's efforts to include its teaching in sermons throughout the deanery.

Sacraments and the Mass

The Council of Trent placed renewed emphasis on the sacraments.[55] Protestants had rejected five of the seven sacraments of the pre-Reformation church and altered the nature of the rites which they kept. Trent's reaction strongly reaffirmed all seven sacraments and stressed the desirability of more frequent confession and reception of communion by the laity. The church sought to create a distinct Catholic lay consciousness through all the sacraments, centring on the Eucharist and its adoration of the body of Christ as the sacrament which best illustrated differences with Protestant doctrines.[56] Both these sacraments illustrated the contrasts between Catholic and Protestant worship practices and served to create a more unique Catholic consciousness in those who actively engaged in them.

Consistent with the ideas of Trent, Rottweil's church took steps to monitor and ensure regular reception of the sacraments, and the *Rat* supported the cause by supplying statutes which threatened punishment for non-fulfilment of sacramental and other religious obligations. Punishments were rarely invoked and the efforts of the church were relied upon to ensure compliance. Rottweil's church began keeping a register of baptisms in the city from 1564 and lists of people receiving other sacraments soon followed.[57] Repression was not an effective method of creating a group consciousness and churches preferred to stress regular participation in group rituals.[58] This was the main reason Catholics established careful record-keeping of the sacraments, especially baptism, marriage, confession, communion and burial.[59] Lack of evidence where punishments were invoked suggests that Rottweil was aware of the potential for failure when using a strategy of repression. The *Rat*'s statutes which required participation in the city's religious life were apparently meant solely as threats, and sentences were not meant to be pronounced on a regular basis. Instead, such statutes were intended to work in tandem with the church's registration of sacramental participation and provide added impetus for compliance through the threat of sanction.

All sacraments were stressed in the reformed Catholicism of the later sixteenth century, but three which appear to have received little attention for reform (or at least leave little evidence in the archives of Rottweil during the period of this study) were confirmation, marriage and extreme unction. Thus, this essay will concentrate on those sacraments upon which the energy of reform was directed: baptism, confession and communion. The first action taken by Rottweil's church to monitor lay reception of the sacraments came in 1564 with the creation of the baptismal register.[60] The practice of keeping registers of sacrament reception was required in the 1567 synodal statutes for the diocese of Constance.[61] Rottweil was one of only two areas in the diocese which began the practice before the decree of the diocesan synod.[62] Johannes Uhl started it and named the Council of Trent as his inspiration for the register's creation.[63] Before the diocesan synod of 1567, Uhl stated here his interest in and knowledge of the Council of Trent. Trent upheld the seven sacraments and declared that participation in them differentiated Catholics from heretics.[64] Trent also mandated the keeping of registers for the recipients of sacraments.[65] This statement had an effect on Uhl and other Catholic reformers who were attempting to stop the spread of Protestantism in their respective regions.[66] Lay knowledge of practices unique to Catholicism through catechisation was not enough for the creation of a Catholic identity and consciousness. In addition,

Uhl understood that societies needed to participate frequently in characteristically Catholic rituals in order to achieve more fully a Catholic identity and the best possible defence against the influence of Protestantism.

Uhl who, it appears, was concerned greatly with the introduction of the new-born into the Catholic community gave the recording of baptisms first priority. Tridentine Catholicism had two premises for the reform of baptismal practices. First, the Council wished to reduce the number of godparents from the late medieval practice of naming multiple godparents to a maximum of two.[67] Second, the Roman Missal directed priests to require saints' names for newly baptised children in the hope that as adults they would maintain a close relationship with that saint, especially those which had strong local cults.[68] The Missal even instructed priests to write a saint's name in the register on behalf of the child if the parents refused one.[69] The aim of both changes was to provide a greater link to God and the sanctified rather than the advancement of extra kinship ties found in late medieval baptismal practice and further reinforced Catholic adherence to specific practices and beliefs labelled superstitious. On a subconscious level this may well have served to remove the sting from the polemic and render it impotent as a tool for undermining Catholics in their belief.

Even though Uhl named Trent as the inspiration for his new baptismal register in 1564, his expectations of the benefits for keeping the register were different from those of the Council.[70] Visitors from Constance noted in their reports from 1608 that the practice of multiple godfathers and one godmother was still allowed in Rottweil and that nothing had been done to correct it.[71] At that time, Uhl had been city priest for forty-two of the forty-four years since the creation of the baptismal register. Any reform of godparent customs could have been initiated by him, but the evidence suggests that he did not devote much attention to them, nor did he concern himself greatly with the assignment of saints' names for the newly baptised. Examination of the three baptismal registers from 1564 to 1601 displays no particular naming patterns for infants.[72] Infant boys often received the common German name of Johannes, but there are very few instances of infant boys being named after the local male patron, St Pelagius.[73]

Rather than stemming from these two Tridentine aims, Uhl's interest in recording baptisms seems to have come from a desire to tie an infant's welcome into the Christian world to one particular church; his church, the Catholic church in Rottweil. Uhl noticed additional advantages to keeping a register of baptisms. He wished to ensure that families and godparents would be reinforced as Catholics and would educate the infant as a Catholic. Baptism in the church served this purpose by bringing all parties involved into contact with Catholic clergy and their churches rather than neighbouring Protestant communities which also offered baptism. The effects of this gathering for the infant's baptism in a Catholic church emphasised that this child was Catholic and that it was the duty of the child's parents and godparents to rear him or her in the Catholic faith. Once the inscription in the register made the event official, there could be no doubt that this child was Catholic, since its baptism was recorded by a Catholic priest and the register was to be for ever held in the Catholic church where the sacrament took place. The low level of literacy in Germany at this time (between 5 and 10 per cent) also aided the priest in reinforcing the ceremony and the roles of all persons involved as Catholic.[74] For some, this may have been the only recording of their name in their lifetime. Modern people append their name to official documents as an almost daily occurrence, which can limit the responsibility that is felt towards each separate commitment. Many people in 1560s and 1570s Rottweil, however, may have seen their name recorded only once, in the baptismal register, and their identification with and responsibility to the Catholic church would have been far greater.

Uhl's dedication to creating a greater Catholic identity in Rottweil is further attested by his willingness to rebaptise in the church infants which had been baptised at their birth by midwives.[75] The midwives were responding to public needs for quick baptism in a world in which nearly half the babies born did not live to see their first birthday.[76] People were also anxious to have infants baptised quickly in order to rid them of original sin which was perceived as something akin to demonic possession.[77] Failure to baptise before death was serious, and it could require a costly contribution to the church in order to have the child buried in the church cemetery.[78] These were integral parts of popular religious culture and Uhl did not see an immediate danger resulting from them. He was, however, quick to give church baptisms in addition to midwives' baptisms. Although this was against church doctrine, further baptism in church was a tool so valued by Uhl in his attempt to create Catholic identity that he saw it as an acceptable breach of practice. Another reason for giving a second baptism was to reinforce the significance of the sacrament by associating it with a fixed location, a Catholic church.[79] The role of pre-Reformation baptism was defined more as a rite of entrance into the citizenry rather than into the community of Christians and often took place somewhere other than a church.[80] New emphasis on the church as the proper setting for baptism attempted to restore a perception of the sacrament as a religious rather than a secular function, which tied individuals to a group of Christian believers rather than to a defined citizenry. Uhl also placed Catholic identity above reforms of godparentage or local saints' devotions. For him, the identification of the individual as a member of the Catholic community of believers was paramount. No doubt he recognised the Tridentine aims as valuable tenets of reform, but saw them as less urgent and gave them a lower priority.

Baptism was not the only sacrament which received Trent's attention. Confession and communion were also given greater emphasis by the Council. In the later Middle Ages there was a movement towards limiting the reception of the Eucharist to those who had prepared themselves extensively through confession. This position was promoted by theologians such as Jean Gerson (1363–1429), who deplored the unworthiness of humanity for eucharistic reception, and what he perceived as popular irreverence for the host which stemmed from the proliferation of feasts and processions.[81] Gerson advocated more frequent confession as the solution, calling for quarterly or even monthly confession.[82] Many German diocesan councils echoed the sentiments of theologians such as Gerson in the 1450s when they limited the number of eucharistic processions and called for more frequent confession.[83] The late medieval Church inextricably linked together the sacraments of confession and communion, establishing confession as 'essentially a form of preparation for communion'.[84] Trent upheld the medieval practice of requiring confession and communion only once per year, while placing additional emphasis on the cleansing of sin with the sacrament of confession as a prerequisite for reception of the Eucharist.[85] In so doing, Trent reinforced the late medieval view that the two sacraments were inseparable and also believed that each confession should be followed by communion.

Trent also opened up the possibility for more frequent confession and communion, instructing Catholics 'to communicate every year, at least at Easter'.[86] The phrase 'at least' implied that a greater frequency was desirable. Already by 1500, attempts had been made in some areas of Europe to increase reception of the two sacraments.[87] Greater efforts were made manifest in synodal statutes after the Council of Trent. The dioceses of Augsburg and Constance confirmed their desire for frequent confession and communion at their diocesan synods in 1567, when they called for confession at the principal feasts of the Church.[88] 'Four or even five separate confessions, scattered regularly throughout the year from Passion Sunday to the Octave of Easter, Christmas, Pentecost, the Assumption of the Virgin (August 15), and the Feast of All Saints, along with "other solemn feasts", became the goal.'[89] Frequent reception of communion was implicit with exhortations to frequent penance since the synods, like their medieval predecessors, did not separate the two sacraments.

One reason why the late medieval church linked confession and communion together was to 'establish sacerdotal control over membership in the sacramental community'.[90] Once achieved, the resulting relationship ideally was used to catechise the penitent with the orthodox teachings of the presiding priest, for by its design, penance demanded conformity.[91] The Eucharist which followed it imparted the grace of God and his intervention in the world for those individuals who had fulfilled the prerequisite soul cleansing which was confession.[92] The two sacraments were thus bound together with the Eucharist serving as a benefit which followed the instruction received in confession.[93] Inseparable, the one sacrament could not achieve its full effects without the other.

Reformed Catholicism in the later sixteenth century stressed the importance of the sacraments, especially confession and communion, as the vehicles of grace which brought people closer to salvation.[94] Confession and communion were singled out for many reasons, one of which was their regular reception throughout life. Baptism, confirmation, marriage (usually), holy orders and extreme unction were meant to be received only once in a lifetime, while confession and communion were meant to be received at least once annually and even more frequent reception became increasingly encouraged. Catholic reformers could also utilise contrasts in penitential and eucharistic practices with those of Protestants to define more clearly the variations between the two confessions and to highlight the 'error' of Protestantism. By stressing these differences they hoped to establish Catholic loyalty and identity in their communities and by labelling Protestants as 'heretics' there was little need to stress the irrationality or 'superstitious' nature of Protestant practice.

Even though Johannes Uhl began reforming the Rottweil church in the 1560s, lay reception of the sacraments of confession and communion was not targeted for reform until the 1580s. The delay can be explained by changes in the expectation of the clergy to administer these sacraments diligently, which also came about in the 1580s. Uhl allowed a generation to elapse from the 1560s to the 1580s before discipline was exacted from clergy for improper behaviour such as concubinage. Reforms in the training of priests began in the 1560s and were given time to germinate before total compliance with clerical behavioural changes was expected. The same leniency was applied to changes in expected diligence regarding the administration of confession and communion. Uhl placed the order of these reforms below priestly training so that more well-trained priests would be in place before the regulation of confession and communion began. By the 1580s, trained priests were being monitored and were more diligent in offering these sacraments and offering them even more frequently, so the laity had greater opportunity to comply with their obligations of confession and communion. As detailed later in this essay, management of regular lay reception of confession and communion also began in the 1580s.

The *Rat* first punished a priest for failure to administer the sacraments in 1537.[95] The next occurrence does not appear in the records until the visitation performed by Johannes Uhl in 1581.[96] There are several explanations for this gap. In 1537, tensions were still high concerning the recent failed Reformation attempt and the *Rat* wished to ensure that all parishes had access to

Catholic sacraments, rather than resort to Lutheran practices which it feared might still be available, especially in the rural parishes. After 1537, the bishops of Constance admonished the *Rat* not to punish priests since that was within the diocese's jurisdiction, advice which caused the *Rat* either to reduce its disciplining zeal or to administer penalties more discreetly.[97] It is also possible that greater concern for popular religious feasts from 1529 to 1563 replaced some of the emphasis on regular reception of sacraments and, therefore, the diligence of priests in offering them. The next period began with Johannes Uhl's appointment as city priest in 1560 and dean of Rottweil in 1574. Uhl was a conscientious and energetic reformer and, at least by 1581, he was actively monitoring the frequency with which priests in his deanery were offering the sacraments of confession and communion. One should not assume, however, that he did not devote his attention to these sacraments in the years 1560 to 1581. More frequent and universal reception of confession and communion was no doubt encouraged during these years, while education of clergy and laity precipitated changes in practice. Uhl decided to enforce regulation of these two sacraments only after he believed sufficient changes in the clergy and their effects on the laity had been achieved, so that he could expect and enforce universal compliance.

Uhl chose to enforce changes with the clergy beginning with the visitation of 1581. His report, dated 13 May 1581, covered eighteen parish priests under the jurisdiction of Rottweil and found two of them negligent in their administration of the sacraments.[98] Joannes Georgius Thomae, the priest in Rottweil-Altstadt, was one of these, and Uhl noted that he had admonished him before for his negligence.[99] The other was Thomae's brother, Georg Thomae, who was the priest in Dauchingen and also took care of the affiliated parish in Weilersbach.[100] The *Rat* levied unspecified fines on 12 September 1581 on both the brothers for failure to perform their duties.[101] On 30 October 1581, after they continued to be negligent, the *Rat* ordered both the brothers to resume their obligations under the penalty of further, more serious sanctions.[102] Further complaints were lodged with the *Rat* by Rottweil-Altstadt parishioners against Joannes Georgius on 25 January 1582.[103] Possibly Joannes Georgius finally took notice of the *Rat*'s threats and changed his ways, since his name no longer appears in the city council minutes and no other priest was appointed to replace him. In May 1582, however, his brother Georg was temporarily replaced as priest in Dauchingen by Paulus Kercker, who was also the priest for the neighbouring village of Dietingen.[104] The next month, Thomas Hauthaber was named as a permanent replacement for Georg.[105]

The example of the Thomae brothers displays the resolve of the *Rat* and Uhl in their new policy to punish priests who failed to provide regular sacraments for their parishes. During the period of this study, only one other priest after the Thomae brothers required admonition for his diligence in administering the sacraments. Lorenz Sichler had been appointed as priest in the village of Balgheim in January 1584.[106] He was admonished by the *Rat* to improve his diligence in administering the sacraments within a month of his appointment.[107] It is unknown whether Sichler improved his sacramental responsibilities or not, but he was eventually dismissed from office in 1589 for refusal to give up his concubine.[108] Sichler's extremely rebellious nature was reported at length in his dismissal proceedings before the *Rat* and other hearings between 1585 and 1589.[109] Apart from Sichler who was chronically insubordinate, the other clergy seem to have heeded the warnings of the Rat and the examples made of the Thomae brothers in 1581 and 1582.

Unfortunately, extant documents do not specify what kind of frequency for offering the sacraments was expected or required of Rottweil priests in the early 1580s. In the early sixteenth century, churches across Europe offered lay eucharistic reception at least once a year at Easter, and at most five times a year.[110] By the beginning of the seventeenth century, lay communion increased across Europe to a minimum of four times a year, while more devout Catholics received the sacrament monthly.[111] The earliest extant records for lay reception of communion are for the main church in Rottweil, Heilig Kreuz, from 1627.[112] In that year, lay reception was offered eleven times.[113] Communion was offered to the laity five times during the Easter season at the Annunciation of the Virgin, Palm Sunday, Maundy Thursday (the most popular), Good Friday and Easter Sunday.[114] The other six occasions were Pentecost, Assumption of the Virgin, Nativity of the Virgin, All Saints, Christmas and the Feast of the Circumcision.[115] As Table 1 demonstrates, lay reception was relatively rare on three of the extra-Easter days: Nativity of the Virgin, All Saints and the Circumcision.[116] The overwhelming comparative popularity of lay reception during Easter and at Pentecost, Assumption of the Virgin and Christmas suggest that there was a tradition of receiving communion at these feasts. Records show that in 1585 Uhl offered lay reception at least at Pentecost and the Assumption of the Virgin in addition to Easter.[117] This suggests that during Uhl's tenure, lay reception was probably expected to be offered at least four times a year; Easter time, Pentecost, Assumption of the Virgin, and at Christmas, with the possibility of the Nativity of the Virgin, All Saints and the Circumcision as well. The Nativity of the Virgin, All Saints and the Circumcision may have been recent additions as eucharistic offerings in the liturgical year in Rottweil, and, if so, this may explain their relative lack of popularity for receiving communion.

Easter time, however, remained the focus for lay reception of communion. The Council of Trent and the 1567 diocesan synod of Constance required Catholics to receive the Eucharist only once a year at Easter.[118] More frequent reception was encouraged but signified devotion rather than fulfilment of

Table 1 Extra-Easter communicants at Heilig Kreuz parish, 1627

Feast-days	Date	Communicants
Pentecost	23 May	736
Assumption of the Virgin	15 August	659
Nativity of the Virgin	8 September	16
All Saints	1 November	52
Christmas	25 December	679
Circumcision	1 January	30
Total		2172

Data for Tables 1 and 2 taken from DAR, Pfarrelarchiv Heilig Kreuz Rottweil, vol. 11: 314. Dates: Adriano Capelli, *Cronologia, cronografia e calendario perpetuo* (Milan, 1988), 62–3.

sacramental obligation. Comparison between the data shown in Tables 1 and 2 shows that more people received communion in Rottweil during Easter time in 1627 than during the rest of the year combined. If the number of Easter-time communicants represents roughly the total number of communicants in Heilig Kreuz parish in Rottweil, then it can be seen that only a portion of parishioners elected to receive communion at the extra-Easter offerings. Even though the totals for extra-Easter and Easter-time communicants are similar, it would be wrong to assume that Rottweilers communicated on average twice per year, once at Easter time and at another feast during the year. It is highly likely that most of the people communicating outwith Easter were receiving the sacrament at one or more of the extra-Easter offerings and probably all three of the most popular: Pentecost, Assumption of the Virgin and Christmas. A handful of people, probably from the same group who communicated regularly outwith Easter time received the sacrament on the Nativity of the Virgin, All Saints or the Circumcision. These people displayed the highest degree of devotion and Eucharistic piety and probably took advantage of every opportunity to receive communion. No lay person would have been able to communicate more than seven times a year in 1627.

Table 2 Easter-time communicants at Heilig Kreuz parish, 1627

Feast-days	Date	Communicants
Annunciation of the Virgin	25 March	247
Palm Sunday	28 March	664
Last Supper	1 April	998
Good Friday	2 April	73
Easter	4 April	391
Total		2373

For source, see Table 1.

Uhl began the practice of monitoring lay reception of communion in the 1580s. By this time he was also regulating the availability of the sacrament in the parishes. Having achieved a sufficient level of clerical education in the deanery, he now expected priests to offer communion on a regular basis. The first attempt to enforce lay communion came on 5 November 1583, when Uhl ordered priests in the deanery of Rottweil to record reception and to report those who did not receive the Holy Sacraments.[119] The order appeared in the city council minutes, where the Rat gave its simultaneous stamp of approval, stating that the monitoring of the sacraments was necessary 'in order to uphold the Catholic old religion'.[120] The statement by the Rat reflects its understanding that Catholic loyalty and the Catholic identity of the populace could be achieved fully only through frequent participation in characteristically Catholic rituals, and that record-keeping was the only dependable means available to ensure universal compliance.

Although the statute of 5 November 1583 denoted the first attempt to govern lay reception of confession and communion in Rottweil, threats of sanction for disobedience did not appear until 28 June 1585. On that date, the *Rat* made a decree that outlined specific punishments for those who failed to uphold their obligation to go to communion at Easter.[121] Since the decree came after Easter (21 April), it was apparently a response to the findings of the record-keeping which began in 1583, and an unspecified number of people were made an example that the populace would become more observant of Easter obligations in the future.[122] Men who failed to fulfil their Easter sacramental obligation were sentenced to be imprisoned until the next available communion at the feast of the Assumption of the Virgin (15 August).[123] By contrast, women who were found guilty were sentenced to go without wine until the Assumption of the Virgin.[124] In the same year, on 9 July 1585, the *Rat* decreed that a servant woman was to be exiled if she failed to take communion at the Assumption of the Virgin.[125] The outcome of the servant woman's case is, unfortunately, unknown. The *Rat* clearly stated in these instances that citizenship in Rottweil depended on each individual's satisfactory fulfilment of Catholic worship obligations. The duration of these sanctions was significant, since it ended with the next available reception of the Eucharist – the ritual which most distinguished Catholics from other German Christians. The lapsed communion recipients reconfirmed their positions as members of a Catholic community once they fulfilled their sacramental obligation. Afterwards, they were welcomed back into the communities of Rottweil, both civic and religious, whose expectations were in unison with each other on the issue of Easter communion. If people could not meet sacramental expectations, they were no longer a viable part of a Catholic community, and, as in the case of the servant woman, would have been excluded from civic membership.

Sacramental expectations for the laity appear to have increased in the 1590s, when they were also required to attend confession before each communion.

On 26 May 1595, Uhl convinced the *Rat* to threaten punishment for all people who went to communion without first attending confession.[126] Shortly after this pronouncement, on 5 July 1595, the *Rat* reinforced Uhl's efforts to record all confessions by making it a civil statute as well.[127] Both these statutes suggest there may have been popular resistance to the recording of confessions. The first decree shows that Uhl felt he needed the support of the *Rat* in order to bring all the laity to confession before each communion, and that possibly the efforts of the clergy to exhort the populace to follow this rule were not universally observed. No record exists to suggest that further punishment or admonition for the offence was necessary, and the *Rat's* threat of sanctions seems to have served as a satisfactory impetus for reluctant confessants. The second decree may have been a response to public fears about the priests keeping records of confessions, when, perhaps, the laity were nervous that details of their individual confessions might also have been recorded along with their attendance. The *Rat's* support for the procedure may not have alleviated fears about what might have been recorded in addition to attendance, but it would have made the point that the responsibility to confess before communion was civic as well as spiritual. Hence, the issue consisted of not only the redemption of souls but also membership of Rottweil society.

Confession received additional emphasis during the period 1579 to 1611 when Rottweil was struck by a series of plagues and bad weather which destroyed the crops in their fields. Johannes Uhl saw the sins of the community as the source of the problem, believing that they had displeased God who was then punishing the people.[128] The belief that natural disasters and epidemics were God's punishments for sin was common across early modern Europe. Villagers in Württemberg, Rottweil's neighbour, attributed the horrors of the Thirty Years' War to God's retribution for their sins.[129] Additionally, sixteenth-century Jesuits believed that disease was God's penalty for the sins of a community and that epidemics served as God's warning for people to change their ways.[130] The solution for both Johannes Uhl and the Jesuits was to exhort the populace to repent their sins and attend the sacrament of confession.[131]

Uhl relied on his own preaching ability to exhort his parishioners to repentance. He appears to have been successful in his attempts, and during his tenure in Rottweil requests were made by the laity for him to hold additional services, which were penitential in nature during these times of great stress.[132] These services consisted of examinations of conscience and a number of prayers for forgiveness.[133] When plague next struck Rottweil in 1610 and 1611 (or four years after Uhl's death), his successor Jakob Khuon also performed the penitential services for the people of Rottweil.[134] Khuon believed that the populace ought not only to confess in order to reconcile the community with God, but also go to communion after their confession.[135] The *Rat* supported him in his endeavour. In March 1611, the *Rat* threatened sanctions against those failing to comply, in an effort to ensure that all persons in Rottweil fulfilled their sacramental duties in order to restore the favour of God to the commune and health to the region.[136] Civic and spiritual duties were concomitant, and once again, the renewable sacraments of confession and communion, specifically Catholic in nature, served to test Catholic loyalty and identity which in their turn conferred full membership in the Catholic society of Rottweil.

Fulfilment of sacramental duties was not only beneficial for the community as a whole, however, but also for the soul of the individual. A high frequency of sacramental reception was desirable and increased piety led to greater spiritual benefits. Even though lay communion might occur only monthly or even less frequently, there was still reason within Eucharistic theology to call for weekly Mass attendance. Actual lay reception was not the only means whereby the individual might receive benefit from communion. Concentration on the Host during its elevation in the Mass and the future redemption which it brought was believed to be spiritually beneficial.[137] Magical-like qualities were perceived in the Host and all things associated with its consecration across many areas of sixteenth-century Germany.[138] The danger in this practice was of course that the laity might believe that gazing at the Host was equal to reception.[139] In the early years of Uhl's attempts to reform the church in Rottweil, this may have been regarded as acceptable to some degree. Those devoted to adoration of the Host would also be devoted to Mass attendance and were therefore exposed to preaching and catechisation. Adoration of the Host, even though potentially dangerous if done to excess, remained a distinctive feature of Catholicism and its practice was an exhibition of loyalty to the faith. As long as the laity continued to behave in Catholic fashion, they remained in the fold and the effects of sermons and catechisation would have the chance to mould them into reformed Catholics.

Once Uhl had brought the clergy in the deanery of Rottweil to offer confession and communion at his determined minimum pace, he pushed for greater frequency of Masses in the parishes. Mass was said irregularly in late medieval Europe, especially in rural areas.[140] Priests who were responsible for multiple parishes were often limited by the necessity to travel great distances, which could require one or more of their parishes to go without Mass on the obligatory Sundays and feast days. Parishioners in rural areas especially were also discouraged by the distances often required of them to travel in order to hear Mass.[141] Attendance remained lax among the laity in these conditions and little effort was made by the church to enforce attendance at Mass until the sixteenth century.[142]

The Mass had also lost some of its theological focus for the laity in late medieval Europe. In some areas, parishioners milled about the door of the church until they heard the bell which signalled the elevation of the Host.[143] At this point, known in Germany as the *Stillmesse*, they would rush into the church and then kneel in reverence to the uplifted Host.[144] This was a supreme moment for the parishioner, a 'transcendental experience'.[145] Afterwards, many would leave the church to go about their daily business or began talking noisily instead of keeping their attention focused on the priest who was about to take communion.[146] Miri Rubin declares church teaching on the elevation of the Host as the source of a lack of interest in the rest of the Mass: 'the benefits of the mass were so closely linked to the moment of the elevation, when Christ was in presence, that it is not surprising that the lengthy ritual that followed it was felt to be an anti-climax'.[147] Many Catholic reformers in the sixteenth century sought to return devotion to the Mass as a whole and not just the elevation of the Host.[148] The Council of Trent echoed their sentiment by emphasising greater liturgical participation of the laity through their more frequent reception of communion rather than their only witnessing the solitary communion of the priest.[149]

For Uhl, multiple Masses each week meant enabling all parishioners to attend Mass at least once a week. If Mass were said only once a week, one member of each household might have been unable to attend, since one person was required to watch the house.[150] Inability to attend Mass also excluded the individual from hearing sermons and catechisation which promulgated reformed Catholicism in the parishes. Parishioners in the Diocese of Speyer responded to the extra availability of Masses there, and in some cases even requested more frequent Masses.[151] The offering of multiple Masses per week served as Uhl's solution to the problem in Rottweil. If the laity were universally able to attend Mass weekly, they were certain not to be excluded from any portion, however slight, of the liturgical calendar, and were privy to the benefits of spiritual and occasional real communion, as well as the full complement of weekly sermons and catechisation.

Trent recognised the common unavailability of Masses as a problem in the mid-sixteenth century and decreed that all bishops ensure that priests 'celebrate Mass at least on the Lord's Days, and on solemn festivals; but, if they have the cure of souls, so often as to satisfy their obligation'.[152] Trent also expounded on its definition of the obligation for those charged with the cure of souls: 'whereas it is by divine precept enjoined on all, to whom the cure of souls is committed, to know their own sheep; to offer sacrifice for them; and, by the preaching of the divine word, by the administration of the sacraments, and by the example of all good works, to feed them'.[153] The duties shown above could be administered only with regular offerings of the Mass. The offering of sacrifice (the Eucharist), preaching, and administration of the sacraments, or at least one of the two renewable sacraments in the Eucharist, all centred on the Mass. Even the words 'to feed them' were obvious allusions to the Eucharist. To charge priests 'to know their own sheep' meant that these, in addition to other pastoral duties, needed to be offered on a frequent basis. By this definition, any priest who did not offer more than one weekly Mass failed in his duties, because multiple Masses per week were essential to ensure universal attendance of his flock.

Analysis of Uhl's visitations of the deanery of Rottweil provides insight into the changes that took place in the frequency of Mass under his leadership. As previously mentioned in this chapter, Uhl began monitoring priests' preaching ability in the 1570s and then the availability of sacraments provided by priests in the 1580s in the deanery of Rottweil. In the 1590s, he started to regulate the frequency with which they said Mass in their parishes as well. For the first time, the visitation of 1597 noted the frequency with which Mass was being celebrated in the deanery.[154] Corresponding information for each parish, however, was not entered into the report. Of the fifteen parishes visited only three commented on this issue. Joannes Monch in Waldmössingen and Joannes Hoch in Fischbach were both recorded as saying the Mass weekly, while the other priest mentioned, Zacharias Glattrin in Epfendorf, was singled out for his diligence as he said two Masses per week.[155] Parishes in the city of Rottweil were excluded from the report on this issue, probably because there had been daily Mass in the city from as early as 1485.[156] On the surface, this may not seem like much of a statement regarding the frequency of Masses in the deanery of Rottweil. As evidenced by Uhl's earlier visitation reports, however, only a few issues which were targets for reform at the time were mentioned in each report. Uhl was also very careful to emphasise positively the particular merits of priests who were performing beyond their obligations. This meant that the 1597 visitation was concerned with Mass frequency and found only one priest who was saying regularly more than one Mass per week. Those parishes in which frequency was unspecified probably fell into two categories; either their priests were saying Mass regularly once a week and were not mentioned, or the discrepancies were not serious enough to warrant disciplinary action beyond Uhl's admonishment since no record exists for the Rat's punishment of priests for this offence in the late 1590s.[157]

Uhl's attempts to increase the number of weekly Masses in the deanery are evidenced by the results of the visitation of 1608. The visitors from the diocese in Constance found in 1608 that many more parish priests were saying multiple Masses per week than had done so in 1597.[158] If one takes into account that Uhl's report in 1597 would have praised any priest who said multiple Masses, then, as shown in Table 3, only one priest out of fifteen was performing at that level. By 1608, that figure jumped to at least nine out of fifteen priests. Even more significant is the fact that by 1608 at least eight out of fifteen priests were saying three or more Masses per week, compared to none who were achieving that level in 1597. So Uhl and his successor as dean from 1606

Table 3 Weekly Mass offerings noted in visitations of 1597 and 1608

Weekly Masses	Parishes (1597)	Parishes (1608)
One	2	0
Two	1	1
Three	0	7
More than three	0	1
Not specified	12	6
Total	15	15

Data from EBAF, HA61, fols 454–8v; HA62, fols 232–57.

to 1608, Joannes Brenneissen, were effective at increasing the numbers of weekly Masses in the deanery's parishes between 1597 and 1608. Priests in the deanery also appear to have supported this reform since no record exists to suggest that any formal warnings or punishments were required to bring about the change. The effect of this achievement was to ensure that all parishioners would be able to attend Mass in these parishes and therefore be exposed further to the Eucharist and its efficacy, as well as to the preaching and catechisation which explained the Eucharist's necessity in the Catholic faith. Once able priests who could restore efficacy to the Mass and explain its teachings were in place, the next move was to provide greater access through increased opportunity to hear and witness the Mass.

This and all of the other efforts described in this essay had as their goal the formation of a distinctly Catholic identity for the people in Rottweil. Church leaders and city council members alike were afraid of a repeat of the failed Reformation years from 1526 to 1529 when a tense battle for believers gripped the city and threatened its livelihood and place in the Empire. They felt that the best defence against another influx of Protestant ideas was to ensure that the people of Rottweil and its territory were as strongly Catholic as possible before any challenge needed to be met. In their view, paramount to this programme was creating a religious environment in the city and the worship practices of the people that reinforced their identity as Catholic and that they were religiously superior to their Protestant neighbours who had failed to hold 'proper beliefs'. Whether this was an effective defence against Protestantism remains unknown since no further attempt to introduce the Reformation to Rottweil was made. It is known, however, that Rottweil did remain strongly Catholic and it is entirely possible that prospective harbingers of the Reformation passed up Rottweil in their search for new lands to reform because they saw that the city possessed an active laity with a strong Catholic identity and believed that other areas would be more responsive to their message.

NOTES

1 Diözesanarchiv Rottenburg (hereafter DAR), AI2a, no. 410, fol. 3.
2 DAR, Pfarreiarchiv Heilig Kreuz Rottweil, vol. 61: 152.
3 Gerhard Oestreich, 'Strukturprobleme des europäische Absolutismus', in G. Oestreich, ed., *Geist und Gestalt des frühmodernen Staates* (Berlin, 1969), 179–97; published in English as B. Oestreich and H. G. Koenigsberger, eds, *Neostoicism and the Early Modern State* (Cambridge, 1982).
4 Ernst Walter Zeeden, *Die Entstehung der Konfessionen. Grundlagen und Formen der Konfessionsbildung* (Munich, 1965).
5 Wolfgang Reinhard, 'Zwang zur Konfessionalisierung? Prologemena zu einer Theorie des konfessionellen Zeitalters', *Zeitschrift für Historische Forschung* 10 (1983), 257–77; Heinz Schilling, 'Confessionalisation in the Empire: Religious and Societal Change in Germany between 1555 and 1620', in H. Schilling, ed., *Religion, Political Culture and the Emergnce of Early Modern Society* (Leiden, 1992), 205–45.
6 Heinz Schilling, 'Nationale Identität und Konfession in der europäischen Neuzeit', in B. Giesen, ed., *Nationale und kulturelle Identität. Studien zur Entwicklung des kollektiven Bewußtseins in der Neuzeit* (Frankfurt, 1991), 192–252; Schilling, 'Die Konfessionalisierung von Kirche, Staat, und Gesellschaft', in Wolfgang Reinhard and Heinz Schilling, eds, *Die Katholische Konfessionalisierung*, in *Schriften des Vereins für Reformationsgeschichte* 198 (Gütersloh, 1995), 1–49, especially 10–12.
7 J. Waterworth, trans., *The Canons and Decrees of the Sacred and Oecumenical Council of Trent* (London, 1848), 213–14, 279.
8 Wolfgang Reinhard, 'Reformation, Counter-Reformation, and the Early Modern State: A Reassessment', *The Catholic Historical Review* 75 (1989), 383–404, especially 391–2.
9 Schilling, 'Nationale Identität', 192–252.
10 Waterworth, *Canons and Decrees*, 208–10.
11 *Constitutiones et decreta synodalia civitatis et dioecesis Constantiensis . . . anno domini M.D.LXVIII. statuta, edita et promulgata, praesidente Marco Sittico S. R. E. tituli S. Georgii in Velabro Presbyterio, Episcopo Constantiensis* (Dillingen, n. pp., 1568).
12 Johannes Greiner, *Geschichte der Schule in Rottweil am Neckar* (Stuttgart, 1915), 22.
13 This idea is present in his visitation reports where he continually emphasised the importance of strong preaching ability. Generallandesarchiv Karlsruhe (hereafter GLAK), 61/7321, fols 45–9v, 151–3; Erzbischöfliches Archiv Freiburg (hereafter EBAF), HA61, fols 97–9r, 454–8v, 610–13.
14 He called these 'Formula'. It is unknown if Uhl intended these to be published or not. There are no known printings, and only one manuscript copy exists. DAR, Pfarreiarchiv Heilig Kreuz Rottweil, vol. 161: 131–54.
15 GLAK, 61/7321, fols 45–9v, 151–3; EBAF, HA61, fols 97–8, 454–8v, 610–13.
16 The volumes are today housed in the parish library of the Heilig Kreuz Kirche in Rottweil, Pfarreibibliothek Heilig Kreuz Rottweil (hereafter PBHKR).
17 PBHKR, XXI 135–6.
18 A detailed examination of these sermons and events surrounding them can be found in Jason Nye, 'Johannes Uhl on Penitence: Sermons of the Dean of Rottweil, 1579–1602', in Katharine Jackson Lualdi and Anne T. Thayer, eds, *Penitence in the Age of Reformations* (Aldershot, 2000), 152–68.
19 DAR, Pfarreiarchiv Heilig Kreuz Rottweil, vol. 161: 139–42.
20 DAR, Pfarreiarchiv Heilig Kreuz Rottweil, vol. 161: 139.
21 Carlos Eire, *From Madrid to Purgatory: The Art and Craft of Dying in Sixteenth-Century Spain* (Cambridge, 1995), 168–231. The Council of Trent also reinforced the doctrine that Masses were beneficial to the living and the dead. Waterworth, *Canons and Decrees*, 232–3.
22 Robert Bireley, *The Refashioning of Catholicism, 1450–1700* (London, 1999), 114.
23 Reinhard, 'Reformation', 393. Chapter 9 of the present volume demonstrates the problems faced by the Protestant revision and rationalisation of the other world.

24 DAR, Pfarreiarchiv Heilig Kreuz Rottweil, vol. 161: 139–40.
25 DAR, Pfarreiarchiv Heilig Kreuz Rottweil, vol. 161: 140.
26 DAR, Pfarreiarchiv Heilig Kreuz Rottweil, vol. 161: 141.
27 The Ten Commandments became increasingly important in the *catechesis* of the late medieval church. Robert Bast, *Honor Your Fathers: Catechisms and the Emergence of a Patriarchal Ideology in Germany* (Leiden, 1997), 6–38.
28 DAR, Pfarreiarchiv Heilig Kreuz Rottweil, vol. 161: 142.
29 Bireley, *The Refashioning of Catholicism*, 102–3.
30 Bireley, *The Refashioning of Catholicism*, 102–3.
31 Bireley, *The Refashioning of Catholicism*, 102–3.
32 Marc Forster, *The Counter-Reformation in the Villages: Religion and Reform in the Bishopric of Speyer, 1560–1720* (Ithaca, 1992), 30.
33 Greiner, *Geschichte der Schule*, 39.
34 GLAK, 82a/50.
35 Bireley, *The Refashioning of Catholicism*, 59.
36 Bireley, *The Refashioning of Catholicism*, 59.
37 DAR, AI2a, Nr. 382.
38 Greiner, *Geschichte der Schule*, 39.
39 Bireley, *The Refashioning of Catholicism*, 103.
40 DAR, Pfarreiarchiv Heilig Kreuz Rottweil, vol. 161: 143–5.
41 Karl Lambrecht, *Rottweiler Narren-Fibel* (Rottweil, 1988).
42 DAR, Pfarreiarchiv Heilig Kreuz Rottweil, vol. 161: 143.
43 Waterworth, *Canons and Decrees*, 279.
44 R. W. Scribner, 'Reformation, Carnival and the World Turned Upside-Down', in his *Popular Culture and Popular Movements in Reformation Grmany* (London, 1987), 71–102.
45 Steven Ozment, *The Reformation in the Cities* (New Haven, 1975), 83.
46 EBAF, HA62, fol. 233v: 'Magna querela et de esa carnium diebus prohibitis, de causa multi scandali, et praesertim rustige facilem oppida nona pravos mores et exempla, vel ex consulo simile perversitate, vel ex simplicitate imitantur.'
47 Stadtarchiv Rottweil (hereafter STAR), Ratsprotkolle, book 1609–16: 410.
48 STAR, Ratsprotkolle, book 1609–16: 410.
49 GLAK 61/7321, fols 45–9v, 151–3; EBAF, HA61, fols 40, 97–8, 182v–183, 359v–360v, 454–8v, 610–13.
50 GLAK, 61/7321, fols 45–9v; EBAF, HA61, fols 454–8v.
51 EBAF, HA62, fols 232–57.
52 EBAF, HA62, fols 232–57.
53 EBAF, HA62, fols 232–57.
54 EBAF, HA62, fol. 240v: 'in doctrina Catechista praesentaliter iuriores tardienses et negligentiores provide admonit Praefectus et superiores ultro huic malo occurrent.'
55 Waterworth, *Canons and Decrees*, 54–6.
56 Reinhard, 'Reformation', 394.
57 DAR, Pfarreiarchiv Heilig Kreuz Rottweil, vol. 1.
58 Reinhard, 'Reformation', 393.
59 Reinhard, 'Reformation', 393.
60 DAR, Pfarreiarchiv Heilig Kreuz Rottweil, vol. 1. The sacrament of holy orders lies outside the scope of this chapter and is, by its very nature, not a sacrament in which the bulk of the Church's adherents participate.
61 Hermann Tüchle, 'Das Bistum Konstanz und das Konzil von Trient', in Georg Schreiber, ed., *Das Weltkonzil von Trient. Sein Werden und Wirken* (Freiburg, 1951), 191.
62 Tüchle, 'Das Bistum Konstanz', 191.
63 DAR, Pfarreiarchiv Heilig Kreuz ottweil, vol. 1: 1: 'LIBER PRIMUS DE HIS, QUI PER LAVACRUM AQUA IN VERBO VITAE a pristinorum sordibus peccatorum repurgati, CHRISTO nomina dederunt: auspicatus iuxta Concilii Tridentini decreta, sub M. Joanne Ullano Parocho

Rotuvilano, die 8 Aprilis, anno Salvatoris 1564'.

64 Waterworth, *Canons and Decrees*, 54–6.
65 Waterworth, *Canons and Decrees*, 198–9.
66 Reinhard, 'Reformation', 393.
67 John Bossy, 'The Counter-Reformation and the People of Catholic Europe', in David M. Luebke, ed., *The Counter-Reformation* (Oxford, 1999), 92–3.
68 John Bossy, *Christianity in the West, 1400–1700* (Oxford, 1985), 17.
69 Bossy, *Christianity in the West*, 17.
70 DAR, Pfarreiarchiv Heilig Kreuz Rottweil, vol. 1: 1.
71 EBAF, HA62, fol. 234v: 'Hactenus admissi sunt patrini duo contra Concili Tridentum et una Matrina, et adhuc admittunt.'
72 DAR, Pfarreiarchiv Heilig Kreuz Rottweil, vols. 1, 3, 4.
73 DAR, Pfarreiarchiv Heilig Kreuz Rottweil, vols. 1, 3, 4.
74 David Bagchi, *Luther's Earliest Opponents: Catholic Controversialists, 1518–1525* (Minneapolis, 1991), 184.
75 Visitors from the diocese reported the practice of rebaptism in the Rottweil churches in 1608, and noted its sacrilegious nature. EBAF, HA62, fol. 234v.
76 I rely here on the evidence gathered by Christopher Friedrichs for the German city of Nördlingen beween 1621 and 1720, where he discovered that 46.5 per cent of infants died before their first birthday. Christopher Friedrichs, *Urban Society in an Age of War: Nördlingen, 1580–1720* (Princeton, 1979), 306–8.
77 Bossy, *Christianity in the West*, 14.
78 For example, in 1603 the Hettinger family paid 100 gulden in order to have their unbaptised child buried. STAR, Archivalien II, Abteilung I, Lade V, Fasz. 16, no. 6.
79 Henry Kamen, *The Phoenix and the Flame: Catalonia and the Counter-Reformation* (New Haven, 1993), 116–17.
80 Bossy, *Christianity in the West*, 14–19.
81 Miri Rubin, *Corpus Christi: The Eucharist in Late Medieval Culture* (Cambridge, 1991), 349.
82 Catherine Brown, *Pastor and Laity in the Theology of Jean Gerson* (Cambridge, 1987), 57–8.
83 Rubin, *Corpus Christi*, 350; David Myers, *'Poor, Sinning Folk': Confession and Conscience in Counter-Reformation Germany* (Ithaca, 1996), 37.
84 Rubin, *Corpus Christi*, 84–5.
85 Waterworth, *Canons and Decrees*, 80–1, 83.
86 Waterworth, *Canons and Decrees*, 83.
87 Myers, *'Poor, Sinning Folk'*, 146.
88 Myers, *'Poor, Sinning Folk'*, 146.
89 Myers, *'Poor, Sinning Folk'*, 146.
90 Rubin, *Corpus Christi*, 84.
91 Rubin, *Corpus Christi*, 84.
92 Rubin, *Corpus Christi*, 85.
93 Rubin, *Corpus Christi*, 84.
94 Outram Evenett, *The Spirit of the Counter-Reformation* (South Bend, IN, 1970), 37–40.
95 GLAK, 82a/261.
96 GLAK, 61/7321, fols 151–3.
97 GLAK, 82a/261.
98 GLAK, 61/7321, fols 151–3.
99 GLAK, 61/7321, fol. 151v.
100 GLAK, 61/7321, fol. 151v.
101 STAR, Ratsprotokolle, book 1580–82: 167.
102 STAR, Ratsprotokolle, book 1580–82: 192.
103 STAR, Ratsprotokolle, book 1580–82: 209.
104 STAR, Ratsprotokolle, book 1580–82: 232.
105 STAR, Ratsprotokolle, book 1580–82: 234.

106 Winfried Hecht, 'Rottweils Magistrat kündigt den Pfarrer von Balgheim (1589)', *Rottweiler Heimatblätter* 52/3 (1991), n. p.

107 STAR, Ratsprotokolle, book 1583–86: 88.

108 STAR, 'Missivbuch der kaiserlichen Reichsstadt Rottweil von 1585–1607', fols 199v–200. Sichler's case and his rebellious nature are treated in detail in chapter 5 and in Hecht, 'Rottweils Magistrat'.

109 Hecht, 'Rottweils Magistrat'.

110 Peter Browe, *Die häufige Kommunion in Mittelalter* (Münster, 1938), 39–42, cited in Myers, 'Poor, Sinning Folk', 34–5.

111 Bireley, *The Refashioning of Catholicism*, 105.

112 DAR, Pfarreiarchiv Heilig Kreuz Rottweil, vol. 11: 314.

113 DAR, Pfarreiarchiv Heilig Kreuz Rottweil, vol. 11: 314.

114 DAR, Pfarreiarchiv Heilig Kreuz Rottweil, vol. 11: 314.

115 DAR, Pfarreiarchiv Heilig Kreuz Rottweil, vol. 11: 314.

116 DAR, Pfarreiarchiv Heilig Kreuz Rottweil, vol. 11: 314.

117 STAR, Ratsprotokolle, book 1583–86: 209, 213.

118 Waterworth, *Canons and Decrees*, 83; Constitutiones et decreta synodalia civitatis et dioecesis Constantiensis.

119 STAR, Ratsprotokolle, book 1583–86: 68.

120 STAR, Ratsprotokolle, book 1583–86: 68.

121 STAR, Ratsprotokolle, book 1583–86: 209.

122 Adriano Capelli, *Cronologia, cronografia e calendario perpetuo* (Milan, 1988), 96–7.

123 STAR, Ratsprotokolle, book 1583–86: 209.

124 STAR, Ratsprotokolle, book 1583–86: 209.

125 STAR, Ratsprotokolle, book 1583–86: 213.

126 STAR, Ratsprotokolle, book 1593–98: 208.

127 STAR, Ratsprotokolle, book 1583–86: 219.

128 For a full discussion of this topic, see Nye, 'Johannes Uhl'.

129 David Sabean, *Power in the Blood: Popular Culture and Village Discourse in Early Modern Germany* (Cambridge, 1984), 61–93.

130 Lynn Martin, *Plague? Jesuit Accounts of Epidemic Disease in the 16th Century* (Kirksville, MO, 1996), 89.

131 Martin, *Plague?*, and Nye, 'Johannes Uhl'. Heinrich Bullinger made similar exhortations to the people of Zürich to combat famine in 1571. Hans Ulrich Bächtold, 'Gegen den Hunger beten. Heinrich Bullinger, Zürich und die Einführung des gemeinen Gebetes im Jahre 1571', in Hans Ulrich Bächtold, Rainer Henrich and Kurt Jakob Rüetschi, eds, *Vom Beten, vom Verketzern, vom Predigen. Beiträge zum Zeitalter Heinrich Bullingers und Rudolf Gwalthers* (Zürich, 1999), 9–44.

132 STAR, Ratsprotokolle, book 1587–92: 371–2.

133 Nye, 'Johannes Uhl'.

134 STAR, Ratsprotokolle, book 1609–16: 153.

135 STAR, Ratsprotokolle, book 1609–16: 192.

136 STAR, Ratsprotokolle, book 1609–16: 192.

137 Rubin, *Corpus Christi*, 63, 150.

138 R. W. Scribner, 'Ritual and Popular Religion in Catholic Germany at the Time of the Reformation', *Journal of Ecclesiastical History* 35 (1984), 47–77.

139 Rubin, *Corpus Christi*, 150.

140 Kamen, *The Phoenix*, 117–18.

141 Kamen, *The Phoenix*, 117–18.

142 Kamen, *The Phoenix*, 118–19.

143 Rubin, *Corpus Christi*, 152.

144 Bossy, *Christianity in the West*, 68.

145 Bossy, *Christianity in the West*, 68.

146 Kamen, *The Phoenix*, 119.
147 Rubin, *Corpus Christi*, 153.
148 Kamen, *The Phoenix*, 121–3.
149 Waterworth, *Canons and Decrees*, 156–7.
150 Bireley, *The Refashioning of Catholicism*, 105.
151 Forster, *The Counter-Reformation*, 31.
152 Waterworth, *Canons and Decrees*, 185.
153 Waterworth, *Canons and Decrees*, 175.
154 EBAF, HA61, fols 454–8v.
155 EBAF, HA61, fols 454–8v.
156 DAR, AI2a, no. 448.
157 STAR, Ratsprotokolle, books 1593–98, 1599–1608.
158 EBAF, HA62, fols 232–57.

3

Traditional practices: Catholic missionaries and Protestant religious practice in Transylvania

MARIA CRAČIUN

The beginning of the Jesuit mission in Transylvania was a mixture of clerical initiative and political decision. In 1579 three youths from the so-called Szekler region, Peter of Ciuc (Csík), Valentine and Thomas went to Lelesz to be ordained. They returned to Cluj (Kolozsvár, Klausenburg) on 25 March, bringing with them a Hungarian Jesuit, Joannes Leleszi. Although he lived at court and only preached on the occasion of festivals, he is believed to have been instrumental in initiating the idea of a Jesuit mission in Transylvania.[1] István Báthory, prince of Transylvania and King of Poland, wanted the Jesuits in Transylvania and imposed his decision on the diet although the latter only accepted them for the purpose of founding schools and colleges. Báthory had met the Jesuits in Vienna and had decided that they could prove instrumental in revitalising Transylvanian Catholicism. Báthory consequently defined the role of the order in educating the young, in reinstating Catholicism to its original position, and creating an educated clergy. Báthory intended to give them the convents of the Franciscans and the Poor Claires at Cluj and the residence of the Benedictine abbey of Cluj-Mănăştur (Kolozsmonostor) with its villages. On 18 July the Jesuits who were meant to found the college arrived in Cluj and established themselves in the former abbey. The mission included the provincial Francisco Sunieri, the Polish Jesuit Jakob Wuyek, Luigi Odescalchi, four other Jesuits and two Szekler priests, Peter Erdösi and Valentine Lado.[2] The team from Poland arrived earlier than the team from Vienna organised by Rome. This had unfortunate consequences for the relations between Jakob Wuyek, the Polish rector of the college and Stephanus Szántó (Arator), one of the Hungarian Jesuits from the other team.[3] The eleven Polish Jesuits were led by Francisco Sunieri, who was the provincial of Poland. They managed to open the school in December 1579 and in the autumn of 1580 they moved the college to Cluj itself, where they had been given the former Franciscan monastery and the convent of the Poor Claires. The college was founded in the spring of 1583.

One is surprised by the fact that on numerous occasions the energy of the Jesuits was spent in petty rivalries, especially between the Hungarian and the Polish Jesuits. The Polish and Hungarian Missionaries did not get on very well. The conflict was acute on the part of Jakob Wuyek, formerly the rector of the college in Vilnius, who had come to Transylvania to head the college in Cluj. This irritated from the start some Hungarian Jesuits, such as Szántó, who had hoped to fill these positions themselves. The two groups had had different experiences of the Counter-Reformation, diverse views on the mission, divergent opinions about the status and the administration of the college and even different experiences of a feudal society and dealings with the serfs. These could be reconciled only with great difficulty and consequently a lot of ink was wasted in letters complaining to the higher Jesuit authorities. The conflict ultimately led to an investigation and Wuyek lost his position while Szántó left to work as a missionary in Oradea (Nagyvárad, Grosswardein). A new Italian rector, Ferrante Capeci was appointed to the college. The conflict between Wuyek and Szántó revolved principally around the issue of the performance of the Polish Jesuits, who could only hold religious services and administer the sacraments but could not preach, because they did not know the language and thus made the mission ineffective.

After the death, on 27 May 1581, of Kristóf (Christopher) Báthory the situation of the Jesuits became more difficult. With Sigismund a minor and Stephen Báthory so far away, the estates tried to block Jesuit activity at every corner. After Báthory's death the expulsion of the Jesuits was openly discussed. The estates in fact applied political pressure in order to expel the Jesuits. At the Diet of Cluj in June 1587, the estates requested the abandonment of idolatry and the expulsion of the Jesuits. They refused to discuss other issues while the religious ones remained unresolved. They were accused of exceeding the duties they had been supposed to perform and of proselytising in places where their presence was not allowed. The efforts of the Jesuits were further hampered by the plague epidemic of 1586, which drastically reduced their numbers, and by the death of Stephen Báthory, which meant a serious loss of support, and by the decisions of the diet of Mediaș (Medgyes, Mediasch) in December 1587, when the Jesuits were asked to leave Transylvania within three weeks.

Thus, the story of the Jesuit mission in late sixteenth-century Transylvania is overall a story of failure. It is nevertheless a story laden with meaning and one that leads us to question the possibility and terms of a Catholic restoration in a state whose political identity had been recently established and where Reformed ideas had made consistent progress throughout the sixteenth century. It also provides the unique opportunity to see Catholicism as the 'new faith' struggling to reform the practices and beliefs of the 'old faith'. This chapter will focus on the changes in religious life in Transylvania during the sixteenth century, within the broader context provided by the character of Counter-Reformation Catholicism in the region. From this perspective, the success or failure of the mission – of re-Catholicisation – becomes irrelevant and allows one to discuss the goals and means rather than fixating on the outcome. This will highlight the way in which the Jesuit missionaries saw the people they worked with, although it will raise difficulties stemming from the analysis both of events and their image in the minds of the people who wished to record and shape them.

An interesting story can be unravelled by looking at the accounts of Jesuit missionaries who tried to reimplement Catholicism in the region at the end of the sixteenth century, during the reign of the Báthory princes. It is significant whether the Jesuit missionaries saw the population of Transylvania as 'heretics', lapsed Catholics or 'shepherdless' Catholics who had survived and forged forms of religious expression in the absence of clerical guidance. One has to assess the extent to which Jesuit missionaries in the area viewed local Protestantism as essentially a distortion of traditional Catholicism, which gave rise to a reluctance on their part to make a clear distinction between 'superstition' and popular piety. The support of the Báthory princes has often been held to account for enthusiasm for re-Catholicisation at the end of the sixteenth century. However, re-Catholicisation could be successful, not so much because of a well-coordinated central policy, but rather because of the continuous vitality of traditional Catholicism, especially within the rural environment.[4] If Protestantism was a distortion, or error-filled version of the true (Catholic) faith, then labelling it superstitious was a dangerous approach which might 'backfire'. Better to stress the 'erroneous' nature of Protestant faith and practice rather than its 'irrationality' or 'baselessness'.

Thus, the main issue in this article could be rephrased and defined as an attempt to clarify whether Catholicism had survived in Transylvania and whether it had felt the need to reform itself even before the arrival of the Catholic missionaries or whether support for Catholicism was solely the result of cooperation between the political authority and post-Tridentine missionary enthusiasm. This leads one to a related and much more relevant question concerning the changes that Transylvanian religious life had undergone during the sixteenth century. We are thus compelled to consider at the same time the survival of Catholicism and the progress of the Reformation within the communities. Beyond the institutional aspect, which can seem relatively clear, the question remains whether the Catholic mission was confronted with a Protestant Transylvania. Can Transylvania be considered Reformed by the end of the sixteenth century? This apparently simple question in fact opens a very complex issue. When can a reforming process be considered complete? When can a territory be considered Reformed? What are the criteria one uses to establish the degree of implementation of Protestant ideas within a given society? One wonders how the Jesuit mission worked and what it aimed to achieve in places where it was allowed to act freely and where the Reformation had made progress. The territorial distribution of the Jesuit mission could be relevant from several points of view.[5] A perfect overlap between the territory of Catholic survival and the territory of the mission could tell us something about the level of adherence to the Jesuit mission in Transylvania and the freedom of movement of the missionaries, while a comparison between the territory of Catholic survival and the reformed Catholic territory in the wake of the mission could be an adequate pointer for the efficiency of the latter.

Finally, one would have to decide whether Transylvania had become Protestant during the sixteenth century. This could be partly evaluated through the response of the wider social body to the effort to reimplement or revitalise Catholicism. This discussion will be restricted to the most obvious changes that had taken place in Transylvanian religious life (noticeable at the level of the communities) which can be established with the help of the reports of the Catholic missionaries from the end of the sixteenth century. In order to evaluate the changes that the Reformation had wrought in the communities, one should take at least three aspects into account: the doctrinal, the ritual and the devotional. One must consider whether the missionaries were trying to implement a reformed Catholicism or merely targeting the major points of difference between Catholicism and Protestantism. A significant criterion for such an investigation, and the only one that will be considered at the present time, is the degree of resistance to the Catholic mission. One must also take the declared aims of the mission into account, whether it defined itself through its evangelical or pastoral dimension – whether it wished to convert the 'heretics' or to strengthen existing Catholics in their faith.[6]

The chapter will focus on one case study, an assessment of the religious experience of the people in the villages of Baciu (Kisbács) and Leghia (Jegenye) which had been returned to the abbey of Cluj-Mănăştur.[7] The advantages of this example are numerous. On the one hand, these villages were not an area of Catholic resistance, because from the moment that they had ceased to be under the control of the Benedictine abbey, Protestant propaganda had had a free rein. On the other hand, when they were returned to the abbey, they became accessible to the Jesuit mission. Consequently, the progress of the Reformation can be assessed with greater accuracy here than elsewhere. Jesuit accounts suggest that the Protestant preachers, some of whom were quite radical (anti-Trinitarians or Anabaptists), had been very active in these villages and consequently the population had been converted to Protestantism. They had been, in any case, deprived for a long time of the Catholic institutional framework which would have ensured the continuity of religious services and the administration of sacraments.[8]

The principal sources for this investigation are the reports and the correspondence of Catholic missionaries who worked in Transylvania. In addition to the reports of two Catholic travellers, who passed through Transylvania in the 1560s and 1570s, most of the material consists of Jesuit letters, written between the moment when their arrival in Transylvania was still being negotiated and their expulsion in 1588. It is necessary to mention some of the limitations of these sources as they most obviously tend to present the Catholic point of view. Most of them were written in order to convince the papacy and the provincial of the Jesuit order of the necessity of a Catholic mission in Transylvania. They thus tend to exaggerate the level of survival of Catholicism and the fact that the Catholic mission would be welcome in this region. One could tentatively presume, in order to achieve a more balanced view of the situation, that the Reformation had made more progress than the Jesuits were willing to admit, and that Catholicism had survived less than they claimed. Their arguments were constructed by presenting Transylvania, seen as an outpost of Catholic Christianity, as a territory in need of Catholic restoration. From this perspective they tended to over-emphasise the survival of Catholicism and to latch on to the smallest shred of evidence of sympathy for Catholicism in the region.[9]

Changes in Transylvanian religious life in the sixteenth century presumably came about because of the progress of the Reformation. This story could be viewed from the Protestant perspective and based on Protestant accounts as a tale of success which led to the emergence of the Transylvanian Reformed principality in the seventeenth century. In this context, the brief episode of Catholic confessionalisation attempted by the Báthory princes constitutes an interesting *intermezzo* which falls within the specific traits of east central European Counter-Reformation Catholicism. As far as the progress of the Reformation is concerned, from a strictly institutional point of view, the different stages of the progress of the Reformation in Transylvania seem relatively clear.[10] In 1543 the diet of Turda (Torda, Torenburg) recognised Lutheranism while in 1545 the *Universitas Saxonum* in Sibiu (Nagyszeben, Hermannstadt) adopted this faith as their own. In 1547 the *Universitas Saxonum* used Honterus' reforming text, *Formula Reformationis Coronensis* in order to prepare a new ecclesiastical order for all the Germans in Transylvania and in 1553 the synod of the Saxon clergy elected its own bishop, Paul Wiener. In 1554 the Hungarian Lutherans founded a separate church and in 1556 Ferenc (Francis) Dávid became the first Hungarian Lutheran bishop. Consequently, in 1557 the Diet of Turda recognised the official status of the three confessions and their equality with Catholicism. In 1564 the synod of Aiud (Nagyenyed, Grossenyed) elected Dávid as its bishop, the diocese thus becoming Calvinist while in 1567 the diet of Turda replaced the Heidelberg Catechism with a more explicitly anti-Trinitarian one. In 1568 the diet of Turda declared religious freedom. On 28 January 1568 the anti-Trinitarians formally separated themselves from the Reformed community. In 1572, the Lutheran synod in Mediaş adopted the *Formula Pii Consensu inter Pastores Ecclesiarum Saxonicarum* and the *Confession of Augsburg*.

The evidence suggests that, until the end of the sixteenth century, all the Saxon towns (Sibiu, Braşov (Brassó, Kronstadt), Bistriţa (Besztercz, Bistriz), Mediaş, Sighişoara (Segesvár, Schässburg), Orăştie (Szászváros, Broos)) were Lutheran. The Reformation had been implemented in the Saxon environment by the magistrates of the towns. On the other hand, all the sources suggest the presence of a deep-seated and almost militant Protestantism among the nobility. The courtly entourage, often dominated by Italian reformers, was strongly supportive of the Reformation. The nobility were able to use all the levers of political power and the legislation of the country in order to defend the new faith from Catholic onslaught. Sources concerning the rural area are not equally informative and suggest that the population of the villages had been converted to Protestantism as a consequence of the exercise of the traditional right of *ius patronatus* when the noble was responsible for bringing in a Protestant preacher. In this region, throughout the Middle Ages the nobility had already enjoyed the right to nominate the clergy as a consequence of *ius patronatus*. During the sixteenth century, the mostly German towns had opted in favour of Lutheranism, the Hungarian nobility was mostly loyal to Calvinism, while the serfs enjoyed little freedom in their religious options and generally followed the lead of the local noble.

The question of the territorial distribution of the mission and its relation with the territories of Catholic survival also needs to be dealt with. The evidence suggests that the areas of Catholic survival were Alba Iulia, where Catholicism had stayed more or less functional through the efforts of the Báthory family, Oradea, which had benefited for a longer time from an institutional framework, the Székely föld (Szekler lands) and the estates of the Báthory family in Şimleuimleu (Somlyó).[11] There is some evidence concerning the survival of a small Catholic community in Cluj. The role of three nuns was emphasised, including an Augustinian nun called Catherine, who lived in a little house which acted as a chapel outside the city walls, and two others, who were Dominican nuns, living in the city in another house next to a chapel dedicated to the Trinity. Their most important contribution was that of keeping a number of liturgical books, homiletic literature and sacred images, which had belonged to the religious orders of the city. The Trinity chapel seems to have become the place of worship for the Catholic community in Cluj. Certainly, Easter was celebrated there in 1576. Undoubtedly, the community was small – for a reception honouring Stephen Báthory could be seated at three tables.

When one takes the territory of the Jesuit mission into account it becomes very clear that the villages which had belonged to the abbey of Cluj-

Mănăştur and had later been taken over by the nobility were especially targeted by the missionaries, because they had been returned to the monastery and were thus accessible (and under the Jesuits' *ius patronatus*). This situation made the work of the Jesuits easier and strengthened their hope that these villages would return to Catholicism.[12] They were also allowed to proselytise in a number of villages where they had been specifically invited by the owner of the estate.[13] Another targeted area was Ciuc, in the Szekler lands, which the Jesuits regarded as an area of Catholic survival.[14] Most of the missions which had visited Transylvania in the second half of the sixteenth century remarked on the survival of Catholicism in this region. One of the local nobles, Paul Becz (of Kormás) was one of the most fervent supporters of Catholicism. He had been tempted by Calvinism, but 'being interested in the truth' and receptive in the face of the Catholic mission, he had returned to his native land intent on supporting the Catholic cause. As far as the towns were concerned, the Jesuits were present in the suburbs of Cluj, where they had taken over the buildings of the Benedictine Abbey of Cluj-Mănăştur, in Alba Iulia (Gyulafehérvár, Weissenburg) and Oradea. They had a college in Cluj and residences in the other two towns.[15] Antonio Possevino would have liked to extend the mission towards areas such as Făgăraş (Fogaras, Fogarasch), Sibiu and Braşov but that was impossible due to the opposition of city magistrates.[16]

Thus, the areas of Catholic survival seem to be more or less identical with the territories of the mission. The Jesuits did not venture into areas where they would have lacked the support of latent Catholicism. In fact they did not benefit from the legal framework for such activities. The Diet of Cluj (1–10 May 1581) conditioned the election of Sigismund Báthory on the reinforcing of the laws concerning religious liberty. This affected the Jesuits directly through the paragraph which said that they were only allowed to act in Cluj, Cluj-Mănăştur and Alba Iulia.[17] The decision of the diet of Cluj meant that the Jesuits were only able to preach among the serfs in the villages they controlled and among the inhabitants of two Transylvanian towns. With the threat of perpetual expulsion hanging over their heads they did not dare venture where they were not invited.

When one contemplates the changes in Transylvanian religious life, the evidence first of all suggests that, during the sixteenth century a significant number of churches had been destroyed or left in ruins.[18] In particular, monastic churches seem gradually to have been abandoned. In some places the buildings had been turned into warehouses or even stables. This latter observation could easily be regarded as part of a scenario concocted by the Jesuits in order to trigger the indignation of the Catholic ecclesiastical authorities. But there could be a grain of truth in these statements. In some regions (especially in isolated places in the rural areas) there had been no interest in holding Protestant services in the former Catholic churches. This seems to have been true especially with regard to monastic churches.[19] In other places, the churches simply under-went some transformations in agreement with the new Protestant religions and there are several mentions of churches which had been taken over by the 'heretics'.[20] The changes in the churches were mostly caused by iconoclastic inci-dents. The evidence suggests that Calvinists inflicted a greater iconoclasm on the churches they expropriated than the Lutherans. These changes refer to the removal/destruction of stained-glass windows and the replacing of the altar stone with a communion table. There is also some evidence that paintings had been destroyed.[21] The Catholic view of Protestants again highlights the error of Protestantism rather than any superstitious quality. Arising from Catholicism, Protestantism was not a 'belief held by many people without foundation' but, instead, was a perversion and distortion of the truth.

Some of the sources suggest that the changes in Lutheran churches were far less significant. The Lutherans did not seem concerned to destroy either the paintings or the statues. They did not necessarily remove the altars or the organs and often preserved liturgical vessels and highly ornate church vest-ments. Pierre Lescalopier, who travelled through Transylvania in 1574, men-tioned the lack of ostensible change to Lutheran churches.[22] While he was visiting Cristian (Kereszténfalva, Neustadt), he entered a church during the evening service, which was held in Latin, and believed himself to be in a Catholic church, until the end of the service when the faithful prayed 'for the destruction of papal and Turkish tyranny'. The stained-glass windows, the mural paintings, and the priests' vestments had given him the misleading impression that nothing had changed.[23]

However, there is also evidence which suggests relatively intense icono-clastic activity in Lutheran churches as well. Data concerning Lutheran churches from the rural area suggests that in several of them wall-paintings had been whitewashed at the time of the Reformation.[24] The removal of the images from Braşov in 1544 had taken place under the influence of Bullinger and shows that there were more radical groups in Saxon towns who would have lobbied for more significant changes.[25] One could also assume that the rural environ-ment was more conservative than the urban one and that could account for the more moderate iconoclastic activity. A similar suggestion comes from instances where the altar stone can be found among other slabs in the pavement of the church, which is a clear indication that it had been removed under Reformed influence.[26] Changes along Reformed lines are suggested by the evidence in Movile (Szászhalom, Hundertbücheln) where there used to be a chapel of St Valentine. A panel from the winged altar, also dedicated to St Valentine, was preserved and ended up serving as a door to one of the storage towers. Litur-gical vessels and vestments, sometimes even books, were removed from the churches.[27] The Protestants had taken all the vestments, liturgical vessels and ornaments from the altar from the abbey in Cluj-Mănăștur. The monks had tried to hide the valuable gold and silver vessels by burying them, but these were discovered and confiscated by the Protestants.

The same types of changes are mentioned by A. A. Rusu for the county of Hațeg (Hátszeg, Hatzeg). Having taken into account both the Orthodox and the Catholic churches in the district of Hațeg, he came to the conclusion that one can demonstrate support for the Reformation among the area's patrons on the basis of the changes to church fabric – generally the removal of the altar stone, the disappearance of the iconostasis and the whitewashing of the wall-paintings.[28] Again the Jesuits could easily be accused of exaggeration but very often their conclusions are supported by archaeological evidence, by the research undertaken by art historians and, surprisingly, even by the reports of Protestant eyewitnesses to events.[29] Thus, a first conclusion could be that the church had suffered material loss and was in a state of institutional disarray.

One must at this point turn to an examination of the religious beliefs and practices which were targeted by the Jesuits in their reports. The fact that the Jesuit mission insisted on the reimplementation of certain practices, which included both doctrinal and ritual and devotional aspects, such as baptism, frequent confession and regular communion, suggests that, in addition to their theological content, these were also the elements which highlighted the differences between the practices of the two religious systems (the Catholic and the Protestant). This would lead us to believe that, in Transylvania, Protestant practices had taken root and that these were primarily targeted by the Jesuits. However, another possible interpretation is that these practices would have been implemented in any case, because they were in agreement with the spirit of the post-Tridentine reform and thus part of the mission's focus on reforming traditional Catholicism.

Nevertheless, an understanding of these events can only come from the study of the actual changes in Transylvanian piety during the sixteenth century. The Catholic aspect of ritual and piety needing to be reinstated would indicate the depth and success of Protestantism in Transylvania. As their primary goal, the Jesuits wished to return the population to Catholicism.[30] They consequently travelled to various communities exercising their sacerdotal duties, administering the sacraments, and, in particular, confessing and baptising. On the other hand, the pastoral dimension was not neglected as the Jesuits preached everywhere in order to convince the 'heretics' to return to Catholicism. The strategy of the mission thus involved several aspects related to language, the importance of which the Jesuits were fully conscious. The role of language, as opposed to religious practice, is a major topic and well beyond the scope of this essay.[31]

The doctrinal issues which do surface in the correspondence are linked to certain crucial tenets of the Protestant faith such as *sola scriptura* (which

highlights issues of authority in doctrinal matters) or *sola fide* (which brings to
the fore the issue of good deeds). They were crucial areas of theological debate
– the issue of sin and redemption – and were coupled with debates on Purgatory and intercession, which related to the rejection of the cult of saints. The
Jesuits claimed that in places such as Cluj, where the Reformation had been
firmly implemented, the Gospel and the prophecies of the Old Testament had
been presented in a distorted way.[32] In many cases the clergy had married, with
widespread popular support. Consequently the Jesuits were condemned by
public opinion because of their insistence on clerical celibacy.[33] The reports also
mentioned, with a certain degree of satisfaction, Ferenz Dávid's fall from grace
as a consequence of his anti-Trinitarian views. Because of his extravagant opinions he had managed to alienate himself completely. He had been imprisoned
in order to explain his doctrinal beliefs.[34] The rejection of the Trinity, central
to the anti-Trinitarian discourse, did reflect a major doctrinal change. Christian doctrine was taught in schools (presumably in both Cluj and Alba Iulia), but
reports admit that this frequently led to controversies. This statement tends to
suggest that doctrine had changed in a significant way and that people had internalised the new teachings to a sufficient degree and felt compelled publicly to
espouse them and even defend them.[35] Clearly one tradition the Jesuits had to
confront was the popularisation of theological debate and the internalisation of
the idea that, to some extent, all men were priests.

Furthermore, the Jesuits were mostly concerned with those ritual and
devotional aspects which had doctrinal implications. There are frequent references to confession, communion, baptism and other sacraments. A reaffirma-
tion of the sacraments in fact had doctrinal value, considering that their number
had been drastically reduced by the Reformation to communion and baptism
and that both these ceremonies were central to the new religion. The Eucharist
was mentioned, because it commemorated the redemptive value of Christ's
sacrifice, while at the same time bringing to the fore the differences regarding
the way in which the divine presence in the eucharistic symbols was understood. The most easily perceivable ritual aspect concerned communion in both
kinds. Baptism, on the other hand, stressed the entrance into the Christian
community through the promise to renounce sin. The degree to which this act
was conscious and internalised had led to fiery disputations in the Protestant
world, especially regarding the age when baptism should be administered –
debates which were not devoid of ritual implications or unimportant in an area
with strong Anabaptist communities. The tendency of the faithful to receive
communion in the Catholic church, to receive baptism or to confess can thus
be understood as a profession of faith.[36] In support of this idea, Ferrante Capeci
stated that some people would have preferred to risk their children's death
without baptism, rather than allow them to be baptised by Protestants. This

occurred because they were not satisfied with the way in which baptism was administered. This attitude suggests a strong attachment to the traditional religious forms and ceremonies as well as a personalised support for Catholic practice.[37] The differences between the Lutherans and the Calvinists were remarked upon and the missionaries stressed the fact that the Lutheran articles of faith were not so different from Catholic ones.[38] Again, the stress of Catholic polemic was not on the 'superstitious' nature of Protestantism but its error.

The most significant ritual changes could be noticed in the liturgy. The Catholic liturgy was no longer a frequent occurrence in Transylvania.[39] Most church ceremonies seem to have changed. The emphases of the Jesuits suggest that the Catholic church did not consider the baptism that had been administered by anti-Trinitarians or Anabaptists to be valid, because of the differences in rite (and, presumably, on the Trinitarian formula). There were differences of opinion regarding adult or infant baptism, sprinkling or total immersion.[40] They also remarked on the fact that the Protestant clergy were ordained in a different ceremony, simply through the laying on of hands.[41] Eventually, being Catholic or not seemed to be very much an issue concerning formal practice, the external manifestations of devotion. The stress placed on confession as one of the sacraments, but also as one of the ways in which a Catholic individual could manifest their faith, argue for this tendency. Confession itself was different in Protestant churches, where it had become communal, while the Catholic church insisted on auricular confession. The wish of the faithful to confess before the major feasts was interpreted by the Jesuits in a positive way.[42] A similar emphasis was placed on baptism. In areas where Anabaptism had become popular, people had not been baptised at all. Odescalchi mentioned that in many places he had baptised a great number of people, up to forty in a village, because in that region, for at least ten years, the Protestant clergy had refused to baptise people.[43] The wish of the people to receive the sacraments was seen as a sign that they wanted to return to Catholicism. Feast-days were especially preferred for the distribution of sacraments. One might conclude that confession and communion, theologically places of sacerdotal power, had been seized upon by the people as individual and voluntary expressions of faith and visible signs of a rejection of Protestant practices.[44]

What seems clear is that these Catholic practices (and beliefs) had proved resistant to Protestant assaults, which would strongly imply that they were retained for more rational and positive reasons than that they were simply traditional and superstitious. While some practices (e.g. the cult of saints; see below) may have been retained because of their 'magical' or 'mystical' value to individuals, the enthusiasm for Catholic communion (never an object of popular participation before the Reformation) and confession would seem evidence of a conscious desire to identify publicly and obviously with the work and faith of the Jesuits. As we will see below, this support is all the more striking when one considers the 'foreign' elements in the Jesuit mission and the opportunities for failure and popular rejection these provided.

The Jesuits tried, on the other hand, to revive the Catholic feasts and ceremonies. For instance, the procession on Palm Sunday, with its festive and even playful dimension, could stimulate the solidarity of the group through communal activity.[45] There was a theatrical dimension to the procession which could appeal to the imagination of the participants. This is supported by István Szántó's attitude to the traditional customs of the area, which were to be treated with respect. Szántó alluded to traditional practices in his dispute with the Polish Jesuits. The latter, because they had a different experience of the Counter-Reformation, wished to implement a series of devotional practices meant to stimulate religious feeling, especially processions, which could presumably induce intense religious emotion. Szántó disagreed with this and upheld local customs instead.[46] Szántó's main objection was that the Polish Jesuits wanted the peasantry to work on feast-days. One of the most interesting features of the complaint is that Szántó objected to the idea that the Polish Jesuits neglected the celebrations of the feast-days of the patron saints of Hungary, especially dynastic saints such as Stephen, Ladislaus and Emericus.[47] Wuyek was also accused of holding additional feasts contrary to the customs of Transylvania. Szántó's wishes fall within the practices of the Catholic church, which were re-emerging at that time and were being used to exploit people's allegiance to traditional devotional patterns. Szántó wished to revive existing feasts and ceremonies, to use them as an appeal to traditional forms of religious expression as a means of strengthening Catholics in their faith. The Polish Jesuits had a different experience of the Counter-Reformation, as in Poland there was an emphasis on the external manifestations of the cult, which fired the imagination of the faithful. There was also strong emphasis on pilgrimages, processions and the cult of relics. They probably tried to introduce these elements into Transylvania as well, a move not supported by the Hungarian Jesuits. Szántó, for instance, criticised the procession organised on Palm Sunday in Baciu. The person who had most offended Szántó's sensibilities was the Polish Jesuit, Petrus Szydlowski, who had compelled the peasantry to enact an episode from his play, *The Dialogue*, under duress.[48]

As a consequence of these complaints, Joannes Paulus Campani, the provincial of Poland, and P. I. Carminata compiled a catalogue of the feasts which should be celebrated in Transylvania, when they visited Transylvania in 1582, in order to clear up the conflict between the Hungarian and Polish Jesuits.[49] The feasts, which they had decided were to be celebrated in Transylvania seem to agree with Szántó's point of view.[50] On several occasions there were detailed instructions concerning the celebrations and it was specified that the peasantry from the estate of Cluj-Mănăștur should not be made to work and thus sin. This seems to come as a response to Szántó's objection that the Polish Jesuits had not respected local custom and tradition and had made the people work on their estates on those particular feast-days. Possevino informs us that in 1582 the Jesuits founded a Marian congregation, no doubt in order to encourage Marian devotion and in 1583 a *Corpus Christi* confraternity was founded, in order to restore a sense of community and to channel devotional patterns along lines totally antithetical to Protestant (especially Calvinist) theology.

Among the devotional models that the Protestants had tried very hard to dislodge were those connected with the cult of the dead. Early Protestantism was generally incapable of eradicating traditional popular concern for the souls of the dead. An attachment to all aspects connected to the rites of passage was still very strong, thus the reimplementation of those models by the missionaries was a lot simpler. Some people requested services for the dead or even a Mass for the dead to be held in Rome. The Mass for the dead had probably disappeared to a large extent in the new atmosphere created by the Reformation.[51] However, the older generation had preserved the memory of Catholic ritual and of Catholic devotional elements.[52] An elderly woman, although she had converted to Protestantism, had requested a Catholic priest on her deathbed. This example highlights the importance of devotional and ritual practices associated with the rites of passage.[53]

The evidence suggests that faith had become a private matter and a degree of caution was exercised in public behaviour. Capeci mentioned the fact that the students of the Jesuit college did not dare to show their faith or display their patterns of piety in front of just anyone. Quite often incidents occurred, especially as a result of devotional practices such as fasting on Fridays or before certain designated feast days. Protestant churches had obviously reduced the number of days which required fasting. The students could thus enter into conflict with their own families.[54]

Some of the facts we have already mentioned do suggest that traditional, medieval religion had been mostly abandoned. Attitudes to processions, pilgrimages, services for the dead, fasting, excesses of devotion, iconoclastic incidents tend to suggest that the religious ethos exposed by the Reformation had taken some hold within the communities. There were occasional violent confrontations even among the faithful. Thus, at a funeral service conducted by Szántó, the Catholics were attacked and the cross was trodden under foot. In 1587, the procession at Easter was attacked. Excesses in eucharistic devotion tended to lead to hostile reactions and to ridicule, which shows that people had fairly clear notions of doctrinally correct attitudes. For instance, in Sibiu, the procession for *Corpus Christi* had been interrupted by onlookers who started to mock the women who carried Christ in their arms. When a crucifix fell to the ground in the church in Viseud (Vessződ, Zied), the reaction of one of the faithful was to demand that it stand up and prove itself.[55] These incidents point to the changes in piety and to the fact that people had become consciously Protestant and, in many cases, were vocal in their rejection of Catholic practices.[56] However, it remains to be seen if the eventual demise of Catholicism was only a generation away or if the Jesuits would be successful in breathing life back into Catholicism in the area.

At this point one has to consider the conclusion suggested by the evidence regarding both the effectiveness of the mission and the degree of the changes. Concerning the first aspect, one feels compelled to say that the Jesuits enjoyed only limited freedom of movement within Transylvania and were mainly active among areas whose rulers still favoured Catholicism, especially those in their care (and power), and those within the college, whom they tried to attract towards the clerical career. They did not come into contact all that much with people who had converted to Protestantism. In this context one should note the importance of the villages of the former monastic estates, as a case study for the effectiveness of the mission where the changes brought about by the Reformation were well implemented and where the people had become Protestants. One can also take into account their actions in the two cities, where they were allowed to establish themselves, Cluj (where they were active through the college) and Alba Iulia (where they were present at court). In the first instance they were in conflict with the magistrates of Cluj, in the second with the Protestant nobles at the court.

Concerning the second aspect, the evidence suggests that by the end of the sixteenth century a number of people had been born and brought up as Protestants with no personal familiarity with Catholicism.[57] Generally speaking, the Jesuits were inclined to admit that the Reformation had made significant progress in Hungary and Transylvania.[58] The attachment to traditional forms of religious expression, such as the rites of passage or fasting, suggests that people did not opt necessarily for theological differences, but rather for certain religious practices, for devotional models whose diversity was increasingly greater than either confession would approve.[59]

Thus, the evidence suggests that during the sixteenth century, Transylvania had undergone significant changes on a doctrinal, ritual and devotional level. It is however much harder to make any definite statements about the extent to which the Reformation had dislodged traditional forms of religious experience. Consequently, judging from the details of the reports, the Catholic church in Transylvania seemed to be primarily concerned with liturgical practice, with the sacraments and with the social aspects of Catholic religious life. Again our conclusions cannot be as clear and well defined as one might wish. Some of the evidence indicates that the Jesuits were targeting religious differences, as they were treating their subjects as 'heretics' they wished to convert. The fact that none of the letters of the Italian Jesuits mention the concept of 'superstition' when referring to the Catholics that have survived in the region seems to suggest that they were not especially concerned with an attack on traditional, pre-Tridentine religion.[60] This is supported by Szántó's attitude to the traditional customs of the area, which should be treated with respect. Szántó was more familiar with the Transylvanian situation and aware that the success of the mission depended on the ability to communicate with the faithful and the need to respect their customs and traditions.

Thus, until the end of the sixteenth century, a percentage of the population of Transylvania, especially in the urban environment or among the nobility was consciously Protestant. Resistance to the policy of re-Catholicisation came especially from the nobility and the burghers, especially the city magistrates. The rural population, ready to change religious affiliation at the bid of the master of the estate, was probably more receptive to the efforts of the Jesuits and more easily inclined to return to Catholicism. They seemed to have a very good practical strategy and their first priority was to convert and then worry about the care of the newly converted and the Catholic survivors. The evidence does not suggest the existence of a need for (Catholic) reform in the wider social body. There was an awareness concerning these (Tridentine) changes in Catholicism only at the level of the elite, and while it was the elite who wished to revitalise Catholicism in this region, their first concern was to return the population to the sacraments and services of the church.

Consequently, the sources would lead one to conclude that the Reformation had made real progress in Transylvania during the sixteenth century. It is possible, even probable that the majority of the people did not understand the more subtle doctrinal changes brought about by the Reformation, but their religious life had changed and their devotional practices had developed in a new direction, to a point whence it would have been difficult to return. Furthermore, the militant attitude of the inhabitants of the majority of Transylvanian towns and the spirited disputations on religious issues suggest a conscious adhesion to the Reformation. The fact that the territory of the mission coincided roughly with the area of Catholic survival tends to suggest that a part of Transylvania under the control of the Protestant nobility and the towns which had adhered to Protestantism did not particularly wish for a Catholic restoration. Society did not react in a positive way to the effort to reimplement or to fortify Catholicism. Focused as it was on conversion and the provision of a minimal core of ecclesiastical life, it can only be stated that Transylvanian Catholicism was militantly 'restorationist' rather than reforming in a more profound sense. The gap between the ideals of the Jesuits and their practical strategy, as well as the limited geographical scope of the mission, make the story of the Catholic mission in Transylvania very much a tale of two cities and three villages.

NOTES

1 Cesare Alzati, *Terra Romena tra Oriente e Occidente. Chiese ed etnie nel tardo '500* (Milan, 1981), 70. An excellent overview of the place, persons and issues discussed in this chapter can be found in Graeme Murdock, *Calvinism on the Frontier 1600–1660: International Calvinism and the Reformed Church in Hungary and Transylvania* (Oxford, 2000).

2 Jakob Wuyek (Vangrovicius, 1541–90) used to be the rector of the Jesuit college in Vilnius and had previously studied in Silesia, Cracow, Vienna and Rome.

3 István Szántó (Stephanus/Stephen Arator, 1540–1612). He was originally from western Hungary. In 1561 he entered the Jesuit Order and studied philosophy and theology in Vienna and Rome. In 1580 he came to Cluj, together with three other Jesuits, at the request of Stephen Báthory. He preached and he was involved in the college. Subsequently, he worked in Oradea for three years. In 1587 he was called to Alba Iulia. After the expulsion of the Jesuits he lived in Olmutz (Olomuc).

4 Marc Forster, *The Counter-Reformation in the Villages: Religion and Reform in the Bishopric of Speyer, 1560–1720* (Ithaca, 1992).

5 Christopher Haigh, 'The Continuity of Catholicism in the English Reformation', *Past and Present* 93 (1981), 37–69, conducted such a study for the Catholic mission in England.

6 Christopher Haigh, 'The Continuity', 37–69; John Bossy, 'The Character of Elizabethan Catholicism', *Past and Present* 21 (1962), 39–59.

7 The villages which had belonged to the abbey of Cluj-Mănăştur were Mănăştur (Monostor), Baciu (Kisbács), Leghia (Jegenye), Chinteni (Kajántó), Tihuţ (Tiborc), and Bagara (Bogártelke). Only the first three had actually been returned to the abbey or, rather, given to the Jesuits. They hoped to get back the revenues of the other three as well, but the issue remained under negotiation for a long time. See the report of 1580, drafted for Jacob Wuyek as the rector of the college, in Maria Holban, ed., *Călători străini despre Ţările Române* (Bucharest, 1968–83), 8 vols, 2: 482–5.

8 Holban, *Călători*, 2: 471 (Odescalchi); Caligari to Galli (Vilnius, 14 June 1579) in Endre Veress, *Fontes Rerum Transylvanicarum. Epistolae et Acta Jesuitarum Transylvaniae (1571–1613)* (Budapest, 1911–13), 2 vols, 2: 12–13.

9 Veress, *Epistolae*, 1: 260–261 (Antonio Possevino to cardinal Ptolemeo Galli; 6 March 1583).

10 Alexander Ungvary, *The Hungarian Protestant Reformation in the 16th century under Ottoman Impact, Essays and Profiles* (Lewiston, 1989); Ludwig Binder, *Grundlagen und Formen der Toleranz in Siebenbürgen bis zur mitte des 17 Jahrhunderts* (Vienna, 1976); Georg Renate Weber, *Luther und Siebenbürgen* (Vienna, 1985); David P. Daniel, 'Calvinism in Hungary: the Theological and Ecclesiastical Transition to the Reformed Faith', in A. Pettegree, A. Duke and G. Lewis, eds, *Calvinism in Europe 1540–1620* (Cambridge, 1994), 201–30; Katalin Peter, 'Hungary', in R. W. Scribner, R. Porter and M. Teich, eds, *The Reformation in National Context* (Cambridge, 1994), 135–67; Daniel, 'Hungary', in Andrew Pettegree, ed., *The Early Reformation in Europe* (Cambridge, 1992), 49–69.

11 Veress, *Epistolae*, 1: 80 (Francesco Sunieri; Cluj, 5 October 1579); 2: 33–8 (Ferrante Capeci; 1584); 1: 284 (Antonio Possevino to Galli; 17 April 1583); 1: 279–80 (Possevino to Gregory XIII; Olmutz, 12 April 1583); 1: 286–8 (Possevino to Galli; 16 July 1583); 2: 63 (Ferrante Capeci; 27 February 1584). In the Szekler lands there were three Catholic regions, Ciuc (Csík), Gheorgheni (Gyorgyó) and Kászon. A. Possevino, *Transilvania* (Budapest, 1913), 91–2, 107; Alzati, *Terra Romena*, 60.

12 Veress, *Epistolae*, 1: 98–100 (Odescalchi to Caligari; 27 March 1580); 2: 17–19 (Odescalchi to Caligari; 30 September 1580).

13 Veress, *Epistolae*, 1: 121–3 (Odescalchi to Caligari; 26 February 1581). The text refers to the village of Şard (Sárd) where one of the Jesuits went to preach, because he had been

invited by the local noble. The population there, except for two people, was inclined to return to Catholicism. Consequently, every fifteen days one of the Jesuits would go there to preach and hold Mass.

14 Veress, *Epistolae*, 1: 121–3 (Odescalchi to Caligari; 26 February 1581); 1: 286–8 (Possevino to Galli; Cracow, 16 July 1583).

15 Veress, *Epistolae*, 2: 61–4 (Ferrante Capeci to Aquaviva; Cluj, 27 February 1584). The mission was active in Oradea were the presence of István Szántó (Arator) had been requested.

16 Veress, *Epistolae*, 1: 286–7 (Possevino to Galli; Cracow, 16 July 1583).

17 Sándor Szilágyi, ed., *Monumenta Comitialia Regni Transylvaniae* (Budapest, 1975–98), 21 vols, 3: 39.

18 Veress, *Epistolae*, 1: 80 (Francesco Sunieri to Caligari; Cluj, 5 October 1579).

19 By 1514 the convent of the Dominican friars from Vinț (Alvinc, Winz) was inhabited by only four friars, Ioan Chrisostomus, Vitalie from Sibiu (Nagyszeben, Hermannstadt), Gáspár from Sebeș (Szászsebes, Mühlbach) and Michael, a lay brother. In 1529 there was only one person left in Vinț. In these circumstances it was easy for the noble Nicholas Kozár to send him away in 1539. The last Dominican inhabitant was Friar Thomas sent to Sebeș and then to Sighișoara (Segesvár, Schässburg). Adrian Andrei Rusu, 'A Glimpse at the Inner Life of a Transylvanian Monastery: The Dominican Monastery of Vinţu De Jos (Alba county)', in M. Crăciun and O. Ghitta eds, *Church and Society in Central and Eastern Europe* (Cluj, 1998), 13–21. The rich monastery of St Michael from Tăuţi (Tótfalud) was turned into a warehouse; see Holban, *Călători*, 2: 437–8 (Lescalopier); the abbey of Cluj-Mănăştur became a castle after the monks had been turned out by the new Protestant owners; see Holban, *Călători*, 2: 489–90 (István Szántó; 1 September 1581). The abbey in Igriş had been abandoned in 1500 and the one in Cârţa (Kerz, Kerc) in 1474, Iuliana Fabritius Dancu, *Cetăţi ţărăneşti din Transilvania* (Sibiu, 1983). At the beginning of the fifteenth century there had been a Franciscan convent in Haţeg (Hátszeg) which had been founded at the end of the reign of Louis I (1342–82). This convent seems to have been abandoned after the Turkish attack of 1479. In 1487 the Franciscans had received a church in Brusturi; see A. A. Rusu, *Ctitori şi biserici din Ţara Haţegului până la 1700* (Satu Mare, 1997), 134–41. Gromo recounts that there had been a very beautiful church, dedicated to the Virgin, in Bistriţa (Besterc, Bistriz) which had been built by a master mason from Bergamo on a commission from the citizens of the town. It had been turned into a Lutheran church. See Holban, *Călători*, 2: 348–9 (Gromo).

20 Holban, *Călători*, 2: 491 (Szántó; 1 September 1581). In Târgu Mureş (Marosvásárhely, Neumarkt), Lugoj (Lugos) and Caransebeş (Karánsebes) the convents had been taken over by Protestants. Holban, *Călători*, 2: 459–62 (Ioannes Leleszi to Aquaviva; Alba Iulia, 8 August 1581). The cathedral in Alba Iulia which the Protestants had acquired in 1565 must have been considered a major loss. The Franciscan convent in Cluj was devastated on Epiphany 1577 and then the Catholic community had to move to the former Benedictine convent of Cluj-Mănăştur.

21 Gromo mentioned that in 1565, when he was passing through Oradea, he witnessed the attempts of the Calvinists to destroy the paintings and the altars of the church. In the church in Alba Iulia only the tombs had remained untouched. The church in Cluj-Mănăştur had been robbed of all its ornaments. The statues had been burned, the stained glass windows broken, and the walls whitewashed; see Holban, *Călători*, 2: 491 (Stephanus Szántó; Cluj, 1 September 1581). In the church at Baciu, the altar had been demolished, see Holban, *Călători*, 2: 471 (Odescalchi to Caligari; Cluj-Mănăştur; 27 March 1580) and Veress, *Epistolae*, 1: 98–100; also Holban, *Călători*, 2: 467 (Leleszi to Aquaviva; Alba Iulia; 10 January 1582) and Veress, *Epistolae*, 2: 33–6 (Ferrante Capeci to Alberto Bolognetti; Alba Iulia, 10 February 1584).

22 Pierre Lescalopier (c.1550–97) was educated in Padova. In 1574 he undertook a journey to Constantinople. Part of his mission was to negotiate a marriage between Stephen Báthory and Renée de Rieux whom Catherine de Medici wanted removed from the French court.

23 Holban, *Călători*, 2: 430 (Lescalopier). In the church in Braşov (Brassó, Kronstadt) the Crucifix had been retained. K. Reinerth, 'Die Reformation der Siebenbürgische sächsischen Kirche', in *Schriften des Vereins für Reformationsgeschichte*, I 73: 61 (Gütersloh, 1956), 43–4.

24 See, for example, Dancu, *Cetăţi, passim*.

25 K. Reinerth, 'Die Reformation', 43–7; E. Roth, *Die Reformation in Siebenbürgen, ihr Verhältnis in Wittenberg und der Schweiz* (Cologne, 1962); Christine Peters, 'Mural Paintings, Ethnicity and Religious Identity in Transylvania. The Context for Reformation', in M. Crăciun and O. Ghitta, eds, *Ethnicity and Religion in Central and Eastern Europe* (Cluj, 1995), 44–63.

26 See examples from Richiş (Rionfalva, Reichesdorf), Motiş (Mártontelke, Mortesdorf), Buzd (Szászbuzd, Busd), Apold (Apold, Trappold), Dancu, *Cetăţi, passim*.

27 Holban, *Călători*, 2: 491 (Stephanus Szántó; September 1581) and Veress, *Epistolae*, 1: 112 (Odescalchi to Caligari; Cluj-Mănăştur, 30 September 1580); 1: 121–3 (Odescalchi to Caligari; Cluj-Mănăştur, 26 February 1581).

28 Rusu, *Ctitori*, 141–333. There is some evidence in Haţeg of ritual mutilation of images as well as in Densuş (Demsus) and Ostrov (Nagyosztró). The eyes of an image were taken out in Colţi Buz and in Răchitova (Reketyefalva) the face of the saint has been scraped off.

29 On 15 March 1556, the Franciscans and Dominicans had to leave Cluj. The notes of Paul Scherer state that the following day the icons were burned: Endre Veress, *Izabella Királyne* (Budapest, 1901), 454; in 1545, under the leadership of he *plebanus* Gáspár Heltai, the entire community of Cluj adopted Lutheranism. As a consequence of this change the entire liturgical fabric of the church was destroyed. Peter Petrovics convinced the people to remove the altars and the portraits of saints; cf. Sandor Székely, *Az unitárius vallás története* (Budapest, 1949); in 1565 the Protestants occupied the cathedral church in Alba Iulia and consequently the decorations were thrown out along with the Catholic clergy: Teuchs, Fornhaber, *Urkundenbuch zur Geschichte Siebenbürgens* (Vienna, 1851), 158, 188, 208; in 1565 at Cluj, the organ was thrown out of St Michael's church; in the cathedral in Alba Iulia, the altars were demolished along with the two organs, the depictions of saints and the sculptures: József Pokoly, *Az erdély református egyház története* (Budapest, 1904), 5 vols, 1: 171–2; G. Mândrescu, 'Altarul de la Guşteriţa', *Ars Transilvaniae* 2 (1992): 73–6; Rusu, 'Bisericile româneşti din districtul Haţeg până la 1700', *Ars Transilvaniae* 1 (1991), 129–42; Elek Jakab, ed., *Oklevéltar Kolozsvár történetéhez* (Budapest, 1870–88), 2 vols, especially vol. 2; Andrei Kertesz Badrus, 'Aspecte privind tematica picturii transilvănene din secolul al 16-lea', *Studii şi cercetări de istoria Artei* 28 (1981), 135–40. In Târgu Mureş, the Franciscan church's paintings were whitewashed, while in Oradea in 1565 the relics of St Ladislaus had been thrown out of the church. The Catholic church in Haţeg was whitewashed during the Reformation when the altar was changed: Rusu, *Ctitori*, 217–22. I would like to take this opportunity to thank my friend and colleague Mária Makó Lupescu for the help she has given me with the Hungarian bibliography.

30 Veress, *Epistolae*, 1: 99–100 (Odescalchi to Caligari; Cluj-Mănăştur, 27 March 1580); 2: 7 (Alphonso Pisano to Eberhard Mercurian; Vienna, 13 November 1575); 2: 12 (Caligari to Galli; Vilnius, 14 June 1579); 2: 92 (Capeci to Piatti; Cluj, 10 March 1585).

31 Maria Crăciun, 'The Use of the Vernacular in Catholic Propaganda during the Last Decades of the 16th Century', in Ambrus Miskolczy, ed., *Europa, Balcanica, Danubiana, Carpathica, 2A, Annales, Cultura, Historia, Philologia* (Budapest, 1995), 130–7. Veress, *Epistolae*, 1: 286–7 (Possevino to Galli; Cracow, 16 July 1583). In Szántó's accusations against Wuyek and the Polish Jesuits the linguistic issue played a prominent role. Szántó stressed the fact that the Polish Jesuits were inadequate as preachers because they had to use a translator. There is also an interesting example for the town of Cluj where it was obvious that sermons were held separately for the two communities, the Hungarian and the German. Possevino insisted on the production of religious literature in the languages of the region; *Transilvania*.

32 Veress, *Epistolae*, 1: 179–80 (Possevino to Gregory XIII; 12 April 1583).

33 Veress, *Epistolae*, 2: 89 (Ferrante Capeci to Girolamo Piatti; Cluj, 10 March 1585). See Alzati, *Terra Romena*, 63; he bases his argument on Possevino's text, *Transilvania*, 92.

34 Veress, *Epistolae*, 2: 10–13 (Caligari to Galli; Vilnius, 14 June 1579).
35 Veress, *Epistolae*, 2: 62 (Ferrante Capeci; 27 February 1584).
36 Veress, *Epistolae*, 1: 121–3 (Odescalchi; 26 February 1581).
37 Veress, *Epistolae*, 2: 96 (Ferrante Capeci to Girolamo Piatti; Cluj, 10 March 1585); Holban, *Călători*, 2: 488 (Stephanus Szántó to Fredericus Rainaldus; 25 February 1580).
38 Holban, *Călători*, 2: 322 (Gromo).
39 Veress, *Epistolae*, 2: 98 (Odescalchi).
40 Veress, *Epistolae*, 1: 98–100 (Odescalchi to Caligari; Cluj-Mănăștur, 27 March 1580).
41 Veress, *Epistolae*, 2: 91 (Ferrante Capeci, 10 March 1585).
42 Colin Morris, *The Papal Monarchy, The Western Church from 1050 to 1250* (Oxford, Clarendon Press, 1989), 371–86. Veress, *Epistolae*, 1: 98 (Odescalchi to Caligari); 1: 98–9 (Odescalchi; 27 March 1580); Holban, *Călători*, 2: 470–1 (Odescalchi).
43 Veress, *Epistolae*, 2: 121–3 (Odescalchi to Caligari; Cluj-Mănăștur, 26 February 1581).
44 Veress, *Epistolae*, 1: 101 (Odescalchi; 27 March 1580); 1: 121–3 (Odescalchi; 26 February 1581); 1: 105 (Odescalchi to Caligari; Cluj, 23 April, 1580).
45 Veress, *Epistolae*, 1: 101 (Odescalchi to Caligari; Cluj-Mănăștur, 27 March 1580); 2: 95–6 (Ferrante Capeci to Girolamo Piatti; 10 March 1581); Holban, *Călători*, 2: 471 (Odescalchi).
46 Veress, *Epistolae*, 1: 160 (István Szántó to Claudio Aquaviva; Cluj, 22 August 1581).
47 Veress, *Epistolae*, 1: 160–1 (István Szántó to Claudio Aquaviva; Cluj 22 August 1581).
48 See *Catalogus Festorum*, in Laszlo Lukács, ed., *Monumenta Antiqua Hungariae* (Rome, 1976), 2 vols, 2 (1580–86): 48.
49 *Catalogus Festorum*, in Lukács, *Monumenta*, 2: 6, 338–44.
50 *Catalogus Festorum*, in Lukács, *Monumenta*, 2: 338–44.
51 Veress, *Epistolae*, 1: 282 (Possevino to Gregory XIII; 12 April 1583).
52 Veress, *Epistolae*, 2: 34 (Ferrante Capeci; 10 February 1584).
53 Veress, *Epistolae*, 2: 93 (Ferrante Capeci to Girolamo Piatti; 10 March 1585).
54 Veress, *Epistolae*, 2: 88 (Ferrante Capeci to Girolamo Piatti; Cluj, 10 March 1585); Holban, *Călători*, 2: 470 (Odescalchi).
55 K. Reinerth, *Die Grundung der Evangelischen Kirchen in Siebenbürgen* (Vienna, 1979).
56 Antal Meszlényi, *A Magyar jezsuitak a XV században* (Budapest, 1931), 177–8.
57 Holban, *Călători*, 2: 478 (Jacob Wuyek; Cluj-Mănăștur, 27 January 1580).
58 Veress, *Epistolae*, 2: 11–13 (Caligari to Galli; 14 June 1579); 2: 58 (Ferrante Capeci to Aquaviva; 27 February 1584); Holban, *Călători*, 2: 493 (Szántó).
59 R. Po-chia Hsia, *Social Discipline in the Reformation: Central Europe 1550–1750*, (London, 1992), 50–1, 131–2.
60 Maria Crăciun, 'Superstition and Religious Difference in Sixteenth and Seventeenth Century Transylvania', in I. G. Toth and E. Andor, eds, *Frontiers of Faith: Religious Exchange and the Constitution of Religious Identities 1400–1750* (Budapest, 2001), 213–31.

4

The Jesuit legend:
superstition and myth-making

ERIC NELSON

Over the past three decades scholars of early modern Europe have increasingly focused their attention on the functions played by legends, myths and superstitions in local communities.[1] They have uncovered evidence in Europe and its colonial possessions of a dynamic interaction between communities and the belief systems that defined their ritual and religious lives.[2] One general conclusion that can be drawn from this research is that superstitious beliefs and practices were frequently created, altered or rejected by communities as they re-evaluated their relationship with their surroundings and the supernatural world. Many developments in ritual and superstitious practice drew upon what were perceived to be ancient beliefs. Nevertheless, societies were also capable of producing new legends, myths and superstitions especially during periods of rapid change or upheaval. These new beliefs often provided a means for understanding the changing world but they could also serve to fulfil the functions of older beliefs and practices that had recently been rejected by the community.

Like their Catholic counterparts, Protestant communities in the sixteenth and seventeenth centuries altered a number of beliefs to help explain the new cultural landscape of the post-Reformation world. A good example of myth formation within this wider set of developments can be found in the anti-Catholic polemic of this period in which Protestant anxiety over the apparent splits and weaknesses within the Reformed movement and the perceived unity of their opponents in the Catholic church inspired literature which described their adversaries in almost superhuman or supernatural terms. The pope was commonly labelled as the Antichrist and his allies, the Spanish and others, as the minions of the devil. For many Protestant polemicists, particularly in the British Isles and the Holy Roman Empire, the construction of myths surrounding the forces of Catholicism provided an explanation for weaknesses within their own states and splits between the European Protestant churches. It allowed the polemicists to recycle in a new format well-worn themes from the

Middle Ages which explained disorder and disunity within societies as a result of the forces of darkness at work in the community.

Probably the most important feature of the Catholic menace constructed by Protestant polemicists was the Jesuit myth or legend.[3] Founded in the 1540s the Society of Jesus' centralised organisation, constitutions and variety of activities as missionaries and educators set it apart from any religious order which preceded it. By the seventeenth century the Society was one of the largest and most influential orders in the Catholic church and a leading force in the international Counter/Catholic Reformation. For many Protestants, the members of this new Society were none other than the loyal minions of the papal or Romish Antichrist and therefore a central feature of the wider Catholic menace.[4] They were broadly defined as a secretive and deceptive fifth-column threat to the state, the church and the social fabric of the community. According to many Protestant polemicists, the Jesuits operated within local communities across Protestant Europe, and were seemingly able to avoid detection even by the most vigilant authorities. Thus, the Jesuits appeared to pose an immanent threat to society and were perceived to be one of the chief threats on the ground to Protestant communities across Europe in the sixteenth and seventeenth centuries. But what makes the legend even more interesting to scholars of superstition in the post-Reformation period is that the Jesuit legend was not strictly a Protestant creation. Instead, important elements of the legend were formed through direct interaction between Protestant and Catholic critics of the Society. Anti-Jesuit pamphlet literature was freely translated, published and read by members of both faiths. That is not to say that the two traditions shared the same purposes; indeed, as will be explained, the individual elements of the legend were similar in both Protestant and Catholic literature, but the role of the legend in the two traditions was very different. For some Protestants, the Jesuits took on almost superhuman or magical powers, and fitted into a wider anti-Catholic polemic defined by an apocalyptic understanding of the Catholic threat. Within the Catholic tradition the Society's menace was interpreted primarily in a political and social context even if the Jesuits were still considered a potent threat to order within communities and states.

The Jesuit legend was a post-Reformation creation; nevertheless, it reflected many of the features seen in similar but much older myths surrounding fifth-column threats to the social order such as witches, demons, Jews and Gypsies. For instance, once it was established in the late sixteenth century, the legend remained relatively static. Evolution hinders legend formation as it complicates what must remain a simple clear message. Moreover, as with other literature designed to promote a myth or legend, there is little room for ambiguity, qualifications or historicism in anti-Jesuit literature. Instead, repetition of familiar themes dominates the corpus of texts. The legend was essentially a tool of polemic, and, while writers used historical events to strengthen their arguments, the complications of historical context were of little concern as such considerations detracted from the clarity of the message. Instead, new examples of Jesuit misdeeds, each of which fitted into the established contours of the legend, defined its development.

Another feature of the Jesuit legend which correlates well with similar myths is its in-built flexibility that allows the legend to remain relevant through time. For over four centuries, critics have drawn upon the Society's legend during times of disorder or uncertainty. While in most cases the Society's misdeeds were interpreted to suit a specific controversy, in each case critics have drawn upon a basic repertoire of evidence concerned with the Society's long-standing predisposition towards secret plots and the sowing of disorder. There is nothing new here; demons and witches have also proved to be enduring figures in European culture, at least in part because it proved impossible fully to uncover and define their ever-changing and mysterious threat to the community. In certain circumstances Jews with their 'bizarre' rituals and Gypsies with their 'unknown' language have also been identified as fifth-column threats to the community in Europe. A self-reinforcing cycle has developed around each of these perceived enemies within the community. Once the presence of a fifth-column threat was established, it proved easy in times of crisis for the authorities or the community at large to identify witches, demons, Jesuits or other enemies as the ultimate source of unrest by pointing to evidence of their previous efforts to sow division and disorder. Consciously or unconsciously, the promoters of the Jesuit legend drew upon time-honoured traditions in myth creation that predate the Society's foundation.

This study sets out to examine the Jesuit legend by focusing on published literature produced in the first hundred years (c.1540–c.1640) following the Society's foundation. Published literature is an appropriate focus for such a study as printed material was the single most important medium for the dissemination of the legend. Moreover, it is appropriate to conclude this study around 1640, as by this date the basic components of the Jesuit legend, which were to remain relatively static into the twentieth century, were already firmly established. Moreover, the year 1640 is also appropriate as it was the publication date for the *Imago primi sæculi Societatis Iesu*.[5] This substantial work produced by Flemish Jesuits was devoted to promoting a very different heroic interpretation of the Society's first century of activity: an interpretation of the Society that has also proved enduring.

The legend is a multi-faceted creation. In order to interpret its meaning within the Protestant tradition we must first consider the individual components and types of evidence that sustained both the Protestant and Catholic versions of the legend. Then, through an examination of how these shared building blocks were interpreted within the different traditions, we can consider the flexibility of myth-making and the confessional requirements that defined its creation.

One feature of the Jesuit legend was the remarkable array of rumours, tales and firmer evidence of Jesuit misdeeds gathered through time from across Europe, the New World and Asia. In the sixteenth and seventeenth centuries, the Jesuits were accused of everything from killing hundreds of thousands of indigenous people in the New World, to overthrowing the Russian tsar, to keeping demons as pets and using crystal balls to spy on their enemies.[6] Such a variety of evidence makes defining the legend and its components difficult. Nevertheless, consideration of three broad themes common to both Protestant and Catholic versions of the Jesuit legend provides a framework for analysis of this rich collection of material.

One important theme taken up by both Protestant and Catholic critics was the rejection of the Jesuits' public image and its replacement with something much more sinister. For promoters of the legend, the Society's public activities were cynically duplicitous, and the Jesuits themselves were guilty of hypocrisy in their public actions.[7] Opponents commonly referred to the Jesuits as wolves dressed in sheep's clothing.[8] Along the same lines one scholarly French critic in the late sixteenth century compared members of the Society to a *manticore*, a mythical beast from India with a human face but the body and nature of a tiger or lion.[9] To support this theme the Society's critics offered a wide array of evidence that the Society's well-known teaching foundations, vows of poverty and missionary work disguised their secret designs. In a tract purporting to be secret guidance from the Jesuit leadership to their brethren around Europe on how to integrate or insinuate the Society into local communities, the author created detailed instructions about the use of public actions to gain influence:

> we ought with all Submissive and Humble deportment frequently visit the Hospitals, the Sick and those that are in Prison, to confess them; and that by a Charity to the Poor not known to other Orders, and being Newcomers, we may have the reverence and respect of the best, and most eminent persons in our Neighbourhood.[10]

Charitable and pious activities pursued in order to gain greater influence within a community was a recurring theme in the opening pages of the tract. Indeed, on the following page Jesuit Fathers were exhorted to show all modesty to gain the goodwill of the clergy and laity 'whose favour or power may avail us any thing'.[11]

According to many critics, any Jesuit who appeared pious and dedicated was either a lowly dupe kept on by the Order to better cover the Society's real designs or a true Jesuit, a master of hypocrisy and deception. The Society's carefully cultivated public mission was just a ruse to cover their true, if secret and only partially understood, purpose of gaining influence and authority wherever they operated. The assertion of duplicity and hypocrisy provided an extremely flexible means to reject the Society's public activities and build a very different image of the Jesuits' purpose. There was no room in the legend for dedicated Jesuit teachers or preachers, so such figures had to be placed in the context of a secret, more sinister, mission. This aspect of the legend took a firm hold in the collective European imagination. Indeed, even today across Europe the term 'Jesuit' continues to carry the connotation of hypocrisy and duplicity.[12] The central question raised by this charge of duplicity in both the Protestant and Catholic traditions was if they lacked dedication to their publicly avowed goals then what were their true intentions?

A second theme which dominated both Protestant and Catholic versions of the legend was how the Jesuits and their minions were operating in the dark corners and recesses of nearly every community across Europe and beyond. For the Jesuits' opponents the hypocritical Fathers conducting the public activities of the Order were dangerous enough, but for many an even greater danger lay in the Society's ability to infiltrate even the most vigilant of communities without being detected. For these critics, the Jesuits were the masters of disguise. Evidence of their penchant for changing identities was found in a variety of their activities. For instance, one particularly imaginative author claimed that the Fathers used costume wardrobes, ostensibly collected to stage drama productions at their colleges, for more sinister designs:

> And with this apparell doe the *Iesuites* habite themselues according to the quality that euery one findeth himselfe ablest to personate, and so practise wonderful Impostures in the world. For at sometimes beeing habited like *Souldiers* very gallant, then walke in the streets and highwayes *Whoring* and *Swaggering* in the publike Stewes. At other times in the ciuil habites of *Citizens* professing themselues to bee of the reformed Religion, they pry vp and downe and listen in Innes, in Playhouses, in Tauernes, vpon the Exchange, and in all places of publike meeting.[13]

This aspect of the legend offered the possibility that the Society could be operating even where they were seemingly absent.

The theme of Jesuits operating secretly in communities was taken even further by a number of Protestant and Catholic polemicists, particularly those writing in regions where few Jesuits were known to operate. For these writers the Society also controlled a secretive and mysterious fifth column of minions or 'Jesuitised' people within the wider community.[14] One author explained this common assertion by defining three types of membership within the Society of Jesus:

> The first consists of certain Lay-people of both Sexes; which having associated Themselves with that Society, live under it in the performance of a certain blind

obedience, steering all Their actions by the Directions of the *Jesuites*, and are ever in a readiness to execute, what They command . . . The second kind takes in only men, of which some are Priests, and others Lay, who though They live abroad in the World, and many times by the *Jesuites* good word obtain Pensions, Canonries, Abbeys and other Revenues, are yet under a Vow to take the habit of the Society upon the first Order from the Father General for which reason they are called *Jesuites* in Vow . . . The third sort is of those Politick *Jesuites*, in whom all the authority rests, who hold the reins of government over their Order.[15]

Thus, the Society's supporters could be men or women in virtually any walk of life whose sole loyalty was to the Society of Jesus as expressed in secret vows. In effect the potential membership of the Society was almost limitless. Indeed, Antoine Arnauld, an important French Catholic critic of the Jesuits who wrote in the late sixteenth and early seventeenth centuries, raised the spectre in one of his tracts that between the different sorts of Jesuits, both secret and open, a whole town may be 'Jesuitical' without the authorities' knowledge.[16]

Who were these secret Jesuits or 'Jesuitised' people? Most polemicists, both Catholic and Protestant, were in agreement that widows and those taught at Jesuit colleges were most at risk of being seduced by the Society, but, according to many authors, the members of the Society possessed an almost superhuman ability to persuade, delude and control individuals in their pursuit of Jesuit goals.[17] The Jesuits were regularly compared to the harpies of Homeric myth or the serpent in the Garden of Eden.[18] Some polemicists emphasised that the Society preyed on weak or malleable individuals and that the whole organisation was geared to finding and recruiting such people.[19] A recurrent theme within this tradition was that members of the Society across Europe persuaded weak or unstable individuals through confession, the sacraments and spiritual guidance to undertake assassinations or other subversive acts for their cause.[20] Indeed, according to their critics the Jesuits excelled at this, and were accused of constructing special chambers of meditation painted black and decorated with images of demons and devils which were used to terrify their potential minions with fear for the safety of their souls.[21] They were even accused of providing special knives or poisons to their minions, but, as always, the Society worked in the shadowy background and their participation in plots only came to light through chance.[22] Many polemicists granted the Jesuits supernatural powers of persuasion drawn from the Society's close relationship with the devil and their knowledge of the black arts. According to their critics the Society could delude and seduce even the most strong-willed mortals. For instance, in his *plaidoyer* against the Jesuits, Antoine Arnauld contended that Jesuits seduced 'the people' with sorcery and enchantments.[23] Moreover, according to one proponent of the legend even monarchs could be seduced by Jesuit sorcerers: 'Now amongst that whole Societie, the prime man for a Magician, is a *French Jesuit*, whom the King of *France* himselfe, had in so high estimation, that hee admitted him not onely to his Princely table, but also to familiar conferences in priuate.'[24] While individual authors drew on different evidence to reach their conclusions, few doubted that for every Jesuit visible in the community there was a whole network of unseen minions seduced into absolute obedience to their Jesuit masters who operated undetected in society.

Disguised Jesuits and their secret Jesuitised minions were essential features of the Jesuit legend. These figures gave the Jesuits an almost limitless ability to be present at or behind an infinite number of plots, assassinations and less well-defined disturbances or divisions in society. Nearly anyone responsible for fomenting religious, political or social disorder could be labelled a disguised or secret Jesuit. The Society gained the image of being an ever present, immanent threat in communities across Europe. At the opening of the seventeenth century the Gallican polemicists Antoine Arnauld and Estienne Pasquier were already accusing the Jesuits of involvement in almost every plot or disturbance in Europe since the Society's foundation in the 1540s.[25] Arnauld's *plaidoyer* against the Society, which was published in 1594, is representative of this approach. Through a flurry of historical examples drawn from across Europe, Arnauld labelled the Society as leaders of rebellion, minions of the Spanish and seducers of the people. The scope of Jesuit action was summarised as: 'all their thoughts, all their designs, all their actions, all their sermons, all their confessions have no other aim than to subjugate the whole of Europe to the domination of Spain'.[26] Jesuit involvement in plots was seemingly limitless. Even the well-respected French historian Jacques-Auguste De Thou in his *Histoire Universelle* repeated as fact rumours of Jesuit plots in localities from England to Poland and Russia.[27] These three French Catholic authors were amongst the most influential promoters of the Jesuit legend and were widely translated and read by Protestants. Their works gave the impression that the Jesuits were active in almost every locality and were behind almost every type of religious, political or social disorder in Europe. For these authors the Society's activities had to be consistent; thus Jesuit involvement in any example of disorder was almost assumed. A powerful component of the Jesuit legend, like all myths or legends, was the Society's seemingly infinite ability and desire to plot secretly and foment disorder almost anywhere in the world.

A third theme that provided an important foundation for the legend concerned the absolute obedience which the Society instilled in its members and the use of this disciplined organisation by the Jesuit Roman hierarchy to gather information which made the Order seem almost omniscient, even in the most secret affairs of state. To many Protestant and Catholic commentators, the perceived presence of the Society across Europe made the Jesuits seem a more immediate threat than even the pope or the Spanish. Further, according to proponents of the

legend, the members of the Society never operated as free agents and their success in fomenting disorder came both from the extraordinary unity of purpose
and the centralised organisation of the Society. Accounts vary as to the exact
details but several elements remain constant. First, Jesuits were carefully chosen
and educated to be obedient to the will of their masters in Rome.[28] Jesuit discipline was authoritarian and those who were not completely trusted by the
Order's leadership were kept in the dark as to the Society's secret plans. Instead
they were used as teachers and preachers to maintain the ruse of the Jesuits'
public mission. This distinction was clearly made in the widely circulated *Doctrines
and Practices of the Societie of Iesvites* when one Jesuit in the dialogue stated:

> I speake not touching your simpler sort of *Iesuites*, from whom these more
> reserued and closer practises of the Societie are altogether concealed, either in
> respect they are not held wise enough (forsooth) to bee acquainted with them,
> or that they are thought too deuout to entertaine them, or else in regard of their
> short continueance in that Society.[29]

Here the author asserted that any good or moral Jesuit must be deluded as to
the true intentions of his Order, which made it even more difficult to undermine the legend by pointing to examples of pious and dedicated members of the
Society. Thus, according to anti-Jesuit polemicists, underneath the carefully
maintained veneer of a simple and pious religious organisation the Society's
General in Rome was able to command absolute obedience from an inner cabal
of his most trusted subordinates across Europe: an obedience which helped to
explain their extraordinary ability to maintain the secrecy of their designs.

An important theme related to the Society's discipline and sense of purpose was the sheer organisational abilities of the Roman central administration.
According to promoters of the legend, Jesuit intelligence-gathering extended
into every princely court in Europe, and the Society's leadership was kept
abreast of even the most secret affairs through a ruthlessly efficient network of
informants in constant communication with Jesuit headquarters in Rome. This
information network was the key to their power as the compromising secrets
collected about both friends and enemies allowed them to blackmail and manip-
ulate behind the scenes to achieve their objectives. One polemicist described in
detail his perception of how the Roman high council of the Society operated:

> Thus when all their Pacquets are come to *Rome*, the Father General calls
> together His Assistants, who lay open to Him the affairs of the whole World
> discovering to Him the interest and practices of all Christian Princes. After
> which when they have consulted about all that is written, and examined
> and compared the several accompts, They draw the conclusion which is to assist
> one Prince, and oppose another, according as it suits with Their interest and
> profit.[30]

The organisational ability of the Society and its detailed knowledge of all affairs across Europe made the Society's scope for activity almost limitless.

For many of their opponents the Society's disciplined organisation made identifying specific Jesuit plots ahead of time nearly impossible. Nevertheless, after the event the Society's opponents were able to provide abundant evidence of the Society working to a common purpose across long distances to carry out their supposed schemes. For instance, one widely disseminated rumour was that the Society experimented with gunpowder during a religious festival in Lisbon just months before they were implicated in the Gunpowder Plot in England.[31] A second rumour current in France in the months following the assassination of Henri IV in 1610 was that the Jesuits in Brussels and Prague knew about Ravaillac's attack on Henri days or even weeks before it occurred. The anonymous author of the *Anticoton* included details in his account that make Jesuit complicity appear all the more likely:

> But from where else than Brussels and Prague (where the Jesuits rule) was the death of the King spoken of twelve or fifteen days before it happened? Many in Rouen have received letters from their friends in Brussels asking if the rumour of the King's death was true, even though it had not yet occurred. Monsieur l'Argentier de Troyes has received letters from Prague from the tutor of his children, which informed him that a Jesuit had already reported the death of the King before it happened.[32]

Although the author left the reader to draw his own conclusions, presumably in this case the Jesuit network was wrongly informed of the date of the attack or Ravaillac was unexpectedly delayed in undertaking his attempt. Whatever the case, Jesuit complicity in the attack was the conclusion which the author expected the reader to draw. The polemicists' vision of Jesuit discipline and organisation played two important roles in the construction of the legend. First, it added to the sense of a secretive organisation working tirelessly to undermine or destroy society from within. Second, it provided evidence of how the Jesuits could operate so successfully and secretly even if local authorities were vigilant in their efforts to prevent Jesuit plots.

The Jesuits of the legend were a dangerous and deceptive enemy. Their ability to operate secretly even in hostile environments and their unity and obedience to the will of their Father General in Rome made the Society something to fear and something to blame for seemingly inexplicable divisions within the community. For their enemies, the Society became the prime suspect in almost any scheme against the state or the church. As their reputation grew so did the polemic which identified their hand behind every plot. The legend, once established, became self-perpetuating and grew rapidly. By the early seventeenth century one polemicist was able to conclude 'that the greatest part of the

Affairs of Christendom pass through the *Jesuites* hands, and that those only succeed which they think not fit to oppose'.[33]

The Society's flexible and only partially understood threat was one reason
for the legend's long-term success. Moreover, the Society's nearly impenetra-
ble secrecy and the impossibility of even identifying Jesuits and their minions
within the community were also key features of the legend since, in the hands
of polemicists, these perceptions allowed the Order to serve as a universal
'bogey' man and a scapegoat for any disunity within a state or church. However, a second reason for the legend's success was that important components
of the legend were based on a core of plausible evidence drawn from the
Society's constitutions, events across Europe and even fabricated *memoirs* or
secret instructions.[34] The evidence in support of the Jesuit legend was rarely
damning, and was often distorted. Nevertheless, the sheer number of examples and the variety of evidence garnered in both Protestant and Catholic contexts brought plausibility to a legend that many were inclined to believe in any
case. While it is not the purpose of this essay to examine the veracity of the
legend, it is useful to consider the evidence employed by opponents of the
Society as a core of verifiable information was often the key to substantiating
accusations which sustained and expanded the legend.

Perhaps the most persuasive evidence used by proponents of the legend
was drawn from the writings of Jesuits, in particular the constitutions of the
Society written by its founder Ignatius Loyola. Two passages from the constitutions attracted regular attention, and helped to substantiate important elements
of the legend. First, Ignatius Loyola advised members of the Order 'to strive to
retain the good will and charity of all, even of those outside the Society, and
especially of those whose favourable or unfavourable attitude toward it [the
Society of Jesus] is of great importance for opening or closing the gate leading
to the service of God and the good of souls'.[35] For critics this passage confirmed
the assertion that the Society was determined to exercise undue influence
amongst the elites of Europe. By the opening of the seventeenth century these
same critics could point to the Society's success in becoming confessors and
advisers to some of the most powerful Catholic monarchs, nobles and churchmen in Europe. A combination of a hostile reading of the constitutions and perceptions of their influence over important personages underpinned wider
speculation over the purpose behind their efforts to seduce powerful figures.
The fourth vow – that of absolute obedience to the pope – was a second passage
from the constitutions upon which the Society's opponents frequently focused.[36]
While other religious orders and bishops took similar oaths, the vow confirmed
for many their suspicions of the Society's secret mission in support of the
papacy. Moreover, by taking the vow a Jesuit established his full membership in
the Society. For many critics this was evidence of an inner cabal of fully

informed Jesuits who were directing the Society's most secret and subversive activities. While neither of these passages from the constitutions could on its own confirm the legend, they provided a solid basis in fact from which critics could extrapolate the Society's hidden purpose.

The Jesuits' opponents were also adept at interpreting seemingly unrelated events from across Europe as proof of the legend's veracity. For instance, critics of the Jesuits were able to collect enough indirect evidence to construct what could be interpreted as a consistent pattern of Jesuit involvement in politically subversive acts. The most important accusations implicated the Society in assassination attempts upon political leaders in France, England and the Dutch Republic. This evidence was then used to speculate about the Society's involvement in other political acts. Many of these accusations were substantiated by little more than circumstantial evidence, as with the assassination attempt in 1598 of Prince Maurice of Nassau, Captain-General of the Dutch Republic's armies. A rumour current in Paris immediately following the attack implicated Jesuits in Douai and Liège along with a Jesuit from Bordeaux who allegedly made a secret trip to the Spanish Netherlands specifically to convince a would-be assassin of the practical and celestial advantages of such an attempt on Maurice's life.[37] The evidence for this accusation was circumstantial at best and even the memoirist Pierre de l'Estoile, a long-standing French Catholic critic of the Jesuits, doubted its veracity.[38] Nevertheless, evidence like this was presented not exclusively on its own merits but in the context of a pattern of such actions which proved convincing to many through the weight of multiple accusations.[39] Indeed, in this respect the Jesuit legend shared a common feature with other legends associated with secretive or fifth-column threats to society. While no single piece of evidence proved the general assertion that the Society of Jesus was an organisation devoted to undermining states and churches across Europe, the sheer number of accusations served to substantiate at least the possibility of such a Jesuit plot and opened the Society to further accusations.

This approach to legend creation is particularly evident in efforts to substantiate the claim that the Jesuits controlled a network of minions through which they gathered information and carried out their secret designs. While recent scholarship on the Society of Jesus has shown that the Society was not able to coordinate its actions across Europe with anything like the efficiency that many of their opponents suggest, the proponents of the legend were able to point to a variety of evidence to support their assertions.[40] Individual examples of widows taking Jesuit confessors or leaving money to the Society were cited by proponents of the legend as evidence of the Society's efforts to recruit loyal servants and financial backers from amongst this group.[41] Moreover, the frequent success of alumni from Jesuit colleges and the role of Jesuit colleges as a focus for networking amongst its graduates provided more fuel for speculation about

secret networks of Jesuitised minions in wider society. But perhaps most important to the assertion of a Jesuit cabal was the culture of regular correspondence
between Jesuit Fathers and the Roman headquarters of the Society. This aspect
of the Society's organisation was extraordinary for the period, and was well
publicised by the dissemination of Jesuit letters from Asia and the New World.
While these letters were intended to promote and glorify the Society's overseas
missions, for their opponents these letters provided apparently solid evidence
that the Jesuits possessed a far-flung news-gathering organisation. These publications made it at least possible that the Society possessed the elaborate and
secret intelligence-gathering network defined in anti-Jesuit literature.

Even some of the more picaresque accusations in the polemics were supported by at least distorted interpretations of reality. The frequent accusations
that Jesuits habitually disguised themselves as anything from prostitutes to
courtiers in order to infiltrate into local communities across Europe was seemingly supported by the Jesuits' unique decision amongst Catholic religious
orders to wear no distinctive habit and their innovative collegiate drama productions which required many of their students to wear costumes. Indeed,
even the most imaginative assertions of their detractors concerning the
Society's penchant for disguise were lent credence by the spectacular examples
of Jesuits like Edmond Campion and Robert Parsons who used elaborate costumes to hide their identities while on their missions to England. Thus many
components of the legend were supported by a variety of evidence widely
known to the public even if their opponents often drew conclusions which the
evidence alone failed fully to substantiate.

The Jesuit legend proved enduring as it drew upon a body of evidence
to support its assertions. However, not all components of the legend could
be supported by offering hostile interpretations of the Society's public writings
or actions. The Society's perceived secrecy needed to be breached on occasion
to provide evidence for their critics, and this in part explains the emergence
of an important type of literature: the *exposé memoire*. These frequently republished works which purported to be written by Jesuit Fathers, novices or
students who had escaped from the clutches of the Order were suitably few in
number. After all a secretive and strictly organised corporation like the Society
of Jesus had the means to stop individuals betraying its secrets. As one German
pamphlet supposedly written by a disillusioned Jesuit explains, in every Jesuit
college there is a subterranean torture chamber specifically designed to

> captivate the vnderstanding of their Desciples, vnto Iesuiticall obedience. For if
> the least mater, they get any hinte of suspition, against any of theyr Novices, that
> he will not be constant, or that he desireth to escape from them, and that he is
> likely to betray the secrets of their Societie, they clap vp such a fellow, in a faire
> paire of stockes, and having macerated him a long time with hunger, and cold,

and want of all bodily comforts; at the last they make an end of him, with some exquisite tortures and killing torments.[42]

Nevertheless, the occasional Jesuit, like the one who purportedly wrote this pamphlet, was able to escape the clutches of their superiors within the Society. Their betrayal of their former masters offered seemingly unassailable evidence of secret Jesuit activities, as did the author of the above account who described in great detail the fate of an unfortunate German novice named Iacobus Cleussus who was dispatched to one of the Jesuit torture chambers for disobedience – never to be seen again.[43]

An important variation on the theme of peering into the secretive workings of the Society was the alleged discovery of secret Jesuit documents. These discoveries served both to provide details of Jesuit activities and to emphasise the perceived hypocrisy of the Jesuits' mission as defined in their public constitutions. The most famous of these works was the *Monita Privata Societatis Jesu*, better known as the *Monita Secreta*.[44] This text was published by a dismissed Jesuit named Hieronymus Zahorowski who claimed that the work consisted of a series of secret instructions from the Jesuit Father General Acquaviva to his provincials and rectors. This tract combined the authority of both an escaped member of the Society and secret Jesuit documents. It proved the single most influential polemic against the Society during the early modern period and ran through twenty-two editions in seven different languages by the end of the seventeenth century. Nevertheless, the *Monita* was just one of several similar tracts that were published, translated and republished across Europe in the seventeenth century.

The Society's Protestant and Catholic opponents used both *exposé* memoirs and 'discovered' papers to add what appeared to be substantive evidence to their accusations, and it was in these writings that many of the most fanciful accusations of magic and torture were made. These texts, however, did not undermine the flexibility which lies at the root of the legend. The works never provided more than a partial view of the Society's activities as they were invariably either written by escaped Jesuit Fathers, novices or students who were only partially aware of their superior's plots or included just one set of secret guidelines for Jesuit Fathers.

This genre of writing, along with evidence taken from their constitutions and incidents across Europe, were the perfect legend-building materials required by the Society's opponents. These sources offered an array of 'evidence' that supported the myth of the Society's plotting, but never provided the complete picture. This allowed the legend to maintain its flexibility, and only added to the uncertainty over what the Society was capable of fomenting in almost any environment. In these texts Jesuit duplicity, secret networks and organisation – the foundation stones of the legend – were all developed. As with any legend or myth it was the perception, not the reality, that was of central importance and, because of the mixture of the plausible with the less plausible, the Jesuit legend maintained a strong resonance amongst both Protestants and Catholics. However, while the polemicists from both faiths used the same building blocks, the Jesuits' wider role in their respective traditions was very differently conceived.

The Society's reputation as a secretive fifth-column threat to communities; the array of partially verifiable evidence which supported their reputation; and their perceived ability to operate in virtually every locality across Europe explain the longevity and flexibility of the legend. Because of the legend's flexibility, polemicists could conceivably use it for a variety of purposes, and it was how some Protestant critics of the Jesuits chose to perceive the Society's ultimate purpose – rather than the elements of the threat itself – which set them apart from their Catholic counterparts. In many Protestant writings the Jesuit threat was described in almost apocalyptic terms and the Society took on nearly superhuman powers in its efforts to undermine godly societies. For Catholic critics, on the other hand, the Society's threat always remained political and social, and their scheming, however crafty, was rarely framed in supernatural terms.

For some Protestants the Jesuit legend was a central feature of a wider anti-Catholic legend. The Society was the chief manifestation on the ground of what was often the distant threat of a united and hostile Catholic church. The Society was well suited to this role. Unlike other potential threats, the Society was perceived to operate across all of the Protestant world. Moreover, their secretive nature made them a more flexible and dangerous threat than even the more numerous Spanish troops which could be identified and opposed by Protestant states. The Jesuit threat transcended categories. Indeed, some Protestant writers argued that the Jesuit menace was part of a wider struggle between good and evil or the godly societies and the devil. For example, in the opening letter to an anti-Jesuit pamphlet published in 1669 one Protestant author reflected on the Society's growing menace over the previous decades: 'For certainly of late Times, the Devil has not found more effectual Insturments of the peacable damnation of Souls than the Jesuites'.[45] Others took the rhetoric even further to link the Society directly to demons: 'And they are also companions of demons, who under the name of Jesus and an outward form of piety come to us, in sheep's clothing, transformed into angels of light. But in their essence and iniquitous works they are ravenous wolves, pseudo-prophets, or, as Christ says, thieves and robbers.'[46] Some authors implied that demons and Jesuits worked hand in hand to advance their goals. For instance, the well-known Jesuit theologian and polemicist Gretser was accused of keeping the Devil in a bottle.[47] For Protestant polemicists the Society of Jesus played an important role in defining the Catholic threat. The pope was the 'Romische Antichrist'; the Jesuits were his demons on the ground.[48]

The association of Jesuits with the demons of the Middle Ages provided an important source for some of the most distinctive features of the Jesuit legend in the Protestant tradition. Jesuits' perceived ability to persuade, to disguise themselves and to work behind a façade of sanctity offered clear parallels with the long-held beliefs that Satan and his minions were primarily adept at creating illusions, fostering confusion, destroying and seducing within Christ's flock. Nevertheless, one does not want to press the parallel with demons too far. According to some of their critics, the Society practised the black arts and at least one tract claimed that Ignatius Loyola, the Society's founder, was the spiritual offspring of the devil, but no polemicist claimed, in more than a figurative sense, that Jesuits in general were demons.[49]

It is perhaps more appropriate to think of the demon analogy as one inspiration for the specific roles attributed to the Society in Protestant anti-Catholic polemic. The Protestant church believed in the existence of demons, but, especially in the Calvinist churches, their role was never fully developed and their threat to the community was never fully defined. In the Middle Ages demons and their minions were the forces of darkness which were most active in the community. They used deception, seduced the weak-willed and worked to sow discord in communities to advance their master's designs. The Jesuits fulfilled a very similar function for their papal masters in the polemic of many Protestant critics. The work of this secretive corporation, which swore obedience to the Antichrist pope, was a threat which could explain weakness and dissension within Protestant communities much as demons had in Catholic communities during the Middle Ages.[50]

Such a well-organised and secretive opponent was a formidable enemy. Indeed, many viewed the Society with apocalyptic concern. The Jesuits were often compared to the locusts of the Old Testament which devoured all in their path.[51] Moreover, allusions to the Society's foundation and growth frequently drew upon the teachings of Revelation 16: 14. For instance, Boquinus, a French Protestant writing in Heidelberg in 1576, asserted in his anti-Jesuit tract:

> And the same doth the spirit of God set forth in the Reuelation, by the image of a whore gorgeously arrayed with purple and scarlet, & attyred with golde, precious stones, and pearles: hauing a cuppe of golde in her hande, full of abominations and filthines of her fornication, wherewith she maketh drunken the kings and inhabitantes of the earth . . . yest especially the same is to be seene at this daye in the new and lately inuented Secte of the Iesuites which the Romishe Antichrist hath set foorth as the laste proppe, and staye of his towering, and ruinous kingdome.[52]

The Jesuits then were the unclean spirits who appeared from the mouth of the Antichrist. They were sent by God to punish the unbelievers in preparation for the second coming.[53] Within the Protestant tradition the Jesuit myth served an important function of providing an immanent threat and an explanation for dissension within the godly community. The Society clearly worked for the forces of darkness, and its members were the chief agents of the Antichrist pope. In the works of the most vehement Protestant polemicists the Society's alliance with the forces of darkness provided them with access to the supernatural powers often associated with demons, and placed them firmly in the apocalyptic setting of Revelation. This in part explained their potent threat to godly communities, and provided the basis for a legend that defined the Society as a more dangerous threat than any normal human enemy. In its most vehement form, Protestant polemicists created the foundation of a legend with strong parallels to medieval traditions centred on demons and the struggle between good and evil. In defining this legend, Protestant writers created a threat which Godly members of Protestant communities feared in much the same way that Catholics feared the threat of demons within their own communities.

Catholic proponents of the legend interpreted the Society's threat along very different lines. In Catholic literature the Society might be minions of the pope or international Catholicism as promoted by Spain, but the pope was not the Antichrist of Revelation. Instead, the Society by the mid-1590s was presented as the chief proponent of papal authority in Catholic kingdoms with strong national church traditions like France and Venice. In France up to 1598 the Jesuits were also often portrayed as the minions of Catholic Spain and again a threat to the French state and the Gallican church as the Society strove to promote a universal Catholic monarchy with the king of Spain as its head. However, when King Henri IV of France made peace with both the pope and Spain in the later 1590s, French polemicists increasingly shifted to a third explanation for Jesuit plotting which was only sporadically reflected in Protestant texts of the period: that the Society undertook its activities for its own aggrandisement rather than for the Pope or the Spanish. The works of the French Gallican polemicist Antoine Arnauld reflected this rapid shift in purpose. In his *plaidoyer* (1594) the Society was portrayed as the chief promoters of the Spanish cause in France and elsewhere in Europe.[54] By 1602 when Arnauld published his *Franc et vray discovrse* in opposition to the Society's return to France his view had changed; now the Society, who were still a real threat to French sovereignty, were only concerned with the promotion and enrichment of their own Order.[55]

All three Jesuit motivations – in support of the pope, in support of the Spanish King, and in pursuit of their own interests – continued to be promoted at different times within the Catholic tradition, but whatever their purpose the Jesuits were consistently accused of undertaking the same actions. One

prominent motif was the Society's efforts to seduce monarchs and other important members of the community so as to increase their influence in affairs of
state. A closely related theme was that the Society actively sought to overthrow
governments and sow discord within kingdoms where the Jesuits were rejected
in order to increase their influence. Finally, the Society's ability to gather in
riches and, through their wealth, increase their influence was another theme
taken up in many Catholic texts. In each of these cases Catholic critics were
able to draw on the basic building blocks of the legend and, indeed, freely used
Protestant evidence of Jesuit misdeeds; however, they used this material to
construct a Jesuit legend based on the premise that the Society was committed
to the promotion of papal, Spanish or its own selfish interests. The Society's
threat was firmly established in political, cultural and social concerns. While
for Catholic critics the Jesuits might be crafty and duplicitous in their efforts to
subvert legitimate authorities in Catholic states and gain in power and influence
themselves, there was little sense of a supernatural underpinning to their
efforts – although occasionally a particularly vehement Catholic polemicist
accused the Jesuits of using sorcery. Moreover, Catholic critics of the Society
failed to construct a cosmology as powerful and all-embracing as the Protestant
one. Instead, the legend was used to define a set of dangerous opponents who
supported an international conception of the Catholic church which threatened
national church traditions in states like France and Venice.

At the beginning of the twentieth century Walter Walsh contributed an
entry on the Society of Jesus to *The Protestant Dictionary*. Walsh's piece reflects
the timeless resonance of the legend as the main components of the legend
around 1640 dominate his account of the Society. For Walsh the Jesuits
remained duplicitous:

> as a rule the professed are men of great subtlety of mind, crafty, worldly-minded
> politicians, more men of the world than anything else, whose great ambition is
> the glorification of their Order by making it the greatest power in the
> professedly Christian world.[56]

Moreover, as Walsh explained, the Society continued to disguise its true
purpose:

> From the ranks of these Fathers who have taken only three vows come the men
> whose work gives to the Society amongst devout Roman Catholics a reputation
> for holiness, and, in the foreign mission field, for heroic devotion for what they
> believe to be their duty . . . yet, after all, they are but the dupes of the real wire-
> pullers. They do the work which gains for the Order renown and praise; when
> evil work has to be done other instruments are generally chosen, though not
> always.[57]

Further, the Society's organisation was still the key to its success:

> They (the professed fathers) hold the strings, and all the other Jesuits are but puppets on the world's stage, who perform mechanically as the strings are pulled by their masters, or rather, by the chief master of the whole organisation – the General of the Jesuits.[58]

As far as Jesuit meddling in worldly affairs and local communities, Walsh summarised his view succinctly when he wrote 'A *History of the Political Influence of the Jesuits* throughout the world would fill several large volumes'. His approach to substantiating this claim is also familiar as he devoted a large portion of his entry to recounting well-worn evidence predictably drawn from now infamous accusations made by the Society's enemies over the previous four centuries.[59]

Nevertheless, while the basic components of the legend remained the same in Walsh's account as those written several centuries earlier, the more apocalyptic Protestant interpretations of the Jesuit threat were absent. There are no claims in Walsh's entry of Jesuits using magic or consorting with demons. Moreover, Walsh's entry lacks the sense that the Society was irresistible because of their powers of persuasion or organisation. Undoubtedly the declining belief in magic and supernatural powers amongst Europeans between the sixteenth and twentieth centuries is one reason behind this shift. Moreover, it is also likely that the perceived threat of Protestant disunity, and indeed of Catholic unity, that resonated in the newly established Reformed churches was no longer so threatening in the stable environment of the early-twentieth-century Anglican British Empire.

In many ways Walsh's interpretation of the legend has taken on the distinctive features of the Catholic interpretation in the sixteenth and seventeenth centuries. The Society of Jesus for Walsh and other twentieth-century Protestants had been and remained 'the most formidable opponent which the Protestant Reformation of the sixteenth century has had to deal'.[60] Yet while the component parts of the legend remained the same, his interpretation of the overall legend closely paralleled early Catholic rather than Protestant concerns. Ultimately it was the political and religious threat to local and national traditions by this successful international Order which fuelled the legend in later periods. Here we can see the dynamism and flexibility in legend formation at work; a twentieth-century Protestant writer altered the myth by removing the magical and apocalyptic features of previous Protestant literature in order to increase its resonance in his audience.

Still for many Protestant opponents in the sixteenth and seventeenth centuries the almost superhuman or irresistible threat which the Society posed to godly communities was very real, and provides an excellent example of Protestant legend creation in the post-Reformation period which, if anything, is more closely related to earlier medieval beliefs than the legend produced by their Catholic counterparts. For Protestants who wished to account for the dissension and disorder in their communities, the Jesuit menace as defined in the legend provided the perfect explanation. Like demons in the Middle Ages, the Society through secret scheming, deception, duplicity and, for some, the use of the black arts was able to undermine even the most stable of godly communities. Here Protestant polemicists fashioned a new threat to society to replace an older partially discredited threat of demons and their minions. In doing so they helped to sustain an older set of beliefs about the threat from within which had long played an important role in defining the communities of Catholic Europe. Nevertheless, some Catholics were also able to use the legend to explain the success of a very different threat to their local church traditions: the rise of post-Tridentine Catholic renewal. Thus, even at a time of great tension between rival Protestant and Catholic churches polemicists from both faiths could interact in legend creation even if for different purposes. It was the Catholic interpretation which ultimately proved more durable and it is in this form that the Jesuit legend continues to be used by polemicists today.

NOTES

I would like to thank Tom McCoog and Tim Watson for reading earlier drafts of this chapter.

1 For the purposes of this chapter I define superstition as a belief held by a number of people but largely without foundation. In this sense, most myths and legends fall under the more general heading of superstition.

2 There is an extensive literature on this topic. See for instance W. Christian, *Local Religion in Sixteenth-Century Spain* (Princeton, 1981). See also M. Forster, *The Counter-Reformation in the Villages: Religion and Reform in the Bishopric of Speyer, 1560–1720* (Ithaca, 1992) and A. Megged, *Exporting the Catholic Reformation: Local Religion in Early-Colonial Mexico* (Leiden, 1996).

3 The terms myth and legend have both been used by scholars to describe the Jesuits' image. I will use these two terms interchangeably in this article. A number of scholarly studies of the Jesuit legend or myth have been produced over the past two centuries. See for instance A. Brou, *Les Jésuites de la légende* (Paris, 1907), 2 vols. See also G. Cubbitt, *The Jesuit Myth: Conspiracy Theory and Politics in Nineteenth-Century France* (Oxford, 1993).

4 For a more detailed account of the development of the Antichrist theme in Protestant propaganda see R. W. Scribner, *For the Sake of Simple Folk* (Cambridge, 1981), 148–65.

5 Anon., *Imago primi sæculi Societatis Iesu a Prouincia Flandro-Belgica eiusdem Societatis repræsentata* (Antwerp, B. Moreti, 1640).

6 The variety of accusations continues to be a feature of the Jesuit legend. For example in the twentieth century, the Jesuits have been linked with the assassination of Abraham Lincoln. See C. Chiniquy, *Fifty years in the Church of Rome: The Thrilling Life Story of Pastor Chiniquy Who was for Twenty-Five Years a Priest in the Roman Church* (London, 1948), 389–409.

7 Both Protestants and Catholics address this theme. See for instance E. Hasenmüller, *Historia Iesvitici Ordinis* (Frankfurt, I. Spies, 1595), 100–1; E. Malescot, *Morologie des Iesvites. Morologie des favx prophetes et manticores Iesuites* (Caen, n. pr., 1593), 8; P. Boquinus, *A defence of the Olde, and True profession of Christianitie, against the new, and counterfaite secte of Iesuites, or fellowship of Iesus* (London, J. Wolf & H. Kirkham, 1581), 77–80, 99–107, 146–7. This text was originally published in Lyon in 1576. For a Catholic example see E. Pasquier, *Le Catechisme des Iesvites* (Paris, Ville-Franche, 1602), *passim*.

8 Anon., 'Charactares Iesuitarum', in Anon., *Doctrinae Iesviticae Praecipva Capita Scripta Qvaedam continens, in quibus Iesuitarum Sophismata solidis rationibus testimoniisque sacrarum Scripturarum & Doctorum veteris Ecclesiae, refelluntur* (La Rochelle, n. pr., 1585), 35.

9   Malescot, *Morologie des Iesvites*, 7.

10 Anon., *The Jesuites Intrigues* (London, n. pr., 1669), 25. This work was originally published in Latin at the opening of the seventeenth century under title *Monita privata Societatis Jesu*; see Brou, *Les Jésuites de la légende*, 1: 275–82.

11 *The Jesuites Intrigues*, 26.

12 For an in-depth discussion of the term's modern usage see A. Lynn Martin, 'The Jesuit Mystique', *Sixteenth Century Journal* 4 (1973), 31.

13 Anon., *The Doctrines and Practices of the Societie of Iesvites, in two books* (London, n. pr., 1630), 41. This text was originally published in Latin as *Profana sectae Jesuiticae vanitas. Dialogus: siue colloquium Jesuiticum de fundamentis sectae Jesuitarum malè fundatis* (Ambergae, n. pr., 1611). See also Robert Tinley, *Two Learned Sermons* (London, W. Halland and T. Adams, 1609).

14 'Jesuited' people or 'Jesuitical' actions are common features in both the Protestant and Catholic traditions across Europe. For one example see Anon., *The Anatomie of Popish Tyrannie* (London, n. pr., 1603), Preamble 11.

15 *The Jesuites Intrigues*, pp. 7–8.

16 A. Arnauld, *Plaidoyé de M. Antoine Arnavld* (La Haye, n. pr., 1594), fol. 4v.

17 Both widows and students are commonly cited. The accusation that the Society seduced the weak and unstable bears a close resemblance to accusations made by Catholics that Protestants focused upon similar vulnerable groups to make conversions. For a detailed account of the Society's interest in widows see *The Jesuits Intrigues*, 35–42. For a discussion of the recruitment of students see *The Jesuits Intrigues*, 43–4, 52–3. See also Boquinus, *A defence*, 4–6, 18–19.

18 Hasenmüller, *Historia*, 20–1, 582.

19 For instance, in one description of a visitation to a Jesuit college, the senior Jesuit inspecting the college asked whether any of its students could be counted upon to sacrifice their lives for the advancement of the Society's designs. The author of the tract implies that this was a standard question posed on such visitations. See *The Doctrines and Practices*, 57.

20 Examples of Jesuit complicity can be found in tracts from across Europe. See for instance Anon., *A trve and plaine declaration of the horrible Treasons* (London, n. pr., 1585). See also Anon., *Anticoton* (n. pl., n. pr., 1610), 35–50. Or for a Protestant account of the same material see D. Hume, *L'assassinat dv roy* (n. pl., n. pr., 1615), *passim*.

21 For this rumour see Bibliothèque Nationale, Manuscrit française 15798, fol. 201–201v ('*Recueil des interrogatoires et des arrests de Jean Guignard et de Jean Chastel*'). This document shows that Chastel's interrogators were well aware of the rumours concerned with special Jesuit meditation chambers.

22 For a discussion of special knives see Hume, *L'assassinat dv roy*, 55–6. For a reference to poison see [Edward Squire], *A lettre written out of England* (London, C. Barker, 1599), 6–7. There are innumerable texts which accuse Jesuits of being the persuasive force behind attacks. For instance see Anon., *A trve report of svndry horrible conspiracies* (London, C. Yetsweirt, 1594).

23 Arnauld, *Plaidoyé*, fol. 2v. On the frequency of such accusations see S. Clark, *Thinking with Demons* (Oxford, 1999), 534.

24 *The Doctrines and Practices*, 51. This is undoubtedly a reference to Father Coton, the Jesuit confessor to Henri IV, who had been accused of questioning demons about Henri's death. See Hume, *L'assassinat dv roy*, 43–4. *The Doctrines and Practices*, 52, offers other evidence of the Society's use of magic.

25 See Arnauld, *Plaidoyé*, *passim*. See also Pasquier, *Catechisme*, *passim*.

26 Arnauld, *Plaidoyé*, fol. 18v.

27 J.-A. De Thou, *Histoire Universelle* (The Hague, n. pr., 1740), 11 vols, 10: 46–73.

28 Hasenmüller, *Historia*, 107–13. See also *The Doctrines and Practices*, 4–6.

29 *The Doctrines and Practices*, 39.

30 *The Jesuites Intrigues*, 4.

31 *A Discourse concerning the original of the Powder-Plot* (London, 1674), 8.

32 *Anticoton*, 48: 'Mais d'où vient qu'à Bruxelles, & à Prague, où les Iesuites regnent, on par- loit de la mort du Roy douze ou quinze iours deuant qu'elle arriuast? A Rouen plusieurs ont reçeu lettres de Bruxelles de leurs amis demandas d'estre aduertis si le bruit de la mort du Roy estoit veritable, combien qu'elle ne fust encores advenue. Monsieur l'Argentier de Troyes a receu de Prague lettres du pedaguogue de ses enfans, qui luy disent qu'un Iesuite les auoit desia advertis de la mort du Roi auant qu'elle aduint.'

33 *The Jesuites Intrigues*, 9.

34 The importance of plausible evidence to the construction of rumour is well documented in T. Shibutani, *Improvised News: A Sociological Study of Rumor* (Indianapolis, 1966), 76–86. While evidence is open to interpretation and often only a distorted view of reality is extrap- olated from the evidence; nevertheless, what is perceived as hard factual evidence, accord- ing to Shibutani, is important for the confirmation of a rumour. R. W. Scribner has argued that a core of factual evidence strengthens propaganda in a similar way. See Scribner, *For the Sae of Simple Folk*, xxiii.

35 I. Loyola, *The Constitutions of the Society of Jesus* (Saint Louis, 1970), 337.

36 Loyola, *The Constitutions*, 238.

37 Archivum Romanum Societatis Iesu Galliae 60, fol. 136 (Oliverius to Aquaviva; 8 July 1598).

38 L'Estoile, *Mémoires-Journaux* (Paris, 1888–98), 12 vols, 7: 117. Furthermore, the most authoritative contemporary tract gives no indication that Bordeaux Jesuits were involved: Anon., *La conspiration faicte par les peres Iesvites de Douay, pour assassiner Maurice, Prince d'Orange, Comte de Nassau*, in S. Goulart, ed., *Memoires de la Ligue* (Geneva, n. pr., 1599), 9 vols, 7: 717–23.

39 For other examples of Jesuit 'implication' in assassination attempts see: R. Mousnier, *L'As- sassinat d'Henri IV* (Paris, 1964), 197–212.

40 On the difficulties experienced in directing the Society of Jesus from Rome see A. Lynn Martin, *The Jesuit Mind* (Ithaca, 1988), 105–23.

41 On the importance of widows in funding Jesuit initiatives see O. Hufton, 'The Widow's Mite', *Transactions of the Royal Historical Society* 8 (1998), 117–37.

42 *The Doctrines and Practices*, 47–8.

43 In this particular manifestation of the theme the torture chamber and its use bears some resemblance to similar myths surrounding the Spanish Inquisition.

44 Although the imprint indicates a publication date of 1612, the text was first published in Cracow in 1614. In this article I have used one of its many translations, *The Jesuites Intrigues*.

45 *The Jesuites Intrigues*, A2.

46 Hasenmüller, *Historia*, 27: 'Et sunt Daemoniorum socij, qui sub nomine IESU, & specie pietatis veniunt ad nos, in vestitu ouium, in angelos lucis transformati: sed reipsa operarij iniquitatis, lupi rapaces, pseudoprophatae, seu, vt Christus dicit, fures & latrones . . .'.

47 For reference to Gretser's travelling companion see Brou, *Les Jésuites de la légende*, 1: 42.

48 The pope as Antichrist was a commonplace in Protestant literature see C. Weiner, 'The Beleaguered Isle. A Study of Elizabethan and Early Jacobean Anti-Catholicism', *Past and Present* 51 (1971), 27–62.

49 See Hasenmüller, *Historia*, 13. See also Boquinus, *A defence*, 12.

50 For more on Protestant conceptions of demons see A. Jelsma, *Frontiers of the Reformation: Dis- sidence and Orthodoxy in Sixteenth-Century Europe* (Aldershot, 1998), 25.

51 For a full discussion of the locust allusion see M. Questier, '"Like Locusts over all the World": Conversion, Indoctrination and the Society of Jesus in Late Elizabethan and Jacobean England', in T. McCoog , ed., *The Reckoned Expense: Edmond Campion and the Early English Jesuits* (Woodbridge, 1996), 265–84, especially 265–6.

52 Boquinus, *A defence*, 8–9.

53 For more context on this issue see Clark, *Thinking with Demons*, 361. For allusions to the Jesuits as a punishment from God see 'Dedicatory Epistle', in *The Doctrines and Practices*.

54 Arnauld, *Plaidoyé*, *passim*.

55 A. Arnauld, *Le franc et véritable discours au roi Henri IV. Sur le rétablissement des Jésuites, 1602*, in J. A. Gazaignes, ed., *Annales de la société des soi-disans Jésuites; ou recueil historique-chronologique* (Paris, n. pr., 1764), 5 vols, 1: 661–95.

56 Walter Walsh, 'The Jesuits', in C. Walsh, ed., *The Protestant Dictionary Containing Articles on the History, Doctrines and Practices of the Christian Church, New Edition* (London, 1933), 349.

57 Walsh, 'The Jesuits', 349.

58 Walsh, 'The Jesuits', 349.

59 Walsh, 'The Jesuits', 350–1.

60 Walsh, 'The Jesuits', 348.

PART II

Superstition, tradition and the other world

'The spirit of prophecy has not wholly left the world': the stylisation of Archbishop James Ussher as a prophet

UTE LOTZ-HEUMANN

In contrast to the Scottish reformer John Knox, who said of himself in 1565 'God hath revealed unto me secrets unknown to the world', the Church of Ireland archbishop of Armagh James Ussher (1581–1656) never claimed to have prophetic powers.[1] However, in 1656 Nicholas Bernard, Ussher's former chaplain and chaplain to Oliver Cromwell during the Interregnum, published a biography of Ussher entitled *The Life and Death of the Most Reverend and Learned Father of Our Church Dr. James Usher*.[2] In this biography, Bernard cast Ussher as a Protestant prophet. Subsequently, Ussher's alleged prophecies were extracted from Bernard's biography and repeatedly published as short pamphlets, which proves that there was a popular interest and thus a 'market' for them.[3]

Prophets and prophecies in sixteenth- and seventeenth-century Protestantism have been variously analysed in recent historiography. Apart from works devoted to pre-Reformation prophecy, different, but related 'variants' of early modern prophecy have been studied.[4] The attitude to, and use of, prophecies in early Lutheranism have been studied by Robin Bruce Barnes and Bob Scribner.[5] Charles Webster in his pioneering study *From Paracelsus to Newton* has drawn attention to the connection between magic, including prophecy, and the development of modern science.[6] Another field of study is political prophecies which played a major role in early modern European politics to bolster resistance movements.[7] In accordance with the general historiographical interest in popular culture, recent research on prophecy has predominantly focused on popular prophets. Studies range from analysis of popular prophecies during the Thirty Years' War[8] including Comenius' acceptance and reception of such prophets,[9] to detailed research into Lutheran popular prophets in Germany and Scandinavia,[10] including such spectacular cases as Hans Keil, a popular prophet in seventeenth-century Württemberg, whose prophecies proved to be fraud.[11] In the English context, the period of the civil war and Interregnum have received considerable attention because 'every kind of prophecy was ventilated'[12] and women were especially prominent as prophets during those years.[13] However, apart from the general overview presented in 1971 by Keith Thomas in his *Religion and the Decline of Magic*, there is as yet no comprehensive work on prophecy in either continental Europe or the British isles and the specialist studies have so far mostly ignored prophecies ascribed to Tudor and Stuart divines.[14]

In this chapter, I will therefore study Nicholas Bernard's biography of Ussher and later pamphlets derived from it as an example of such 'ascribed' prophecies. Proceeding from an analysis of the contents of Bernard's tract, this chapter will then put Bernard's 'stylisation' of Ussher as a prophet in its contemporary context of Civil War/Interregnum popular prophecy and in the context of Protestant preaching and prophecy in general. Finally, this essay will look at the pamphlets which were derived from Bernard's biography and which – in contrast to Bernard – focused solely on Ussher's alleged prophecies. How this changed the impression conveyed to readers and how these tracts reflect popular Protestant identity in early modern England and Ireland will be analysed.

In his biography of Ussher, Bernard made his case for the archbishop's prophetic powers by introducing and developing biblical parallels. He began by juxtaposing Ussher with Samuel as a preacher and prophet, first in general and then adding particular points which he considers especially noticeable as parallels. First, Samuel and Ussher began their preaching 'when the word of God was precious, or rare'.[15] Second, both began ministering in their youth; third, Samuel and Ussher were both in favour with both God and men. Fourth, just as Samuel came to be known to all of Israel, not just one tribe, Ussher was 'known far and neer, to the whole Reformed Church'.[16] Fifth, like Samuel, Ussher was first popular with 'the vulgar', but later had to flee his country.[17] Sixth, as Samuel saw great changes in the government of his native country, so Ussher lived to see the Irish rebellion of 1641; and lastly,

> as the devil took upon him to prophesie in the name of Samuel after his death, so we do expect the like from his instruments; nay, some have already attempted to set forth Sermons, and Books of errors in this our Samuels Name, and like to proceed, if not prevented by the Government.[18]

Finally, Bernard stresses that as there was universal mourning among the Israelites for Samuel, so there is for Ussher 'throughout the reformed Church'.[19]

Bernard then embarked on Ussher's biography, which he related in a strictly chronological order. It is noticeable that in large parts of the tract, Ussher is not at all portrayed as, or even juxtaposed with, a prophet, but rather praised as a scholar whose learning and wisdom were respected by Protestants and Catholics alike.[20] In addition, Ussher's special status as a 'holy man' (as he is repeatedly called) and as a Protestant saint – he is, for example, described as having had 'an Apostolical Saint-like spirit' – are stressed.[21] Among the many parallels from the Bible and church history which are introduced to describe Ussher, that between Christ and Ussher is most striking.[22] This is of course only alluded to – in the context of Ussher's having been tempted by the devil in his youth and when Ussher is said to have rather turned to the 'poorest and weakest person' than to the more learned – but as an image it is very powerful to underline the representation of Ussher as a man of extraordinary spiritual powers who had a special relationship to God.[23]

When describing Ussher's prophecies and prophetic powers, Bernard gradually leads the reader into the theme. He starts by relating that Ussher's first sermon in 1601 was preached on the text: 'Thou hast a name that thou livest, and art dead' (Revelation 4:1) during a service held in Dublin to pray for Mountjoy's campaign against Hugh O'Neill.[24] According to Bernard, Ussher preached his sermon at exactly the time that the Battle of Kinsale was fought and won by the English. Bernard then hints that, as Ussher's sermon had been his first, this 'might possibly' have made it 'more efficacious'.[25] After that Bernard reported that Ussher had in fact been tempted to defer his ordination because of a rumour that Protestant clergymen would be the first target of Irish Catholics if they won the Nine Years' War. However, Ussher 'resolved the rather upon it, conceiving he should in that Office of the Ministery, and for that Cause, die the next door to Martyrdome'.[26]

Having thus 'warmed the reader up', Bernard then proceeded to give us the first 'full-blown' prophecy from Ussher. This prophecy was also supposed to have taken place in a sermon in 1601 or early 1602, roughly forty years before the Irish rebellion.[27] Ussher preached 'before the State at Christs Church Dublyn' on Ezekiel 4:6 ('where the Prophet by lying on his side, was to beare the iniquity of Judah forty dayes, I have appointed thee a day for a year, even a day for a year'), expounding this text with regard to Ireland thus: 'From this year will I reckon the sin of Ireland, that those whom you now imbrace [i.e. the Catholics] shall be your ruine, and you shall beare this iniquity'.[28] Bernard then argued indirectly that Ussher predicted the Irish Catholic rebellion of 1641 forty years beforehand. He was, however, very cautious in ascribing prophetic powers to Ussher:

> Now, what may be thought of this, I leave to the judgement of others; onely give me leave to say, 'tis a very observable passage, and if it may be conceived to be a Propheticke impulse in those years, he was the liker this our Samuel, who in his youth was sent with the like massage to Eli, relating the ruine of his native Country.[29]

On the other hand, in order to bolster his case for Ussher's status as a prophet, Bernard stressed that Ussher always expected such a judgement to come upon

Ireland and that he grew more and more fearful of it although 'there being nothing visibly tending to the feare of it'.[30]

Almost fifty pages further on in the biography, Bernard introduced Ussher's next alleged prophecies of 1624/25, referring, on the one hand, to the 'changes' (i.e. the rebellion and civil war, in Ireland and Britain) and, on the other hand, to his own poverty as a consequence of these events.[31] Bernard lists sermons and passages from Ussher's book *Ecclesiarum Britannicarum Antiquitates*, in which he foretold confusions, divisions and destructions of the sinfulness and wickedness 'of all sorts and degrees'.[32] More specifically, Ussher is reported to have said in 1624 'That he was perswaded the greatest Stroak to the Reformed Church was to come yet'.[33] And Bernard related that Ussher attributed the divisions 'in matter of Religion' during the civil war and Interregnum to the machinations of the Catholic clergy and concluded that if this was not stopped, 'Popery, or Massacres, or both' would be the consequence.[34]

Bernard's narrative strategy in this context is very interesting. First, he does his best to persuade the reader that these utterances of Archbishop Ussher were guided by God by claiming that 'He hath often acknowledged, that sometimes that which he hath fully resolved in his Sermon not to utter, when he came to it, was like Jeremiahs fire, shut up in his bones, that he could not forbeare, unlesse he would have stood mute, and have proceeded no further'.[35] And Bernard stressed that 'Hundreds alive at this day have laid [Ussher's prophecies] up in their hearts, and by what hath fallen out already, do measure their expectation for the future'.[36] But at the end of this passage, Bernard is more careful in his judgement:

> Now, howsoever I am as farre from heeding of Prophesies this way as any; yet with me 'tis not improbable, that so great a Prophet, so sanctified from his youth, so knowing, and eminent throughout the Universall Church, might have at some speciall times more then ordinary motions and impulses in doing the Watch-mans part, of giving warning of Judgements approaching.[37]

Only three pages further on, when Bernard came to the year 1640, he again reverted to a more emphatic statement of Ussher's prophetic powers. Speaking first of 'Gods speciall providence for his [i.e. Ussher's] preservation' because the archbishop left Ireland before the rebellion of 1641, he then recalled another of Ussher's predictions of 'heavie sorrowes and miseries' soon to come, which, Bernard says, 'put me in minde of that in Amos 3:7: Surely the Lord will do nothing, but he will reveale it unto his servants the Prophets; (at least so great an one, and of that Nation.)'.[38] Finally, Bernard related another of Ussher's warnings of 'afflictions and trials, which he was perswaded were not farre from us' (this time in 1656, shortly before his death).[39]

In early modern Protestantism, the attitude towards prophecies was decidedly mixed. While Protestants – in contrast to Catholics – regarded the age of miracles as having passed and did not believe in the appearance of saints, prophecies remained the last possibility of a direct revelation from God about the future.[40] Even in the established churches of England, Scotland and Ireland, opinions about prophecy varied considerably. For example, while the Church of Ireland bishop, Dopping, argued that the age of prophecies was over, John Knox and John Hacket, the Restoration bishop of Coventry and Lichfield, believed that revelation could still occur through prophecy.[41] The Protestant sects (e.g. the Quakers) firmly believed in the continuing presence and significance of prophecy.[42] We have thus, on the one hand, a considerable spectrum of attitudes towards prophecy within Protestantism and, on the other hand, we also have a wide range of prophecies.

Prophecies can be variously differentiated. Besides the biblical prophecies, there were so-called 'ancient prophecies' (for example, prophecies attributed to Merlin, Bede or Edward the Confessor).[43] Similar to 'contemporary' prophecies like astrological prophecies and prophecies based on all kinds of prodigies, these required interpretation as well as application to contemporary situations.[44] In contrast, 'contemporary' prophecies uttered by, or attributed to, specific persons usually already contained direct references to contemporary events – often wars and crises – and predictions for the future were related to, or derived from, statements about the present.

In this context, we can again differentiate between so-called popular prophets (e.g. Lutheran laymen in sixteenth and seventeenth-century Germany or women and even children especially during the Civil War and Interregnum in Britain), on the one hand, and prophecies uttered by, or attributed to, 'godly persons' in a broad sense of the word, on the other hand. The latter included Luther, the martyrs of the Marian persecution as well as many Tudor and Stuart divines (e.g. Richard Hooker, Lancelot Andrewes and George Abbot).[45] With regard to the clergymen-prophets, there were always two possibilities of prophesying which Luther had originally identified and which resulted in another ambiguity about prophecy within Protestantism. One was the 'extraordinary' prophecy which foretells the future upon a direct revelation from God, the other was biblical exegesis as an 'everyday' kind of prophecy by the preacher.[46]

The contemporary context to Bernard's stylisation of Ussher as a prophet has already been hinted at above. When Bernard published his biography of Ussher in 1656, prophesying by members of different Protestant sects was rampant. In the atmosphere of religious toleration created by Cromwell and because of the absence of censorship, Protestant sects and their radical religious ideas proliferated. As a consequence, there was unrestrained preaching and prophesying by laymen and laywomen, in particular Quakers. Millenarian prophecies mixed with social and political forecasts. Prophets claimed to have received their revelations from angels or even from Christ himself.[47]

Seen in this context, Bernard's portrayal of Ussher as a prophet appears extremely cautious and 'conservative', but nevertheless does not lack elements of popular appeal. First of all, it is striking that almost all of Ussher's alleged prophecies related by Bernard are said to have been uttered as parts of sermons. This mixture of preaching and prophecy put Ussher firmly into the Protestant tradition of 'preaching-prophesying' mentioned above. It also placed Ussher in a long line of Protestant clergymen-prophets, many of whom had only been styled as prophets after their deaths.[48] The first and most prominent among these was Luther, and it is remarkable how many elements of stylisation which were used in the popular pamphlets about Luther also appear in Bernard's text. Luther, like Ussher, was described as a pious teacher, as a preacher, as a 'holy man' or 'man of God' and also as a saint.[49] From this resulted the belief that Luther was a divinely inspired preaching prophet.[50] Similarly, Bernard's careful description of Ussher as a 'holy man' underscored the popular belief that 'a man who was holier than his contemporaries was likely to be endowed with a special gift of foreknowledge'.[51] This 'special gift' of prophecy was underlined by the fact that Ussher's prophesying was explicitly described as going beyond his normal preaching: 'sometimes that which he hath fully resolved in his Sermon not to utter, when he came to it, was like Jeremiahs fire, shut up in his bones, that he could not forbeare'.[52] Moreover, parallels were drawn between both Luther and Ussher and, among others, Christ, Moses, Daniel and St Paul.[53]

In addition, Bernard made the mixed attitude of sixteenth and seventeenth-century Protestants towards prophecies a direct subject of discussion in his text: 'I am as farre from heeding of Prophesies this way as any; yet with me 'tis not improbable, that so great a Prophet . . . might have at some speciall times more then ordinary motions and impulses'.[54] The careful balance in Bernard's description of Ussher as a prophet makes it clear that Bernard was not writing for the more radical Protestant sects, to which much wilder claims about Ussher's prophesying would have appealed. As with the rest of the work, which, for example, carefully stresses Ussher's Calvinism, Bernard's biography was written for more 'conservative' or 'moderate' Protestants of the Interregnum like Cromwell himself.[55]

All in all, Bernard's stylisation of Ussher as a prophet must be called 'moderate' when viewed in its contemporary context. Nevertheless, the contents of Ussher's alleged prophecies reflect Protestant traditions of apocalyptic preaching and of popular apocalyptic prophesying.[56] Both, apocalyptic sermons and apocalyptic prophecies, proceeded from a description of the enormity of sins in society in order to warn of God's imminent judgement. The aim of such sermons and prophecies was to exhort people to repent their sins – for example, drunkenness, whoring, swearing, Sabbath-breaking – to ask God for forgiveness and to sin no more, so that the country or nation would be spared from God's retribution which would otherwise come in the form of plagues, natural disasters or wars.[57] These exhortations included drawing a parallel between the 'nation', which could be England and/or Protestant Ireland, and Israel.[58]

The contents of Ussher's alleged prophecies reflect such apocalyptic sermons. In the sermon in which he predicted the Irish rebellion, the sin that is denounced is connivance of Catholicism and (Protestant) Ireland is paralleled with Israel: both were destroyed after forty years.[59] Repeatedly, Bernard stressed that Ussher warned of 'a judgement upon that his native Country [i.e. Ireland]', which was coming nearer and nearer.[60] While these predictions for Ireland seemed already to have come true, Ussher's last sermon in England on 'Sinne when it is finished, brings forth death' (James 1: 15) was concerned with judgement yet to come.[61] Bernard related that 'his full application of it to the fulnesse of the sins of this Nation [i.e. England], which certainly would bring forth destruction . . . affected much the auditory'.[62]

This brings us, thus, to the end of Bernard's biography of Ussher. As mentioned above, Ussher's prophecies were afterwards extracted from Bernard's work and printed in different versions and under different titles. In the following, I will look at two of these pamphlets in order to analyse how they differ from Bernard's original account. In this context, two aspects will be emphasised. First, how these pamphlets managed to achieve a more popular appeal than Bernard and second, how these pamphlets were related to Protestant national identity in England and Ireland.

First of all, the titles of these pamphlets are – in contrast to Bernard's *Life and Death of . . . Dr. James Usher* – completely geared to the prophetic utterances ascribed to Ussher: *Strange and Remarkable Prophesies and Predictions Of the Holy, Learned, and excellent James Usher, Late L. Arch-Bishop of Armagh, and Lord Primate of Ireland* and *The Fulfilling of Prophecies: or the Prophecies and Predictions Of the late Learned and Reverend James Usher, Ld. Archbishop of Armagh, And Lord Primate of Ireland, Relating to England, Scotland, and Ireland.*[63] While the first title drew upon Bernard's text in describing Ussher as 'holy' and thus implying his special relationship to God, the second title stressed that some of Ussher's prophecies had already been fulfilled – from which one might logically infer that those as yet unfulfilled would one day become true.

Second, both pamphlets took all the passages relating to prophecies from Bernard's biography, then added comments and passages of their own. Thus, while in Bernard's biography the prophecies only took up a comparatively small portion of the text and were scattered in between relations of Ussher as a churchman and scholar, these pamphlets focus solely on the prophecies. Through their focus and conciseness these pamphlets have of course a much greater popular appeal than Bernard's tract. In addition, the pamphlets are – again in marked contrast to Bernard – much more assured and direct in their statements about

Ussher as a prophet and about the prophecies ascribed to him. There is no careful consideration, no balanced account as in Bernard. Rather, everything that Bernard formulated as a possibility, is here presented as a certainty.

For example, the title page of the 1678 pamphlet (*Strange and Remarkable Prophecies*) proceeded from a numbered list of Ussher's prophecies drawn from Bernard's biography, but formulated them much more directly and absolutely:

> Giving an Account of his [Ussher's] Foretelling
> I. The Rebellion in Ireland Forty Years before it came to pass.
> II. The Confusions and Miseries of England, in Church and State.
> III. The Death of King Charles the First.
> IV. His own Poverty and want.
> V. The Divisions in England in matters of Religion.
> Lastly, of a great and Terrible Persecution which shall fall upon the Reformed Churches by the Papists, wherein the then Pope should be chiefly concerned.[64]

In addition, the pamphlet's aim was explicitly stated as being that of an apocalyptic warning: 'publisht earnestly to perswade us to that Repentance and Reformation which can only prevent our Ruin and Destruction'.[65] All of this was 'topped up' by a verse from the Bible: 'And the Lord said, Shall I hide from Abraham the thing which I do?' (Genesis 18:17).[66]

Both pamphlets make certainties of what were tentative formulations in Bernard's tract: It is, for example, notable how Bernard's statement that Ussher had preached on 1 Samuel 12:25 ('But if ye still do wickedly, you shall be consumed, both you and your King') in 1625, is flatly 'converted' into Ussher having predicted King Charles' death.[67] Similarly, both pamphlets failed to relate Bernard's doubts as to whether the sermon predicting the Irish rebellion was preached in 1601 or 1602.[68] Rather, it is asserted that 'he foretold the Irish Rebellion Forty years before it came to pass, with the very time it should break forth, in a Sermon Preached in Dublin in 1601'.[69]

Interestingly, both pamphlets took up the question of the existence and validity of prophecies in Protestantism in their introductory paragraphs as well as in their conclusions. The 1678 pamphlet is very affirmative about prophecies in general and Ussher's prophetic powers in particular, although it retains a hint at Ussher's own rather sceptical attitude towards prophecies:

> he was wonderfully endued with a Spirit of Prophecy, whereby he gave out several true Predictions and Prophesies of things great while before they came to pass, whereof some we have seen fulfilled, and others remain yet to be accomplished. And though he was one that abhor'd Enthusiastick Notions, being too Learned, Rational, and knowing, to admit of such idle Freaks and Whimsies. Yet he protest, 'That several times in his Life he had many things imprest upon his mind, concerning future Events, with so much warmness and importunity, that

he was not able to keep them secret, but lay under an unavoidable necessity to make them known.[70]

Once again, it is especially interesting how the careful wording in Bernard's text, which says that Ussher had voiced thoughts in his sermons which he had been resolved not to utter, has been changed to a direct claim that Ussher had received revelations from God about the future.[71]

In contrast to the assured assertiveness of the 1678 pamphlet, the 1689 pamphlet (*The Fulfilling of Prophecies*) begins by discussing the Protestant attitude towards prophecies and thus seems to address a potentially more doubtful audience: 'Though in these latter Ages of the Church, many Learned and Pious Men, have made it a question, whether God now speaks to any by a prophetick Spirit; yet surely 'twere a great Boldness and Presumption for any preemptorily to determine that he does not.'[72] The pamphlet goes on to discuss this in detail, blaming the suspicion of prophecies upon 'the Frauds and Forgeries of Lying Popish Priests, who by counterfeit Miracles have strove each one to establish their several Orders'.[73] Ussher is then presented as proof that prophecy has not left the world:

> Now to confirm what I have been saying, that the Spirit of Prophecy has not wholly left the world, even in this Age, I have here proposed this great Man, Archbishop Usher, for an Example . . . And certainly let any Man lay aside Prejudice, and reflect on what has been already accomplished, as to his own particular, as well as in some part to Ireland formerly, and what is now sadly fulfilling in that miserable Kingdom, and he will be forced to confess, that this holy Man was indeed a Prophet.[74]

The 1689 pamphlet then repeats the introduction of the 1678 pamphlet as outlined above and both pamphlets end with a verbatim transcription of Bernard's carefully worded affirmation of Ussher being a holy man and prophet.[75]

The second part of the text of both pamphlets, however, does not quote or reproduce passages from Bernard's text with only slight changes or additions, but presents a new episode about Ussher as a prophet to the reader. This passage is implied as also being related by Bernard, but it is not to be found in detail in Bernard's biography of Ussher.[76] In this passage, Ussher is asked by the narrator in 1655

> what his present apprehensions were concerning a very great Persecution which should fall upon the Church of God in these Nations of England, Scotland, and Ireland, of which this Reverend Primate had spoken with great confidence many years before . . . I asked him whether he did believe those sad times to be past, or that they were yet to come. To which he answered, That they were yet to come, and that he did as confidently expect it as ever he had done . . . I then asked him, By what Means or Instruments this great Tryal should be brought on? He answered, By the Papists.[77]

This prophecy was then reinforced by the narrator as well as through the alleged testimony of Ussher's daughter and another lady. The narrator stressed that Ussher's countenance when uttering the above was not normal but 'a serious and irefull look, which he usually had when he spake God's word, and not his own; and when the Power of God seemed to be upon him'.[78] In order to bolster Ussher's status as a prophet even more, his daughter Phoebe, Lady Tyrrell, is then cited as a witness:

> She found him with his Eyes lift up to Heaven, and the Tears running apace down his Cheeks, and that he seemed to be in an Ecstasie, wherein he continued for about half an hour, not taking any notice of her, though she came into the Room; but at last turning to her, he told her, That his Thoughts had been taken up about the Miseries and Persecutions that were coming upon the Churches of Christ.[79]

And finally, the testimony of Lady Bysse was presented to the reader, to whom Ussher allegedly said that the predicted persecution of Protestants might be delayed a little longer if the King returned to England, but that it would nevertheless eventually take place.[80]

This leads us directly into the final question of this chapter: if and how these tracts on Ussher as a prophet were connected with national identity in England and Ireland. These interrelated questions can best be approached from a rather unusual angle: their publication dates. The first of these was licensed in London on 16 November 1678. This was at the height of the excitement about the popish plot.[81] The second pamphlet discussed here, *The Fulfilling of Prophecies*, was printed in London in 1689, when the Glorious Revolution had taken place but was not yet secure, especially in Ireland. Another reprint of Ussher's prophecies appeared in Dublin in 1714, 'probably during the early summer, when the Protestant succession seemed once more to be hanging in the balance'.[82]

These highly symbolic publication dates show that every time the Protestant king or succession were or seemed to be in danger, the resulting scare of an overthrow of Protestantism by Catholicism was heightened by appropriate predictions. The prophecies ascribed to Archbishop Ussher fitted this bill perfectly. They were vague enough to be applicable to different situations ('the greatest stroke upon the Reformed Churches was yet to come'), but by laying the blame firmly on 'the Papists', they appealed to the strong anti-Catholic element in English and Protestant Irish national identity.[83] Moreover, the alleged slight 'delay' in the fulfilling of the prophecies because of the restoration of the monarchy made a date towards the end of the seventeenth or at the beginning of the eighteenth century even more likely.

All in all, it has become clear that there was a development in the stylisation of Archbishop James Ussher as a Protestant prophet which led to an increasing explicitness and to a strengthening of the popular appeal of Ussher's alleged prophecies. His biographer, Nicholas Bernard, was still very careful in his judgement and interpretation. His case for Ussher as having been a prophet was introduced very subtly in his tract and was formulated more as an offer to the reader than as an assurance. And it only constituted a small part of Bernard's description of Ussher, who was above all portrayed as a scholar of international renown. In contrast, the later pamphlets were short and focused almost wholly on the subject of prophecy. Ussher's prophecies became absolute certainties here; they were expressed as definitive statements. In order to heighten their popular appeal, those prophecies that had already come to pass were, on the one hand, made more specific than they had originally been (for example, the prediction of the death of Charles I). On the other hand, those predictions that had not yet been fulfilled became more detailed and their testimony was carefully corroborated so as to make them more credible. It says a lot for the strength of this popular appeal that, for example, in a tract entitled *Compleat History of Remarkable Providences* (1697) by William Turner, it was alleged that Ussher had received a premonition of his own death and, moreover, that Ussher's prophecies were included in an almanac in 1704.[84] Thus, Bernard's relation of Ussher's prophecies had been, and continued to be, geared to popular tastes and, being infinitely malleable, could be used to heighten Protestant national identity in times of crisis.

NOTES

1 Cited in: Keith Thomas, *Religion and the Decline of Magic. Studies in Popular Beliefs in Sixteenth and Seventeenth Century England* (London, 1971), 131. On Ussher see Richard Parr, *The Life of the Most Reverend Father in God, James Ussher, late Lord Archbishop of Armagh* (London, N. Ranew, 1686); Charles Richard Elrington, *The Life of the Most Rev. James Ussher, D.D.* (London, 1848); *Dictionary of National Biography* (London, 1899), 63 vols. (1885–1900), 58: 64–72; R. Buick Knox, *James Ussher, Archbishop of Armagh* (Cardiff, 1967); Hugh Trevor-Roper, 'James Ussher, Archbishop of Armagh', in Hugh Trevor-Roper, *Catholics, Anglicans, and Puritans. Seventeenth Century Essays* (Chicago, 1988), 120–65, 289–92; Amanda L. Capern, 'Slipperye Times and Dangerous Dayes. James Ussher and the Calvinist Reformation of Britain, 1560–1660', unpublished Ph.D. thesis (University of New South Wales, 1991); Capern, 'The Caroline Church. James Ussher and the Irish Dimension', *Historical Journal* 39 (1996), 57–85. See also Raymond Gillespie, *Devoted People. Belief and Religion in Early Modern Ireland* (Manchester and New York 1997), 141.

2 Ussher died on 21 March 1656 and Barnard's biography was in fact an extended version of his funeral sermon for Ussher. See Nicholas Bernard, *The Life and Death of Dr. James Usher* (London, E. Tyler, 1656). Bernard had also been Dean of Kilmore and Ardagh in Ireland. On his biography see *DNB*, 4: 384–6.

3 See below, note 75.

4 See e.g. Ottavia Niccoli, *Prophecy and People in Renaissance Italy* (Princeton, 1990); Sabine Tanz and Ernst Werner, *Spätmittelalterliche Laienmentalitäten im Spiegel von Visionen, Offenbarungen und Prophezeiungen* (Frankfurt am Main, 1993).

5 See Robin Bruce Barnes, *Prophecy and Gnosis. Apocalypticism in the Wake of the Lutheran Reformation* (Stanford, CA, 1988); R. W. Scribner, *For the Sake of Simple Folk. Popular Propaganda for the German Reformation* (Oxford, 1994), especially, 136–47, 184–5, 255–6; Scribner,

'Luther Myth. A Popular Historiography of the Reformer', in Scribner, *Popular Culture and Popular Movements in Reformation Germany* (London, 1987), 301–22.

6 See Charles Webster, *From Paracelsus to Newton. Magic and the Making of Modern Science* (Cambridge, 1982); see also Richard H. Popkin, 'Predicting, Prophecying, Divining and Foretelling from Nostradamus to Hume', *History of European Ideas* 5: 2 (1984), 117–35.

7 See Sharon L. Jansen, *Political Protest and Prophecy under Henry VIII* (Woodbridge, 1991); Nicolette Mout, 'Chiliastic Prophecy and Revolt in the Habsburg Monarchy during the Seventeenth Century', in Michael Wilks, ed., *Prophecy and Eschatology* (Oxford, 1994), 93–109; see also Howard Dobin, *Merlin's Disciples. Prophecy, Popetry, and Power in Renaissance England* (Stanford, 1990).

8 See, for example, John Theibault, 'Jeremiah in the Village. Prophecy, Preaching, Pamphlets, and Penance in the Thirty Years' War', *Central European History* 27 (1994), 441–60.

9 See, for example, Hans-Joachim Müller, 'Kriegserfahrung, Prophetie und Weltfriedenskonzepte während des Dreißigjährigen Krieges', in *Jahrbuch für historische Friedensforschung* 6 (1997), 26–47; Joachim Friedrichsdorf, *Umkehr. Prophetie und Bildung bei Johann Amos Comenius* (Idstein, 1995).

10 See Jürgen Beyer, 'Lutherische Propheten in Deutschland und Skandinavien im 16. und 17. Jahrhundert. Entstehung und Ausbreitung eines Kulturmusters zwischen Mündlichkeit und Schriftlichkeit', in Robert Bohn, ed., *Europa in Scandinavia. Kulturelle und soziale Dialoge in der frühen Neuzeit* (Frankfurt am Main, 1994), 35–55; Beyer, 'Lutheran Popular Prophets in the Sixteenth and Seventeenth Centuries. The Performance of Untrained Speakers', *ARV. Nordic Yearbook of Folklore* 51 (1995), 63–86; Beyer, 'A Lübeck Prophet in Local and Lutheran Context', in R. W. Scribner and Trevor Johnson, eds, *Popular Religion in Germany and Central Europe, 1400–1800* (London, 1996), 166–82, 264–72.

11 See Norbert Haag, 'Frömmigkeit und sozialer Protest. Hans Keil, der Prophet von Gerlingen', *Zeitschift für Württembergische Landesgeschichte* 48 (1989), 127–41; David Warren Sabean, 'A Prophet in the Thirty Years' War. Penance as a Social Metaphor', in Sabean, *Power in the Blood. Popular Culture and Village Discourse in Early Modern Germany* (Cambridge, 1984), 61–93.

12 Thomas, *Religion*, 140.

13 See Phyllis Mack, 'Women as Prophets during the English Civil War', *Feminist Studies* 8: 1 (1982), 19–45; Mack, *Visionary Women. Ecstatic Prophecy in Seventeenth-Century England* (Berkeley, 1992). On women prophets in general see Diane Watt, *Secretaries of God. Women Prophets in Late Medieval and Early Modern England* (Cambridge, 1997).

14 But see chapter 6 on John Knox by Dale Johnson in this volume. Thomas lists John Hooper, Hugh Latimer, Richard Hooker, Lancelot Andrewes, George Abbot, Thomas Jackson, Nicholas Ferrar and Robert Catlin as divines to whom prophecies were ascribed; Thomas, *Religion*, 131–2.

15 Bernard, *Life and Death*, 3.

16 Bernard, *Life and Death*, 4.

17 Bernard, *Life and Death*, 4.

18 Bernard, *Life and Death*, 5; for all the parallels see, 3–5.

19 Bernard, *Life and Death*, 6.

20 See Bernard, *Life and Death*, 6–15.

21 See, for example, Bernard, *Life and Death*, 4, 112 and 106. On the concept of Protestant sainthood as developed in the martyrologies of Bale and Foxe see, for example, Leslie P. Fairfield, *John Bale. Mythmaker for the English Reformation* (West Lafayette, IN, 1976), 121–43; William Haller, *Foxe's Book of Martyrs and the Elect Nation* (London, 1963), 19–47; John N. King, *English Reformation Literature. The Tudor Origins of the Protestant Tradition* (Princeton, 1982), 71–5, 436–43.

22 Among these are Moses, Daniel, St Paul, St Peter and St Augustine (see Bernard, *Life and Death*, 99, 108–11).

23 See Bernard, *Life and Death*, 24 and, especially 58.

24 See Bernard, *Life and Death*, 35–6.

25 Bernard, *Life and Death*, 36.

26 Bernard, *Life and Death*, 36.

27 Bernard was himself not sure whether the sermon had really been preached in 1601 and he therefore argued: 'And whether preached in 1601 or in the beginning of 1602 the account is the same; for though that Massacre began in Octob. 23. 1641 yet they were continuing their murders, and proceeding in their destroying us, till 1642' (Bernard, *Life and Death*, 40). Elrington has shown that the sermon was most likely only given in 1602/03 (see Elrington, *Life of Ussher*, xxx; Philip Styles, 'James Ussher and His Times', *Hermathena* 88 (1956), 12–33, especially 21).

28 Bernard, *Life and Death*, 38–9.

29 Bernard, *Life and Death*, 40.

30 Bernard, *Life and Death*, 40. This fits into the general account of the years between the Nine Years' War and the Irish rebellion of 1641, i.e. that this was a period of peace for Ireland which obviously led the New English Protestants into believing that Ireland was finally under control. Accordingly, many Protestants are said to have been surprised by the 1641 rebellion; see Aidan Clarke, 'Ireland and the General Crisis', *Past and Present* 48 (1970), 79–99, here 86. However, Ussher's whole career shows that he was very conscious of what he perceived to be the Catholic threat in Ireland (see, for example, his reaction to the so-called 'graces') and it is therefore not surprising that he feared another Catholic uprising (see Ute Lotz-Heumann, *Die doppelte Konfessionalisierung in Irland. Konflikt und Koexistenz im 16. und in der ersten Hälfte des 17. Jahrhunderts* (Tübingen, 2000), 310–11).

31 See Bernard, *Life and Death*, 86.

32 Bernard, *Life and Death*, 87. See James Ussher, *Ecclesiarum Britannicarum Antiquitates* (Dublin, n. pr., 1639).

33 Bernard, *Life and Death*, 89.

34 Bernard, *Life and Death*, 90–1.

35 Bernard, *Life and Death*, 88.

36 Bernard, *Life and Death*, 90.

37 Bernard, *Life and Death*, 91.

38 Bernard, *Life and Death*, 93.

39 Bernard, *Life and Death*, 106.

40 See Beyer, 'Lübeck prophet', 168; Beyer, 'Lutheran Popular Prophets', 64; Müller, 'Kriegserfahrung', 31; Thomas, *Religion*, 128.

41 See Gillespie, *Devoted People*, 141; Thomas, *Religion*, 130.

42 See Thomas, *Religion*, 138–44.

43 See Thomas, *Religion*, 389–96.

44 See Benigna von Krusenstjern, 'Prodigienglaube und Dreißigjähriger Krieg', in Hartmut Lehmann and Anne-Charlott Trepp, eds, *Im Zeichen der Krise. Religiosität im Europa des 17. Jahrhunderts* (Göttingen, 1999), 53–78; Heike Talkenberger, *Sintflut. Prophetie und Zeitgeschehen in Texten und Holzschnitten astrologischer Flugschriften 1488–1528* (Tübingen, 1990).

45 See Scribner, 'Luther Myth', 307–11; Thomas, *Religion*, 131–2.

46 See Thomas Klingebiel, 'Apokalyptik, Prodigienglaube und Prophetismus im Alten Reich. Einführung', in Lehmann and Trepp, eds, *Im Zeichen der Krise*, 17–32, here 23–4; Theibault, 'Jeremiah', 446.

47 See Mack, 'Women as Prophets', 24; Thomas, *Religion*, 138–40. For the general background see, for example, Claire Cross, *Church and People, 1450–1660* (London, 1987), 207–20.

48 See, for example, Katherine R. Firth, *The Apocalyptic Tradition in Reformation Britain, 1530–1645* (Oxford, 1979), 228; Thomas, *Religion*, 131–2. Thomas lists Ussher also among the so-called 'ancient prophecies' (at 393), which seems rather misleading to me because he refers to Ussher above all in the context of Tudor and Stuart divines styled prophets by their biographers, which seems a more appropriate 'classification'.

49 See Scribner, 'Luther Myth', 303.

50 See Scribner, 'Luther Myth', 303, 307, 309.

51 Thomas, *Religion*, 132, see also 144.

52 Bernard, *Life and Death*, 88.
53 See Scribner, 'Luther Myth', 305–7; for Ussher see note 27 above.
54 Bernard, *Life and Death*, 91.
55 See Trevor-Roper, 'James Ussher', 121. Ussher is, for example, brought in connection with Calvin by stressing that both had been meant for the law by their fathers; Bernard, *Life and Death*, 30.
56 Patrick Collinson uses the term 'prophetic preaching' in this context. For Collinson, it means the 'everyday' kind of prophecy by preachers. See Patrick Collinson, *The Birthpangs of Protestant England. Religious and Cultural Change in the Sixteenth and Seventeenth Centuries* (London, 1988), 8. This is of course derived from the so-called 'prophesyings', the gatherings of Puritan clergy to expound the Scriptures, often attended by the laity. But the term 'prophetic preaching' could, as explained above, also denote extraordinary prophecies made public through sermons, and it is therefore an ambiguous term.
57 See Collinson, *Birthpangs*, 17–20; Beyer, 'Lübeck Prophet'; Haag, 'Frömmigkeit'; Sabean, 'A Prophet'.
58 See Collinson, *Birthpangs*, 18; for Ireland see Alan Ford, *The Protestant Reformation in Ireland, 1590–1641* (Dublin, 1997), 191–4.
59 See Bernard, *Life and Death*, 39.
60 Bernard, *Life and Death*, 40, see also 87.
61 Bernard, *Life and Death*, 89.
62 Bernard, *Life and Death*, 89–90.
63 Anon., *Strange and Remarkable Prophesies* (London, R. G., 1678 and London, n. pr., 1681) and Anon., *The Fulfilling of Prophecies* (London, R. Baldwin, 1689). See also Anon., *Bishop Ushers second prophesie which he delivered to his daughter on his sick-bed* (London, John Hunt, 1681); Anon., *The prophesy of Bishop James Ussher* (London, n. pr., 1687).
64 *Strange and Remarkable Prophesies*, 1.
65 *Strange and Remarkable Prophesies*, 1.
66 *Strange and Remarkable Prophesies*, 1.
67 Compare Bernard, *Life and Death*, 86, and *Strange and Remarkable Prophesies*, 1, 3; *The Fulfilling of Prophecies*, 2.
68 See above note 32.
69 *Strange and Remarkable Prophesies*, 2; see *The Fulfilling of Prophecies*, 1.
70 *Strange and Remarkable Prophesies*, 2.
71 See above text belonging to note 43.
72 *The Fulfilling of Prophecies*, 1.
73 *The Fulfilling of Prophecies*, 1.
74 *The Fulfilling of Prophecies*, 1.
75 See above text belonging to note 45.
76 This seems to be an elaboration of a short passage in Bernard, in which he tells of his leave-taking of Ussher in 1655, when Ussher told him 'to prepare for afflictions and trials, which he was perswaded were not farre from us'. Bernard, *Life and Death*, 106.
77 *The Fulfilling of Prophecies*, 2; see *Strange and Remarkable Prophesies*, 4–5.
78 *The Fulfilling of Prophecies*, 2; see *Strange and Remarkable Prophesies*, 5. A similar statement is made a few lines below this one; see *The Fulfilling of Prophecies*, 2; *Strange and Remarkable Prophesies*, 6.
79 *The Fulfilling of Prophecies*, 2; see *Strange and Remarkable Prophesies*, 7.
80 See *The Fulfilling of Prophecies*, 2; *Strange and Remarkable Prophesies*, 8.
81 See Styles, 'James Ussher', 21. There were several reprints of Ussher's prophecies in the following years, which attest, first, to the continuing popish plot scare (until 1681–82) and later probably to the developments in the reign of the Catholic James VII and II.
82 Styles, 'James Ussher', 21.
83 *The Fulfilling of Prophecies*, 2; see *Strange and Remarkable Prophesies*, 4.
84 See St John D. Seymour, *Irish Witchcraft and Demonology* (New York 1992), 103, and Gillespie, *Devoted People*, 142.

6

Serving two masters:
John Knox, Scripture and prophecy

DALE JOHNSON

The Renaissance and Reformation movements promoted complementary and sometimes contradictory goals, but they agreed on at least one proposition. Icons, relics, indulgences, pilgrimages and other fashionable religious practices were superstitious rubbish, which impeded the progress of reform. Scots reformer John Knox agreed wholeheartedly with this assessment. Unlike other reformers, Knox did not train in the humanist method but gave all of his energies to battling superstitious idolatry which he equated with the Roman Catholic religion in general and the mass in particular. In his crusade against idolatry Knox held inconsistently to the doctrine of *sola scriptura*. Knox also moved beyond the practice of John Calvin and fitted into a category which, Calvin conceded, existed only under extraordinary circumstances.

Almost without exception the Protestant reformers of the sixteenth century affirmed the progressive nature of divine revelation and likewise contended that in Christ and the apostles, God has spoken his last word so that revelations such as theophanics, dreams and audible voices have ceased. John Knox the Scots reformer was one of these exceptions. Knox did state his agreement with the Protestant, Reformed view that post-biblical revelation had ceased, yet in practice Knox disagreed, for he believed he was God's prophet in Scotland. While Scripture remained his primary authority he did not depend exclusively on the Bible. Knox guided his hermeneutic by Deuteronomy 12: 32, agreeing to follow only what the Lord commanded without any addition, but he could also make prophetic pronouncements with a clear conscience and confidence that he spoke the Word of God, and could interpret the work of God in nature and in history.

He acknowledged the importance of the first four ecumenical councils of the church, but explicitly denied their infallibility. Some councils, according to the *Scots Confession of Faith* (1560), 'have manifestly erred in matters of great weight and importance'.[1]

In a letter to some friends dated July 1556, Knox, the exiled preacher, admonished the Christians to heed God's Word, 'without which knowledge shall not increase, nor godliness appear, nor fervency continue among you. The Word of God is the beginning of spiritual life, without which all flesh is dead in God's presence'.[2] The *Scots Confession of Faith*, of which he was the principal author, declares: "As we believe and confess the Scriptures of God sufficient to instruct and make the man of God perfect, so do we affirm and avow the authority of the same to be of God, and to depend on neither men nor angels'.[3]

Knox's view of Scripture

Knox did not produce a systematic theology, nor was he a theologian *per se*, but it is possible to identify his view of Scripture from his extensive writings.[4] Like other reformers, Knox taught the perspicuity of Scripture. He repeatedly used the phrases 'God's plain Word' and the 'plain Scriptures' to underscore his argument.[5] Knox warned that 'all interpretation disagreeing with the principles of our faith, repugnant to charity, or that which stands in plain contradiction to any other manifest place of Scripture, is to be rejected'.[6] In one of his famed meetings with Mary Queen of Scots, Knox lectured the Queen on biblical hermeneutics. 'The Word of God is plain . . . and if there appear any obscurity in one place, the Holy Ghost, which is never contrarious to himself, explains the same more clearly in other places so that there can remain no doubt but unto such as obstinately remain ignorant.'[7] Knox applied a literal interpretation of Scripture whenever possible. 'We stick . . . to the literal sense of these former words of the Apostle, [and] then the rest of Scripture . . . teach[es] us.'[8] The literal hermeneutic enhanced the vehemence of Knox's preaching and exhortation.

Knox affirmed progressive revelation from the Old to the New Covenants. The Old Testament foreshadowed the New, but the New Testament did not supersede the Old Testament.[9] Furthermore, Knox believed in the sufficiency of Scripture. 'He hath revealed unto us so much as is profitable . . . of such sufficiency, that if an angel from heaven, with wonders, signs, and miracles, would declare to us a will repugnant to that which is already revealed . . . we would hold him accursed and in no wise to be heard.'[10]

The *Scots Confession of Faith* echoes those same sentiments: 'But if men, under the name of a Council, pretend to forge unto us new articles of our faith, or to make constitutions, repugning to the word of God, then utterly we must refuse the same as the doctrine of devils.'[11] This vigorous affirmation led one admiring biographer to call Knox's reliance on Scripture alone his 'master principle', one which the reformer applied to worship, for which he required an explicit biblical warrant for every religious practice.[12] In an informative article titled 'John Knox and the Bible', Professor G. D. Henderson declares that

the Bible provided Knox with a guide for 'theology, worship, discipline, government and even politics'.[13] Knox told the Scottish nobility 'the scriptures of
God are my only foundation and substance in all matters of weight and importance'.[14] Knox, however, went beyond John Calvin, for his Genevan mentor
contended that Scripture neither affirms nor forbids some worship practices
which the church should regard as *adiaphora* (things indifferent). In April of
1561, Calvin even wrote a letter requesting that Knox moderate his strict conviction and allow some ceremonies which lacked explicit biblical support.[15]
While a recent scholar called Calvin 'a prophet without a prophecy', Knox was
a prophet with prophetic claims and the ability to interpret the hand of God.[16]

Knox's doctrine of Scripture in practice

Knox affirmed a view of Scripture similar to the other major Protestant
reformers, but in practice he sometimes deviated from his own doctrine of
authority. He followed the typological principle of finding the type in the Old
Testament and its corresponding antitype in the New Testament, but he took
this procedure one step further by identifying other antitypes in contemporary
Scotland and England. Knox's practice stemmed from his desire to see and
interpret the hand of God in history. It seems that Knox blended the interpretation and the application of Scripture and thus employed an exotic exegesis.
As one modern writer has observed, 'in a sense this method stands typological
exegesis on its head . . . the antitype is now extra-biblical . . . taken from
events . . . it illumines the antitype, rather than vice-versa'.[17]

Despite his praise for the Bible, Knox took liberties with it, since he
appeared more interested in contemporary applications than in the precise
meaning of Scripture. One biographer, perhaps unaware of the implications of
his remark, gleefully said of Knox, 'He hurries quickly from the exposition to
the application; the text being only a point of departure for his own [opinion]
. . . It does not seem to matter much which text he chooses'.[18] Such practice,
however, is damning to someone who affirms the absolute authority of the
Bible. Thus, Knox, the activist, in his rush to rid the kirk of idolatry failed to
employ careful exegesis. Knox, in fact, lacked both the temperament and the
mastery of biblical languages to exegete the Scripture with precision. He began
to tread on a slippery landscape, and he slipped precariously when he made
prophetic claims.

In the opinion of Richard Kyle, the doctrine of God's immutability shaped
Knox's understanding of revelation. When the reformer applied that doctrine to
Scripture, he could logically argue for continuing revelation. Because God never
changes, he could in any era speak through individuals to proclaim his will, and

Knox believed that he had inherited the mantle of the biblical prophets.[19] His own 'prophecies' then were divinely inspired and were intended to aid the reform of the Scottish kirk. His zeal for reform, therefore, led him to promote his own prophetic gifts, which led to an inconsistent doctrine of revelation.

Knox's belief about his God-given authority becomes clear as one examines his sense of prophetic consciousness. He saw himself standing in the tradition of the Old Testament prophets; that is, he actually believed that God had anointed him to foretell events.[20] Many of his followers considered Knox's prophecies credible, a fact which surely enhanced his leadership among people. This prophetic consciousness seems to be a key to understanding Knox's self-image, but it also raises questions about his doctrine of revelation. Historian John Gray certainly had it right when he wrote of Knox: 'He was no political philosopher, systematic theologian or ecclesiastical theorist. He was more like Luther or George Wishart, his own predecessor, than he was like Calvin. He was primarily a preacher, a prophet, a seer'.[21]

Lord Eustace Percy claimed that Knox's career as a reformer began with his association with George Wishart, who had risked his life preaching Protestant views in Scotland.[22] Knox travelled with Wishart and served as his bodyguard for five weeks. Wishart prophesied his own death at Haddington and predicted divine judgement upon that town.[23] Knox interpreted the arrest of Wishart that same week as fulfilment of the prophecy. Wishart warned that terrible plague and bondage to foreigners would fall upon the town of Haddington. In his *History of the Reformation in Scotland*, Knox recorded that there was indeed much devastation in Haddington, and a plague hindered the burial of the dead. Knox concluded, 'and so did God perform the words and threatenings of his servant Master George Wishart'.[24] Convinced that Wishart 'was clearly illuminated with the spirit of prophecy', Knox saw him as an example of the prophet he hoped to become in Scotland.[25]

Knox began his own preaching career with a sermon from the book of Daniel, chapter 7. This became the occasion of his first prophecy, which he delivered to a group of renegade Protestants at the castle of St Andrews. There he preached to killers of David Cardinal Beaton, who avenged the murder of George Wishart. Knox and the other Castilians waited for military help from England. Knox's version of the events makes him something of a seer. He contradicted the boasting of the Castilians.

> John Knox was of another judgment, for he ever said, 'that their corrupt life could not escape punishment of God' and that was his continual advertisement from the time he was called to preach. When they triumphed of their victory . . . he lamented, and ever said, 'they saw not what he saw.' When they bragged of the force and thickness of the walls, he said, 'they shall be but egg-shells.' When they vaunted, 'England will rescue us,' he said, 'ye shall not see them;

but ye shall be delivered in your enemy's hands, and shall be married to a strange country'.[26]

In July 1547 the French sailed into St Andrews harbour and compelled the rebels besieged in the castle to surrender to Catholic forces. Although Knox's predictions now may seem more common sense than prophecy, Knox believed that they vindicated his powers.[27] Knox saw himself as both an interpreter and a leader in an apocalyptic battle against the forces of Satan. His *History of the Reformation in Scotland* teaches this philosophy of history on virtually every page. 'Satan', Knox wrote, 'ever travails to obscure the light; and yet how God by his power, working in his weak vessels, confounds his craft, and discloses his darkness.'[28] Knox saw any battle against the papist French as a part of the larger battle between Satan and Christ. It is in this context that Knox recorded a skirmish in which one hundred French soldiers fell when English troops fired only two bullets. 'For the bullets rebounded from the friar kirk, to the wall of Saint Katherine's chapel . . . and from the wall of the said chapel . . . so oft, that there fell more than an hundred of the French at these two shots only.[29]

Because of his association with the renegades in the castle, the French forced Knox into service as a galley-slave, and that setting became the site of his next prophecy. Many slaves died from exposure and poor nutrition. Knox himself became very ill. From their floating prison, James Balfour asked Knox to look at the coast and to identify their location. Knox saw the steeple of St Andrews, where God first called him to preach, and he made that the occasion of an unlikely prediction. 'I am persuaded fully, however weak that I now appear, that I shall not depart this life until my tongue shall glorify his [the Lord's] name in that same place.'[30] Knox's *History* has James Balfour repeating this prediction in the 'presence of many famous witnesses' so as to memorialise the prediction and its 'fulfilment'. Ten years later he preached again in St Andrews. Historian Katherine Firth argues that the events in St Andrews and the galley service contributed to Knox's prophetic consciousness. 'The success of his sermon . . . and . . . the French galleys gradually convinced Knox that he, like Wishart, had the gift of illumination, an ability not only to interpret the word of God but also to speak it.'[31] After his release from the French he preached in Berwick, England, and warned that disease would strike the town. When the 'sweating sickness' appeared there in 1551–52, he reminded the congregation of his prediction. With great confidence Knox assured the people that their calamities came from the hand of God.[32] Many of Knox's contemporaries offered similar forecasts but the confidence with which he spoke is a powerful demonstration of Knox's prophetic self-image. Such assurance in his ability to deduce the providence of God in history led his critics to complain that Knox believed he held a chair on God's Privy Council.[33]

Knox's prophecies occasionally extended beyond general, vague, or common-sense forewarnings. He pronounced divine judgement on the new English regent, John Dudley, Duke of Northumberland, that God would avenge any violence against the former Protector, Edward Seymour, Lord Somerset. Disastrous foreign and domestic policies forced Somerset from power, and Dudley personally engineered the arrest and imprisonment of the Protector in the Tower of London. Knox stood nearly alone when he proclaimed Somerset's innocence. Dudley ignored Knox's warning, and Somerset was executed in January 1552. The next year Dudley was beheaded for his role in the scheme to alter the succession of Mary Tudor. The violent death of Dudley convinced Knox that God had fulfilled another of his 'prophecies'. He used the event to authenticate his prophetic claims and no doubt for self-promotion at the church in Newcastle. In case they had forgotten, Knox told them to 'Remember, that whatever was spoken by my mouth that day, is now complete and [has] come to pass'.[34]

One of the most amazing of Knox's prophecies was the prediction of the hanging of William Kirkcaldy of Grange. Knox despised him because Kirkcaldy had abandoned Knox's party of reform for the Queen's party now exiled in England. Near death in November 1572, Knox sent messengers to inform Kirkcaldy that: 'unless he is yet brought to repentance, he shall die miserably . . . He shall be dragged from his nest to punishment and hanged on a gallows in the face of the sun, unless he speedily amend his life and flee to the mercy of God.'[35]

Kirkcaldy remained unmoved. He neither repented nor ceased his support for the Queen's cause. Jasper Ridley has related the details surrounding the rather strange death of Kirkcaldy. 'When Grange was hanged at the market cross of Edinburgh on a sunny afternoon, he was hanged facing toward the east; but before he died, his body swung around to face the west; so he hanged as Knox had foretold, in the face of the sun'.[36] When some of his contemporaries had challenged this prophecy, Knox countered by claiming, 'God is my warrant, and you shall see it'.[37] According to James Melville, who was in a position to know, Knox even predicted the exact words Kirkcaldy would utter on the occasion of his hanging. Such amazing predictions led Melville to attest confidently that Knox was a 'true prophet of God'.[38]

Knox's prophecy about Kirkcaldy became famous, and it provided the basis for a play by John Davidson, who composed it as entertainment for a wedding in St Andrews. Melville recorded in his diary that Knox attended the play and there promised the imminent fulfilment of his prediction.[39] The hanging of Kirkcaldy occurred about a year later.

To some observers Knox's predictions may appear to be simple deductions from Scripture: God blesses obedience and judges disobedience. Knox, in fact, on occasion invoked that very principle in explaining them. From the port in Dieppe, France, he addressed a *Letter to the Faithful in London, Newcastle, and Berwick* to warn them of the disaster and plagues which would accompany their practice of idolatry (1554):

> My assurances are not the Marvels of Merlin, nor yet the dark sentences of profane prophecies: but (1) the plain truth of God's Word; (2) the invisible justice of the everlasting God; and (3) the ordinary course of his punishments and plagues from the beginning, are my assurance and grounds. God's Word threatens destruction to all [who are] disobedient; this immutable justice must require the same. The ordinary punishments and plagues show examples.[40]

Knox's disclaimer seriously weakens his prior prophetic claims. The above letter was not, however, his final word on the matter. William Croft Dickinson, modern editor of Knox's *History of the Reformation in Scotland*, noted that the reformer's 'conviction of prophetic powers grew with the years'.[41] At least a dozen references to fulfilled prophecies appear in Knox's *History*, where he cited divine judgements through deaths, destruction and unusual weather. We know that Knox wrote his *History* years after the fact and may very well have embellished the record to ensure that his own prophecies were in fact 'fulfilled'. The validity of Knox's prophecies is not the point of the chapter. Knox used this prophetic mantle as a strategy to promote his own leadership among his followers and against his enemies. The claim to be a prophet of God is the ultimate technique of one-upmanship. Knox wore the prophet's mantle but held it in tension with the leading Protestant reformers, who believed that prophetic powers ended with the Apostles in the New Testament era.

Although some of Knox's biographers have called him a prophet, they did not necessarily mean thereby that he possessed such ability, and his consciousness of a prophetic self-image increased throughout his career. Duncan Shaw noted that in his later years, Knox quoted often from Daniel and the Apocalypse, and that he identified himself closely with the prophets of the Old Testament.[42] Knox came to see himself blessed with prophetic powers, for use in the battle against the mass and other superstitions. He believed that he stood in the same tradition with biblical seers.[43]

Fairly late in his ministry, Knox preached a remarkable sermon at St Giles Church in Edinburgh, on 19 August 1565, from I Timothy 4. In the preface to it, he made clear his claim to divine inspiration.

> I decreed to contain myself within the bounds of that vocation whereunto I found myself especially called. I dare not deny (lest that in so doing I should be injurious to the giver) that God has revealed to me secrets unknown to the world; and also . . . to forewarn realms and nations, yes, certain great personages, of translations and changes, when no such things were feared, nor were yet appearing, a portion whereof cannot the world deny . . . to be fulfilled.[44]

In addition to this public declaration of his gifts, Knox prayed to thank God for the prophetic insight, 'Thou hast given to me knowledge above the common sort of my brethren'.[45] Knox's contemporaries sometimes hastened to verify his prophetic ability. John Spottiswoode, Protestant archbishop of St Andrews, for example, testified that many people esteemed Knox's pronouncements as 'oracles' from God.[46]

For many years Thomas M'Crie's *Life of John Knox* (1811) was the standard biography of the reformer.[47] M'Crie cautiously but clearly credited Knox with prophetic powers. M'Crie noted that Knox's contemporaries considered him a prophet, and his predictions 'received an exact accomplishment'.[48] The author understood that crediting Knox with prophetic abilities was dangerous because of its theological implications. As an honest writer he felt compelled to address the potentially explosive subject.

> The most easy way of getting rid of this delicate question is by dismissing it at once and summarily pronouncing that all pretensions to extraordinary premonitions, since the completing of the canon of inspiration, are unwarranted, that they ought, without exception, to be discarded and treated as fanciful and visionary . . . I doubt much if this method of determining the question would be consistent with doing justice to the subject.[49]

M'Crie believed that only figures of 'singular piety' have received such special gifts, and that only in unusual circumstances were men such as Knox 'occasionally favoured with extraordinary premonitions'.[50] M'Crie appears to conclude that the context of the Reformation in Scotland constituted an extraordinary time in history in which God would intervene in miraculous ways.

Knox's enemies also acknowledged that he possessed some extraordinary powers. At the very least the perception circulated to the point where his critics had to address this issue. In attempts to undermine his influence, Catholics sometimes acknowledged his power, but they accused Knox of practising witchcraft.[51] They claimed he was a wizard and that he raised demons, including Satan himself, from the churchyard at St Andrews.[52] Knox referred to his enemies in Edinburgh who accused him of using magic and practising necromancy.[53] Some of his opponents thus attributed Knox's powers to the devil explicitly.[54] Ninian Winzet, perhaps 'Knox's ablest opponent',[55] debated with the reformer at Linlithgow in March 1562, and there he posed the question, 'Where are your miracles?'[56] Knox answered from his Edinburgh pulpit the following Sunday. He challenged the notion that a calling from God necessarily implies miracles. He cited Amos and John the Baptist as men of God who had no miracles to their credit.[57] It is interesting to note that Knox did not at this time defend himself with appeals to his own prophecies. The debate with Winzet took place three years before his sermon at St Giles in which Knox publicly claimed the gift of prophecy.

Further evidence of some inconsistency in Knox's attitude towards Scripture and the gift of prophecy appears in discussions which led to the publication of the *Book of Discipline*. Knox and some of his co-workers provided for a church officer called a superintendent to meet the crisis of a severe shortage of ministers in the Reformed church. Critics of this proposal feared that it would lead to a Protestant bishopric.[58] The superintendent was to travel and preach in different parishes, but unlike a bishop, he would possess no authority over churches.[59] Knox participated in commissioning the superintendents, but he refused to lay hands on those who were inducted into the office 'in case it might symbolize the transmission of miraculous gifts, [which] he held . . . had ended with the apostolic church'.[60] The *Book of Discipline* stated that, though 'the Apostles had laid hands, [now] the miracle had ceased'.[61] Here we see a rather glaring inconsistency by the Scots reformer. In this case, abiding by the procedure in the *Discipline*, Knox upheld the common Reformed view of revelation, despite his personal claim to prophetic gifts.

Further examination reveals additional inconsistency by Knox. In a lengthy debate with William Maitland of Lethington, Knox disclosed once again his belief in post-biblical revelation. The debate centred on the prophetic roles of ministry in the sixteenth century. He argued for an end of prophetic gifts, yet not a *final* end: 'for Jesus Christ being anointed in our nature, by God his father, King, Priest and Prophet, has put an end to all external unction. And yet, I think, you will not say that God has now diminished his graces for those whom he appoints ambassadors between him and his people'.[62]

The exchange with Maitland reflects clearly Knox's mediating image of himself as continuing the work of the biblical prophets before him. God had not diminished his gifts and graces and Knox deemed himself one of the recipients. That is, his belief in the unchanging character of God enabled him to contend for the ongoing revelation of God's will through the voice of prophecy. Knox could argue that prophetic powers had ceased in the Apostolic age, yet God's power aided those singular ambassadors in extraordinary times.

Knox affirmed both a theoretical subscription to *sola scriptura* and gave some role to his own prophetic utterances.[63] During the reign of Queen Mary Tudor (1553–58), Knox found express scriptural reasons for opposing the Catholic tyrant. Just as Moses and other prophets resisted godless rulers, so did Knox,[64] for in his view, 'It is evident . . . that the power of God's Word pronounced by the mouth of man prevailed at one time in a great number against nature and compelled [God's prophets] to be executors of God's vengeance'.[65]

Since Knox believed that he was God's special messenger of justice, he sought and found biblical examples 'sufficient to prove as well that God's Word draws his elect after it, against worldly appearance, against natural affections, and against civil statues and constitutions: so that such as obey God's speaking by his messengers never lack just reward and recompense'.[66] Knox's argument nearly compelled God to grant power to his virtuous servants.

In his treatise, *On Predestination*, Knox once more affirmed his contention that God continued to speak in the sixteenth century by means of prophets as he had done in biblical times, 'for we find that God communicates his power with his true messengers and ambassadors, that whatever they loose on earth, he will loose in heaven'.[67] Just as God put words into the mouth of Jeremiah (Jeremiah 1: 9), so through his sixteenth-century messenger, John Knox, the Lord addressed his will to Scotland and England where 'these words witness that the effectual power of God works with the word which he puts in the mouths of his true messengers, that either it edifies, enlightens or brings salvation, or else it destroys, darkens, and hardens'.[68]

Knox's doctrine of prophecy, of course, shaped his attitude towards, and relationship with, civil rulers. He believed that God appointed him to instruct and rebuke rulers on the basis of special directives which he received from the Holy Spirit.[69] Knox informed them that 'God shall always raise up some to whom truth shall be revealed, and unto them you [civil authorities] shall give place, even though they sit in the lowest places'.[70] In explaining why magistrates lacked the knowledge of God that he possessed, Knox cited the noetic effects of sin, which high birth and education cannot overcome, and he once again claimed the ability to know the will of God.[71]

Views regarding Knox's prophecies

Virtually every Knox scholar acknowledges the prophetic role of the Scottish reformer. Writers fall into five overlapping categories when they explain Knox's prophetic activities.

1   Some contend that Knox's prophetic claims stem from his overemphasis on the continuity of the Old and New Testaments and the unchanging nature of God.[72] The combination of these convictions then led Knox to wear the prophet's armour in his struggle for the soul of Scotland.

2   Richard Kyle cites a sixteenth-century practice called the 'prophetic hermeneutic' to account for Knox's prophecies.[73] According to this view, congregations actively participated in the exegesis of Scripture. This 'prophesying', practised by many Reformed churches, especially during the Marian exile, followed the guidelines of I Corinthians 14: 'Let the prophets speak two or three, and let the others judge . . . For ye may all prophesy one by one, that all may learn, and all may be comforted.'[74] John a' Lasco practised this in his

London church, and the English exiles witnessed it in Geneva.[75] This method moved back and forth from the sixteenth century to Old or New Testament times and directly applied biblical precepts to contemporary issues. This hermeneutic gave little or no consideration to the context of Scripture. Upon his return to Scotland in May of 1559, Knox organised public prophesying based on the instruction of the apostle Paul in I Corinthians 14: 29–31.[76] Knox practised this method when he compared Canaan's sins to his opponents who supported the *Book of Common Prayer*. Canaan sinned because he exposed Noah's drunken and naked condition. According to Knox, some things should be kept secret, while others must be revealed. He could not hide the errors in the *Second Prayer Book*, and it was his duty to reveal them. While this is called 'prophesying', Ronald Vander Molen clarifies the issue by calling it 'analogical' rather than 'prophetical'.[77] This is an interesting contribution, but it fails to account for the crucial predictive nature of Knox's prophecies. The forthtelling or 'prophesying' practised by sixteenth and seventeenth-century Puritans is clearly a different species from the predictive prophecies of Knox.

3 Some writers cite his vivid call to the ministry to explain Knox's prophetic inclination. In this respect, anyone called to preach is a 'prophet' because they proclaim the Word of God.[78] Greaves, Kyle, and Firth agree on this point but disagree regarding the nature of Knox's prophecies. Greaves interprets Knox as a prophet-preacher whose task was to proclaim boldly the truth of God. Firth contends that over time, Knox increasingly cited the Old Testament prophets for courage and example, and eventually found in them the 'example of his own vocation'.[79] Firth traces a prophetic vocational lineage from George Wishart to Knox. She holds that his success 'gradually convinced Knox that he, like Wishart, had the gift of prophecy of special illumination, an ability not only to interpret the Word of God but also to speak it'.[80] Knox himself interpreted Wishart in this light. Wishart 'was so clearly illuminated with the spirit of prophecy, that he saw not only things pertaining to himself, but also such things as some towns and the whole realm afterward felt, which he forespoke not in secret, but in the audience of many, as in their own places shall be declared'.[81]

4 Likewise, Kyle acknowledges the traumatic sense of calling Knox experienced, and, like Firth, links it with apocalypticism and occasional predictions.[82] Knox saw himself engaged in a cosmic struggle between the forces of good and evil. Perhaps these were the 'unusual circumstances' to which Thomas M'Crie referred when he wrote of Knox's 'extraordinary premonitions'. This apocalyptic sense steadily intensified with his experiences at the hand of Catholic oppressors.[83] The desperate conditions demanded a prophet

of God equipped with supernatural gifts to do battle with the enemies of God. Professor Authur Williamson saw Knox engaged in a desperate struggle which demanded that he both admonish and prophesy.

> John Knox unequivocally identified with the prophetic tradition and came to see himself as a latter-day prophet along the lines of Isaiah, Elijah, Daniel, Jehu, Amos or Jeremiah. The reformer believed that God had endowed him with the ability for both types of prophecies: the word of admonition and the knowledge of future events. In Knox's prophetic ministry the two models overlapped, but on the whole, admonition clearly took precedence over prediction.[84]

5   All of the explanations above touch on the vexing subject of Knox's prophetic self-image. Some are more successful than others but none adequately explains it. Michael Walzer's model of the 'oppositional man' perhaps best portrays the prophetic sensibilities of Knox.[85] Walzer argues that the Tudor Protestants in the Marian exile developed the ecclesiastical office of prophet, the oppositional man, or saint-out-of-office to promote Protestantism during the extraordinary reign of Mary Tudor.[86] The gentry held the numerical advantage in the Marian exile, but they were largely impotent. The gentlemen left behind their lands in England, but the clergy in exile brought their books and co-opted power from the gentry and established both a new intellectual tradition and prophetic office. Some of the Protestants, including Knox, suffered a double exile when they were forced to leave Frankfurt for their refusal to accept the liturgy of the second Edwardian Prayer Book. Alienated from England, and then from fellow exiles, this group found a refuge in Geneva. Free from the laws of England, the exiles in Geneva held no official status except in the small congregation which they formed. It can be argued that Knox, a leader among the exiles in Frankfurt and Geneva, suffered more trauma than most, since circumstances forced him to flee from Scotland, England and Frankfurt. Walzer argued that Knox and others created a new office from which to carry on the task of the Reformation. In this calling 'they sought a new office and found it not in men's constitutions, but in divine prophecy . . . in the person of the Old Testament prophet, the men of Geneva found their new public character'.[87] Knox and his closest associate, Christopher Goodman, 'described prophecy as a Calvinist office, in which individual inadequacy and corruption were overcome by the discipline of duty and divinely ordained status'.[88] Knox personally transformed this calling into a prophetic task, because of the growing apostasy in England, which he addressed in the Godly Letter.[89] Knox claimed a prophetic calling by labelling the Romanism of Mary Tudor idolatry, and he compared it with the same idolatry condemned by the Hebrew prophets.[90] Knox saw the task of the prophet primarily as one of denunciation, and he personally applied God's anointing of the prophet Jeremiah: 'See, today I appoint you over nations

and kingdoms to uproot and tear down, to destroy and overthrow, to build and to plant', Jeremiah 1: 10 (NIV).[91] The *Godly Letter* is the counsel of Knox the exiled prophet/preacher delivering a 'Jeremiad' to his covenant congregations in England. Knox explicitly modelled his letter on the prophet Jeremiah, citing the text nearly sixty times. In 1558, Knox defended the condemnation he suffered by identifying with Jeremiah and other persecuted prophets.

> It is not unknown that the prophets had revelations of God which were not common to the people . . . Jeremiah did foresee the destruction of Jerusalem and the time of their captivity. And so divers other prophets had divers revelations of God, which the people did not understand but by their affirmation; and therefore in those days were the prophets named Seers, because God did not open into them that which was hid from the multitude.[92]

Knox followed a prophetic model by rallying support for the reforming party. Walzer called this strategy 'the enlistment of soldiers which became a prophetic task'.[93] During the exile, Knox cultivated support for the Reformed party through his letters to the Scottish nobility.[94] When he returned to Scotland in 1559, his preaching against idolatry produced a widespread iconoclasm which he censured without enthusiasm.[95] Knox believed his power came from supernatural illumination of the Holy Ghost. In his famous *First Blast of the Trumpet*, he explained his God-appointed task – 'God shall always raise up some to whom the verity shall be revealed and unto such ye shall give place'.[96] Knox believed he was one of those prophets whom God raised up with special powers of prescience. In an effort to link himself with the prophets and their unjust treatment Knox wrote, 'Neither ought any man think it strange, that I compare myself with them, with whom I sustain a common cause'.[97] He then applied the biblical example appealing to the nobility to defend him just as the princes of Judah defended their prophet Jeremiah. 'Neither ought you, my lords, judge yourself less indebted and bound to me, calling for your support, than did the princes of Judah think themselves bound to Jeremiah.'[98]

Knox versus Calvin on prophetic gifts

It is the argument of this writer that Knox's prophetic self-image is out of character with mainline Protestant reformers and inconsistent with his own claim of *sola scriptura*. A comparison of Knox with John Calvin (1509–64) will thus highlight the distinctive nature of Knox's view. Protestant reformers generally agreed that the prophetic and miraculous gifts given to the Old Testament prophets and New Testament apostles ended with the close of the canon of Scripture. When the last apostle died, the apostolic age ended, and with it, the miraculous gifts, signs and wonders. Calvin held this view, though with distinctive nuances.[99]

It is possible to determine Calvin's views by an examination of his comments in his commentaries of a few key New Testament passages which speak of the gift of prophecy. St Paul's epistles to the Ephesian and Corinthian churches are similar texts which describe the variety of offices given by Christ Jesus to individual New Testament Christians for the express purpose of the promotion of the church. Ephesians 4: 11 mentions five offices: 'It was he who gave some to be apostles, some to be prophets, some to be evangelists, and some to be pastors and teachers' (NIV). John Calvin says of the prophetic office, 'Paul applies the name "prophets" not to all those who were interpreters of God's will, but to those who excelled in a particular revelation'.[100] In his commentary on Ephesians, Calvin says of Paul's use of the word prophet that some have an interpretative gift more than a predictive.[101]

Calvin's comments on I Corinthians 12: 28, which lists the offices of apostles, prophets, and teachers, echoes those in Ephesians. 'I am certain in my own mind, that he [Paul] means by those prophets, not those endowed with the gift of foretelling, but those who were blessed with the unique gift of dealing with Scripture.'[102] The prophet, according to Calvin's interpretation of Paul, 'devotes himself to consolation, encouragement, and teaching, but these activities are quite distinct from predictions'.[103] While Calvin clearly rejects the predictive element, he does consider the interpretive gifts supernatural. 'I take the term prophecy to mean that unique and outstanding gift of revealing what is the secret will of God, so that the prophet is, so to speak, God's messenger to men.'[104] Calvin continued to nuance his teaching regarding the miraculous interpretive powers by declaring them temporary gifts. Calvin believed the offices of apostle, prophet and evangelist were 'raised up . . . at the beginning of [God's] kingdom, and now and again [he] revives them as the need of the times demands'.[105] More specifically, Calvin says of the office of prophet, 'this class either does not exist today or is less commonly seen'.[106] Calvin kept the door slightly ajar for the resurfacing of miraculous gifts after the apostolic era.

> I do not deny that the Lord has sometimes at a later period raised up apostles, or at least evangelists in their place, as has happened in our own day. For there was need for such persons to lead the church back from the rebellion of Antichrist. Nonetheless, I call this office 'extraordinary,' because in duly constituted churches it has no place.[107]

According to John T. McNeill, the distinguished editor of Calvin's *Institutes*, Calvin was referring to Martin Luther in the above quotation.[108] Calvin believed that God raised up Luther to fight the Antichrist in the sixteenth century. John Knox also saw himself engaged in a life and death battle with the Antichrist whom he linked with the Roman papacy.[109] It appears that Knox included himself in this category of a latter-day prophet, supernaturally gifted by God, to reform the church and rid it of superstitious practices like the Mass. Brutal conditions and personal catastrophes also contributed to Knox's apocalyptic views and subsequently his claim to prophetic powers. Knox's arrest in Scotland, his slavery in France, his exile from England, the martyrdom of personal friends and the restoration of the dreaded Mass led Knox to revive the prophetic office.[110] Knox saw himself living in extraordinary times and believed that God called him to reform the church, in Calvin's words, 'where religion has fallen into decay'.[111] Calvin saw a limited role for a prophet whom God used during critical times to expound the Scriptures and restore religion.[112] Consciously or unconsciously, Knox fitted himself into this exceptional category that Calvin identified. Knox's self-image as a prophet led to an exaggerated attraction to see the hand of God in history and relate it to current events.

In his commentary on the Old Testament prophet Isaiah, Calvin encouraged his readers to imitate the prophets:

> It is of high importance to us to compare the behavior of the men of our own age with the behavior of that ancient people, and from their histories and examples we ought to make known the judgements of God; such as, that what he formerly punished he will also punish with equal severity in our own day, for he is always like himself.[113]

Calvin's emphasis on the 'consolation, encouragement and teaching' nature of the prophetic office suggests that a calling to preach may prepare the way for a prophetic office.[114] It may also explain why Catholic critic, Ninian Winzet, challenged Knox so forcefully on the nature of Knox's call to preach. Calvin taught that an inward call to preach must be confirmed by a call from a congregation.[115] Knox's 'congregation' among the Castilians in 1547 included a bizarre collection of murderers, renegades and reformers. Even if Knox's 'call' came under extraordinary circumstances, the vindication of his call came through the amazing prescience God gave him.

Calvin also gave instructions to distinguish between a true and false prophet using Knox's favourite prophet Jeremiah as a model: 'Then the Lord put forth his hand, and touched my mouth: and the Lord said unto me, Behold I have put my words in thy mouth.'[116] Calvin says of this passage:

> Here Jeremiah speaks again of his calling, that his doctrine might not be despised, as though it proceeded form a private individual. He, therefore, testifies again, that he came not of himself, but was sent from above, and was invested with authority of a prophet. For this purpose he says, that God's words were put in his mouth.[117]

Knox made the same kinds of claims that he spoke with the certainty that God gave him the words to speak. Jeremiah suggests that the prophet becomes a kind of empty vessel, stripped of his own ideas. No prophet or teacher ought to be counted true and faithful, except those through whom God speaks, who invent nothing themselves, who teach not according to their own fancies, but faithfully deliver what God has committed to them.[118]

It appears that Knox modelled himself more along the line of Old Testament than New Testament prophets. Knox, as we argued above, claimed both forthtelling and foretelling powers. The predictive element is a significant component of Knox's prophetic claim, and more consistent with the Old rather than the New Testament prophet. Knox appears to have especially revered Jeremiah among all of the Old Testament prophets, and in his crusade against idolatry he served two masters, Scripture and prophecy. Knox argued that both came from God, but in his epistemological shift from Scripture alone to Scripture and prophecy Knox unwittingly used weapons outside the arsenal of most Protestant reformers.

NOTES

1 John Knox, *Johns Knox's History of the Reformation in Scotland*, trans. and ed. William C. Dickinson, (New York, 1950), 2 vols, 2: 267.

2 John Knox, *The Works of John Knox*, ed. David Laing (Edinburgh, 1846–64), 6 vols, 4: 133 (hereafter cited as *Works*). The quotations taken from the Laing edition of collected works contain 'corrected' spelling to reflect modern usage. In 'A Letter of Wholesome Counsel', Knox cited the *Shema* (Deuteronomy 6: 4ff.) as a principle which reveres the importance of Scripture in daily activity, *Works*, 4: 134. Knox affirmed Scripture alone in his battle with Dr Richard Cox in the English exile church in Frankfurt. He opposed the Second Prayer Book because some of its practices lacked strict biblical proof. See Knox, *Works*, 4: 61. Roger Mason agrees that Knox held the doctrine of *sola scriptura*: 'If sixteenth century Protestantism was pre-eminently the religion of the Word, Knox was certainly one of those who pressed the doctrine of *sola scriptura* to extremes. Intense biblicism . . . is the hallmark of his thought.' See Roger A. Mason, 'Introduction', in his *John Knox on Rebellion* (Cambridge, 1993), x, xxiv.

3 Knox, *Works*, 2: 112. See also W. Ian O. Hazlett, 'The Scots Confession 1560: Context, Complexion and Critique', *Archiv für Reformationsgeschichte* 78 (1987), 287–320.

4 See Richard G. Kyle, 'The Hermeneutical Patterns in John Knox's Use of Scripture', *Pacific Theological Review* 17: 3 (1984), 19–32. In this interesting article it is possible to deduce four principles of Knox's interpretation of Scripture: 1 Emphasis on the Old Testament, 2a Literal interpretation, 2b Infallibility of Scripture, 3 Witness of the Holy Spirit (though Knox gives this less emphasis than Calvin or Bucer), 4a Prophesying, or 'prophetic hermeneutic', within the context of I Corinthians 14, 4b. Interpretation by the Congregation. Several of these points are examined below.

5 Knox, *Works*, 2: 184; 3: 166, 168.

6 Knox, *Works*, 2: 243.

7 Knox, *History*, 2: 18.

8 Knox, *Works*, 5: 196. Kyle describes Knox's method as 'pronounced literalness', in his 'The Hermeneutical Patterns', 20. See also Mason, 'Introduction', x.

9 Richard L. Greaves, *Theology and Revolution in the Scottish Reformation* (Grand Rapids, 1980), 20–1.

10 Knox, *Works*, 5: 312.

11 Knox, *History*, 2: 267.

12 James Stalker, *John Knox: His Ideas and Ideals* (London, 1904), 129.

13 G. D. Henderson, 'John Knox and the Bible', *Records of the Scottish Church History Society* 9 (1947), 97–110, especially 108. The author states his thesis on page 100: '[Knox] is clearly much closer to the pre-reformation conception of the bible than he is to that of the post-Wellhausen age to which we belong.' This article shows several similarities between the views of Knox and some early church Fathers on the doctrine of Scripture.

14 John Knox, *Selected Writings of John Knox*, trans. Kevin Reed (Dallas, 1995), 485.

15 John Calvin, *Letters of John Calvin*, ed. Jules Bonnet, trans. Marcus Robert Gilchrist (New York, 1972), 4 vols, 4: 184. This letter to Knox touches on the Mass and other practices the reformers found repugnant. Calvin's letter is also found in Knox, *Works*, 6: 123–4.

16 Max Engammare, 'Calvin! A Prophet without a Prophecy', *Church History* 67 (1998), 643–61.

17 Martha Abele MacIver, 'Ian Paisely and the Reformed Tradition', *Political Studies* 35 (1987), 362–78, especially 362. See also Richard Kyle, 'John Knox's Concept of History: A Focus on the Providential and Apocalyptic Aspects of His Religious Faith', *Fides et Historia* 18 (1986), 5–19, especially 7–8.

18 Stalker, *John Knox*, 133.

19 Many scholars acknowledge Knox's prophetic consciousness, but too few follow it to its logical conclusion. See, for example, Richard Kyle, 'John Knox: A Man of the Old Testament', *Westminster Thelogical Journal*, 54 (Spring 1992): 66; Christopher Hill, *The World Turned Upside Down* (Middlesex, 1984), 91, and Howard Dobin, *Merlin's Disciples: Prophecy, Poetry, and Power in Renaissance England* (Stanford, MA, 1990), 43–7; Paul M. Little, 'John Knox and the English Social Prophecy', *Presbyterian Historical Society of England* 14 (1970), 117–27, and an older work, Andrew Lang, *John Knox and the Reformation* (London, 1905), 18–19. Richard Greaves is another very important source for this point of view, see Greaves, *Theology and Revolution*, 1–4.

20 Knox's most dramatic claim to prophetic powers is found in the sermon he delivered, on 19 August 1565, at St Giles's Church in Edinburgh, *Works*, 6: 229. Knox acknowledged a personal identity with Old Testament prophets. In the *Godly Letter*, written to his English congregation, Knox cites the prophet Jeremiah over sixty times. See also George Johnston, 'Scripture in the Scottish Reformation', *Canadian Journal of Theology* 9 (1963), 40–9. Johnston says, 'Knox built his case . . . on the role of the prophet in the history of God's people, Israel', 43. His own work depended on the recognition that he too was a prophet. Johnston found that Knox claimed to be in succession with 'Elijah, Isaiah, Jeremiah, John the Baptist and the Apostle Paul', and that he claims for himself 'direct inspiration', 44–5.

21 John R. Gray, 'The Political Theory of John Knox', *Church History* 8 (1939), 132–47, especially 134.

22 Lord Eustace Percy, *John Knox* (London, 1937), 21. See also Katharine R. Firth, *The Apocalyptic Tradition in Reformation Britain 1530–1645* (Oxford, 1976), 117, and Lang, *John Knox and the Reformation*, 18–19.

23 Knox, *History*, 1: 65.

24 Knox, *History*, 1: 68, 113, for quotation, see 1: 60. See also Edwin Muir, *John Knox: Portrait of a Calvinist* (London, 1929), 15, where he says '[Knox] noted that Wishart had the power of prophecy . . . might he not . . . possess it himself, although it had not yet manifested itself?' Jasper Ridley calls Muir's biography 'entertaining but unsound', *John Knox* (Oxford, 1968), 533. Katharine Firth says, 'Not least among the reasons why Knox admired Wishart was his ability as a prophet, not only as one who admonished but also as a man given prescience by special illumination', *The Apocalyptic Tradition*, 114.

25 Knox, *History*, 1: 95–6.

26 Knox, *History*, 1: 95. See also W. Stanford Reid, *Trumpeter of God* (New York, 1974), 53. William Croft Dickinson the modern translator of Knox's *History* interpreted these prophecies as self-fulfilling. Dickinson wrote in the introduction to the *History*, 'Knox certainly uses

every endeavor to ensure the fulfillment of the prophecy', 1: lxxi. This essay, of course, does not stand or fall upon the credibility of Knox's prophecies. Whether true or not, Knox and his followers believed them.

27 Knox, *History*, 1: 92.

28 Knox, *History*, 1: 106.

29 Knox, *History*, 1: 109. In a letter (31 December 1559) to Mrs Anne Locke, Knox reflected on his galley service and wrote, 'Then was I assuredly persuaded that I should not die till I had preached Christ Jesus, even then as now', Knox, *History*, 1: 109 and *Works*, 4: 104. See also Firth, *The Apocalyptic Tradition*, 117. Reid, in *Trumpeter of God*, 69, ignores the prophetic issues and highlights the leadership of Knox in the galleys.

30 Knox himself cites the fulfilment. See Knox, *History*, 1: 182; Firth, *The Apocalyptic Tradition*, 117. Cf. D. Hay Fleming who argues that several reformers in the sixteenth and seventeenth century possessed the gift of prophecy. His lists includes Bullinger, Luther, Latimer, Bradford, Hooper and Archbishops Sandys and Ussher. By contrast, Fleming said of Knox, 'On various occasions, Knox himself made predictions which duly came to pass but most of them were in general terms'. See D. Hay Fleming, 'John Knox In the Hands of the Philistines', *The British Weekly* 33 (26 February 1903), 518. It appears that Erasmus did not deny the existence of miracles (like prophecies) in his own day but argued that they were unnecessary. Similarly, William Tyndale cautioned that miraculous claims could slip into superstition. Miracles served only as confirming signs of God's word. I believe Knox saw himself in this mode, receiving prophetic utterances from God as a confirmation of the power of the Gospel. Knox stood on dangerous ground here because these prophetic claims unwittingly associated him with the identical errors he condemned in the Anabaptists. For Erasmus and Luther, my reference is Beth Langstaff, 'A World without Wonders? Erasmus, Tyndale, and the Cessation of Miracles', an unpublished paper delivered at the *Sixteenth Century Studies Conference* (Toronto, 28 October 1994).

31 Knox, *Works*, 3: 167–9. See also Peter Lorimer, *John Knox and the Church of England* (London, 1895), 82.

32 Knox, *Works*, 6: 146.

33 Knox, *Works*, 3: 277–8.

34 Knox, *Works*, 6: 657.

35 Ridley, *John Knox*, 519. Ridley, however, on pages 519–20, questions the truth of this prophecy because it was repeated only by Knox's 'ardent' followers, and only after the fact. See also Sir William Kirkaldy, *Memoirs and Adventures* (London, 1849), 355–60. The author blames the 'superstitious [David] Calderwood' for this account of the events; see 360. Maitland's biographer also reluctantly 'credits' Knox for the fulfilled prophecy; see John Skelton, *Maitland of Lethington and the Scotland of Mary Stuart, A History* (London, 1888), 424–7.

36 Quoted by James Melville, *The Autobiography and Diary of Mr. James Melville*, ed. Robert Pitcairn (Edinburgh, 1842), 33.

37 Melville, *Autobiography*, 34.

38 Melville, *Autobiography*, 27; see Robert Moffat Gillon, *John Davidson of Prestonpans* (London, 1936), 34–5, 245–6.

39 Knox, *Works*, 3: 168–9.

40 Knox, *History*, 1: lxxi.

41 Duncan Shaw *et al.*, *John Knox: A Quartercentury Reappraisal* (Edinburgh, 1975), 3.

42 Kyle, 'John Knox's Concept of History', 7. See also Greaves, *Theology and Revolution*, 56.

43 Knox, *Works*, 6: 229; see also Dobin, *Merlin's Disciples*, 43–7.

44 Knox, *Works*, 6: 483.

45 John Spottiswoode, *History of the Church of Scotland* (Edinburgh, 1851), 2 vols, 1: 373.

46 Robert Lindesay of Pitscottie in A. J. G. MacKay, ed., *The History and Cronicles of Scotland* (Edinburgh, 1899–1911), 3 vols, a contemporary of Knox, recorded some of these prophecies of Knox but is not a consistently reliable source. See, Knox, *History*, 1: 95, n. 95 and 2: 347.

47 Malcom B. MacGregor, *The Sources and Literature of Scottish Church History* (Glasgow, 1934), 117.

48 Thomas M'Crie, *The Life of John Knox* (Glasgow, 1976), 283.

49 M'Crie, *The Life of John Knox*, 283.

50 M'Crie, *The Life of John Knox*, 284–5.

51 Ridley, *John Knox*, 433. For helpful discussion of Knox's critique of magic, sorcery, conjuring and their relationship to liturgy, superstition and idolatry see Euan Cameron, 'Frankfurt and Geneva: The European Context of John Knox's Reformation', in Roger Mason, ed., *John Knox and the British Reformation* (Aldershot, 1998), 51–73, especially 63–5.

52 Knox, *History*, 2: 15–16.

53 Charles Kirkpatrick Sharpe, *A Historical Account of the Belief in Witchcraft in Scotland* (New York, 1972), 47.

54 Protestant reformers Martin Luther and Robert Barnes attributed some Catholic 'miracles' to Satan. See James Edward McGoldrick, *Luther's English Connection* (Milwaukee, 1979), 73–88.

55 Gordon Donaldson, *The Scottish Reformation* (Cambridge, 1960), 1.

56 Ridley, *John Knox*, 409.

57 Hugh Watt, *John Knox in Controversy* (New York, 1950), 43.

58 C. L. Warr. *The Presbyterian Tradition* (London, 1933), 279–81. Quoted in W. Standford Reid, 'Knox's Attitude to the English Reformation', *Westminster Theological Journal* 26 (1963), 1–32, especially 2.

59 W. Stanford Reid, 'French Influence on the First Scots Confession and Book of Discipline', *Westminster Theological Journal* 35 (1972–73), 1–14, especially 13.

60 R. A. Finlayson, 'John Knox, His Theology', *The Bulwark* (1975), 1–11, especially 7.

61 Knox, *History*, 2: 286; see Hill, *The World Turned Upside Down*, 91 and Ridley, *John Knox*, 409, 451, 519.

62 Knox, *History*, 2: 128. Knox also predicted the judgement of God upon Maitland's family. William Croft Dickinson cites the prophecy and its 'fulfilment'. Dickinson writes in a footnote, 'The death of his [Maitland's] only son in poverty and exile was believed by many to be the fulfilment of Knox's prophecy', Knox, *History*, 1: 335, n. 15. It was Maitland's younger brother, however, not his son, that Dickinson intended to cite. For a view which rejects the fulfilment of Knox's prophecy, see William S. McKechnie, 'Thomas Maitland', *Scottish Historical Review* 4 (1907), 274–93.

63 Richard G. Kyle, 'John Knox: The Main Themes of His Thought', *The Princeton Seminary Bulletin* 9 (1983), 102–4; see John Calvin, *Institutes of the Christian Religion*, ed. and trans. Henry Beveridge (London, 1949), 2 vols, 2: 393–4 (4. 8. 7) where Calvin argued, after asserting that special divine revelation ceased with Christ and the New Testament: 'God will not henceforth, as formerly, speak by this one and by that one, that he will nod add prophecy to prophecy, or revelation to revelation, but has so completed all the parts of teaching in the son, that it is to be regarded as his last and eternal testimony . . . in other words, [God] has so spoken [in Christ] as to leave nothing to be spoken by others after him'. Compare Calvin's comments on I Peter 1: 25 in *Commentaries on Catholic Epistles*, ed., and trans. John Owen (Grand Rapids, 1948), 59–60.

64 Knox, *Works*, 3: 310.

65 Knox, *Works*, 3: 311.

66 Knox, *Works*, 3: 312–13. See Richard L. Greaves, 'The Nature of Authority in the Writings of John Knox', *Fides et Historia* 10 (1978), 4 24, especially 24.

67 Knox, *Works*, 5: 385.

68 Knox, *Works*, 5: 385.

69 Knox, *Works*, 6: 230–1.

70 Knox, *Works*, 4: 379. Quoted in Michael Walzer, *The Revolution of the Saints* (London, 1969), 101. See also Greaves, 'The Nature of Authority', 45. Greaves argues that Walzer did not understand the facts. Even those with only a passing knowledge of Knox are familiar with his 'Blast of the Trumpet' against female (particularly Catholic) rulers.

71 Knox, *Works*, 5: 28.

72 Kyle, 'The Hermeneutical Pattern', 20–1, 23. See also Firth, *The Apocalyptic Tradition*, 125.

73 Kyle, 'The Hermeneutical Pattern', 29. See also Richard Kyle, 'John Knox's Method of Biblical Interpretation: An Important Source of His Intellectual Radicalness', *Journal of Religious Studies* 12: 2 (1986), 57–70, especially 62.

74 Kyle, 'Biblical Interpretation', 62 quoted in Kyle, 'The Hermeneutical Patterns', 29.

75 M. M. Knappen, *Tudor Puritanism: A Chapter in the History of Idealism* (Chicago, 1966), 253–5. See Little, 'Social Prophecy', 117, 119, 120–1.

76 Knox, *Works*, 2: 242–5.

77 Knox, *Works*, 4: 7–68, especially 39, cited as *A Brief Discourse*, 38–40, Ronald J. Vander Molen, 'Providence as Mystery, Providence as Revelation: Puritan and Anglican Modifications of John Calvin's Doctrine of Providence', *Church History* 47 (1978), 27–47, especially 40, and Vander Molen, 'Anglican against Puritan: Ideological Origins during the Marian Exiles', *Church History* 42 (1973), 45–57, especially, 47.

78 Arthur H. Williamson, *Scottish National Consciousness in the Age of James VI: The Apocalypse, the Union and Shaping of Scotland's Public Culture* (Edinburgh, 1979), 4.

79 Greaves, *Theology and Revolution*, 1, and 218. See also Firth, *The Apocalyptic Tradition*, 121.

80 Firth, *The Apocalyptic Tradition*, 117.

81 Knox, *History*, 1: 60.

82 Richard Kyle, 'John Knox and Apocalyptic Thought', *Sixteenth Century Journal* 15 (1984), 449–69, especially 449, 454–7.

83 Kyle, 'Apocalyptic Thought', 449–55. See also Williamson, *Scottish National Consciousness*, 20–2.

84 Kyle, 'Apocalyptic Thought', 456. Cf. also 455: 'Knox saw the drama of the Old Testament reenacted in Scotland, with himself as Moses, Joshua, Isaiah, Jeremiah, Ezekiel, and Daniel all combined into one.' He believes Knox limited his predictive elements to warnings of judgement, or the promise of victory or triumph; see 457.

85 Walzer, *The Revolution of the Saints*, 112. I am mindful of Greaves's criticism of the Walzer model; see note 78 above.

86 Walzer, *The Revolution of the Saints*, 112.

87 Walzer, *The Revolution of the Saints*, 94–6, 98. Cf. P. Hume Brown, *John Knox: A Biography* (London, 1929), 2 vols. Brown also noted Knox's close identification with the Hebrew prophets and wrote: 'To possess the gift [of prophecy] in a certain degree was in Knox's day even regarded as the natural cause of special services in the cause of the church', 1: 84–6.

88 Walzer, *The Revolution of the Saints*, 98.

89 John Knox, *Select Practical Writings of John Knox* (Edinburgh, 1845), xvi, 60–2, and Knox, *Works*, 3: 159.

90 Martha Abele MacIver, 'Militant Protestant Political Ideology: Ian Paisley and the Reformation Tradition', unpublished Ph.D. dissertation (University of Michigan, 1984), 44. The author wishes to thank Dr W. Fred Graham for bringing this dissertation to his attention.

91 Knox cited, quoted or alluded to Jeremiah repeatedly in the *Godly Letter* and *The Appellation*; see Knox, *Works*, 3: 165–201, and 4: 465–520, also see note 20 above.

92 Knox, *Selected Writings*, 509.

93 Walzer, *The Revolution of the Saints*, 104.

94 See, for example, *The Appellation*, Knox, *Works*, 3: 165–201, and *Supplication and Exhortation to the Nobility*, Knox, *Works*, 4: 523–38.

95 Knox condemned the so-called 'rascail [sic] multitude' for the riots which followed his anti-idolatry sermon in Perth; Knox, *History*, 1: 161.

96 Knox, *Works*, 4: 379, quoted in Walzer, *The Revolution of the Saints*, 101, n. 100.

97 Knox, *Selected Writings*, 487.

98 Knox, *Selected Writings*, 487.

99 See also Engammare, 'Calvin: A Prophet without a Prophecy', 644, n. 9.

100 John Calvin, *The Institutes of the Christian Religion*, ed. John T. McNeill, and trans. Ford Lewis Battles (Philadelphia, 1960), 2 vols, 2: 1057.

101 John Calvin, *Commentaries on the Epistle of Paul to the Galatians and Ephesians*, trans. William Pringle (Grand Rapids, 1979), 279.

102 John Calvin, *Calvin's New Testament Commentaries: The First Epistle of Paul to the Corinthians*, ed. David W. Torrance and Thomas F. Torrance, and trans. John W. Fraser (Grand Rapids, 1960), 271.

103 Calvin, *Corinthians*, 271.

104 Calvin, *Corinthians*, 271. Calvin was commenting on I Corinthians 12: 10.

105 Calvin, *Institutes*, 2: 1056.

106 Calvin, *Institutes*, 2: 1057. See also Leonard Sweetman, Jr., 'The Gifts of the Spirit: A Study of Calvin's Comments on I Corinthians 12: 8–10, 28; Romans 12: 6–8; Ephesians 4: 11', in David E. Holwerda, ed., *Exploring the Heritage of John Calvin: Essays in Honor of John Bratt* (Grand Rapids, 1976), 273–303, 285–6.

107 Calvin, *Institutes*, 2: 1057.

108 Calvin, *Institutes*, 2: 1057 and n. 4. James Atkinson also argues that Luther was a self-perceived prophet. See, James Atkinson, *Martin Luther: Prophet of the Catholic Church* (Grand Rapids, 1983), 18.

109 Kyle, 'Apocalyptic Thought', 449–51.

110 See Walzer, *The Revolution of the Saints*, 61–5, 99–101.

111 Calvin, *Commentaries on Galatians and Ephesians*, 280.

112 Calvin, *Intitutes*, 2: 1056–7.

113 John Calvin, *Commentary on the Prophet Isaiah*, trans. William Pringle (Grand Rapids, 1979), 45 vols, 1: xxx. I am indebted to Martha Abele MacIver's dissertation for this reference to Isaiah and other insights which confirm my own research. Dr MacIver argues that the Northern Irish preacher and politician adopted the prophetic mantle of John Knox. See MacIver, '*Militant Protestant Political Ideology*', 36.

114 Calvin, *Commentary on First Corinthians*, 271, and MacIver, '*Militant Protestant Political Ideology*', 37.

115 Calvin, *Institutes*, 2: 1062–3. Luther also offered suggestions for determining legitimate from false prophets. In a letter to Philip Melanchthon dated January 1522, Luther said that 'a true prophet mush be called through men or at least attested to by signs, and must have experienced spiritual distress and the divine birth, death and hell'. Luther had the Zwickau prophets in mind when he gave these instructions, which are quoted from Mark U. Edwards, Jr., *Luther and the False Brethren* (Stanford, 1975), 22. See also MacIver, '*Militant Protestant Political Ideology*', 37–8, and n. 15.

116 John Calvin, *Commentaries on the Prophet Jeremiah and the Lamentations*, ed., and trans. John Owen (Grand Rapids, 1979), 45 vols, 1: 42. This is a quotation from Jeremiah 1: 9.

117 MacIver, '*Militant Protestant Political Ideology*', 42.

118 Calvin, *Commentary on the Prophet Jeremiah*, 43.

7

A Protestant or Catholic superstition? Astrology and eschatology during the French Wars of Religion

LUC RACAUT

The opposition between superstition and reason has coloured our understanding of the Reformation debate since the Enlightenment. Around this time Protestantism was irremediably associated with reason and Catholicism with superstition.[1] It is useful to re-place the terms of this debate in the context of sixteenth-century discussions about astrology because it was thought to be intrinsically superstitious. Catholic and Protestant attitudes towards astrology and superstition can be usefully compared. In *Les guerriers de Dieu*, Denis Crouzet posited that Protestants had been more critical of astrology than Catholics.[2] This conclusion was reached from studying literature that contributed to what Crouzet calls a civilisation of eschatological anguish. Crouzet does not really discuss the problem of superstition that was nonetheless at the heart of contemporary debates about astrology. Astrology was not a monolithic whole, and there were deep divisions drawn between natural and superstitious astrology. A survey of the literature can help to illuminate the distinction and refine Crouzet's hypothesis that Protestants rejected astrology whereas Catholics embraced it.

The Renaissance saw renewed interest in classical forms of divination, including astrology. A particular concern of humanists was to reconcile interest in classical divination and Christian theology. The Scriptures added a layer of complexity to the issue of divination, as it provided many examples of prophets who had to be distinguished from the pagans.[3] Although the Scriptures implied that knowledge of the future could be derived from observation of the sky, classical forms of divination were looked upon with extreme suspicion by theologians.[4] Astrology was superstitions because it implied that the stars had the power to determine events and interpreted their influence as causes rather than signs.[5] Here St Augustine was very explicit in his *City of God*:

> But it may be said that the stars give notice of events and do not bring those events about, so that the position of the stars becomes a kind of statement, predicting, not producing, future happenings; and this has been an opinion held by

men of respectable intelligence. Now this is not the way the astrologers normally talk. They would not say, for example, 'This position of Mars signifies
murder'; they say, 'it causes murder'.[6]

Ascribing agency to the stars was superstitious because it was a transgression
of the first commandment, defined by Thomas Aquinas as incorrect worship of
God or worship of something other than God.[7] In the most extreme case, associated with the pre-Christian practice of astrology, the stars and planets themselves had literally been worshipped.[8]

Astrology was more commonly thought to be superstitious because it
ascribed undue efficacy to the movement and influence of the stars. As such it
was a token of false worship, vain and empty because it appealed to causal relationships that simply were not there. This strict theological definition of superstition changed in the course of the sixteenth century as it became increasingly
associated with magic, witchcraft and devil worship. To quote Clark: 'The
devil was invoked whenever methods of acquiring knowledge assumed causal
connections in nature that did not exist or intellective capacities that humans
did not possess.'[9] Commentators associated astrology with superstition
because they saw its practice as synonymous with rendering homage to the
devil. To illustrate this, we can find nothing better than the papal bull published
by Sixtus V in 1586:

> These, in a similar attempt to divine hidden things . . . openly make a pact with
> the Devil . . . They beg that same Architect of Deception to show them the future
> or whatever is hidden . . . or they seek the truth about the future and hidden mat-
> ters through that same Father of Lies . . . by means of . . . various superstitious
> ceremonies, and so try to foretell it to other people.[10]

This had not always been the case, as many contemporary discussions of
magic and astrology found them perfectly respectable. Superstition did not rest
in the belief that the stars had influence on men. Even the most virulent critics
of astrology conceded that there was a hidden relationship between the world
and the zodiac (often compared to the effect of magnets on metal). The occult
was part of the arsenal of technologies that were used to understand the world
and, as such, participated in the elaboration of the modern concept of
science.[11] Although it would be anachronistic to speak of a debate between
science and superstition, there existed a contemporary distinction between the
natural and the superstitious.[12] The association with devil worship and superstition forced practitioners of astrology to emphasise the scientific aspect of
their art. But in order to dissociate astrology from superstition, commentators
spoke of natural astrology rather than scientific astrology.

The most difficult question, for Christian commentators, seems to have
lain in distinguishing between natural, diabolical and divine signs. Spiritual

divination, effectively divine revelation, was thought to be extremely rare and bestowed on very few individuals, mainly biblical prophets. Early modern thinkers were very reluctant to bestow the title of prophet on any of their contemporaries or themselves because of the biblical injunction against false prophets, though an interesting corrective to this general prohibition can be found in the chapters by Johnson and Lotz-Heumann in this volume. This was particularly acute during the Reformation, as opponents on different sides of the confessional divide were quick to call each other false prophets. Natural divination was basically deductive reasoning, based on the observation of natural phenomena, a science in the modern sense. At the opposite end of the spectrum to spiritual divination was the demonic, a form of deception that the devil and evil spirits used to lead men away from the worship of God. Defenders of astrology had to demonstrate that their knowledge of the future derived from the observation of nature (natural) rather than from the devil (superstitious).

In the French context, the humanist Pontus de Tyard relayed these arguments in his *Mantice ou Discours de la verité de Divination par Astrologie* (1558). In this treatise, Pontus de Tyard proposed to prove or disprove the ability to divine future events from the movement of the planets:

> If human understanding is capable of predicting the future, and if Divination is in some way true: it seems to me to be only acceptable, if it is freed from all superstition, and practised through knowledge of some natural cause . . . I cannot see how this jumble of superstitions so devoid of reason or proof could be received.[13]

Pontus went back to the distinction that was made by Augustine between signs and causes: 'Regardless of whether astrological predictions come true or not, it remains to be established if the stars, through the observation of which the astrologer can divine, are the causes of the thing predicted, or only signs and clues that it will happen'.[14] Having concluded that astrology did not work naturally, Pontus declared it to be superstitious and associated it with other branches of the occult:

> Such is the fabulous and superstitious Magic, leading astray all sorts of simple and ignorant people, under the magnificent guise of Occult Philosophy, with its servants, like Necromancy, and other such rubbish such as sorcery, vain, ridiculous and good for nothing, except to scare old women and little children. Such is this sublime and haughty Judicial Astrology, that has perniciously engendered an incredible number of follies of the same kind, like Geomancy, Onomancy, and other such Mancies.[15]

In keeping with his contemporaries, Pontus was nonetheless convinced that the planets had indeed an influence on men: 'the Stars inspire our lives through the influence of their rays that work within us according to the constitution of our being'.[16] Astrology was uncontroversial as long as it concerned birth charts, divining character (phlegmatic, sanguine, melancholic, etc.) from the position of the stars at birth and when used in medicine to determine the optimum time to administer a cure. As such, humanists argued that it could be subsumed under the broader category of natural science. It cannot be said therefore that astrology was a 'science of eschatology', as Crouzet suggests, because it was only elevated to the status of science precisely when it was *not* eschatological.[17]

The controversy surrounding astrology had been going on for many years when it was rendered even more complex with the advent of the Reformation. This debate crystallised around the prophecies of Nostradamus in the middle of the sixteenth century. The arguments that were used by critics of astrology were given a new spin in the light of the events of the French Wars of Religion. Nostradamus was attacked by his contemporaries for combining astrology and prophecy. As such, Nostradamus was an exception and cannot by himself account for the prophetic astrology described by Crouzet in *Les Guerriers de Dieu*. On the contrary, prophecy and astrology were clearly distinguished again and again by many commentators during those years. Prophecy, in the biblical sense, was handed down from God, whereas judicial astrology, or astrology turned to prediction of the future, was highly controversial and was associated with superstition and devil worship. Criticism of judicial astrology and Nostradamus did not come exclusively from reformers, as Crouzet argues, but also from many Catholics.

If the success of the prophecies of Nostradamus is anything to go by, we can forgive Crouzet for thinking that France was a civilisation of eschatological anguish. Nostradamus was also famous because of his appointment as court physician by Catherine de' Medici, who shared her family's passion for astrology. Nostradamus, however, was not without his critics and the reactions to his publications testify to their impact on contemporaries. Claude Haton records in his memoirs that his prophecies, published between 1547 and 1566, were either welcomed as the work of a prophet or condemned as the erring of a dangerous sorcerer.[18] The terms of this debate were borrowed from a controversy that is outlined above about the validity of astrology as a form of divination. With the advent of the Reformation, both Catholics and Protestants accused the other of having resuscitated the superstitions of the ancients. Nostradamus was caught in the middle of this confessional crossfire and was posthumously 'bequeathed' to the Catholic side, when Ronsard and later Jean-Aimé de Chavigny turned him into a staunch defender of Catholicism.[19] But this is not to say that his work was welcomed uncritically, as Crouzet suggests, and his fiercest critics were indeed Catholics.

Chronologically, the first criticism came from a pamphlet published in 1556, under the title *Les Propheties du Seigneur du Pavillon Les Lorriz*, reacting to the first prophecies that had been published in 1555. The author, Antoine Couillard, wrote a second pamphlet in 1560 where he tried to establish whether the prophecies of Nostradamus were legal or not. Antoine Couillard admitted that he did not know any more about the stars than he did about 'coquesigrues marines'.[20] This did not prevent him, he argued, from making prophecies and he complied in listing a series of satirical commonplaces.[21] Couillard also made fun of the obscure language of Nostradamus, designed to confuse his readership.[22] But under this apparent light-heartedness, Couillard made some very serious points, summarising previous scholarship, regarding the desirability of predicting the future and denying God's prerogative to determine the course of events.[23] He concluded, like his predecessors, that it was permissible to plot the course of the stars, but not to rely on them to predict the future.[24]

The second treaty is discussed by Crouzet as 'de sensibilité protestante' and 'une attaque très calvinienne . . . contre l'astrologie juidiciaire'.[25] There is little in the first treatise, of 1556, to determine whether Couillard was sympathetic to the Reformation or not. In the course of this first treatise, Couillard made a jibe at heretics, the court, the universities of Louvain, Paris, Montpellier, the Cardinal de Lorraine and du Bellay, but that hardly makes him a Calvinist.[26] It is possible to infer from the second treatise that Couillard is a humanist, blaming the success of astrology on the decline of learning between antiquity and the reign of François I: 'All sciences were buried by cruel wars and lethal divisions of most of Christendom for the last twelve hundred years . . . until the beginning of the reign of our great and magnanimous king Francis.'[27] Antoine Couillard clearly acknowledged the progress of the Reformation in France between these two anti-Nostradamus commentaries published respectively in 1556 and 1560.[28] In the first tract, Antoine Couillard attributed the success of the prophecies of Nostradamus to an unhealthy curiosity that led men to forget that it was God who dictated the course of events.[29] In the second tract, Couillard refused to blame the unchecked publication of books in the vernacular for inspiring new ideas and false interpretations. The case for the use of the vernacular and the progress of the Reformation was made over and over, in anti-Protestant polemic and by historians alike.

The new climate of religious strife led Couillard to associate the debate about Nostradamus with an increasing concern about the progress of the Reformation.[30] We could forgive Crouzet for thinking that Couillard was a sympathiser if it was not for the following extract where he does not spare his criticism for Geneva:

> Why do they come so close to the fire to die? It would have been better for them
> to fall on the side of those who burn the others. But what? They take pride in
> dying in error, in order to go and perform miracles and to be canonised in
> Geneva and to be registered in the catalogue of their unfortunate preachers,

who are too afraid to come any closer for fear of dying from the heat: several others, in order to follow their libertine doctrine sold . . . their benefices . . . others went bankrupt, stole from or destroyed their creditors: and others, priests or laymen, deflowered virgins and nuns [who] were ravished, taken as their wives to this receptacle of all those banished and exiled.[31]

It seems that Crouzet missed this essential quote, otherwise he would not have argued that Couillard was veering towards Calvinism. One may ask what this piece of anti-Calvinist bravura (making reference to Crespin's *Histoire des Martyrs*) is doing in a tract about Nostradamus. This diatribe against Geneva is very similar to Catholic propaganda that became very prominent during this period.[32] Couillard's second tract indicates that by 1560, the debate about astrology came second to the more pressing need to address the threat of the Reformation.

Another commentary discussed by Crouzet is Laurens Videl's *Declaration des abus, ignorances et seditions de Michel Nostradamus* (1558). Crouzet argues that Videl's piece was part of a systematic campaign orchestrated from Geneva against Nostradamus.[33] On the contrary, I have found nothing to suggest that Videl was anything other than who he claimed to be: a rival astrologer who was probably jealous of Nostradamus' notoriety. Drawing on the distinction that was commonly made between superstitious and natural astrology, Videl accused Nostradamus of giving astrology a bad name:

> I pray the reader to reconsider his bad opinion of astrology, knowing that no malevolent spells have any relation nor anything in common with astrology, but are completely contrary, and are abominable, to the Christian religion . . . most people today believe that those who meddle in prediction, or make prognostics, use superstitious magic, which spurred me to write treatises to show that true astrologers do not meddle in such spells.[34]

Later in the treatise, Videl denied Nostradamus the title of prophet and accused him of being a false prophet denounced in the Scriptures. Prefiguring the papal bull of 1586, Videl called for the extermination of false prophets by fire, echoing similar demands that were made in contemporary anti-Protestant polemic:

> Who can save those who practise such things from destruction by fire? It is undeniable that those who presume to make predictions, not by virtue of the power of our lord but through the illusions of evil spirits, and vain magic, incantations, exorcism and other diabolical works . . . will perish with . . . Simon the Magician.[35]

Crouzet also describes Videl as falling on the Reformed side. But there is no indication in the text that Videl was anything other than a rival astrologer. Crouzet argues that the tract must be Reformed because it accused Nostradamus of being a false prophet. Because this accusation was also used against Protestants at the time, its reversal would indicate that it originated from a Protestant: 'Il lui est attribué d'être ce que l'ancienne religion accuse les ministres d'être. Ce retournement de l'attaque prouve, à mon avis, l'origine calviniste du libelle.'[36] Crouzet argues that Nostradamus was being accused of being a false prophet in a reversal of a Catholic attack against Protestants. But the fact that astrologers were accused of being false prophets as well as Protestants does not prove anything. Furthermore Olivier Millet concurs that nothing in this work indicates a confessional commitment to one side or the other.[37]

Anti-Protestant propaganda that was published in the same year demonstrates that Catholics indeed associated Protestantism with divination and superstition. Antoine de Mouchy, a senior members of the Faculty of Theology of the University of Paris, was particularly virulent in his condemnation of Protestantism. For example, he fell back on the biblical injunctions against consulting wizards, to condemn Protestantism:

> This divine verdict shows that male and female sorcerers and diviners and those that believe in them, and follow them, deserve death. They bewitch Christians with dangerous doctrine, and turn the Scriptures on their head. [Protestants] also deserve death, as it is shown by this law against idolaters . . . Moreover we can demonstrate that the heretics deserve to be burned, because wizards and sorcerers were also burned . . . We have also noted that the heretics keep company with several diviners, magicians, astrologers and philosophers that share their unhealthy curiosity.[38]

This attack was answered by the Calvinist Nicolas des Gallars in 1559 in a pamphlet turning the accusation on the Catholics:

> As for witchcraft, I don't know what motive has impelled this fine defender to bring this up at the wrong moment, unless God is forcing him to stir up the dreadful crimes which hold sway under the cover of papal darkness. For where are magicians, sorcerers, charmers, necromancers and diviners more tolerated and shown greater favour than among you? I'm not saying this merely about a few inquisitive people, but about people who are much more conspicuous, and even about those members of the clergy who are not ashamed to mix themselves up in it.[39]

Just before the outbreak of the French wars of religion, Jean Gay, a member of the *parlement* of Toulouse, accused Protestants outright of being responsible for the renewal of interest in astrology and other forms of divination:

> These people have revived the ancient superstitions of the auguries and divinations of ancient idolaters, and they believe them. By a similar route and path of error and heresy, modern heretics have revived them in peculiar novelties, the revival of judicial astrology, and other divinatory methods similar to those

> ancient superstitions; and it is to give greater colour to their heresy . . . that the Devil has caused them all to revive all the condemned arts of divination, judicial astrology and necromancy.[40]

These accusations had become stock phrases that were used indiscriminately by Protestants and Catholics alike and does not prove that Videl was a Protestant sympathiser. Antoine Couillard, for example, also used the accusation of false prophet against Nostradamus, arguing that astrologers were even more dangerous than false preachers:

> Their doctrine is more dangerous than the one preached in the pulpit: because false preachers cannot preach in all places: but the words of the astrologers . . . are preached, written down, published and inscribed in the hearts of everyone. That is why I resort to a sentence pronounced against the false preachers as well as the false prophets: because what greater heresy can be preached than to say and publish that the celestial bodies rule in the sky?[41]

It could be argued that during the wars of religion, the arguments against astrologers were recycled, by both Catholics and Protestants, who accused the other of being versed in magic, sorcery and divination. No conclusions can be drawn, therefore, from the fact that Videl called Nostradamus a false prophet, as this was a stock accusation that was turned against astrologers, Protestants and Catholics alike. The above passages, however, suggest that Catholics associated astrology, superstition and magic with Protestantism much more consistently than the reverse. Another example is provided by an anti-Protestant tract that was published by the Leaguer polemicist Jean Porthaise in 1579, *De la Vraie et Faulse Astrologie contre les Abuseurs de nostre Siecle*. Porthaise adopts the terms of the debate about true and false astrology outlined above for the purpose of writing anti-Protestant propaganda:

> It is notorious that those who began to stir trouble in our French monarchy, put much of their trust in the destiny of the stars than in the cause of their religion . . . they even say that the stars even threaten the Papacy . . . We show them the ruin of . . . the religion of the . . . so-called Reformed, without resorting to the influence and astronomical conjunctions.[42]

Porthaise's assessment of true and false astrology is in keeping with Pontus de Tyard, Laurens Videl or Antoine Couillard: 'Judicial astrology does not deserve the name of science . . . Moses and Daniel . . . prophesised the future state of the world through divine inspiration, and not through the false and uncertain judicial astrology that is full of superstition.'[43] The fact that Nostradamus had mixed prophecy and judicial astrology is precisely the reason why he was attacked so vehemently by his contemporaries. Catholicism did not embrace astrological prophecy as Crouzet suggests; on the contrary,

Catholics were just as quick to associate astrology and superstition with Protestantism.

The debate surrounding divination in general, and astrology in particular, cannot be dissociated from the confessional debate that was beginning to emerge in this decade. Catholic attacks against Nostradamus share some traits with anti-Protestant polemic. The fact that Nostradamus published his prophecies in the vernacular was not lost on his critics, who accused him of leading the common folk astray, an allegation frequently used against Protestants. The opening sentences of Couillard's second attack against Nostradamus could be interpreted in this light: 'knowing the foolish multitude, the vulgar opinion . . . left the true light to fall into the darkness of error'.[44] Couillard also accused Nostradamus of denying free will, assigning the salvation and damnation of souls to the stars, in an argument borrowed from St Augustine.[45] Naturally, anti-Protestant authors were quick to associate the pagan notion of Fate with the Calvinist doctrine of predestination. For example, Jean Gay compared the idea that the stars determined the course of one's life to 'Calvin's fatal predestination'.[46] I have shown elsewhere how, during the French Wars of Religion, Catholic authors turned consensus values and current debates against the Protestants.[47] It is not surprising that arguments emerging in the closing years of the 1550s against Nostradamus were recycled for the purpose of religious polemic during the Wars of Religion.

Denis Crouzet, in *Les Guerriers de Dieu*, gives pride of place to astrology. It was instrumental, he argues, in fostering a civilisation of eschatological anguish. On numerous occasions, Crouzet uses the words astrology, prophecy and eschatology in succession, implying a correlation between the three. He writes of 'prophétisme astrologique' and argues that the prophetic tradition found in the Scriptures colluded with astrology to exacerbate eschatological anguish in the mid-1550s. In fact, many authors went to great pains to distinguish between the two traditions, in an attempt to separate different strands of divination, those that were acceptable and those that were not. In the course of this controversy astrology, or to be more precise judicial astrology, came under great suspicion. This criticism came from both Catholics and Reformed alike and not, as Crouzet suggests, exclusively from Calvinist circles.[48] Catholics also condemned judicial astrology as superstitious and moreover accused the Protestants of practising astrology as a form of devil worship. I should also like to suggest that Catholics and Protestants can no more be differentiated in terms of their approach towards eschatology.

It is possible to identify, among Catholic critics of Nostradamus, strands of scepticism regarding the ability to predict the end of time. Antoine Couillard and Laurens Videl, for example, argued that it was impossible to predict the end of time with any certainty. Of particular concern to Couillard is the prediction that the world would end at a precise date, concluding that the world 'will be full of years and almost eternal'.[49] Laurens Videl, as well as Couillard, pointed out some contradictions in the prophecies of Nostradamus. On the one hand he announced that the end of time was imminent, and on the other declared that the world would endure for another 3797 years.[50] Videl directly challenged Nostradamus, 'How do you know the world is going to last so long?' but also pointed out that in subsequent editions, Nostradamus had suggested that the end was near.[51] Couillard mentioned another prophecy stating that the world would end 235 years after 1555 (in 1790) and that he was convinced that it would last for much longer than that.[52] Both authors denied Nostradamus and other astrologers the ability to predict the end of time. The time of the Last Judgement, announced in the Scriptures, was hidden from men for all eternity, as in Matthew 24: 36: 'But about that day and hour no one knows, neither the angels of heaven, nor the Son, but only the Father.'

The refusal to believe that the end of the world was imminent, at least among these authors, moderates the picture of an 'eschatologie catholico-astrologique' described by Crouzet.[53] Furthermore, translations into French of classical works on astrology challenged the Christian eschatological tradition, in arguing that the world was eternal and would not end at all. Discussion of the *Corpus Hermeticum* indicates that the mere possibility of the world being eternal was envisaged once more.[54] These texts, ascribed to the mythical figure of Hermes Trismegistus, are thought by modern scholars to have emerged from the tradition of religious syncretism that existed in the second century AD in North Africa. Early modern editions of the *Corpus Hermeticum*, however, suggest that its editors and translators thought it even more ancient, predating the Old Testament and the Jewish astrological tradition embodied by Moses. In fact, the Hermetic tradition really emerged during the Renaissance with the translation into Latin of the *Hermetica* by Marsilo Ficino in the late fifteenth century.[55] The *Corpus Hermeticum* then took on a life of its own in the sixteenth century as subsequent authors used it as a precedent to justify their own contemporary understanding of the occult.[56] What is known as the *Corpus Hermeticum* is a collection of texts that include two dialogues dealing with the power, wisdom and will of God. It was these dialogues that were translated into French by Gabriel du Preau in 1557, and gave the debate surrounding astrology and eschatology a new spin.

The *Corpus Hermeticum* is relevant to astrology because it clearly states the influence of the planets and the stars on human affairs, flowing from one of the sentences of the Hermetic Emerald Table: 'As below, so above, and as above, so below.' Hermeticism is the origin of an expression that was appropriated by the scientific revolution: 'Nothing dies, nothing is born, everything is transformed.' According to this tradition, the history of creation is in a constant flux that is mirrored in the movement of the celestial bodies. Hermeticism clashed with Christianity, when it promoted the quasi-deification and worship of the planets.[57] Furthermore, it also promoted the idea of the irreversible course of Fate that could not be diverted by the free will of men. What is more relevant, it also argues that the world, in the image of God, had no beginning and no end, and was eternal: 'This restoration of the world, which will take place after the revolution of some time, will be a general reformation and atonement of all good things, and a great holy renewal of the whole of nature, which is, has been, and will be without any beginning or end.'[58] Hermes Trismegistus talks of the transformation rather than the end of the world.

Du Preau also added in his commentary that the end of the world had been announced in the Scriptures, and that the notion of the eternity of creation was a pagan superstition.[59] But Couillard could not resist the temptation to point out that Hermes Trismegistus, who was thought to be the father of astrology, had denied the possibility that the world could end: 'Given that the age cannot cease, the world therefore cannot end: being eternal no part of it can ever perish. Let our philosophers and astrologers discuss this as much as they want, there is here matter that has no bottom nor banks: but I could not resist.'[60] The irony used by Couillard indicates that Catholics were not uncritical, and could be very sceptical of eschatological astrology.

Astrology was either considered as a science (when it dealt with natural causes) or as an illicit form of divination (condemned as superstition) but was very rarely thought to be a form of prophecy. Few commentators accepted the prophecies of Nostradamus uncritically, and when they did, it was for polemical purposes. Couillard and Porthaise ascribed the popularity of Nostradamus to superstition and linked it with the coming of the Reformation. Later Ronsard praised Nostradamus as a prophet because he interpreted one of his prophecies as a defence of the papacy in the face of the Reformation.[61] After the end of the French Wars of Religion, the prophecies of Nostradamus were no longer controversial and even served to celebrate the providential accession of Henri IV. Jean-Aimé de Chavigny published his *Janus François* in 1594, ascribing specific prophecies of Nostradamus to individual events of the French wars of religion from 1534 to 1589. Chavigny used the prophecies of Nostradamus to provide a very providential vision of the reign of Henri IV whom he complimented on his conversion to Catholicism: 'in the hope that your Majesty will persevere in your happy conversion to the Roman and Apostolic Catholic Church'.[62] The only concession that was made to the earlier controversy was that the University of Paris had Chavigny remove the title of prophet from his work.

On the opposite side of the confessional debate, French Calvinists were equally preoccupied with prophecy and eschatology during this period. In the Anglican and Lutheran tradition, the battle between the true church and the antichrist had found echoes in their respective struggles with the papacy. The antichrist of Revelation was identified as the pope, and the true church as the Protestant church. Calvin, by contrast, had refused to comment on the Revelation of John, because it was too contentious.[63] These reservations were swept aside in the 1580s when French commentaries on Revelation started to appear, reproducing the apocalyptic interpretation that had been championed by Lutherans and Anglicans. This process culminated in the inclusion, by Simon Goulard, of a calculation of the reign of antichrist in Crespin's posthumous editions of the *Histoire des Martyrs*.[64] This aspect of Reformed apocalypticism, that had loomed large in Lutheran and Anglican ecclesiology, had been absent from French Calvinism until that point.[65] But at that time Simon Goulard translated the works of Flacius Illyricus and other Lutherans that offered a very eschatological reading of ecclesiastical history.[66] It seems that the new interest in the Revelation of John sprang from a crisis of identity of the Calvinist church, in the aftermath of the St Bartholomew's Day Massacre. This trend was intensified in the reign of Henri IV, when Nicolas Vignier was commissioned by the Reformed National Synod to write a comprehensive treatise on the papal antichrist.[67]

Goulard also translated a key Lutheran discussion of divination and astrology, Caspar Peucer's *Les Devins ou Commentaire des principales sortes de devinations* (1584). This treatise reproduced many of the arguments that had been relayed by the Catholics Pontus de Tyard, Couillard, Videl and Porthaise, namely that there were licit and illicit forms of astrology. Peucer relayed the distinction that had been made in other works between true (natural) and false (superstitious) astrology: 'true astrology is a part of natural philosophy . . . true natural astrology is a science'.[68] Goulard also translated the work of another Lutheran, Philippe Camerarius *Les Meditations Historiques*, published in 1610. This work is very eschatological in arguing that although astrologers could not predict the end of time, it did not mean that it was not imminent: 'I do not bring these arguments forward, because I think the last day . . . is far: on the contrary I firmly believe that the signs that precede it, predicted by our Saviour, have already happened.'[69] Simon Goulard was instrumental in introducing this largely Lutheran eschatological view of ecclesiastical history in the French context. Goulard's editions of the *Histoire des Martyrs* reflect the influence of Lutheran authors that he translated and edited during those years. But eschatology is conspicuous by its absence in French Calvinism of the earlier period when it refrained from lambasting Rome as the seat of the Antichrist. The first commentaries of the Revelation of John published in the French language that clearly identified the pope as Antichrist were mostly Dutch in origin.[70] This is also consistent with Crouzet's analysis of the first half of the sixteenth century, when he mentions German and Dutch examples of eschatological tracts making inroads into France.[71] Rather than look for an explanation along confessional lines, as Crouzet does, one might want to fall back on cultural and political differences between France and the Empire.

The fact that these arguments were not previously used in France points to the differences that existed between the French Calvinist and the other Protestant traditions. In England and the Empire, anti-papal arguments had been instrumental in rallying the political elite to the Protestant cause. The conflict between the Pope and secular rulers over the control of church appointments and revenues was central to the Lutheran and English arguments. The arguments had no clout in France because of the specificity of the Gallican church. Whereas the support of secular rulers played a considerable part in the success of the Reformation in England, the Netherlands and Germany, that was not the case in France. Yet a providential, and in many ways eschatological, reading of ecclesiastical history was imported from those parts of Protestant Europe and integrated into Calvinist ecclesiology by Simon Goulard in the 1580s. It is difficult to determine why French Calvinists adopted the very eschatological notion of the papal Antichrist at this time. For England, Peter Lake has argued that by the 1580s the pope had become a convenient 'other' against whom Protestants could make common cause beyond their doctrinal differences.[72] Could it be argued that French Protestants' anti-popery was motivated by a need to show a concerted front in the face of the Catholic Reformation the impact of which was beginning to be felt?

There were no fundamental differences between Catholic and Protestant attitudes towards astrology. As a transgression of the First Commandment it was uncontroversial and thought on both sides to be superstitious. Notwithstanding these theological reservations, both Catholics and Protestants counted supporters of astrology in their ranks. Protestants and Catholics nonetheless accused one another of practising astrology, giving it a sinister varnish of magic and superstition. The adoption of eschatological themes and accusations of superstition were at least partly dictated by rhetorical and polemical imperatives. On the Catholic side, the prophecies of Nostradamus were used by Ronsard and Chavigny. On the Protestant side, the concept of the papal Antichrist was imported from other parts of Europe and included in Calvinist ecclesiology. The fact that astrology and eschatology had become weapons in the polemic of the French Wars of Religion does not necessarily mean that France was a civilisation of eschatological anguish. It is possible to argue that the Reformation contributed to the gradual fall from grace of astrology that became irreversibly associated with superstition. It would be wrong, however, to try to find the origin of modern scepticism in either Catholic or Protestant ideology.

NOTES

1 Denis Crouzet, *Les Guerriers de Dieu: la violence aux temps des troubles de religion, vers 1520–vers 1610* (Paris, 1990), 2 vols.; Crouzet's association of Protestantism and modernity is clear on 625–6 where he follows Weber in attributing a *Zweckrational* (means to an end) thinking process to the Protestants: 'La violence réformée . . . ne peut être pensée que rationellement . . . Se devine, en cette tension de programmation réfléchie de l'action, une certaine "modernité".'

2 Crouzet, *Guerriers de Dieu*, 1: 135–53.

3 Jean Céard, *La Nature et les prodiges: l'insolite au XVIe siècle* (Geneva, 1996), 87–105.

4 Luke 21: 25 (all biblical quotations from the NRSV): 'There will be signs in the sun, the moon, and the stars'.

5 Stuart Clark, *Thinking with Demons: The Idea of Witchcraft in Early Modern Europe* (Oxford, 1000), 181.

6 St Augustine, *Concerning the City of God against the Pagans*, ed. and trans. H. Bettenson (London, 1987), 180.

7 Exodus 20: 4: 'You shall have no other gods before me. You shall not make for yourself an idol'; Clark, *Thinking with Demons*, 472–88, especially 474–6.

8 Gabriel du Preau, ed., *Deux Livres de Mercure Trismegiste Hermés* (Paris, E. Groulleau, 1557), fol. 98: Hermes Trismegistus recommends the worship of the planets.

9 Clark, *Thinking with Demons*, 479–84, especially 481.

10 See Sixtus V's bull, *Coeli et Terrae* (1586), translated by P. G. Maxwell-Stuart, *The Occult in Early Modern Europe: A Documentary History* (Basingstoke, 1999), 59–60.

11 Peter Dear, *Revolutionizing the Sciences: European Knowledge and Its Ambitions, 1500–1700* (Houndsmill, 2001), 25.

12 Clark, *Thinking with Demons*, 235, 479–80.

13 Pontus de Tyard, *Mantice ou Discours de la verité de Divination par Astrologie* (Lyon, J. de Tournes & G. Gazeau, 1558), 3–4, 17.

14 De Tyard, *Mantice*, 27.

15 De Tyard, *Mantice*, 7–8.

16 De Tyard, *Mantice*, 81.

17 Crouzet, *Guerriers de Dieu*, 1: 117.

18 L. Bourquin, ed., *Mémoires de Claude Haton, Tome 1 1553–1565* (Paris, 2001), 39–40.

19 Olivier Millet, 'Feux croisés sur Nostradamus au XVIe siècle', *Divination et controverse religieuse en France au XVIe siècle*, Cahiers V. L. Saulnier 4 (1987), 103–21.

20 Antoine Couillard, *Les Propheties du Seigneur du Pavillon Les Lorriz* (Paris, A. le Clerc, 1556), sig. C4.

21 Couillard, *Les Propheties*, sigs. E1v, G1.

22 Couillard, *Les Propheties*, sigs. E2v, D4v.

23 Couillard, *Les Propheties*, sig. B3v.

24 Couillard, *Les Propheties*, sig. C3.

25 Crouzet, *Guerriers de Dieu*, 1: 141.

26 Couillard, *Les Propheties*, sigs. B2, C4–C4v, G4v.

27 Antoine Couillard, *Les Contredicts du Seigneur Du Pavillon, lez Lorriz, en Gastinois, aux faulses & abbusifves propheties de Nostradamus, & autres astrologues* (Paris, C. l'Angelier, 1560), sig. †2v.

28 Millet, 'Feux croisés', 106.

29 Couillard, *Les Propheties*, sig. B3v.

30 Couillard, *Les Contredicts*, sig. †4v

31 Couillard, *Les Contredicts*, sigs. †4, †5.

32 Francis Higman, 'The Origins of the Image of Geneva', in J. B. Roney and M. J. Klauber, eds, *The Identity of Geneva: The Christian Commonwealth 1564–1864* (London, 1998), 21–38.

33 Crouzet, *Guerriers de Dieu*, 1: 140; Millet, 'Feux croisés', 106.

34 Laurens Videl, *Declaration des abus, ignorances et seditions de Michel Nostradamus, de Salon de Craux en Provence oeuvre tresutile & profitable â un chacun* (Avignon, P. Roux & J. Tramblay, 1558), sigs. A2–A4.

35 Simon the Magician was thought to be the father of all heretics. Videl, *Declaration des abus*, sigs. D3v–D4.

36 Crouzet, *Guerriers de Dieu*, 1: 140.

37 Millet, 'Feux croisés', 112–14.

38 Leviticus 19: 31: 'Do not turn to mediums or wizards; do not seek them out, to be defiled by them'; Antoine de Mouchy, *Responce a quelque apologie que les heretiques ces jours passés ont mis en avant sous ce titre: Apologie ou deffence des bons Chrestiens contre les ennemis de l'Eglise catholique* (Paris, C. Fremy, 1558), sigs. B1, B2, C7v, H5v.

39 Nicolas des Gallars, *Seconde apologie ou defense des vrais chrestiens, contre les calomnies impudentes des ennemis de l'Eglise catholique* (n. pl., n. pr., 1559), sig. B4; translated by Maxwell-Stuart, *The Occult*, 167–8.

40 Jean Gay, *Histoire des scismes et heresies des Albigeois conforme à celle du present* (Paris, P. Gaultier, 1561), 8, 31; translated by Maxwell-Stuart, *The Occult*, 168.

41 Couillard, *Les Contredicts*, sigs. G7v, G8.

42 Jean Porthaise, *De la Vraie et Faulse Astrologie contre les Abuseurs de nostre Siecle* (Poitiers, F. le Paige, 1579), 25, 272.

43 Porthaise, *De la Vraie et Faulse Astrologie*, 195, 253, 274, 284.

44 Couillard, *Les Contredicts*, sigs. A1v, C5, H2v.

45 Couillard, *Les Contredicts*, sig. A2v.

46 Gay, *Des Scismes*, 7–8, 31.

47 Luc Racaut, *Hatred in Print: Catholic Propaganda and Protestant Identity during the French Wars of Religion* (Aldershot, 2002).

48 Crouzet, *Guerriers de Dieu*, 1: 138: 'Les textes, dont l'analyse est proposée dans les lignes qui suivent, font plutôt entrevoir une situation de course de vitesse entre la religion du Verbe et une eschatologie catholico-astrologique.'

49 Couillard, *Les Contredicts*, sigs. L2v, D4v, G3, H1v.

50 Videl, *Declaration des abus*, sig. E1; Couillard, *Les Propheties*, sig. D4v; Michel Chomarat, 'De Quelques Dates Clairement Exprimées par Michel Nostradamus dans ses "Prophéties"', *Prophètes et prophéties au XVIe siècle*, Cahiers V. L. Saulnier 15 (1998), 83–93, especially 85–6.

51 Videl, *Declaration des abus*, sigs. E1r, F1r.

52 Couillard, *Les Propheties*, sig. G3.

53 Crouzet, *Guerriers de Dieu*, 1: 138.

54 Du Preau, ed., *Deux Livres de Mercure*; Roger Bacon, ed., *Des Choses Merveilleuses en nature, ou est traicté des erreurs des sens, des puissances de l'ame, & des influences des cieux* (Lyon, n. pr., 1557).

55 Céard, *La Nature et les prodiges*, 87–94.

56 I owe thanks to Dr P. G. Maxwell-Stuart (St Andrews), for these remarks.

57 St Augustine condemns Hermes Trismegistus in *City of God*, 8: 23–4.

58 Du Preau, *Deux Livres de Mercure*, fol.103.

59 Du Preau, *Deux Livres de Mercure*, preface.

60 Couillard, *Les Contredicts*, sigs. L3v, L5v.

61 Céard, *La Nature et les prodiges*, 215.

62 Jean-Aimé de Chavigny, *La Premiere Face du Janus François* (Lyon, P. Roussin, 1594), sig. Ã4.

63 Irena Backus, *Les Sept Visions et la fin des temps: les commentaires genevois de l'Apocalypse entre 1539 et 1584* (Geneva, 1997).

64 Jean Crespin, *Histoire des Martyrs persecutez et mis a mort pour la verité de l'Evangile*, ed. Simon Goulard (Geneva, P. Aubert, 1619), fol. 22.

65 Luc Racaut, 'Religious Polemic and the Protestant Self-Image', in R. Mentzer and A. Spicer, eds, *Society and Culture in the Huguenot World, 1559–1665* (Cambridge, 2002), 29–43.

66 Matthias Flacius Illyricus, *Catalogus Testium Veritatis*, ed. Simon Goulard (Geneva, M. Stoer & Chouet, 1597).

67 J. Aymon, ed., *Tous les Synodes Nationaux des Eglises Reformées de France* (The Hague, 1710), 2 vols, 1: 36; Nicolas Vignier, *Theatre de L'Antechrist* (Saumur, n. pr., 1610).

68 Caspar Peucer, *Les Devins ou Commentaire des principales sortes de devinations* (Antwerp, H. Connix, 1584), 550, 605.

69 Philippe Camerarius, *Les Meditations Historiques* (Lyon, A. de Harsy's widow, 1610), 3 vols, 1: 205.

70 François du Jon, *Apocalypse ou Revelation de S. Jean Apostre Evangeliste de nostre Seigneur Jesus Christ* (Geneva, P. de St-André, 1592).

71 Crouzet, *Guerriers de Dieu*, 1: 106–20.

72 P. Lake, 'Anti-popery: The Structure of a Prejudice', in R. Cust and A. Hughes, eds, *Conflict in Early Stuart England: Studies in Religion and Politics, 1603–1642* (London, 1989), 72–106, especially 82.

8

Rational superstition:
the writings of Protestant demonologists

P. G. MAXWELL-STUART

In 1863 a Welsh farmer had a cow which fell sick on the Sabbath. He dosed her with medicine, but she seemed to become worse rather than better and so, fearing she was about to die, the farmer ran back to his house, brought out the family Bible, and read a chapter to her. In Norway, a nineteenth-century Protestant minister maintained he was able to recognise that a woman who came forward to receive communion was a witch because the wine in the chalice swirled widdershins. At much the same time, in the Protestant Cévennes, local women used to bring with them to divine service a sachet of silkworm eggs hidden in their corsages, an action which they intended to have two magical effects: the avoidance of future diseases and the insurance of a good harvest.[1] Thus, in three places with a long tradition of various types of Protestantism, official disapproval of magical beliefs and operations had had little practical effect, and people continued to react and behave in ways which equally disparate Catholic communities would not have found in the least odd or confessionally peculiar.

Examples of similarity between Catholics and Protestants in relation to magic are almost too numerous, but three areas of experience will serve to illustrate the whole. First, then, bad weather was seen by both as a sign of divine or preternatural perturbation. Thus, in 1521 Johann Eberlin von Günzberg addressed a pamphlet to Charles V, blaming recent hail-storms, bad weather in general, and the outbreak of plague on the continuance of abuses within the church, monasticism in particular; and this was also the general import of the message preached by the sixteenth-century pastors of Strasbourg to their congregations; while the English Puritan clergyman, Ralph Josselin, saw the weather as God's way of coercing reluctant people to attend divine service.[2] On the Catholic side we have the mordant witness of Montaigne who observed, 'Quand les vignes gelent en mon village, mon prebstre en argumente l'ire de Dieu sur la race humaine'; Saint Francis of Assisi told the inhabitants of Greccio that the wolves which were attacking both them and their flocks, and the annual hail-storms which destroyed their fields and vine-yards were a sign of God's anger against them: and sure enough, when the people did penance, the devastations ceased; while in Munich there was dreadful weather in the spring of 1590 and a newly built church tower collapsed, a misfortune which many blamed on the activity of witches.[3]

There is an interesting parallel, too, between St Thomas Aquinas who said that, with God's permission, evil spirits might raise up strong winds and make fire fall from the sky, and Luther's view that aerial manifestations such as comets or St Elmo's fire were either a sign sent by God to inspire terror in humankind, or visible marks of the sport of evil spirits.[4] If there is a difference between the two confessions, it may be seen in the Catholics' greater willingness to attribute bad weather to the activity of evil spirits, while Protestants were perhaps more inclined to view it as a direct message from God. Nevertheless, one should not be too ready to draw a distinction between them, and one may note that Protestants, for all their cries of superstition against Catholics, did not hesitate to accommodate in both their thinking and their practice the notion that adverse weather was not simply a natural occurrence, but contained either a preternatural or a supernatural element which humanity ignored at its peril.

Monstrous births of one kind or another also served as divine or demonic signs in need of interpretation. Sometimes they were *lusus naturae* caused, perhaps, by their mothers being frightened or otherwise receiving the imprint of a disturbing sight during their pregnancies. But, while not denying the immediate natural causes of these monsters, writers both Catholic and Protestant followed the line of Konrad Wolffhart (Lycosthenes) who wrote bluntly in 1557 that 'it is impossible to deny that a monster is an imposing sign of divine wrath and malediction'. Hence, Melanchthon interpreted a monstrous birth found dead in the Tiber in 1496 as a symbol of the multiple corruptions of the papacy, while the Catholic Pierre Boaistuau deduced that the increased numbers of monsters between 1567 and 1573 had happened because God was angry with the Protestant heretics' attempt to take up arms against the true faith in France. Once again, this mode of thinking and interpretation outlasted the immediate impact of the Reformation, and can be seen in a community Protestant from the beginning. John Winthrop, governor of the Massachusetts Bay Colony in the 1630s and early 1640s, inferred that a deformed child born to Mary Dyer, a woman of unorthodox religious opinions and suspected (perhaps *propter hoc*) of witchcraft, was evidence of her traffic with Satan; and when another suspected heretic and witch, Anne Hutchinson, 'brought forth not one . . . but . . . 30 monstrous births or thereabouts, at once', Winthrop noted, 'see how the wisdom of God fitted this judgement to her sin in every way, for look as she had vented mis-shapen opinions, so she must bring forth deformed monsters'.[5]

Thirdly, the vexed problem of demonic possession exercised both confessions as each sought to display its superior efficacy (and therefore its superior hold on theological truth), in the use of exorcism to expel the offending spirit.[6] Following Catholic ritual practice, Luther was prepared to countenance exorcism during the baptismal rite. His *Order of Baptism*, published in 1523, directs the officiating minister to blow three times under the child's eyes and say, 'Depart, thou unclean spirit', and thereafter to command the departure of the evil spirit by making three signs of the cross. In the revised version of this rite (1526), the blowing has been dropped, but everything else is retained. When it came to exorcising adults, however, forcible methods might well be used. In February 1564, for example, an English Puritan clergyman exorcised an evil spirit from an adolescent girl by holding her down and squirting vinegar into her nostrils, meanwhile leading the crowd of spectators in recitations of the Lord's Prayer and the Te Deum. As Kathleen Sands, who cites the case, comments, 'This event bore all the marks of the Jesuit exorcisms which would be the target of Protestant ire into and throughout the following century. These very practices . . . would form the subject of countless chapbooks and broadsides lampooning Catholic superstition and blasphemy.'[7]

Not that such exorcisms were regular practice among the various Protestant communities. Indeed, the general assertion made by Protestants that the age of miracles was over and that miracles claimed by Catholics were no more than wonders created and manipulated by Satan, tended to argue against the supernatural reality of demonic possession and more in favour of Satanic illusions or human fraud, neither of which required the counter-operations of either God or priest.[8] Moreover, the majority of Protestants became uncomfortably aware that they lacked the ritual means to command the dispossession of evil spirits. In the words of the English bishop, Joseph Hall, 'we that have no power to bid must pray', and so prayer and fasting, allied to Griselda-like patience, became the regular resort of Protestants faced with trials sent by God or tribulations inflicted by Satan. A jettisoning of ritual, however, and semantic play with the word 'miracle', came nowhere near to destroying Protestants' belief in the activity of evil spirits, and as late as the eighteenth century we can find a Presbyterian minister praying over a possessed woman and arguing with the spirit speaking through her, or resolutely facing Satan, whether the fiend was disguised as a respectable gentleman or as a little black dog.[9]

In these three areas alone, therefore – and parallels between Catholic and Protestant belief and practice could be shown to exist in almost every department of daily existence – it is evident that the various Protestant confessions did not succeed, in spite of their pious hopes and rhetoric, in expelling from the minds and lives of their adherents what their spokesmen were pleased to call 'superstition'. But did they also develop, independently of Catholic tradition, practices or beliefs of their own which, when viewed from an outsider's stand-point, might be called 'superstitious'? The answer must be yes and no. The various Protestant groupings were not religions entirely divorced from Catholi-cism, and therefore some of their distinctive traits which strayed over the border between piety and superstition were simply confessional exaggerations of aspects of the faith all held in common.[10] Appeals to various and particular work-ings of Providence, for example, were scarcely more than substitutes for Catholic references to miracles, and Protestant 'providentialist' interpretations of signs, wonders, and portents in the natural world as a weapon to lambast Catholics were no less opportunistic and just as sincere as the equivalent Catholic allegations that God was thereby displaying his wrath against heresy.

Yet there is here much more than simple parallelism.[11] The Protestants' doctrine of providence stemmed largely from their insistence that the indivi-dual human soul stood alone in a relationship with God, which admitted of no intermediaries, and in consequence the intense and minute scrutiny of the divine omnipotence became a matter of the utmost importance to human sen-sibilities heightened by their awareness on the one hand of God's overwhelm-ing power, and on the other of their own impotence and scarcely regenerate proclivity to sin. Providential instances, then, were to be read and interpreted as messages from God to sinners in general and as tokens, perhaps, to individ-uals of their standing in his eyes – an open invitation, as Calvin recognised, to the uncontrolled development of personal superstitious beliefs and practices.[12]

The Bible itself was employed as a magical object, to be used in testing for witchcraft or as a protective amulet against the unwelcome activities of preternatural beings. Thus it was reported by *The Morning Post* on 28 January 1780 that a clergyman at Bexhill had weighed two women against the Bible in response to a request from his parishioners that he discover whether or not they were witches, an experiment which actually resulted in their acquittal; while in 1658 the witchcraft indictment of a Scotswoman, Janet Miller, included the charge that she had been consulted by a man with a sick child, and had advised him to make sure that his daughter always had a Bible near at hand (even though the child could not read), because she was being troubled by fairies.[13] Fasting, too, developed as a peculiar magical rite among certain Pro-testant sectaries. Fasts were ordained by both the state and individual congre-gations for such diverse purposes as bringing favourable weather or turning away bad, curing the sick, or appeasing God's anger in time of war or rebel-lion, Calvinist theologians in particular stressing that these Protestant fasts were quite different from the childish superstition of Catholic fasts, since the latter encouraged God's wrath whereas the former tried to assuage it.[14] We can therefore discern distinctive Protestant trends in magical usage, which had their origin in Catholic practice or belief, but achieved over time their own life and momentum in Protestant community life and thus became 'Protestant' as it were by adoption.

Protestants, then, as much as Catholics lived in a magical universe and were fully aware that they did so. If there is a difference between Catholic and Protestant explanations of the manifestations of magic within that universe and their solutions to the moral dilemmas which it posed, it may be found perhaps less in theological niceties over the degree of power God was allowing Satan to exercise throughout creation, and more in the driving energy behind the polemics of inter-confessional rivalry after the Reformation. Protestants found it important, for the sake of emphasising God's omnipotence and thus avoiding any taint of Manichaeism in their theology, to designate all manifestations of preternatural power illusions or natural phenomena as yet unknown to, or imperfectly understood by, human beings.[15] In consequence, Catholic controversialists were almost obliged to take the opposite point of view and maintain the reality of demonic operations, a tendency which inevitably resulted in their giving the impression that Satan's abilities were extensive and that God was permitting him a remarkable degree of freedom in the world.[16]

What this means for Protestant demonologies is quite important. Both these and their Catholic counterparts are usually read in isolation, as though they were intellectual monographs produced by scholars with an almost abstract interest in the topic, whereas they were actually works of heated religious controversy, written in high passion and deeply informed by the immediate circumstances of their composition, a particularity which makes them as difficult to apprehend, in their way, as an Aristophanic comedy. Let us take two examples and note how closely they conform, or not, to these expectations. The first is the *Demonologie* of François Perreaud, written around 1613 but not published until 1653.

Perreaud cannot be counted as one of the great luminaries of the continental Reformation. Certainly he was a pastor much respected by his ecclesiastical equals and superiors and had what appears to have been a long and honourable career, dying amid general plaudits in 1657 at the age of eighty-five. But had it not been for one slight, though intriguing, claim to fame, his death would have wrapped him in permanent obscurity. As it is, he claims our attention because in 1612, soon after he had arrived in Mâcon to start his ministry, both he and his household were subjected to a series of almost unremitting attacks from an evil spirit which plagued them in poltergeist-fashion from mid-September until 22 December that same year. Once they were over, he wrote a detailed account of them, prefacing this with a demonology which serves it in the office of introduction or prefatory sermon-cum-explanation, and which has been more or less ignored by those who have taken a greater interest in the ghost-account which follows.

Perreaud begins with a short preface in which he explains that in 1652 he visited Bern for the first time for fifty years, and there congratulated the city on passing a law against witches, which declared its intention henceforth to investigate charges of witchcraft with a due measure of thought, lengthy deliberation, a ripe regard for the attendant circumstances and ramifications thereof. This reminded Perreaud, he says, of three things: first, an older but similar ordinance published by Venice, which curbed the abuse of allowing those who accused others of witchcraft to benefit from their escheated goods; second, the attacks he himself had suffered at the hands of Catholics who had drawn attention to the large numbers of witches burned in the Pays de Vaud and inferred therefrom that Reformed religion is to blame for the infestation – to which Perreaud replied that if Satan was bold enough to attack Adam and Eve in Eden, he was quite apt to do as much in places where the pure Gospel was preached; and third, his experiences in Mâcon when he arrived to take up his ministry. He believed it possible to show that all these incidents were not unconnected and so, stimulated by his visit to Bern and the judicious Witchcraft Act of its city council, he had decided to make available his treatise on demonology 'wherein', he says, 'I have tried to explain by reliable grounds and principles what one must believe, the strength and weakness of evil spirits, and the proper remedies and safeguards one may undertake against them'.[17]

The treatise is divided into twelve short chapters and reads like an extended sermon. Perreaud begins by addressing himself to the problem of those people who do not believe in the existence of angels, good or bad. There are two ways of proving something, he says: the word of God and experience. He furnishes the usual examples from Scripture to show that both good and bad angels exist, and then makes the observation that just as a secular state needs executioners and people to carry out the ordinances of justice, so demons are necessary to punish sin and test the faith of believers. Experience, too, confirms the existence of these beings. Houses and châteaux all over Europe have been abandoned because they are infested with evil spirits whose numbers are so vast, they cannot be counted. Perreaud then adds the unexpected comment: so why is there only one devil? Because 'devil' is a collective noun.[18]

This procedure of appeal to Scripture and experience is followed throughout the remaining chapters. Perreaud goes on to argue that witches and sorcerers undoubtedly exist and that maintaining their non-existence is simply one of Satan's tricks. (Here Perreaud takes a side-swipe at Montaigne who actually did not question the existence of witches so much as suggest that one must be quite convinced of the possibility of the reality of their crime before one burned them for it). Satan imitates God, says Perreaud, by sending visions to his witches as God sent visions to his prophets; and the devil's marks are the equivalent of circumcision among the Jews or baptism among Christians. Nevertheless, it is as dangerous to be over-credulous as it is to be unbelieving. Certain phenomena may have a natural explanation. Deliberate fraud must not be discounted. Misunderstanding by the ignorant should be taken into account. Malicious accusation is always possible, as when an evil spirit suddenly began to make appearances at night in the city of Tours. The citizens called him *le Roy Hugon* or *Huguet*, and Protestants in the city were henceforth known as Huguenots because they held their meetings only at night under the aegis of this evil spirit.

Popular belief that witches can raise hail-storms and tempests is both wrong and impious. Only God can do such things. Certainly the devil does have great power on earth and in the air, but neither he nor his evil spirits can do anything except by God's permission and licence. If storms do occur, they are more likely to be signs of God's anger at our sins, and it should be a consolation to us to know both that calamity comes either from God or from Satan acting under God's directions, and that God will not permit us to be tested beyond our endurance.

The word *demon* means 'someone who knows', says Perreaud – actually it does not, but no matter – and demons are possessed of two qualities: the power to know and the power to act. Demons apparently know what is going on in the present, for they can enter people's minds and read their unspoken thoughts, although only God can *really* know what is going on in someone's mind. (If that is not altogether clear, it is because Perreaud himself seems confused about this point.) Demons can also predict the future, not because they know it, but because they are immensely skilled both at reading signs and drawing correct inferences from the past, and these they use to give what appear to be an extraordinarily accurate forecast of the future.

Nevertheless, demons operate principally through illusion, and they may persuade people to believe their illusions either by working upon the individual imagination or upon the exterior senses of sight and sound. As an example of the former, Perreaud refers to the story of a man who refused to sit down because he believed his buttocks were made of glass and that if he rested them on a chair they would crack in pieces. Such mistaken beliefs, he says, are caused by melancholy, an excess of black bile in the system, which causes fumes to rise from the stomach to the brain where they interfere with the natural spirits resident there and so produce something akin to hallucination. Hence, says Perreaud, witches merely imagine they fly to their Sabbats and nocturnal assemblies, while Satan also makes use of their melancholic proclivities to manufacture illusions in their brain. Demons, in fact, are expert conjurors and can deceive the eye and ear, either by creating illusions themselves or having magicians and witches create them on their behalf.

But demons can also do things impossible to humans. For example, they can use other bodies for their own purposes – the corpses of those who have been hanged are a common choice – or manufacture false bodies from congealed air. Once in the new body, they can make it speak by striking the air so that it vibrates through the corpse's lungs and mouth and so reaches the ear of the listener, so that it appears as though real speech and real articulation are taking place. This, says Perreaud, is how the poltergeist at Mâcon was able to speak and we were able to hear an apparent voice. Demons can use human bodies because their own are so much lighter, and lighter things have power over heavier. Thus they can carry witches through the air, as a wind carries objects heavier than itself. Therefore a demon's ability to throw stones or domestic utensils, ring bells and create other noises should not be regarded as strange or unlikely.

Nor are such manifestations illusory. Satan's repertoire of tricks is immense and aimed entirely at achieving a single goal: the destruction of humanity. He misleads people through idolatry (for example, via the church of Rome or, even worse, by means of those who claim to effect cures by means of popular magic), through heresy and false doctrine, perfidy and atheism, murders, duels, religious wars, debauchery and the corruption of justice. The end of the world is not far off; therefore Satan is constantly inventing new stratagems to ensnare and destroy the faithful. What, then, can one do to protect oneself against him? He is not to be restrained by superstitious means such as crosses, relics, holy water, and exorcisms. A strong faith in the mercy of God, prayer, vigil, and fasting are the appropriate weapons with which we must fight, and if we live our lives as in the presence of God, we may be assured of God's protection from ultimate harm.

While the logical progression of the argument of the *Demonologie* may not be altogether coherent, the main thrust of Perreaud's disquisition is clear.

1 Evil spirits do exist and are capable of doing harm to human beings. They operate, however, only with permission from God and cannot go further in malignancy than he allows.
2 Much of what they do is sheer illusion.[19] That it appears real to us is simply because evil spirits exist on a more subtle plane and have a much greater knowledge of and control over nature than we.
3 Having been fettered by God for a thousand years, Satan has now been released and is working havoc against humanity. With the advent of true religion in Europe, he is making even greater efforts to ruin souls. (This last point raises the question, how far did inter-confessional hostility at this time both create and magnify both sides' conviction that they were living in the final times and that witches and other magical operators were proliferating before their eyes?)[20]
4 But we must not allow ourselves to fall into superstitious over-credulity and see demonic activity where there is none. A judicious vigilance and a constant trust in God will see us safely through any demonic nightmare.

There is nothing here which is in the least novel or unorthodox. Indeed, there is very little which is distinctively Protestant (an interesting aspect of the work, since Perreaud was a faithful Calvinist). Demonologies by Catholic and Protestant writers from the late sixteenth century onwards in fact tended to make fairly similar points. Girolamo Menghi, for example, suggested that 'the most powerful remedies against these diabolical nightmares are a sorrowful and tearful contrition for one's sins, confession, the Lord's Prayer devoutly said, holy communion, devotion of the holy cross, exorcism . . . meditation on Christ's passion, giving alms, fasting, pilgrimage, and prayer to the saints'.[21] *Mutatis mutandis*, the emphasis here is upon contrition for sin, prayer and fasting, all of which Perreaud would have been happy to approve. Both parties tended to refer to the same authorities with an almost tedious regularity, and Protestants quoted Catholic authors quite readily as magisterial texts worthy of absolute credence. Perreaud himself, for example, cites Bodin, Boguet and Pierre de Lancre. Any differences between them tend to lie in their illustrative details, often contemporary anecdotes, which might lend themselves to confessional manipulation and which could be used for sectarian purposes to underline a desired doctrinal point; while another source of difference can be found in the remedies and safeguards the writer recommended. Catholics had an immense repertoire of what one might call 'counter-magic' to range against the devil and his servants. Protestants, on the other hand, were in theory supposed to rely principally upon prayer and steadfast hope, gritting their teeth, like Job, and waiting patiently until the storm had passed: an austere, even bleak advice which not everyone could like or follow. Nor, in fact, did Protestants regularly follow it: for, as we have seen, the gap between their precept and practice was usually large.

But the *Demonologie* was not written as a free-standing treatise. Its significance therefore derives from its being a preface to *L'Antidemon de Mâcon*, a highly personal account of an extended haunting which Perreaud explains by referring to maleficent magic. After describing the poltergeist activity at length, he then informs the reader that some people thought the trouble lay in his wife's maid who was already suspected of being a witch and came from a suspect family. Perreaud himself thought she may have been practising witchcraft, but he does not pursue the point in his essay, nor does he seem to agree that she was the agent of the demonic manifestations. Another observation, too, he records and quietly puts to one side. A former owner of the house had been murdered and it is well known, he says, that demons do appear in places such as this. His favoured explanation, however, involves a third person altogether. Perreaud's narrative does not make it clear, but he had obviously moved into the house by the time the poltergeist activity had started. The previous owner, a woman, had had to be dispossessed by judicial judgement in order to make way for the Perreauds, and naturally she was resentful. Unable to bend or persuade the law to her point of view, it seems she took matters into her own hands, for Perreaud tells us she was discovered one day, kneeling beneath the chimney, calling upon the devil to do harm to him and his family. Perreaud thereupon made a formal complaint, and the woman was ordered to appear before the authorities and explain herself to them. This she did and it is interesting to note that they did no more than bind her over to keep the peace, perhaps an indication that the local magistrates were accustomed to be lenient, or perhaps that Perreaud's action in moving house had not gone down well with certain sections of the town. But the episode ended with a coincidence. The date of her court appearance was 22 December, and on that very day all poltergeist activity ceased for good. 'In my opinion', says Perreaud, 'this woman was the most likely cause.'

His opinion should not come as a surprise. Protestants did not always opt for what would now be called the rational explanation of events. The magical world was real and could furnish causes of extraordinary phenomena in the natural world, often by employing agents within that world to do their business for them. Perreaud, indeed, has signalled from the start that this will be his explanation of the haunting, for the title of his account is significant. L'Antidemon de Mâcon is unusual because of that word 'antidemon'. At first glance, one might assume that antidemon means 'someone opposed to a demon', just as Antichrist is someone opposed to Christ. In this case, the most likely antidemon of Mâcon would be François Perreaud himself. But this is too bizarre an explanation, and we must surely turn to the other meaning of the Greek preposition anti, 'standing in place of'. This, I think, makes sense. Someone standing in place of a demon seems to indicate that Perreaud suspected a human agency behind the demonic and, as he says at the end, the woman ejected from her house to make way for him is a very good candidate.

We should not, however, jump to any premature conclusion that because Perreaud is pointing the finger at a human being he is therefore implying the whole thing was a fraud. This is completely to misread his convictions. Nothing could be more likely, according to contemporary belief, than that a woman with a grudge should have turned to harmful magic to right what she saw as her wrongs, and there is no reason for us to doubt that Perreaud made every effort to leave us an accurate record of what he saw and heard and thought he knew; and what he saw and heard and thought he knew was that for more than twelve weeks at the end of 1612, a prolonged operation of maleficent magic had been directed against him and his household, either by Satan at the behest of God as a test of their faith and endurance, or by some malign spirit acting under the control of a nondemonic agent whose identity might be guessed but was not known for certain.

Perreaud's experience, then, reluctantly published so long after the event, provides us with a reminder of seventeenth-century Protestant attitudes towards preternatural phenomena. *L'Antidemon*, along with the prefatory *Demonologie*, supports traditional Protestant views on possession and witchcraft, for it acknowledges that Satan's power is real but limited and that his attacks are part of God's plan for humanity which must suffer them, like Job, with prayer and exemplary patience; it gives an edifying account of Protestant piety, thereby affording a useful counterbalance to Catholic works on the same subject, which suggest that only the Roman church can provide an effective panoply against diabolical assault; and because Perreaud himself was considered to be truthful and reliable, and because his account contains few details which might be regarded as overblown or fantastic, his book gained a respectful readership.[22] Curiously enough, it also foreshadows in certain ways the experience and opinions of John Wesley and his family. During the winter of 1716–17, their household was subject to a type of haunting characterised by Samuel Wesley as the visitation of an evil spirit. The disturbances lasted for about two months and then abruptly ceased. Emily Wesley gave her opinion that they had been caused by witchcraft, since a year previously the neighbouring town had been troubled by witches.[23] John Wesley, who meditated on this episode for a considerable time, then produced his famous dictum that 'the giving up of witchcraft is in effect giving up the Bible', an assertion which mirrors Perreaud's earlier opinion that 'those who deny devils and witches tacitly deny God, heaven and hell'.

Perreaud's *Demonologie*, then, neatly summarises the principal lines taken by a Protestant divine when discussing magic, its manifestations in the created world and the way humans may cope with these. The *Antidemon* which follows gives a particular instance of a preternatural happening and an illustration of how a devout Calvinist family dealt with it. Most significantly, perhaps, while the *Demonologie* had reiterated orthodox teaching anent Satan's tendency to work through illusion, Perreaud was in no doubt that his ghostly experiences had been real and had been caused by a deliberate operation of maleficent magic. Orthodoxy and experience, it seems, were not necessarily always in agreement.[24]

Our second example of a Protestant demonology, Lambert Daneau's *De Veneficiis*, illustrates some of the other difficulties and inconsistencies attendant upon inquiry into the subject. Daneau (1530–95) was, like Perreaud, a Calvinist minister.[25] He had studied law in his youth and been a councillor of the *parlement* of Paris; but then he went to Geneva where he took the cloth, and also became professor of theology at the university, producing a large number of works, mainly theological, but including a voluminous tome, *Christianae Physicae*, which sought to show that the account of the physical world given in the Bible, and that described by contemporary natural philosophers, were in perfect concordance: and the short treatise on witchcraft we are about to consider.

De Veneficiis is written in the form of a dialogue, and was stimulated (so Daneau says), by recent events in France.

> Some people have recently come back from Paris with stories about extraordinary things . . . They say (and there is no reason to disbelieve them), that three months ago an almost uncountable number of workers of poisonous magic [*venefici*] were arrested in France. Their offence has now been judged by the *parlement* of Paris, and every day various people from various provinces are referred to it after being found guilty of this crime, and are subject to its sentences. What you may find even more remarkable is that those who appear in the court records come from every rank in society, starting with aristocrats and then going on to men and then women – even people who are well educated and have a reputation for learning! So what shall I say when it comes to the common rank and file who have no experience and no knowledge? – people such as farmers, vineyard workers, shepherds, villeins, craftsmen, and the rest of that sort of person, not to mention the old, and the adolescent, almost uncountable numbers of whom (and there is absolutely no doubt about this), are workers of poisonous magic and witches [*sortiarii*].[26]

It should be noted that the Latin vocabulary for magical operators is extensive and cannot be reduced to the single French word *sorcier/sorcière* or English *witch* without serious distortion of the intended meaning of the text. This is a point to which I shall return. Daneau's message to the reader is straightforward. Witches do exist. Their transvection to the Sabbat is not contrary to nature, although there can be differences of opinion about whether it is illusory or not.[27] The Sabbat itself, however, is undoubtedly real. 'Theophilus', Daneau's speaker in the dialogue, produces a fairly standard description of what goes on there and is asked by 'Antonius' how he knows this account to be true.[28] Theophilus answers by referring to confessions almost without number, which have been made by participants, and which are absolutely consistent with each other in every detail. Antonius still demurs, thinking these people must be deceived, but Theophilus produces a further argument.

> Have there not been found many people who have gone to these assemblies out of idle curiosity, and have been physically present in those places where the witches [*sortiarii*] were being gathered together as a body, after which they have come back home on a journey which has cost them much pain and trouble to their neighbours' certain knowledge and eye-witness? . . . The consistency of witches' [*sortiarii*] confessions, and a limitless number of testimonies, contradict you and your opinion, Antonius.[29]

Theophilus/Daneau likewise accepts the reality of the witch's mark.

> Let me make this point quite clear to you. There is no witch [*sortiarius*] who has not made a pact and a bargain with Satan, and dedicated him or herself to him;

and they carry about on some part of their body confirmation that they are his property by means of an imprint which Satan has burned upon them.[30]

As for illness and the use of counter-magic to amend it,

> If someone is said to be a witch [*sortiarius*], he or she cannot cure us by any superstitious method or any traffic with Satan – only in accordance with doctors' precepts and recommendations, and the remedies they prescribe. Under these circumstances it is permissible for us, in the saving fear of God, to make use of his or her hand, work, and help . . . Therefore it would be better for us to lie sick in our bed for the rest of our lives than have recourse to the power [of magic] and skills belonging to Satan.[31]

According to Daneau, then, witches and evil spirits do exist. Transvection to the Sabbat may or may not be real, but the Sabbat certainly is, and so is the witch's mark. Witches make a pact with Satan who misleads them into thinking they have effective power. Witches, however, cannot cure illness by magic, only with the help of natural means such as doctors also use; but it is dangerous for people to have recourse to magical practitioners in times of illness because of their link with or subservience to Satan. Almost any Catholic demonologist would have been happy enough to agree with these proposals. But like Perreaud – and, indeed, like the majority of Protestant demonologists – Daneau is not laying out for his readers a distinctive Protestant explanation of magic or witchcraft. The confessional variances lie in the details and emphases, not in the principal thesis.[32]

Now, Daneau's particular thrust is made clear in his Latin title, translated as *Workers of Poisonous Magic, Once Called Diviners, but Now Commonly Known as Witches/Sorcerers*. The English version, produced in 1575, ignores *Venefici*, the key-word of the title: *A Dialogue of Witches, Aforetime Named Lot-tellers, and Now Commonly Called Sorcerers*; while the German version of 1576 is worse: *Von den Zauberern, Hexen, und Unholden*.[33] It is essential, as I pointed out earlier, not to reduce the variety of Latin terms for magical operators to a single word. Workers of poisonous magic were, by definition, people who used herbs, minerals, and other natural substances in combination with magical words and sometimes gestures either to produce a cure for an otherwise intractable illness, or to induce sickness or death in a human or animal. The physical components of such an operation might be dangerous; hence the possibility that they could kill, whether intentionally or not. A *veneficus* (feminine, *venefica*) was someone who employed these means. Such a person could be a witch, as defined by local or national statute, but equally she or he need not be. Hence it is very misleading to translate *veneficus* as 'witch' or 'sorcière'.

In this treatise, Daneau is obsessed with poisoning. The words *intoxicare* ('to poison') and *venenum* ('poisonous substance' and 'poisonous substance used in magic') appear constantly in his text once he gets down to the business of describing what these people do and how they do it. At the Sabbat, Satan gives them powders, roots and poisons so that they may avenge themselves secretly on those they hate, and 'so that they may poison anyone they please without anxiety or fear of retribution'.[34] He questions them 'so that he can find out from them how thoroughly and how diligently they have made use of his gifts of poisoning', and teaches them how to make and blend poisons for themselves.[35] They poison us subtly and secretly while we eat, drink and walk from one place to another.[36] Once imprisoned, however, witches cannot poison anyone, first, because they cannot readily lay their hands on their special poisons, and, second, because once in custody they dare not communicate with Satan who is at once their master in the art and their teacher.[37]

Magical poisoning, then, is the activity which concerns Daneau most and is the main thrust of his discourse, a point which is obscured by his own remarkable confusion over terminology. At the end of the preface, Antonius asks Theophilus to explain the meaning and etymology of the word *sortiarius*, and this Theophilus proceeds to do in chapter 1 which turns out to be a mishmash of misunderstanding flecked with apparent ignorance. *Sortiarius*, he says, is derived from *sortilegus* which refers to someone who foretells the future by throwing lots. So far so good, since both are related to the Latin *sors* meaning both 'lot' and 'divinatory response', and hence 'an individual's destiny'.[38] He then goes through the standard list of Greek, Hebrew and Latin terms for magicians, enchanters, diviners, astrologers and necromancers, not to mention stage illusionists and those with the evil eye (*fascinatores*), lumping them all together as *sortiarii* and as people who derive their power from their enslavement to Satan.

Antonius, however, interrupts to point out that he remembers his teacher telling him that *sortilegus* did not have the same meaning as *veneficus* – the first reference in this chapter to the magical poisoner of the title. Theophilus is therefore obliged to practise verbal sleight of hand.

> What you say is quite correct, Antonius; for if we want to be absolutely accurate, we ought not to call *sortiarii* [witches, sorcerers] *sortilegi* [diviners], but rather 'diabolical workers of poisonous magic' [*venefici*] and 'users of toxic substances' [*intoxicatores*]. But, you see, when they do harm in this fashion, they have learned how to do it from Satan himself; and they have entered into a pact with him, just as those earlier people known as *sortilegi* did: and they enslave themselves completely to Satan, just like the *sortilegi*. Now, what actually happened was, they were called *sortilegi* and *sortiarii* by a set of people not as careful or as scrupulous about words as we are, who used *sortilegi* and *sortiarii* to refer to those who make divination by lot under Satan's instruction, *and* to those who carry off both humans and animals by means of poison, with that very same Satan providing the toxic substances.[39]

This convenient slippage made, Theophilus/Daneau can then assume that the two terms are interchangeable and that other classical Latin words for 'witch/female operator of magic' – *saga, Thessala, lamia, strix* – all of which actually have distinct implications and nuances of their own, can be amalgamated with *venefica*. Antonius readily accepts this. 'Because we should be using common parlance [instead of Latin], let us call the Satanic workers of poisonous magic [*venefici*] *sortiarii*, and their administration of toxic substances "harmful magic" [*maleficium*].[40] At best this is intellectually slovenly, at worst dishonest, and one can comment only that Lewis Carroll seems to have had it right. 'When I use a word', Humpty Dumpty said, in a rather scornful tone, 'it means just what I choose it to mean – neither more nor less'.[41]

In sum, then, we may deduce that Catholic and Protestant writers on demonology were very alike. Each confession had its adherents and sceptics over various points, and both took for granted the reality of a preternatural world of non-human beings who were capable, with God's permission, of interfering in, modifying or changing the regular laws of nature. Each writer differs from the rest in the emphases he chooses to put on certain aspects of his subject-matter, and this he does in accordance with the motive which impelled him to write his treatise in the first place, and with the requirements of his personal side in confessional controversy. Protestant demonologies were thus no more 'rational' than their Catholic counterparts. It is the propagandistic element in their treatments of magic which have persuaded people otherwise – a neat example, in fact, of the way history has been rewritten, or at best re-emphasised, in cultures which adopted some form of Protestant faith and believed the eighteenth century when it told them that the (Catholic) Middle Ages were dark and superstitious, while the (Protestant/Deist) eighteenth century was 'enlightened' and rational.

NOTES

1 E. Owen, *Welsh Folk-Lore* (Oswestry and Wrexham, 1896), 245. R. Kvideland and H. K. Sehmsdorf, eds, *Scandinavian Folk Belief and Legend* (Oslo, 1991), 198–9. P. Joutard, 'Protestantisme populaire et univers magique: le cas cévenol', *Religion populaire: le Monde alpin et rhodanien* 5 (1977), 154.

2 S. Ozment, *The Reformation in the Cities* (New Haven, 1975), 94. L. J. Abray, *The People's Reformation: Magistrates, Clergy, and Commons in Strasbourg, 1500–1598* (Cornell, 1985), 82. R. Josselin, *Diary, 1616–1683*, ed. A. MacFarlane (Oxford, 1976), 132. The Second Prayer Book of the English king Edward VI included in the Litany a prayer for fair weather, which contains the supplication, 'We humbly beseche thee, that although we for our iniquities have worthely deserved this plague of rayne and waters, yet upon our true repentaunce thou wilt send us such weather whereby we may . . . learne . . . by this punishment to amende our lives, and for thy clemency to geve thee prayse and glory'.

3 M. Montaigne, *Œuvres complètes: Essais* (Paris, 1962), 1: 26 (p.156). St Bonaventure, *Life of Saint Francis*, in E. Cousins, trans., *Bonaventure* (London, 1978), 260–1. W. Behringer, *Witchcraft Persecutions in Bavaria* (Cambridge, 1997), 160, and compare 168–9. Witches (or perhaps one should say *tempestarii*) were regularly blamed for stirring up bad weather. See,

for example, Kramer and Sprenger, *Malleus Maleficarum*, pt 2: question 1, cap. 15. There were one or two sceptics – J. Wier, *De praestigiis daemonum* (Basil, n. pr., 1677), 3: cap. 16, for example – but they were a minority.

4 St Thomas Aquinas, *Expositio in Job* (Rome, n. pr., 1562), cap. 1: lectio 3. M. Luther, *In primum librum Mose enarrationes* (Nuremburg, Montanus, 1550), on Genesis 9: 16.

5 Martín Del Rio, *Disquisitiones Magicae* (Leiden, 1608), 1: cap. 3, quaestio 3. Luther, *Mose enarrationes* on Genesis 30: 39. Cf. A. E. Fife, 'Birthmarks and Psychic Imprinting of Babies in Utah Folk Medicine', in W. D. Hand, ed., *American Folk Medicine, A Symposium* (Berkeley, 1976), 273–83. Luther regarded severely-handicapped children as changelings, substituted by the devil for children created by God. His advice in one case was that the child be taken away and drowned, and then that it be exorcised by having the Lord's Prayer said over it daily in church until the evil spirit departed. See A. Jelsma, *Frontiers of the Reformation: Dissidence and Orthodoxy in Sixteenth-Century Europe* (Aldershot, 1998), 29; Wolffhart, cited in L. Daston and K. Park, *Wonders and the Order of Nature, 1150–1750* (New York, 1998), 183. Melanchthon and Boaistuau also cited in Daston and Park, *Wonders*, 188–9; Winthrop, see M. J. Westerkamp, *Women and Religion in Early America, 1600–1850* (London, 1999), 56–7.

6 On this point see further D. P. Walker, 'Demonic Possession Used as Propaganda in the Later 16th Century', in P. Rossi, ed., *Scienze, Credenze Occulte, Livelli di Cultura* (Florence, 1982): 237–48.

7 M. Luther, *Works*, ed. U. S. Leupold (Philadelphia, 1965), 55 vols. (1958–86), 53: 95–103, 106–9. The use of exorcism in baptism became a subject of controversy between Lutherans and Calvinists, the former talking in terms of heresy, the latter in terms of Catholic magic. See B. Nischan, 'The Exorcism Controversy and Baptism in the Late Reformation', *Sixteenth Century Journal* 18 (1987): 31–51. K. R. Sands, 'The Doctrine of Transubstantiation and the English Protestant Dispossession of Demons', *History* 85 (2000), 447–8, 461. Cf. S. Clark, *Thinking With Demons* (Oxford, 1997), 418: 'There was no bar to the use, among some Protestant communities, of exorcisms as elaborately figured as anything in the apocalyptic language of the Catholic manuals.'

8 P. Soergel, 'From Legends to Lies: Protestant Attacks on Catholic Miracles in Late Reformation Germany', *Fides et Historia* 21 (1989): 21–9. It is perhaps no accident that this tendency in Germany was stimulated by an exorcism held in Altötting in 1571. Cf. Richard Bovet, *Pandaemonium* (London, J. Walthoe, 1684), 89: 'Roman Miracles . . . are the effect of Diabolical Confederacies and Impostures.'

9 R. Willock, *A Shetland Minister of the Eighteenth Century* (Kirkwall, 1897), 90–2, 97–102.

10 A. Walsham: *Providence in Early Modern England* (Oxford, 1999), 225: 'By enhancing a doctrine of a vigilant and interventionist deity, Calvinist theology merely intensified a cluster of assumptions which had long been part of the machinery of pre-Reformation minds.'

11 Although parallelism there is a-plenty. Thus, to give only one example, Catholics had a crucifix which refused to be burned at the hands of Swedish soldiers during the Thirty Years' War, and Protestants an engraving of Luther, which emerged unharmed from a fire in the house wherein it was hanging in 1634; R. W. Scribner, 'Incombustible Luther: The Image of the Reformer in Early Modern Germany', *Past and Present* 110 (1986), 65, 38.

12 G. Zimmermann, 'Freiheit und Aberglaube in der Theologie des Genfer Reformators', in *Zwingliana* 21 (1994), 59–81. See also Walsham, *Providence*, 8–20. Curiously enough, German Reformed clergy often made use of astrology to project their teachings into the understanding of their flocks. See C. Scott Dixon, 'Popular Astrology and Lutheran Propaganda in Reformation Germany', *History* 84 (1999): 403–18. The peculiar frame of mind which providentialism could engender may be illustrated by Ralph Josselin: 'Stung I was with a bee on my nose. I presently pluckt out the sting, and layd on honey, so that my face swelled not. Thus divine providence reaches to the lowest things', ed. A. MacFarlane *Diary*, 19 (5 September, 1644). Cf. the report of an eighteenth-century missionary to India. 'Brother Carey, while very sea-sick, and leaning over the ship to relieve his stomach from that very oppressive complaint, said his mind was even then filled with consolation in

contemplating the wonderful goodness of God', quoted in Sydney Smith, *Works* (London, 1848), 3 vols, 3: 223–4. Note, too, the self-absorption which constant scrutiny of providence could produce. Richard Baxter, and English Puritan divine, interpreted the death of his wife, probably from cancer, as God's way of reminding him of his sins; see his *Autobiography* (London, 1974), 249.

13 SRO, JC (Records of the Court of High Justiciary in Edinburgh) 26/24: item 11 on the indictment. We have already noted the Welsh farmer who read from the family Bible to cure his sick cow. Cf. the recommendation to Welsh asthmatics that they put a Bible under their pillow for three successive nights in order to effect a cure, Owen, *Welsh Folk-Lore*, 267. Further examples of magical uses of the Bible by Protestants are given in K. Thomas, *Religion and the Decline of Magic* (London, 1971), 83, 123, 139, 254.

14 Thomas, *Religion*, 134–5. William Cramond, *Extracts from the Records of the Kirk Session of Elgin* (Elgin, 1897), 18 December 1745 and 16 August 1750. Walsh, *Providence*, 143–7.

15 In 1612, Agnes Wilson was accused of being a witch and was asked how many gods she acknowledged. 'Two,' she replied, 'God the Father and the Devil', cited in Thomas, *Religion*, 568.

16 This does not mean that either Catholic or Protestant demonologists were necessarily unanimous with their fellows in points of controversial explication. Denial of such key concepts in witchcraft theory such as the devil's mark or the reality of witches' flight to the Sabbat, for example, could be, and indeed were made by both sides. I note only a general tendency in their works.

17 F. Perreaud, *Demonologie* and *L'Antidemon de Mâcon* (Geneva, P. Aubert, 1653).

18 'Ce mot Diable est un mot collectif', Perreaud, *Demonologie*, 16.

19 The most obvious Catholic parallel is contained in the tenth-century *Canon Episcopi* which maintained that women who believed they flew through the air with the pagan goddess Diana were suffering from illusions caused by evil spirits.

20 Cf. Del Rio who prefaced his *Disquisitiones Magicae* with a prologue explaining that the pride and malice of God's enemies were increasing, and that evil spirits were on the loose, seeking to take possession of foolish, deluded souls. Del Rio attributes this on the one hand to weakness of faith among Catholics and on the other to the spreading of heresy, especially in Germany, France and Britain.

21 Girolamo Menghi, *Fustis Daemonum* (Bologna, Giovanni Rossi, 1584), cap. 17.

22 Lazare Meysonnier, a doctor in Mâcon, included an account of Perreaud's experience in his introduction to his translation of Della Porta's *Magia Naturalis* (Lyon, P. Compagnon, 1650), 12–18. This was very much more theatrical than Perreaud's own version. See further E. Labrousse, *Conscience et conviction, études sur le XVIIe siècle* (Oxford, 1996), 36.

23 See *Arminian Magazine* 7 (1784), 548–50, 606–8, 654–6.

24 In spite of (or perhaps because of) official prohibition, books, songs and pamphlets about witches and magic as a whole exercised a continuing fascination over the general public. See Abray, *The People's Reformation*, 171–2.

25 L. Daneau, *De veneficiis* (Geneva, Eustace Vignon, 1574).

26 Daneau, *De veneficiis*, 378.

27 The English demonologists Scot and Gifford regarded the flight as illusory. James VI and I, on the other hand, was undecided.

28 There is a translation of the relevant passage in P. G. Maxwell-Stuart, *The Occult in Early Modern Europe* (Basingstoke, 1999), 173–4.

29 Daneau, *De veneficiis*, 390.

30 Daneau, *De veneficiis*, 388.

31 Daneau, *De veneficiis*, 397.

32 With the occasional side-swipe at the opposite confession. Daneau's treatise is largely free of this; even so, he cannot resist a sneer at the Jesuit Juan de Maldonado whom he criticises, not for delivering a public lecture on demonology, but for 'discoursing upon this topic in such a laboured fashion that he made his audience sick, in spite of the fact that they had been very eager to hear him on the subject', 379.

33 The French title of 1579 merely gives us *Deux traitez nouveaux, tres-utiles pour ce temps. Entretien sur les malefices et Traité des sorciers* (Frankurt, Jacques Baumet, 1579); *Von den Zauberern* (Cologne, J. Gymnicus, 1576); *A Dialogue of Witches* (London, Watkins, 1575).

34 Daneau, *De veneficiis*, 388.

35 Daneau, *De veneficiis*, 389.

36 Daneau, *De veneficiis*, 398. Putting magical devices on the lintel of a door or under its threshold so that anyone passing under or over them would be trapped and affected by the bewitchment was a common device of malefice. Witches attempting to murder James VI of Scotland, for example, tried to have toad-poison, magically enhanced in power, placed in just such a position that it would drip upon the King's head as he walked beneath it.

37 Daneau, *De veneficiis*, 395.

38 Del Rio pointed out that *sortiarius* was a late mediaval derivation based upon 'sortilegus', *Disquisitiones Magicae*, 1: cap. 2.

39 Daneau, *De veneficiis*, 381.

40 Daneau, *De veneficiis*, 381.

41 The Protestant Wier is not so cavalier. His preferred word for 'witch' is *lamia*, *De praestigiis daemonum*, 3: cap. 1, although he discusses other Latin terms accurately enough, and he keeps *veneficus/venefica* separate (2: cap.1). Del Rio, on the other hand, is inclined to use *strix* or *saga*. His discussion of Latin, Greek and Hebrew terms for magical practitioners is, as one might expect, both learned and reliable (*Disquisitiones Magicae*, 1: cap. 2, n. 28). Jean Bodin does not engage in this kind of disquisition but, writing in the vernacular, defines 'witch' (*sorcier*) as 'someone who knowingly tries to accomplish something by diabolical means', *Démonomanie des sorciers* (Rouen, n. pr., 1604), 1: cap. 1. The Protestant Reginald Scot, on the other hand, does not try to define the word 'witch' but tells us that witches are silly, old, superstitious women who are also Catholics, *Discoverie of Witchcraft* (London, W. Brome, 1584), 1: cap. 3.

9

Deceptive appearances: ghosts and reformers in Elizabethan and Jacobean England

PETER MARSHALL

Over the two generations or so during which the Protestant Settlement of 1559 put down roots in English society, few issues seemed to reformers to epitomise so clearly the link between the Catholics' false doctrine and their degenerate superstitious devotion, as belief in the appearance of ghosts. Associated indelibly with the abrogated teachings on purgatory and intercessory masses, stories about ghosts encapsulated the ignorance, credulity and corruption of papists, whereas the rejection of them by Protestants was symptomatic of a sober, scriptural faith. In a sermon of 1552, Robert King contrasted the spirit, which relies on the unadorned Word of God, with the flesh which 'sekethe the trueth at the deade . . . geveth credite to spirites'.[1] The Jacobean bishop, Thomas Morton, argued that Romanists displayed an 'infatuation' with 'ghostly apparitions, which Protestants dare not beleeve', making them 'speciall grounds for the defence of their doctrines of Purgatorie, power of *Indulgences*, and . . . praier for the dead'.[2] That Catholic authorities habitually and promiscuously appealed to the authority of ghosts to prop up their imaginary purgatory was a recurrent refrain throughout the period.[3] Indeed, it was commonly asserted that a belief in ghosts was not some waste-product of the popish Purgatory, but the foundation of the whole edifice. In a sermon of 1564, the bishop of London, Edmund Grindal, alleged that the doctrine of Purgatory was 'maintained principally by feigned apparitions'.[4] To the Elizabethan preacher Henry Smith, it was notorious that 'they had never heard of Purgatorie, but for these spirites which walked in the night, and tolde them that they were the soules of such and such, which suffred in fire till their masses, and almes, and pilgrimages did raunsome them out'.[5]

Small wonder then, that in his magisterial survey of popular belief in early modern England, Sir Keith Thomas asserted that belief in ghosts was 'a shibboleth which distinguished Protestant from Catholic almost as effectively as belief in the Mass or the Papal Supremacy'. He went on to suggest that in the first century of the Reformation, ghosts 'presented no problems' to reformers, who knew exactly what they thought about them.[6] Yet the emphasis in this

chapter will be on ghosts as a distinctly problematic feature in the mental landscape of late-sixteenth and early-seventeenth-century English Protestantism. I
will argue that the intellectual rationalisation of ghostly experience was a
somewhat uncertain exercise, which threatened to expose tensions within
English Protestantism, and also that teaching the people about the nature of
apparitions posed pastoral problems of considerable magnitude. It will further
be argued that in engaging with these problems in a variety of genres and contexts, English Protestant writers sometimes remained closer to traditional
ways of thinking than they would have cared to recognise.

In their efforts to discredit popish visions of the dead, Protestant authors
instinctively turned, not to reason but to Scripture. While a huge array of texts
could be deployed against Purgatory, there were fewer places in the Bible that
seemed to have specific application to the question of ghosts. Mention was frequently made of the warnings to the Israelites in Deuteronomy and Isaiah not to
consult with the dead, but only two proof-texts were construed at any length,
one Old Testament, and one New.[7] The latter was the parable of the rich man
and Lazarus in Luke 16. The rich man in hell spies Lazarus afar off in 'the bosom
of Abraham', and pleads with Abraham to send Lazarus to his father's house to
warn his five brothers of the fate awaiting them if they do not mend their ways.
Abraham replies that they have Moses and the prophets, and that if they will
not listen to them they would not repent even if one were to rise from the
dead. Here surely was an unambiguous assertion of the primacy of the word of
scripture as the sole source of revelation, over visions, apparitions and human
traditions. In the words of the Elizabethan bishop of Exeter, William Alley, 'by
this place it is most certaine, and evidently confuted that the soules have not,
nor can not appeare after their death'.[8] A series of sermons on the rich man and
Lazarus by the Jacobean preacher Robert Horne concluded that 'the doctrine of
teaching man, by men from the dead, is a doctrine from hell'.[9]

More widely canvassed than the Lazarus parable, however, was a passage
which was, from the Protestant point of view, rather less straightforward: the
account in the first book of Samuel of Saul's encounter with the Witch of
Endor, describing how Saul had asked God how he would fare in battle with the
Philistines, and the Lord declining to answer him, how he had turned to 'a
woman that hath a familiar spirit'. The witch then summoned up the spirit of
the dead prophet Samuel, who correctly foretold Saul's imminent death. Aside
from the miracles associated directly with Christ, this was the sole instance of
the appearance of a dead soul attested to in Scripture – a text that, as the bishop
of Winchester, Thomas Bilson, put it in 1599, 'hath moved much question in
the church of God, whether it were *Samuel* in deede that rose and spake, or
whether it were the divell transforming himselfe into the likenesse of *Samuel* to
drive *Saul* into dispaire'.[10] With some qualifications, the former interpretation

was upheld by Catholic exegesis.[11] Bilson, along with virtually all shades of opinion in the Church of England, insisted on the latter. Thus in marginal annotations to verse 14 – 'And Saul perceived that it was Samuel' – both the Geneva and Bishops' Bibles had, 'To his imagination, albeit it was Sathan in dede'.[12] As William Perkins helpfully explained, Scripture often speaks of things 'not as they are in themselves, but as they seeme to us'.[13] The delusion was called Samuel, explained Henry Smith, 'as the Bookes of Calvin are called Calvine . . . as he that playeth the King upon a stage, is called a King'.[14] There were numerous reasons why the apparition could not be the soul of the prophet: the souls of the dead are at rest; the Lord had refused to answer Saul by 'ordinary means'; the true Samuel would have reproved Saul for resorting with witches, and could not have prophesied that Saul (a reprobate) would be with him the next day.[15] Moreover, commentators noted that Saul had bowed down before the apparition: a true prophet would not have suffered himself to be worshipped, whereas Satan desires his followers 'to adore him as a God'.[16] To Protestants, the message of I Samuel 28 was clear: it provided a confutation, in the words of the Coventry minister, Thomas Cooper, of 'that which the *Church of Rome* doates concerning the *walking of dead men*'.[17] It was also, suggested Perkins, a caveat 'not easily to give credit to any such apparitions. For though they seeme never so true and evident, yet such is the power and skill of the devill, that he can quite deceive us'.[18]

Yet the text used to establish this point was itself an ambivalent and potentially deceptive one. In the first place, Catholic controversialists could point out that another book of the Bible, Ecclesiasticus, asserted unambiguously that Samuel prophesied after his death.[19] To Protestants, of course, Ecclesiasticus was not a canonical book, and therefore open to relativist readings. 'Most Jews of those times did imagin ther might be some conference with spirits and soules of men', remarked Henry Holland, and the congruence of Catholic and Jewish superstition about ghosts was itself a polemical trope.[20] Yet the Book of Common Prayer sanctioned the use of apocryphal books in public worship – a source of irritation and embarrassment to some Protestants. In December 1584 the issue was raised at a conference at Lambeth between Archbishop Whitgift and the puritans Thomas Sparke and Walter Travers. Whitgift was compelled to admit that the relevant chapter of Ecclesiasticus was appointed to be read in church, prompting Lord Grey to ask 'what error the people might be in daunger to learne by the hearing of this read, and by believing of it?' To this, in Travers's account, the archbishop had no satisfactory answer.[21]

At much the same time a yet more unsettling interpretative trajectory from I Samuel was discharging from the pen of Reginald Scot, whose interpretation of the incident in his *Discoverie of Witchcraft* shockingly broke ranks with the orthodox Protestant one in arguing that there was no manifestation of the devil, but merely 'an illusion or cousenage practised by the witch'. 'Samuel' was an accomplice kept in the witch's closet, whose prophecies were provided by the ventriloquist skills of the witch herself 'speaking as it were from the bottome of hir bellie.' In an objection remarkably similar to those made by Catholic commentators, Scot argued that 'if it had beene a divell, the text would have noted it in the same place of the storie'.[22] Scot's scepticism about the appearance of the devil was crucial to his argument that witches had no real power to harness or channel the powers of Satan. This was the central theme of his *Discoverie*, in which ghosts *per se* play a merely subsidiary role. Nonetheless, he had little hesitation in applying the template generally: 'in all ages moonks and preests have abused and bewitched the world with counterfet visions'. The biblical prohibitions on seeking counsel of the dead, or attempting to raise them, did not signify that these things were possible, but that 'men beleeve they doo them, and thereby cousen the people . . . some one knave in a white sheete hath cousened and abused manie thousands that waie'.[23] Scot's thoroughgoing scepticism about the intervention of any supernatural forces in the world made him pretty much unique among contemporary authors.[24] Nonetheless, there were echoes of his attitude towards ghosts in later texts, most notably Samuel Harsnett's *Declaration of Egregious Popish Impostures* (1603), which argued that 'all these brainlesse imaginations of . . . house-hanting and the rest, were the forgeries, cosenages, Imposturs, and legerdemaine of craftie priests and leacherous Friers'.[25] Harsnett's fellow bishop, Gervase Babington, accepted that devils might assume the shape of the deceased, but laid greater emphasis on the 'many a thousand times' that 'false iuggling hypocrites abused Gods people to establish their idolatry, superstition and error'.[26] There was a considerable tradition to draw on here. Fraudulent apparitions had featured in Erasmus's *Colloquies*, and monkish tricks of this sort were enthusiastically exposed by continental writers such as Johan Weyer and Ludwig Lavater.[27] Even the Catholic writers Pierre Le Loyer and Noel Taillepied accepted that many apparitions were the product of human ingenuity, albeit of youthful practical jokers, not priests.[28]

If for Scot the encounter between Saul and the Witch of Endor was the pattern and precursor of popish knavery, for many other Protestants it was no less than the archetype of demonic witchcraft. It is a measure of how corrosive Scot's theory was to the prosecution of witchcraft, that over the succeeding decades English demonological writers turned repeatedly to attack the idea of 'a meere cosenage of the witch'.[29] If the one scripturally attested ghost was in fact the devil, then it followed that subsequent appearances served an explicitly Satanic agenda. Here indeed the devil took a more direct and personal role than in any other manifestation of popish superstition, he, or his demons, taking on 'the similitude of some person, that was lately, or had been long dead' to deceive the ignorant.[30] Deuteronomy 18: 10–11 seemed to identify seeking counsel of the dead as a species of witchcraft, and while 'necromancy' in this period served as a loose synonym for demonic magic of all sorts, in the taxonomies elaborated by Elizabethan and Jacobean demonologists, it retained its specific sense of a means of divining by attempting illicit communication with the dead.[31] To some, I Samuel 28 was the key unlocking the pattern of demonic heresy underpinning popish devotions. That Saul had worshipped the apparition was particularly significant. As perhaps the most potent symbol of the inversion of all right religion, idolatry firmly fixed the link between feigned ghosts, demonic witchcraft and superstitious popish practice. In the influential *Christian Disputations* of the Swiss reformer, Pierre Viret, translated into English in 1579, it is the ultimate indictment of Catholicism that it had

> set up & erected a necrolatrie . . . an adoration and worshipping of the dead, and the most greatest Idolatrie that ever was upon the earth: And have made the bodies of men to serve ye divell, & have made him to be worshiped, under the name and title of them, even as Saul worshiped him under the name of Samuel.[32]

The theories that visitations of ghosts were elaborate frauds perpetrated by avaricious priests, and that they were personal appearances by the devil or one of his minions, were by no means mutually exclusive. Thomas Beard, for example, argued that all the 'strange stories . . . touching walking ghosts' found in old popish books fell into one of two categories: 'eyther they were jugling tricks of imposters to deceive the simple, or deceits of devils to delude the learned'.[33] Another Jacobean writer equally hedged his bets: 'if they be not popish which make such false apparitions for gaines sake, they are certain evil spirits'.[34] In a sermon preached at St Mary's in Cambridge towards the end of James I's reign, Robert Jenison similarly asserted that many apparitions were fained popish miracles, but that 'many also have the devill, who is false and a lier, for the chiefe author of them; by which, the supposed miracle-workers his instruments, doe not only delude others, but are deluded themselves'.[35] Papists were thus both perpetrators and victims of the delusions and falsehoods which apparitions fathered upon the world. In Elizabethan and Jacobean England, therefore, ghosts validated a spectrum of anti-Catholic views. To some they did no more than epitomise the credulity and knavery of papists, though to others they conveyed more transcendent meanings. Papist endorsement of demonic apparitions (starting with that of 'feigned Samuel') could slot effortlessly into that system of antithesis, contrariety and inversion which permeated early modern intellectual thought, and by which popish religion as a whole could come to be associated with the anti-type of God, Satan, and with Satan's worship on earth, witchcraft.[36] As the puritan Richard Bernard remarked in 1627, Satan is ever ready 'to further popish Idolatry', and 'sorcery is the practice of that

whore, the Romish synagogue'.[37] A rather different conclusion was drawn, however, in one of John Donne's sermons of the same year, finding connections
between 'the easiness of admitting Revelations . . . and Apparitions of spirits,
and Purgatory souls' by papists on the one hand, and the 'super-exaltation of
zeale, and . . . captivity to the private spirit' characteristic of schismatics on the
other.[38] Echoes of a conformist anti-Puritan rhetoric are also audible among the
anti-Catholic trumpetings of Harsnett's *Declaration of Egregious Popish Impostures*.[39]

   Ghosts were thus a very multivocal instrument of theological controversy
and polemic. But on this issue reformers could not simply face backwards
towards the repudiated popish past, or outwards, towards Rome and the folly
(or heresy) of her doctrines and adherents. Their gaze was also of necessity
drawn inwards, on to the church and people of Protestant England. What was
the meaning of appearances of 'dead souls' in an England which had abandoned
Purgatory and intercession, what were the people to be taught regarding them,
and what did the alleging of such apparitions say about the progress of godly
reformation itself? From one perspective it could seem that these were questions
which did not demand anguished or extended answers. One recurrent theme of
English Protestant writing about ghosts was that they were simply no longer a
problem, part of the superstitious dross which had clogged up the house of English Christianity, but had now been swept out by the new broom of the Gospel.
This opinion was voiced as early as 1543 by the Henrician reformer, Robert
Wisdom, who asserted that 'sowles departed do not come again and play boo
peape with us', adding that 'thankes to god, ever since the word of god cam in
thei be nether herd nor senne'.[40] Under Elizabeth, a number of authorities were
keen to confirm Archbishop Sandys's emphatic assurance that 'the gospel hath
chased away walking spirits'.[41] The theme was a recurrent one of Lavater's ghost
treatise: 'there were farre more of these kindes of apparitions and myracles seen
amongest us, at such tyme as we were given unto blindnesse and superstition . . .
The clere light of Gods word driveth away al such spirits.'[42] Unsurprisingly, one
of the most emphatic assertions that ghosts were now an infrequent occurrence
came from Reginald Scot. Thanks to the preaching of the Gospel, the sighting of
apparitions was much reduced, and would shortly vanish away completely. In
Germany, he reported on good authority, spirits had ceased to appear since the
time of Luther. In distinctly triumphalist mode, Scot propounded that

> through ignorance of late in religion, it was thought, that everie churchyard
> swarmed with soules and spirits: but now the word of God being more free, open,
> and knowne, those conceipts and illusions are made more manifest and apparent
> . . . Where are the soules that swarmed in times past? Where are the spirits? Who
> heareth their noises? Who seeth their visions? Where are the soules that made
> such mone for trentals, whereby to be eased of the paines in purgatorie? Are they
> all gone into Italie, bicause masses are growne deere here in England?[43]

Scot was again echoed here by Samuel Harsnett, who scoffed that in the time of 'popish mist' children, old women and maids were afraid to cross a churchyard, and if tithes or Peter's Pence were unpaid 'people walked in fear of spirits'.[44] The claim that ghosts were more usual when popery held sway was made by other early Stuart anti-Catholic writers, including John Donne, Richard Bernard and Edward Hoby, the latter referring contemptuously to those night-ghosts 'which the world hath now for many yeares since forgotten to believe'.[45]

The question of whether apparitions were more common in 1500 than in 1600 unfortunately does not lend itself to any kind of meaningful historical analysis. The vanishing of spirits was in any case less an empirical observation than a rhetorical and polemical trope in the campaign against Catholicism. In other contexts, Protestant writers were quite ready to affirm that popular belief in ghosts was far from moribund. In 1571, for example, the preacher John Northbrooke insisted that souls 'wander not abroade as foolishly is furnished.'[46] Such admonitions against superstitious survivalist beliefs were to be expected in the early years of Elizabeth's reign, but in fact they supplied a constant refrain throughout the period, a range of divines attributing belief in the apparition of souls to 'the unskilled multitude', 'the simple people', 'the common people' and 'many ignorant persons among us', finding it 'still in the mouth and faith of credulous superstition at this day'.[47] In the theophrastic dialogues beloved of puritan writers, bucolic characters are sometimes made to confess their desire to communicate directly with the dead. In Jean Veron's *The Huntyng of Purgatorye to Death*, Dydimus, 'a poore simple and ignoraunt person', confesses that he does not know what to think about Purgatory 'except peradventure, I shoulde chaunce too mete with some of those spirits & soules, which (as our priests wil make folkes to believe) arte wont to appeare after their deathe, for to crave good deedes'.[48] Four decades later, in Arthur Dent's dialogue *The Plaine Man's Pathway to Heaven*, the character of Antilegon refuses to accept assurances about the small number of the elect unless 'there should come two soules, one from heaven, and another from hell, and bring us certaine newes how the case stood'.[49]

Didymus and Antilegon were of course straw men, literary stereotypes whose dialectical function was to underscore true doctrine by articulating objections that could easily be dismissed. Taking Protestant writing on ghosts as a whole, however, it seems fairly clear that in expressing concerns about popular beliefs, many authors were not merely constructing an artificial 'other', an inversion of orthodoxy whose postulation provided the logical and philosophical basis for their own attitudes. Rather, they were speaking to and from experience, and directly confronting a pastoral reality. Underpinning the ghost treatise of the Swiss reformer, Ludwig Lavater, was the conviction that 'daily experience teacheth us that spirits do appear to men'.[50] His translator, Robert

Harrison, justified turning the treatise into English on the basis of pressing pastoral need. Not only were there still superstitious persons who had been taught to believe that 'mens soules returne agayne on earth, cravyng helpe of the lyvyng', but there were also those 'otherwise well trayned up in religion' whose views on this issue were confused and uncertain, and did not conform to those of orthodox Protestantism. Like Lavater, Harrison confirmed that 'there be many also, even nowe a dayes, which are haunted and troubled with spirites'.[51] Reginald Scot found it bitterly ironic that while his contemporaries gave no credit to tales of Purgatory souls wandering the earth in puruit of trentals and masses, 'we thinke soules and spirits may come out of heaven or hell, and assume bodies'.[52]

Some leading reformers could confirm from first-hand experience that this was the case. In around 1564 Bishop Pilkington of Durham wrote to Archbishop Parker about events at Blackburn, where a young man had been conversing with a neighbour who died four years before. The curate, schoolmaster and other neighbours had seen the apparition also, and Pilkington despairingly commented that 'these things be so common here, and none of authority that will gainsay it, but rather believe and confirm it, that every one believes it'.[53] Despite (or perhaps because of) this unsettling experience, Pilkington does not seem to have been impelled to consider ghosts at any length in his writings. But some who went into print on the question clearly did so in response to actual sightings or affirmations among their parishioners. In a 1581 treatise, the puritan minister Anthony Anderson included a long discursus 'beating down to death this error . . . that the soules of the dead depart not so from us, but that after buryall they walke in the earth, and appeare unto men'. His motive for doing so was that even as he composed the work 'a most slanderous report is raysed of an honest and vertuous Minister departed this lyfe, that hys soule nowe walketh at this daye in his Parsonage house'.[54] In a printed funeral sermon of 1619, John Preston took occasion to reprove the 'many who affirme that they have seene and heard dead men to walke and talke, to frequent their premises, and to say, I am the soule of this man, or of that woman'.[55] Preachers sometimes imaginatively anticipated (or perhaps echoed) the scepticism of the people towards orthodox Protestant interpretations. 'Thou wilt say', remarked Anderson, 'what shall we say to this, there is much iumblyng in suche a house, and there is seene lyvely such a man walke before us, whome we cannot but say to be our friend departed, to all our sences judgement.' 'How then?', ventriloquised Henry Smith, 'what is this which I see in the night like such a man, and such a man?'[56] Asked by a parishioner if spirits might haunt a house, the renowned Elizabethan pastor Richard Greenham replied that it was possible, but that 'it is not undoubtedly the soule of any departed'.[57]

Some reformers made serious efforts not merely to denounce, but to explain to the laity why apparitions could not be the souls of the dead. Smith patiently expostulated that such an entity could not be a soul, since souls are spirits and by definition invisible. Nor could it be a body, since a body cannot walk without a soul, and a look in the grave of a dead man would confirm his body to be still there. In short, the apparitions of the age were none other than that which appeared to Saul, a dangerous delusion of the devil 'to draw us from the word of God, to visions, & dreams, and apparitions, upon which manie of the doctrines of the papists are grounded'.[58] In his *Exposition of the Catholike Faith*, Gervase Babington proceeded in a similarly syllogistic fashion. Such spirits could not come from hell, whence there is no escape, and if they came from heaven, 'who should send them there hence to wander on earth?' Not the devil, who has no rule in heaven; nor God 'for he hath thousands of Angels to doe his will'. If the dead could return of their own volition, they would seek to be with us always 'they being not now deprived of love, and become cruel'. Like other commentators, Babington cited Augustine's remark that if the dead were able to return his loving mother Monica would never have left him alone.[59]

Protestant preachers and writers could thus with great confidence and clarity tell people what ghosts were not — they were not the souls of dead persons returning from heaven, hell or a non-existent Purgatory. Rather more problematic was the task of accounting for what they actually were, and about this there was no certainty or infallible test. Very commonly, of course, ghosts were supposed to be devils, but this was not the only theory canvassed. Nor was it always clear with what aims and by whose authority such devils operated on earth. In the process of telling the people what to think about ghostly apparitions, reformers were working it out for themselves, and they adumbrated a number of overlapping interpretative models.

To begin with the most esoteric of contemporary speculations, some reformers showed an awareness of the theory, propagated by the Renaissance magus Cornelius Agrippa, that apparitions of the dead represented a kind of temporary and natural projection from the body of the deceased, though they generally did so only to reject it.[60] Ironically, here the postulations of learned natural magic may have coincided with a long-standing popular intuition that the souls of the dead lurked for a transitional period near the places where they had been buried.[61] For neither reason did the idea recommend itself to the proponents of godly reformation. The explanation which some Protestants had used to account for the proliferation of visions and apparitions in medieval times, namely that they were frauds engineered by the duplicity of popish clergy, obviously had more limited application after Elizabeth's accession, though it was still periodically trotted out. A 1582 tract by Barnaby Rich described how a teenager in Flintshire 'had been seduced by a ronegate priest, and how by his instructions she had feined to see certain visions' including that of a recently deceased local girl.[62] In 1624, the pamphleteer John Gee accused the Jesuits of faking two recent ghostly appearances in London, for the purpose of conning gullible women to part with their fortunes and enter nunneries. One of the victims reportedly told Gee that she thought 'some of those things could not be done without witchcraft, or some strange helpe by the devill', but Gee's own conclusion was that the apparitions were 'some iugling tricke', adding sarcastically that 'apparitions from the dead might be seen farre cheaper at other Play-houses. As for example, the Ghost in Hamlet, Don Andreas Ghost in Hieronimo'.[63] The Jesuits, however, could not plausibly be blamed for all the walking spirits infesting Protestant England.

One rather different approach to the problem was to imply that many of these were not true apparitions at all, but rather the product of timorousness, over-active imaginations and that characteristic Elizabethan malady, melancholy. It was a cliché of contemporary commentators on spectres and apparitions, English and continental, that the groups most likely to believe they had seen a ghost were melancholics, madmen, cowards, those with guilty consciences, the sick, the aged, children, women (especially menstruating women).[64] As Babington remarked, 'many times the corrupt humours that are in our heads will make us thinke we see formes, and faces and shapes and shadowes that indeed are not at all there'.[65] Scot had put it more bluntly: on a dark night 'a polled sheepe is a perillous beast, and many times is taken for our fathers soule'.[66] There was, however, no necessary and intrinsic contradiction, and certainly no hard and fast dividing line, between the idea of subjective illusion and that of objective delusion, between 'natural' and 'supernatural' explanations for the phenomenon of ghosts. Melancholics, like sinners and papists, were expected targets for the devil to insinuate himself upon, a truism reflected in contemporary theories of suicide, as well as in Hamlet's poignant concern that the devil 'out of my weakness and my melancholy – as he is very potent with such spirits – abuses me to damn me'.[67] The *locus classicus* of early modern treatments of melancholia, Robert Burton's *The Anatomy of Melancholy*, cited it as axiomatic that 'melancholy men are most subject to diabiolical temptations and illusions, and most apt to entertain them'.[68]

If the overwhelming consensus of commentators was that at least a proportion of apparitions possessed some kind of objective reality, did it follow that they were necessarily evil? As Michael MacDonald has observed, 'Elizabethans believed that the world was vibrant with supernatural forces and invisible beings'.[69] Many of these beings were God's servants, the angels; might they not on occasion manifest themselves visibly for the furtherance of God's purposes? The possibility was admitted by the pre-eminent Protestant ghost authority of the age, Ludwig Lavater. Lavater began his treatise observing that spirits were 'not the souls of dead men . . . but either good or evill Angels', and he went on firmly to maintain that good angels sometimes appear. But Lavater was also quick to insist that since all that was necessary for salvation was contained in the Word of God, 'good angels appeare to us more seldom in this oure tyme'.[70] Indeed, a number of Protestants raised the possibility of angels appearing in bodily form only immediately to dash it. Predictably perhaps, Reginald Scot took this view: the age of miracles was past, and God no longer sent his 'visible angels'.[71] But Scot was here in good company. Elizabethan England's leading theologian, William Perkins, was of the opinion that angels 'appeare not nowe as in former times'.[72] The king of Scots agreed. In his *Daemonologie*, James denied that angels could appear in the forms of dead men, and insisted that 'since the comming of Christ in the flesh, and establishing of his Church by the Apostles, all miracles, visions, prophecies, & appearances of Angels or good spirites are ceased'.[73]

Despite this authoritative testimony, however, the issue was not a closed one in James's English Kingdom, as events at Hidnam House near Launceston in Cornwall make clear. The divine Daniel Featley was here house-guest to Sir Thomas Wise, who sounded him out on 'the truth of apparitions . . . and notes of difference betweene good angels and bad', and then confessed that about a month earlier his household had been haunted. A ghostly vision of a woman appeared in the bed-chamber of his maids, who told their master 'they were frighted with a walking spirit'. Sir Thomas initially dismissed this as 'vaine fancy of womanly feare', but the following night the apparition appeared in his own chamber, standing at the foot of his bed for half an hour before gradually vanishing. Wise, previously 'ever of the opinion that there were no such apparitions', had by his own account behaved in an exemplary Protestant fashion, praying fervently, confessing his heinous and grievous sins, and charging the apparition 'in the name of the God of heaven to come no nearer'. After the event he sought the counsel of an archdeacon who pronounced it 'an angellical apparition and not a diabolicall illusion', on the grounds that it did him no hurt, that he had the power to speak to it, and that it had appeared in white and shining raiment. Featley, however, judged 'rather it was an evill spirit'; firstly because 'miraculous revelations and angelicall apparitions are ceased', but also because an angel would have delivered a message, and because it was unheard of for an angel to appear in the form of a woman. He advised Sir Thomas not to enquire curiously about the apparition, 'but to examine his owne conscience, and give God thanks for his deliverance'.[74]

The Hidnam haunting opens for us a range of perspectives on the same event: that of the terrified servants, of the educated Protestant layman (Sir Thomas), and of the learned divines he consulted about the affair. Even when the latter had had their say, the happening remained numinous and uncertain.

The remaining part of this chapter will attempt to explore how cultural constructions of the ghost in Protestant England were refracted through dialogues between elite and popular culture (albeit less literal ones than at Hidnam) and how in the process traditional ideas helped to shape, and to some extent mitigate the demonic apparition of Protestant orthodoxy.

An essential point of departure here is the recognition that to Protestants, no less than to Catholics, ghostly apparitions might serve didactic and exemplary purposes. It is revealing that Featley's final advice to Sir Thomas was 'to sinne no more, lest a worse thing befell him'.[75] It was a commonplace of Protestant rhetoric that the devil and his minions 'can do us no harme . . . excepte God give them leave thereto', and that they might on occasion be directly employed to execute the judgements of God.[76] Ghosts, therefore, might be subsumed into that mind-set of providentialism, which, as Alexandra Walsham has demonstrated, saturates the discourses of early modern England.[77] This could lead to the expression of a certain amount of ambivalence about the status and nature of ghosts, even in rather surprising places. In the 1563 edition of his *Acts and Monuments*, for example, John Foxe retold a story from the medieval chronicle of Mathew Paris. Innocent IV had excommunicated the bishop of Lincoln, Robert Grosseteste, for rebuking the pope's corruption, and two years after his death, the bishop appeared in the night to Innocent and beat him up with his staff. In the second, 1570 edition, Foxe repeated the story, though this time adding 'a note to the reader concerning the appearing of dead men' to the effect that though images of things unseen through the permission of God can come to men in their sleep, 'certaine it is, that no dead man materially can ever rise againe, or appeare, before the judgement day'.[78] Despite this delayed disclaimer, the moral and dramatic force of the story clearly lay in the idea of the dead as instruments of God's justice avenging wrongs committed against themselves, an idea commonly found in the popular sermon collections of the late middle ages.[79] A 1581 pamphlet by the moralist Philip Stubbes told a similar, if more homely cautionary tale. An avaricious Leicestershire woman, who refused to remit the debt of a dying poor man, was visited by the devil in the guise of the pauper, who struck her and turned her body black as pitch.[80] Stubbes at least proposed that the visitant was the devil in appropriate disguise. The issue was less clear-cut in another providential pamphlet, *A Strange and Fearful Warning to all Sonnes and Executors* (1623). As the title suggests, this concerned a dutiless son, the heir of John Barefoote, a tailor of Sunning in Wiltshire, who held back legacies intended for his sisters. In consequence his house and belongings were wrecked by a poltergeist until he finally relented. In rehearsing these events, the pamphlet displayed considerable ambiguity about the identity of the supernatural force at work. It is described initially as the work of the devil and an 'evil spirit', but later as 'Gods Angel and no evill'.

Moreover, the author reported that certain children of the town had seen old Barefoote 'walke in the churchyard in a most strange and fearefull manner'. The pamphlet offered the convoluted hypothesis that

> it may be, that they might see some vision or representation of him, for some spirit (through Gods sufferance) might assume an apparant likeness of him: a thing only appointed to make men know and beleeve, that he was shewed in the likenesse of a Spirit, as a cause of all these present evils, in regard that he being wronged, that all these things (for his sake) happened to the wronger.[81]

Remarkably, there were some Protestant tellers of providentialist anecdotes who did not even go this far in conforming to orthodox doctrine about the spirits of the dead. A work by the Scottish writer, David Person, published in London in 1635, unselfconsciously related the tale of a man who broke his promise to bury his wife in the churchyard. As a result, 'this woman's ghost . . . did so incessantly both haunt and affright, both him, his children, and family, that there was no resting for them at any time'.[82]

In these exemplary cases of spirits (in the likeness of identifiable dead individuals) haunting malefactors of various kinds, it is possible to see Protestantism involved in a kind of dialogue with more perdurable elements of popular beliefs about the behaviour and rationale of ghosts. This is a pattern for which we have been prepared by the work of Walsham on providential literature more generally, of Peter Lake on murder pamphlets, and of Tessa Watt on cheap print and godly ballads.[83] In the field of ghost-lore, however, it is possible to suggest that the writings of reformers not only engaged with popular belief, but were themselves structured by it, that English Protestant typologies of the demonic apparition were in fact substantially shaped by traditional expectations about the ghostly revenant.

In the first place, there was the question of what was considered to be the characteristic, even defining activity of apparitions and spirits. In attacking Catholic traditions and superstitious popular beliefs about ghosts, reformers overwhelmingly typified them as 'walking' or 'wandering' spirits.[84] These rather aimless-sounding activities seem somewhat at odds with official Catholic teaching, which held that ghosts appeared by special permission of God for highly specific reasons, but they undoubtedly reflected a widespread popular sense about the restless, troubled spirits of some of the dead. It seems highly likely too that this was how people in Reformation England continued to represent to themselves the nocturnal behaviour of spirits, whether malevolent or benign. As we have seen, the maidservants of Sir Thomas Wise were 'frighted with a walking spirit'.[85] Looking back from the later seventeenth century, John Aubrey remembered how 'when I was a child (and so before the Civill Warres) . . . the fashion was for old women and mayds to tell fabulous stories nightimes of Sprights and walking of Ghosts'.[86] Protestants knew of course that the souls of the dead did not walk; it was the devil who simulated this to deceive the unwary. The logical corollary of this, however, was that in Protestant demonology one of the most direct and overt forms of Satanic activity in the world was patterned after the folk-beliefs of medieval Catholicism. As Sir Thomas Browne put it, writing in the 1630s, 'those apparitions, and ghosts of departed persons are not the wandring soules of men, but the unquiet walkes of Devils . . . instilling, & stealing into our hearts, that the blessed souls are not at rest in their graves, but wander solicitous of the affaires of the world'.[87]

A similar structural congruence between learned Protestantism and unlearned opinion relates to the places where this walking was most likely to take place. John Bossy has written that the traditional ghost 'was personal not real; he haunted people not places'.[88] In fact, this is probably only half true. The leading authority on medieval ghosts, Jean-Claude Schmitt, asserts that 'countless tales of apparitions' were linked to parish cemeteries.[89] Reginald Scot sarcastically noted that in the past 'every churchyard swarmed with souls'.[90] There was no particular reason in Catholic theology why souls from Purgatory should have manifested themselves pre-eminently in churchyards. That ghosts were seen there was probably linked to a more naturalistic popular conception of the dead which associated their spirits with the places where their bodies were buried. Nor was there an overwhelming rationale for the devil to make the churchyard his base of operations, other than the fact he appeared to do so. Inventive reasons were sometimes advanced by Protestant writers to account for this. Thomas Nashe stated that 'if anie aske why [the devil] is more conversant and buysie in churchyards and places where men are buried, than in anie other places', this was because he wanted to make us believe that 'the bodies & soules of the departed rest entirely in his possession', and that 'the boanes of the dead, the divell counts his chiefe treasure, and therfore is he continually raking among them'.[91] Thomas Browne adduced a similar explanation: the reason that phantoms 'doe frequent Cemiteries, charnall houses, and churches, it is because those are the dormitories of the dead, where the Devill like an insolent Champion beholds with pride the spoyles and Trophies of his victory in *Adam*'.[92]

Some echoes of genuine popular concerns may also be faintly audible in discussions of whether the *bodies* of the dead were ever disturbed from their rest. As Nancy Caciola has recently demonstrated, belief in the power of the malevolent dead to reanimate their corpses was characteristic of non-learned culture in medieval Northern Europe, and a particularly prominent feature of the series of ghost stories recorded by a monk of Byland Abbey in Yorkshire in the early fifteenth century.[93] Whether or not the devil had the power to automate the bodies of the dead was a question that divided Protestant authorities.

Some, including Lavater, denied it outright.[94] Others were more agnostic, but thought it unlikely that the devil could do so.[95] The champion of the contrary view was James VI and I, who argued that if demonic possession of the living was permitted by God, appropriation of corpses certainly would be. As a consequence the devil could become visible to men 'and as it seemes unto them naturallie as a man converses with them'.[96] Significantly, the Jacobean witchcraft statute of 1604 added to the list of capital offenders those who dug up the bodies of the dead to use for any kind of sorcery.[97] In his 1596 treatise *The Divell Conjured*, Thomas Lodge agreed that evil angels can 'appeare in assumpted bodies, appropriat to their intents'. Furthermore, he subscribed to the popular (and erroneous) belief that the hair, beards and nails of the recently dead could continue to grow.[98] It is likely that these were issues that resonated outside the world of theological polemic and demonological scholarship. In *The Vow Breaker* (1636) by the provincial playwright, William Sampson, the ghost of a scorned lover returns to haunt his false sweetheart. However, the apparition is held by one of the other characters to be the result of sorcery:

> Hell can put life into a senseless body,
> And raise it from the grave, and make it speake;
> Use all the faculties alive it did,
> To worke the Devill's hellish stratagems![99]

As *The Vow Breaker* reminds us, ghosts in Reformation England were not just a topic of theological discourse, or an occasional and exceptional facet of genuine experience. They were also a cultural type affording the opportunity for imaginative representation. Ghosts, of course, made regular appearances on the Elizabethan and Jacobean stage. It has been calculated that in the period 1560–1610, fifty-one ghosts featured in twenty-six plays.[100] They were also a mainstay of the genre of 'news' or 'letters from hell' which was in vogue in the 1590s and early 1600s, the ghosts here usually acting as mouthpieces for satire or social criticism.[101] Occasionally, representations of ghosts in literary works might carry rather self-conscious health warnings. When the ghost of the actor Richard Tarleton appears to the narrator at the start of the late-Elizabethan burlesque *Tarleton's News out of Purgatory*, the latter starts back, crying '*In nomine Jesu*, avoid, Satan, for ghost thou art none, but a very devil. For the souls of them which are departed (if the sacred principles of theology be true) never return into the world again till the general resurrection.' The ghost, however, is unimpressed, responding, 'Oh there is a Calvinist'.[102] Many dramatists who employed ghosts did not unduly agonise over their precise ontological status, or they evaded sensitive theological issues by rationalising them as spirits from Hades in the Senecan tradition. A good number of critics have noted that Shakespeare's *Hamlet* is highly unusual among Elizabethan and Jacobean plays in explicitly addressing the question of whether the apparition is really the spirit of Hamlet's father, or a demonic illusion, and making it central to the action of the play.[103] It does not by any means follow that authors of works employing ghosts necessarily rejected the orthodox view that the souls of the dead could not appear again to the living: even so fervent an opponent of walking spirits as John Donne could in verse imagine himself returning as a ghost to haunt a faithless lover.[104] Rather it points to the somewhat limited utility of the Protestant demon-ghost as an embodiment of dramatic meaning. The literary ghost, whether seeking revenge, showing solicitude for a loved one or tormenting a guilty conscience, usually implied some direct association with the dead person whose likeness it bore. The cultural patterning of the ghost in English Renaissance theatre was a compounded one: it certainly recognised the ideas of the Reformation, and generally contained no hint (*Hamlet* is a possible exception) of Catholic notions of Purgatory and intercession. Nonetheless, its emotive and imaginative energy seems predicated on assumptions other than the doctrinally sound one that the dead had no interest in the state of affairs they left behind them, or the obligations and deserts of the living.

It is no new discovery that the Reformation failed to eradicate a widely held belief in the possibility of the dead making contact with the living. In 1659, a full century after the Elizabethan settlement, it could be asserted that examples of people returning as ghosts after their deaths were 'numerous and frequent in all mens mouths'.[105] This failure was not, I think, as Ronald Hutton has recently argued, because of an 'instinctive assumption on the part of Protestants' that folk beliefs about wandering spirits were 'essentially harmless', and a wise pastoral decision to leave the subject well alone.[106] The evidence cited in this chapter argues that the continuing propensity of English people to believe in ghosts was of concern not just to a handful of Puritan zealots, but to a broad spectrum of Protestant opinion. Although writers and preachers construed apparitions and their significance in diverse and un-uniform ways, there was a clear bottom line. In the words of Henry Smith, he that departs from this life 'hath no more societie with them that live upon the earth'.[107] Yet this was a message mediated through a culture which unashamedly continued to employ quasi-traditional ghost-figures in its literature and drama, and which was at times problematised by Protestant authorities themselves, as they attempted to press-gang ostensible appearances of the dead into a framework of providentialist justice and the sanctioning of social norms. Approaches to ghosts and apparitions might appear to be a clear marker between popular and learned religious cultures, between 'superstitious' and authoritative understandings of the ordering and operation of the supernatural world. But as the reformers themselves well knew, appearances can be deceptive.

NOTES

1 R. King, *A funerall sermon that was prepared to have bine preached* (London, Richard Grafton, 1552), sigs. G3v–4.

2 T. Morton, *A Catholike Appeale for Protestants* (London, R. Field, 1609), 428.

3 J. Véron, *The Huntyng of Purgatorye to Death* (London, J. Tysdale, 1561), fol. 201v; J. Calfhill, *An Answer to John Martiall's Treatise of the Cross*, ed. R. Gibbings (Cambridge, 1846), 90; H. Bullinger, *The Decades: The Fourth Decade*, ed. T. Harding (Cambridge, 1851), 400; L. Lavatr, *Of Ghostes and Spirites Walking by Night*, ed. J. Dover Wilson and M. Yardley (Oxford, 1929), 110; W. Fulke, *Two Treatises Written against the Papistes* (London, T. Vautrollier, 1577), 163–4; G. Wither, *A View of the Marginal Notes of the Popish Testament* (London, E. Bollifant, 1588), 74; M. Sutcliffe, *Adversus Roberti Bellarmini de Purgatorio Disputationem* (London, Bishop, Newberie & Barker, 1599), 101; E. Hoby, *A Letter to Mr T. H.* (London, Eld & Snodham, 1609), 42; S. Purchas, *Purchas his Pilgrimage* (London, W. Stansby, 1613), 179; T. Beard, *A Retractive from the Romish Religion* (London, W. Stansby, 1616), 414; R. Horne, *Certaine Sermons of the Rich Man and Lazarus* (London, B. Alsop, 1619), 135; R. Jenison, *The Height of Israels Heathenish Idolatrie* (London, G. Eld, 1621), 143; J. Donne, *Sermons*, ed. E. M. Simpson and G. R. Potter (Los Angeles, 1953–62), 10 vols, 10: 145–6; A. Cooke, *Worke, More Work, and a Little More Worke for a Masse-Priest* (London, W. Jones, 1630), 46.

4 E. Grindal, *Remains*, ed. W. Nicholson (Cambridge, 1843), 24.

5 H. Smith, *Sermons* (London, T. Orwin, 1592), 540–1.

6 K. Thomas, *Religion and the Decline of Magic. Studies in Popular Beliefs in Sixteenth and Seventeenth Century England* (London, 1971), 703–4.

7 Calfhill, *Answer to Martiall*, 90; A. Anderson, *The Shield of our Safetie Set Foorth* (London, H. Jackson, 1581), sig. H2; R. Scot, *The Discoverie of Witchcraft* (London, W. Brome, 1584), 139; G. Gifford, *A Dialogue concerning Witches and Witchcraftes* (London, J. Windet, 1593), sig. F2; Horne, *Certaine Sermons*, 134.

8 G. A[lley], *Ptochomouseion. The Poore Mans Librarie* (London, J. Daye, 1571), fol. 53v. See also Bullinger, *Fourth Decade*, 401; Anderson, *Shield of our Safetie*, sig. H2.

9 Horne, *Certaine Sermons*, 122.

10 T. Bilson, *The effect of Certaine Sermons . . . preached at Pauls Crosse* (London, P. Short, 1599), 204.

11 R. Bellarmine, *Liber de Purgatorio*, in *De Controversiis Christianae Fidei adversus Huius Temporis Haereticos* (Ingolstadt, A. Sartrius, 1601), 5 vols, 2: 791–2; G. Martin, ed. and trans., *The Holie Bible Faithfully Translated into English . . . by the English College of Doway* (Douai, L. Kellam, 1609–10), 2 vols, 1: 631–2; N. Taillepied, *A Treatise of Ghosts*, trans. M. Summers (London, 1934), 152–7. A more agnostic attitude is evident in W. Allen, *A Defense and Declaration of the Catholike Churches Doctrine touching Purgatory* (Antwerp, J. Latius, 1565), fol. 110v.

12 M. Parker, ed. and trans., *The Holie Bible* [Bishops' Bible] (London, R. Jugge, 1568), fol. 50; T. Sampson, ed. and trans., *The Bible* [Geneva version] (London, R. Parker, 1599), 109. The story is treated in detail by Lavater, *Of Ghostes*, 127–45; Anderson, *Shield of our Safetie*, sigs. H2v–I1; P. Martyr, *The Common Places*, trans. A. Marten (London, Denham & Middleton, 1583), 72–7; Scot, *Discoverie*, 139–52; G. Gifford, *A Discourse of the Subtill Practises of Devilles by Witches and Sorcerers* (London, T. Orwin, 1587), sigs. E1v–E3v; H. Holland, *A Treatise against Witchcraft* (Cambridge, J. Legatt, 1590), sigs. C1v–C3; A. Willet, *Synopsis Papismi* (London, T. Orwin, 1592), 305–6; R. Hutchins, *Of Specters*, ed. & trans., V. B. Heltzel and C. Murley *Huntingdon Library Quarterly* 11 (1947–8), 424–6; J. Deacon and J. Walker, *Dialogical Discourses of Spirits and Divels* (London, G. Bishop, 1601), 120–6; W. Perkins, *A Discourse of the Damned Art of Witchcraft* (Cambridge, J. Legat, 1608), 108–20; T. Cooper, *The Mystery of Witchcraft* (London, N. Okes, 1617), 151–4.

13 Perkins, *Discourse of the Damned Art*, 113.

14 Smith, *Sermons*, 538.

15 Holland, *Treatise against Witchcraft*, sig. C2; W. Perkins, *A Golden Chaine* (Cambridge, J. Legat, 1600), 515; *Discourse of the Damned Art*, 109–10, 112, 115; Deacon and Walker, *Dialogical Discourses*, 121–2; Cooper, *Mystery of Witchcraft*, 151–2.

16 Willet, *Synopsis Papisimi*, 306; Perkins, *Discourse of the Damned Art*, 111; *Golden Chaine*, 50; Gifford, *Discourse of the Subtill Practises of Devilles*, sig. E1v; Holland, *Treatise against Witchcraft*, sig. C2.

17 Cooper, *Mystery of Witchcraft*, 152.

18 Perkins, *Discourse of the Damned Art*, 118.

19 Bellarmine, *De Purgatorio*, 792; *Douai Bible*, 2: 441; Taillepied, *Treatise of Ghosts*, 153.

20 Holland, *Treatise against Witchcraft*, sig. C2; Purchas, *Pilgrimage*, 179: 'poore Purgatorie with Jewes and Romists is preached by walking ghosts'.

21 A. Peel, ed., *The Seconde Parte of a Register* (Cambridge, 1915), 2 vols, 1: 279. A later conformist response to Puritan objections to this passage admitted that the verse reflected 'the general voice of those times, and the opinion of *Saul* and the Witch then generalie currant': T. Hutton, *Reasons for Refusal of Subscription to the booke of common praier* (Oxford, J. Barnes, 1605), 116.

22 Scot, *Discoverie*, 139, 142–50, 152.

23 Scot, *Discoverie*, 462, 139, 152.

24 See S. Anglo, 'Reginald Scot's *Discoverie of Witchcraft*: Scepticism and Sadduceeism', in S. Anglo, ed., *The Damned Art: Essays in the Literature of Witchcraft* (London, 1977), 106–39.

25 S. Harsnett, *A Declaration of Egregious Popish Impostures*, reprinted in F. W. Brownlow, *Shakespeare, Harnett, and the Devils of Denham* (London, 1993), 309.

26 Gervase Babington, *Workes* (London, G. Eld, 1622), 2 vols, 2: 189.

27 D. Erasmus, *The Colloquies*, trans. C. R. Thompson (Chicago, 1965), 230–7; J. Weyer, *De praestigiis daemonum*, in G. Mora *et al.*, eds. and trans, *Witches, Devils, and Doctors in the Renaissance* (Binghampton, NY, 1991), 439–41; Lavater, *Of Ghostes*, chs. 5–9.

28 Taillepied, *Treatise of Ghosts*, ch. 6; P. Le Loyer, *A Treatise of Specters*, trans. Z. Jones (London, V. Simmes, 1605), fols 75v–79v.

29 Perkins, *Discourse of the Damned Art*, 118; *Golden Chaine*, 50; Gifford, *Subtill Practises of Devilles*, sigs. E3–3v; Holland, *Treatise Against Witchcraft*, sig. C2; Cooper, *Mystery of Witchcraft*, 154; Deacon and Walker, *Dialogical Discourses*, 125–6.

30 G. Strode, *The Anatomie of Mortalitie* (London, W. Jones, 1632), 205. See also P. Du Moulin, *The Waters of Siloe* (Oxford, J. Barnes, 1612), 395; Hutchins, *Of Specters*, 426.

31 R. Kieckhefer, *Magic in the Middle Ages* (Cambridge, 1989), 152; Holland, *Treatise of Witchcraft*, sig. D4; Perkins, *Discourse of the Damned Art*, 107–8; *Golden Chaine*, 50; J. Cotta, *The Triall of Witchcraft* (London, G. Purslowe, 1616), 37.

32 P. Viret, *The Christian Disputations*, trans. J. Brooke (London, J. Brooke, 1579), fol. 104v.

33 Beard, *Retractive*, 437.

34 J. Preston, *A Sermon Preached at the Funeral of Mr Arthur Upton Esquire in Devon* (London, W. Jones, 1619), 33.

35 Jenison, *Height of Israel's Idolatrie*, 141.

36 On inversion and witchcraft, see S. Clark, 'King James's *Daemonologie*: Witchcraft and Kingship', in Anglo, ed., *Damned Art*, 156–81; and his *Thinking with Demons: The Idea of Witchcraft in Early Modern Europe* (Oxford, 1997), ch. 6.

37 R. Bernard, *A Guide to Grand-Iury Men* (London, F. Kingston, 1627), 34, 99. See also Cooper, *Mystery of Witchcraft*, 22; J. Napeir, *A Plaine Discovery of the Whole Revelation of Saint John* (Edinburgh, R. Waldegrave, 1593), 46; N. Jones, 'Defining Superstitions: Treasonous Catholics and the Act Against Witchcraft of 1563', in C. Carlton *et al.*, eds, *State, Sovereigns and Society in Early Modern England* (Stroud, 1998), 187–204.

38 Donne, *Sermons*, 7: 168; 8: 135.

39 See Brownlow, *Devils of Denham*, 74–5, for the view that Harsnett's tract was aimed as much at the Puritan exorcist John Darrell as at the Catholics who were its ostensible targets.

40 BL, Harleian MS 425, fols 4–7.

41 E. Sandys, *Sermons*, ed. J. Ayre (Cambridge, 1841), 60.

42 Lavater, *Of Ghostes*, 89, 183.

43 Scot, *Discoverie*, 152–3, 463. He was ill-informed about the situation in Germany: see S. Karant-Nunn, *The Reformation of Ritual. An Interpretation of Early Modern Germany* (London, 1997), 185–6.

44 Harsnett, *Declaration*, 306–7.
45 Donne, *Sermons*, 10: 145–6; Bernard, *Guide to Grand-Iury Men*, 99–100; Hoby, *Letter to Mr T. H.*, 42.
46 J. Northbrooke, *Spiritus est Vicarius in Terra* (London, J. Kingston, 1571), fol. 15.
47 Hutchins, *Of Specters*, 410; Smith, *Sermons*, 536; Perkins, *Golden Chaine*, 515; *Discourse of the Damned Art*, 115–16; Strode, *Anatomie of Mortalitie*, 204–5.
48 Véron, *Huntyng of Purgatorye*, fols 197v–198v.
49 A. Dent, *The Plaine Mans Pathway to Heaven* (London, R. Dexter, 1605), 265–6.
50 Lavater, *Of Ghostes*, 71.
51 R[obert] H[arrison], 'To the Reader', in Lavater, *Of Ghostes*.
52 Scot, *Discoverie*, 532.
53 M. Parker, *Correspondence*, ed. J. Bruce (Cambridge, 1853), 222.
54 Anderson, *Shield of our Safetie*, sig. H1v.
55 Preston, *Sermon Preached at the Funeral of Mr Arthur Upton*, 33.
56 Anderson, *Shield of our Safetie*, sig. H2; Smith, *Sermons*, 537–8.
57 K. L. Parker and E. J. Carlson, *'Practical Divinity': The Works and Life of Revd Richard Greenham* (Aldershot, 1998), 217.
58 Smith, *Sermons*, 540.
59 Babington, *Workes*, 2: 188–9; Anderson, *Shield of our Safetie*, sig. H4.
60 Scot, *Discoverie*, 141; Hutchins, *Of Specters*, 424. On Agrippa and ghosts, see R. H. West, *The Invisible World: A Study of Pneumatology in Elizabethan Drama* (New York, 1969), 52–3.
61 N. Z. Davis, 'Some Tasks and Themes in the Study of Popular Religion', in C. Trinkaus and H. O. Oberman, eds, *The Pursuit of Holiness in Late Medieval and Renaissance Religion* (Leiden, 1974), 333; R. Muchembled, *Popular and Elite Culture in France 1400–1750*, trans. L. Cochrane (London, 1985), 64.
62 B. Rich, *The true report of a late practise enterprized by a papist with a yong maiden in Wales* (London, J. Kingston, 1582).
63 J. Gee, *New Shreds of the Old Snare* (London, J. Dawson, 1624), 1–25.
64 Lavater, *Of Ghostes*, chs. 2–4; Scot, *Discoverie*, 152, 462; Taillepied, *Treatise of Ghosts*, chs. 3–5, 7; Hutchins, *Of Specters*, 412; T. Nashe, *The Terrors of the Night*, in *The Works of Thomas Nashe*, ed. R. B. McKerrow and F. Wilson (Oxford, 1958), 5 vols, 1: 348, 378; T. Lodge, *The Divell Coniured*, in *The Complete Works of Thomas Lodge*, ed. E. Gosse (London, 1883), 4 vols, 3: 33; Harsnett, *Declaration*, 304–5; Le Loyer, *Treatise of Specters*, fols 104–12v; Donne, *Sermons*, 7: 168; T. White, *The Middle State of Souls* (London, n. pr., 1659), 170.
65 Babington, *Workes*, 2: 189.
66 Scot, *Discoverie*, 152.
67 M. MacDonald and T. Murphy, *Sleepless Souls: Suicide in Early Modern England* (Oxford, 1990), 34–41; *Hamlet*, 2: ii. 600–4. On melancholy, see M. MacDonald, *Mystical Bedlam: Madness, Anxiety, and Healing in Seventeenth-Century England* (Cambridge, 1981), 150–60.
68 Cited in Macdonald, *Mystical Bedlam*, 169.
69 Macdonald, *Mystical Bedlam*, 157.
70 Lavater, *Of Ghosts*, sig. B2, 145, 159–63, 193, 196, 199.
71 Scot, *Discoverie*, 152, 462.
72 W. Perkins, *A Reformed Catholike* (Cambridge, J. Legat, 1598), 247.
73 James VI and I, *Daemonologie*, ed. G. B. Harrison (London, 1924), 61, 65–6; originally published as James VI, *Daemonologie, in Forme of a Dialogue* (Edinburgh, R. Waldegrave, 1597).
74 Bodleian MS Rawlinson D 47, fols 42–43v.
75 Bodleian MS Rawlinson D 47, fol. 43v.
76 Lavater, *Of Ghostes*, 175, 191; James VI and I, *Daemonologie*, 58.
77 A. Walsham, *Providence in Early Modern England* (Oxford, 1999), *passim*.
78 J. Foxe, *Actes and Monumentes* (London, J. Daye, 1563), sig. **I*(v); *Actes and Monuments* (London, J. Daye, 1570), 409–10. Foxe was not the first English Protestant to retell the story: Thomas Swinnerton, *A mustre of scismatyke bysshoppes of Rome* (London, J. Byddell, 1534), sig. B4.

79 See, for example, T. Erbe, ed., *Mirk's Festial* (London, 1905), 270; J. de Voragine, *The Golden Legend*, trans. W. Ryan (Princeton, 1993), 2 vols, 2: 290.

80 P. Stubbes, *Two wunderfull and rare examples of the undeferred judgement of God* (London, W. Wright, 1581).

81 Anon., *A Strange and Fearful Warning to all Sonnes and Executors (that fulfill not the will of their dead Fathers)* (London, E. Allde, 1623).

82 D. Person, *Varieties: or a Surveigh of rare and excellent matters* (London, Badger & Cotes, 1635), 165.

83 Walsham, *Providence*; P. Lake, 'Deeds against Nature: Cheap Print, Protestantism and Murder in Early Seventeenth-Century England', in K. Sharpe and Lake, eds, *Culture and Politics in Early Stuart England* (Basingstoke, 1994); T. Watt, *Cheap Print and Popular Piety 1550–1610* (Cambridge, 1991).

84 BL, Harl. 425, fol. 6v; Northbrooke, *Spiritus est Vicarius Christi*, fol. 15; Sandys, *Sermons*, 60; Bullinger, *The Fourth Decade*, 404; Anderson, *Shield of our Safetie*, sigs. H1v–2; Martyr, *Common Places*, 326; Scot, *Discoverie*, 462; Smith, *Sermons*, 525, 541; Hutchins, *Of Specters*, 426; Perkins, *Golden Chaine*, 515; *Discourse of the Damned Art*, 33; R. Pricke, *A Very Godlie and Learned Sermon treating of Mans Mortalitie* (London, T. Creede, 1608), sig. D4v; Harsnett, *Declaration*, 306; Purchas, *Pilgrimage*, 179; Beard, *Retractive*, 437; Cooper, *Mystery of Witchcraft*, 152; Babington, *Workes*, 2: 188–9; Strode, *Anatomie of Mortalitie*, 205.

85 Bodleian MS Rawlinson D 47, fol. 43.

86 R. Finucane, *Appearances of the Dead: A Cultural History of Ghosts* (London, 1982), 124.

87 T. Browne, *Religio Medici*, in his *The Major Works*, ed. C. A. Patrides (Harmondsworth, 1977), 108.

88 J. Bossy, *Christianity in the West 1400–1700* (Oxford, 1985), 29.

89 J.-C. Schmitt, *Ghosts in the Middle Ages: The Living and the Dead in Medieval Society*, trans. T. Fagan (London, 1998), 137.

90 Scot, *Discoverie*, 462.

91 Nashe, *Terrors of the Night*, 348–9.

92 Browne, *Religio Medici*, 108.

93 N. Caciola, 'Wraiths, Revenants and Ritual in Medieval Culture', *Past and Present* 152 (1996), 3–45.

94 Lavater, *Of Ghostes*, 171; Veron, *Huntynge of Purgatory*, fol. 245v; Deacon and Walker, *Dialogical Discourses*, 101–2, 104; Cotta, *Triall of Witchcraft*, 37; *No Man is an Island: A Selection from the Prose of John Donne*, ed. R. Scott (London, 1997), 169.

95 Cooper, *Mystery of Witchcraft*, 151; Preston, *Sermon Preached at the Funeral of Mr Arthur Upton*, 33. See also Whitgift's admission at the 1584 conference at Lambeth that it was 'a question among the learned' whether witches had power to raise the bodies of the dead: Peel, *Seconde Parte of a Register*, 1: 279, a comment wrongly attributed to Travers by Thomas, *Religion*, 706.

96 James VI and I, *Daemonologie*, 59, 67, 73; Hutchins, *Of Specters*, 416.

97 G. L. Kittredge, *Wtchcraft in Old and New England* (New York, 1929), 312.

98 Lodge, *Divell Coniured*, 23, 30. For the very long-standing popular intuition that the corpses of the dead continued to possess some degree of sentience or life-force, see Caciola, 'Wraiths, Revenants and Ritual'; R. Richardson, *Death, Dissection and the Destitute* (London, 1987), ch. 1.

99 Cited in K. M. Briggs, *The Anatomy of Puck: An Examination of Fairy Beliefs among Shakespeare's Contemporaries* (London, 1959), 137.

100 E. Prosser, *Hamlet and Revenge* (Stanford, 1967), 255. General treatments of ghosts in Elizabethan drama are provided by Briggs, *Anatomy of Puck*, ch. 9; West, *Invisible World*, ch. 9.

101 J. Belfield, 'Tarleton's News out of Purgatory (London, 1590): A Modern-Spelling Edition', unpublished Ph.D. thesis (University of Birmingham, 1978), 116–33.

102 Belfield, 'Tarletons News', 284.

103 J. Dover Wilson, *What Happens in Hamlet?* (Cambridge, 1951), ch. 3; M. Joseph, 'Discerning the Ghost in Hamlet', *Publications of the Modern Language Association of America* 76

(London, 1961), 493–502; C. Devlin, 'Hamlet's Divinity', in *Hamlet's Divinity and Other Essays* (London, 1963); Prosser, *Hamlet and Revenge*; R. West, *Shakespeare and the Outer Mystery* (Lexington, 1968), ch. 4; R. M. Frye, *The Renaissance Hamlet: Issues and Responses in 1600* (Princeton, 1984), 14–28; A. McGee, *The Elizabethan Hamlet* (New Haven, 1987), chs. 1–3; S. Greenblatt, *Hamlet in Purgatory* (Princeton, 2001).

104 J. Donne, *Selected Poems*, ed. J. Hayward (Harmondsworth, 1950), 52.

105 Henry More, *The Immortality of the Soul* (London, J. Flesher, 1659), 286.

106 R. Hutton, 'English Reformation and the Evidence of Folklore', *Past and Present* 148 (1995), 114.

107 Smith, *Sermons*, 532.

Bibliography

Primary sources (unpublished)

Archivum Romanum Societatis Iesu
    Galliae 60

Bibliothèque Nationale
    Manuscrit française 15798 (*'Recueil des interrogatoires et des arrests de Jean Guignard et de Jean Chastel'*)

Bodleian
    MS Rawlinson D 47

British Library
    Harleian MS 425

Diözesanarchiv Rottenburg (DAR)
    AI2a, nos. 382, 410, 448
    Pfarreiarchiv Heilig Kreuz Rottweil, vols. 1, 3, 4, 11, 161

Erzbischöfliches Archiv Freiburg (EBAF)
    HA61
    HA62

Generallandesarchiv Karlsruhe (GLAK)
    61/7321
    82a/50
    82a/261

Pfarreibibliothek Heilig Kreuz Rottweil (PBHKR)
    XXI 135–6

Scottish Record Office
  JC (Records of the Court of High Justiciary in Edinburgh) 26/24

Staatsarchiv Nürnberg (StaatsAN)
  Rep. 44e, Losungsamt, Akten, SIL. 131, no. 14

Staatsarchiv Nürnberg
  Rep. A6, Sammlung der (gedruckten) Mandate, Urkunden und Verordnungen
     der Reichsstadt und Stadtverwaltung Nürnberg, 1219 bis Gegenwart
     1525 Mai 24 and 1526 März 3
  Rep. B14/III (Inventarbücher), nos. 8, 12
  Rep. E1 (Familienarchive Spengler), nos. 4, 47

Stadtarchiv Augsburg
  Reichsstadt, Ratserlasse (1507–99), 14/8 (1537)

Stadtarchiv Rottweil (STAR)
  Archivalien II, Abteilung I, Lade V, Fasz 16, no. 6
  Missivbuch der kaiserlichen Reichsstadt Rottweil 1585–1607
  Ratsprotokolle, book 1580–82
  Ratsprotokolle, book 1583–86
  Ratsprotokolle, book 1587–92
  Ratsprotokolle, book 1593–98
  Ratsprotokolle, book 1599–1608
  Ratsprotokolle, book 1609–16

Primary sources (published)

Allen, W., *A Defense and Declaration of the Catholike Churches Doctrine touching Purgatory*
     (Antwerp, J. Latius, 1565)
A[lley], G., *Ptochomouseion. The Poore Mans Librarie* (London, J. Daye, 1571)
Anderson, A., *The Shield of our Safetie Set Foorth* (London, H. Jackson, 1581)
Anon., *The Anatomie of Popish Tyrannie* (London, n. pr., 1603)
Anon., *Anticoton* (n. pl., n. pr., 1610)
Anon., *Bishop Ushers second prophesie which he delivered to his daughter on his sick-bed*
     (London, John Hunt, 1681)
Anon., 'Charactares Iesuitarum', in Anon., *Doctrinae Iesviticae Praecipva Capita Scripta
     Qvaedam continens, in quibus Iesuitarum Sophismata solidis rationibus testimoniisque
     sacrarum Scripturarum &Doctorum veteris Ecclesiae, refelluntur* (La Rochelle, n. pr.,
     1585)
Anon., *La conspiration faicte par les peres Iesvites de Douay, pour assassiner Maurice, Prince
     d'Orange, Comte de Nassau*, in S. Goulart, ed., *Memoires de la Ligue* (Geneva, n.
     pr., 1599), 9 volumes

Anon., *A Discourse concerning the original of the Powder-Plot* (London, n. pr., 1674)

Anon., *The Doctrines and Practices of the Societie of Iesvites, in two books* (London, n. pr., 1630)

Anon., *The Fulfilling of Prophecies* (London, R. Baldwin, 1689)

Anon., *Imago primi sæculi Societatis Iesu a Prouincia Flandro-Belgica eiusdem Societatis repræsentata* (Antwerp, B. Moreti, 1640)

Anon., *The Jesuites Intrigues* (London, n. pr., 1669), 25

Anon., *Profana sectae Jesuiticae vanitas. Dialogus: siue colloquium Jesuiticum de fundamentis sectae Jesuitarum malè fundatis* (Ambergae, n. pr., 1611)

Anon., *The prophesy of Bishop James Ussher* (London, n. pr., 1687)

Anon., *A Strange and Fearful Warning to all Sonnes and Executors (that fulfill not the will of their dead Fathers)* (London, E. Allde, 1623)

Anon., *Strange and Remarkable Prophesies* (London, R. G., 1678 and London, n. pr., 1681)

Anon., *A trve and plaine declaration of the horrible Treasons* (London, n. pr., 1585)

Anon., *A trve report of svndry horrible conspiracies* (London, C. Yetsweirt, 1594)

Aquinas, St Thomas, *Expositio in Job* (Rome, n. pr., 1562)

Aquinas, St Thomas, *Summa Theologica*, translated by the Fathers of the English Dominican Province (London 1920), 22 volumes

Arminian Magazine 7 (1784), 548–50, 606–8, 654–6

Arnauld, A., *Le franc et véritable discours au roi Henri IV. Sur le rétablissement des Jésuites, 1602*, in J. A. Gazaignes, ed., *Annales de la société des soi-disans Jésuites; ou recueil historique-chronologique* (Paris, n. pr., 1764), 5 volumes

Arnauld, A., *Plaidoyé de M. Antoine Arnavld* (La Haye, n. pr., 1594)

St Augustine, *Concerning the City of God against the Pagans*, ed. and trans. H. Bettenson (London, 1987)

Aymon, J., ed., *Tous les Synodes Nationaux des Eglises Reformées de France* (The Hague, 1710), 2 volumes

Babington, Gervase, *Workes* (London, G. Eld, 1622), 2 volumes

Bacon, Roger, ed., *Des Choses Merveilleuses en nature, ou est traicté des erreurs des sens, des puissances de l'ame, & des influences des cieux* (Lyon, n. pr., 1557)

Beard, T., *A Retractive from the Romish Religion* (London, W. Stansby, 1616)

Bellarmine, R., *Liber de Purgatorio*, in *De Controversiis Christianae Fidei adversus Huius Temporis Haereticos* (Ingolstadt, A. Sartorius, 1601), 5 volumes

Bernard, Nicholas, *The Life and Death of Dr. James Usher* (London, E. Tyler, 1656)

Bernard, R., *A Guide to Grand-Iury Men* (London, F. Kingston, 1627)

Bilson, T., *The effect of Certaine Sermons . . . preached at Pauls Crosse* (London, P. Short, 1599)

Bodin, Jean, *Démonomanie des sorciers* (Rouen, n. pr., 1604)

St Bonaventure, *Life of Saint Francis*, in E. Cousins, trans., *Bonaventure* (London, 1978)

Boquinus, P., *A defence of the Olde, and True profession of Christianitie, against the new, and counterfaite secte of Iesuites, or fellowship of Iesus* (London, J. Wolf & H. Kirkham, 1581)

Bourquin, L., ed., *Mémoires de Claude Haton, Tome 1 1553–1565* (Paris, 2001)

Bovet, Richard, *Pandaemonium* (London, J. Walthoe, 1684)

Browne, T., *Religio Medici*, in *The Major Works*, Browne, ed. C. A. Patrides (Harmondsworth, 1977)

Calvin, John, *Calvin's New Testament Commentaries: The First Epistle of Paul to the Corinthians*, ed. David W. Torrance and Thomas F. Torrance and trans. John W. Fraser (Grand Rapids, 1960)

Calvin, John, *Commentaries on Catholic Epistles*, ed., and trans. John Owen (Grand Rapids, 1948)

Calvin, John, *Commentaries on the Epistle of Paul to the Galatians and Ephesians*, trans. William Pringle (Grand Rapids, 1979)

Calvin, John, *Commentary on the Prophet Isaiah*, trans. William Pringle (Grand Rapids, 1979)

Calvin, John, *Commentaries on the Prophet Jeremiah and the Lamentations*, ed., and trans. John Owen (Grand Rapids, 1979)

Calvin, John, *Institutes of the Christian Religion*, ed., and trans. Henry Beveridge (London, 1949), 2 volumes

Calvin, John, *The Institutes of the Christian Religion*, ed. John T. McNeill, and trans. Ford Lewis Battles (Philadelphia, 1960), 2 volumes

Calvin, John, *Letters of John Calvin*, ed., Jules Bonnet and trans. Marcus Robert Gilchrist (New York, 1972), 4 volumes

Camerarius, Philippe, *Les Meditations Historiques* (Lyon, A. de Harsy's widow, 1610), 3 volumes

Chavigny, Jean-Aimé de, *La Premiere Face du Janus François* (Lyon, P. Roussin, 1594)

Constitutiones et decreta synodalia civitatis et dioecesis Constantiensis . . . anno domini M.D.LXVIII. statuta, edita et promulgata, praesidente Marco Sittico S. R. E. tituli S. Georgii in Velabro Presbyterio, Episcopo Constantiensis (Dillingen, n. pr., 1568)

Cooke, A., *Worke, More Work, and a Little More Worke for a Masse-Priest* (London, W. Jones, 1630)

Cooper, T., *The Mystery of Witchcraft* (London, N. Okes, 1617)

Cotta, J., *The Triall of Witchcraft* (London, G. Purslowe, 1616)

Couillard, Antoine, *Les Contredicts du Seigneur Du Pavillon, lez Lorriz, en Gastinois, aux faulses & abbusifves propheties de Nostradamus, & autres astrologues* (Paris, C. l'Angelier, 1560)

Couillard, Antoine, *Les Propheties du Seigneur du Pavillon Les Lorriz* (Paris, A. le Clerc, 1556)

Cramond, William, *Extracts from the Records of the Kirk Session of Elgin* (Elgin, 1897)

Crespin, Jean, *Histoire des Martyrs persecutez et mis a mort pour la verité de l'Evangile*, ed. Simon Goulard (Geneva, P. Aubert, 1619)

Daneau, L., *Deux traitez nouveaux, tres-utiles pour ce temps. Entretien sur les malefices et Traité des sorciers* (Frankurt, Jacques Baumet, 1579)

Daneau, L., *A Dialogue of Witches* (London, Watkins, 1575)

Daneau, L., *De veneficiis* (Geneva, Eustace Vignon, 1574)

Daneau, L., *Von den Zauberern* (Cologne, J. Gymnicus, 1576)

Deacon, J., and Walker, J., *Dialogical Discourses of Spirits and Divels* (London, G. Bishop, 1601)

Del Rio, Martín, *Disquisitiones Magicae* (Leiden, 1608)

Dent, A., *The Plaine Mans Pathway to Heaven* (London, R. Dexter, 1605)

Donne, John, *No Man is an Island: A Selection from the Prose of John Donne*, ed. R. Scott (London, 1997)

Donne, J., *Selected Poems*, ed. J. Hayward (Harmondsworth, 1950)

Donne, J., *Sermons*, ed. E. M. Simpson and G. R. Potter (Los Angeles, 1953–62), 10 volumes

Erasmus, D., *The Colloquies*, trans. C. R. Thompson (Chicago, 1965)

Erbe, T., ed., *Mirk's Festial* (London, 1905)

Foxe, J., *Actes and Monumentes* (London, J. Daye, 1563; 1570)

Fulke, W., *Two Treatises Written against the Papistes* (London, T. Vautrollier, 1577)

Gallars, Nicolas des, *Seconde apologie ou defense des vrais chrestiens, contre les calomnies impudentes des ennemis de l'Eglise catholique* (n. pl., n. pr., 1559)

Gay, Jean, *Histoire des scismes et heresies des Albigeois conforme à celle du present* (Paris, P. Gaultier, 1561)

Gee, J., *New Shreds of the Old Snare* (London, J. Dawson, 1624)

Gifford, G., *A Dialogue concerning Witches and Witchcraftes* (London, J. Windet, 1593)

Gifford, G., *A Discourse of the Subtill Practises of Devilles by Witches and Sorcerers* (London, T. Orwin, 1587)

Grindal, E., *Remains*, ed. W. Nicholson (Cambridge, 1843)

Gryse, N., *Spegel des Antichristlichen Pawestdoms Vnd Lutterischen Christendoms / Na Ordenung der V. Höetstücke vnsers H. Catechismi vnderscheiden* (Rostock, Steffen Muellman, 1593)

Hamburger Kunsthalle, *Luther und die Folgen für die Kunst*, ed. W. Hofmann (Munich and Hamburg, 1983)

Hampe, T., ed., *Nürnberger Ratsverlässe über Kunst und Künstler im Zeitalter der Spätgotik und Renaissance* (Vienna and Leipzig, 1904), 2 volumes

Harding, Thomas, ed., *The Decades of Heinrich Bullinger* (Cambridge, 1848–52), 4 volumes

Hasenmüller, E., *Historia Iesvitici Ordinis* (Frankfurt, I. Spies, 1595)

Hoby, E., *A Letter to Mr T. H.* (London, Eld & Snodham, 1609)

Holban, Maria, ed., *Călători străini despre Ţările Române* (Bucharest, 1968–83), 8 volumes

Holland, H., *A Treatise against Witchcraft* (Cambridge, J. Legatt, 1590)

Horne, R., *Certaine Sermons of the Rich Man and Lazarus* (London, B. Alsop, 1619)

Hume, D., *L'assassinat dv roy* (n. pl., n. pr., 1615)

Hutchins, R., *Of Specters*, ed. & trans., V. B. Heltzel and C. Murley *Huntingdon Library Quarterly* 11 (1947–8)

Hutton, T., *Reasons for Refusal of Subscription to the booke of common praier* (Oxford, J. Barnes, 1605), 116

Illyricus, Matthias Flacius, *Catalogus Testium Veritatis*, ed. Simon Goulard (Geneva, M. Stoer & Chouet, 1597)

Jakab, Elek, ed., *Okleveltar Kolozsvár történetehez* (Budapest, 1870–88), 2 volumes

James VI, *Daemonologie, in Forme of a Dialogue* (Edinbrugh, R. Waldegrave, 1597)

James VI and I, *Daemonologie*, ed. G. B. Harrison (London, 1924)

Jenison, R., *The Height of Israels Heathenish Idolatrie* (London, G. Eld, 1621)

Jon, François du, *Apocalypse ou Revelation de S. Jean Apostre Evangeliste de nostre Seigneur Jesus Christ* (Geneva, P. de St-André, 1592)

Josselin, R., *Diary, 1616–1683*, ed. A. MacFarlane (Oxford, 1976)

King, R., *A funerall sermon that was prepared to have bine preached* (London, Richard Grafton, 1552)

Kirkaldy, Sir William, *Memoirs and Adventures* (London, 1849)

Knox, John, *Johns Knox's History of the Reformation in Scotland*, trans. & ed. William C. Dickinson (New York, 1950), 2 volumes

Knox, John, *Select Practical Writings of John Knox* (Edinburgh, 1845)

Knox, John, *Selected Writings of John Knox*, trans. Kevin Reed (Dallas, 1995)

Knox, John, *The Works of John Knox*, ed. David Laing (Edinburgh, 1846–64), 6 volumes

Kramer and Sprenger, *Malleus Maleficarum*, ed. M. Summers (New York, 1971)

Lavater, L., *Of Ghostes and Spirites Walking by Night*, ed. J. Dover Wilson and M. Yardley (Oxford, 1929)

L'Estoile, M., *Mémoires-Journaux* (Paris, 1888–98), 12 volumes

Le Loyer, P., *A Treatise of Specters*, trans. Z. Jones (London, V. Simmes, 1605)

Lodge, T., *The Divell Coniured*, in *The Complete Works of Thomas Lodge* , ed. E. Gosse (London, 1883), 4 volumes

Loyola, I., *The Constitutions of the Society of Jesus* (Saint Louis, 1970)

Lukács, Laszlo, ed., *Monumenta Antiqua Hungariae* (Rome, 1976), 2 volumes

Luther, M., *D. Martin Luthers Werke. Kritische Gesamtausgabe* (Weimar, 1883–1983), 61 volumes

Luther, M., *D. Martin Luthers Werke. Tischreden* (Weimar, 1912–21) 6 volumes

Luther, M., *In primum librum Mose enarrationes* (Nuremburg, Montanus, 1550)

Luther, M., *Works*, ed., U. S. Leupold (Philadelphia, 1965), 55 volumes

MacKay, A. J. G., ed., *The History and Cronicles of Scotland* (Edinburgh, 1899–1911), 3 volumes

Malescot, E., *Morologie des Iesvites. Morologie des favx prophetes et manticores Iesuites* (Caen, n. pr., 1593)

Martin, G., ed. and trans., *The Holie Bible Faithfully Translated into English . . . by the English College of Doway* (Douai, L. Kellam, 1609–10), 2 volumes

Martyr, P., *The Common Places*, trans. A. Marten (London, Denham & Middleton, 1583)

Menghi, Girolamo, *Fustis Daemonum* (Bologna, Giovanni Rossi, 1584)

Montaigne, M., *Œuvres complètes: Essais* (Paris, 1962)

More, Henry, *The Immortality of the Soul*, (London, J. Flesher, 1659)

Morton, T., *A Catholike Appeale for Protestants* (London, R. Field, 1609)

Mouchy, Antoine de, *Responce a quelque apologie que les heretiques ces jours passés ont mis en avant sous ce titre: Apologie ou deffence des bons Chrestiens contre les ennemis de l'Eglise catholique* (Paris, C. Fremy, 1558)

Moulin, P. Du, *The Waters of Siloe* (Oxford, J. Barnes, 1612)

Müller, G., and Seebass, G., eds, *Andreas Osiander d. Ä. Gesamtausgabe* (Gütersloh, 1975–97), 10 volumes

Murr, C. Gottlieb von, *Beschreibung der vornehmsten Merkwürdigkeiten in des H. R. Reichs Freyen Stadt Nürnberg und auf der hohen Schule zu Altdorf* (Nuremberg, 1778)

Napier, John, *A Plaine Discovery of the Whole Revelation of Saint John* (Edinburgh, R. Waldegrave, 1593)

Nashe, T., *The Terrors of the Night*, in *The Works of Thomas Nashe*, ed. R. B. McKerrow and F. Wilson (Oxford, 1958), 5 volumes

Nider, Joannes, *Preceptorium Divine Legis* (Basle, n. pr., c. 1470)

Northbrooke, J , *Spiritus est Vicarius in Terra* (London, J. Kingston, 1571)

Parker, M., *Correspondence*, ed. J. Bruce (Cambridge, 1853)

Parker, M., ed. and trans., *The Holie Bible* [Bishops' Bible] (London, R. Jugge, 1568)

Parr, Richard, *The Life of the Most Reverend Father in God, James Ussher, late Lord Archbishop of Armagh* (London, N. Ranew, 1686)

Pasquier, E., *Le Catechisme des Iesvites* (Paris, Ville-Franche, 1602)

Peel, A., ed., *The Seconde Parte of a Register* (Cambridge, 1915), 2 volumes

Pelikan, J., ed., *Luther's Works* (Philadelphia, 1958–67), 55 volumes

Perkins, W., *A Discourse of the Damned Art of Witchcraft* (Cambridge, J. Legat, 1608)

Perkins, W., *A Golden Chaine* (Cambridge, J. Legat, 1600)

Perkins, W., *A Reformed Catholike* (Cambridge, J. Legat, 1598)

Perreaud, F., *L'Antidemon de Mâcon* (Geneva, P. Aubert, 1653)

Perreaud, F., *Demonologie* (Geneva, P. Aubert, 1653)

Person, D., *Varieties: or a Surveigh of rare and excellent matters* (London, Badger & Cotes, 1635)

Peucer, Caspar, *Les Devins ou Commentaire des principales sortes de devinations* (Antwerp, H. Connix, 1584)

Porthaise, Jean, *De la Vraie et Faulse Astrologie contre les Abuseurs de nostre Siecle* (Poitiers, F. le Paige, 1579)

Preau, Gabriel du, ed., *Deux Livres de Mercure Trismegiste Hermés* (Paris, E. Groulleau, 1557)

Preston, J., *A Sermon Preached at the Funeral of Mr Arthur Upton Esquire in Devon* (London, W. Jones, 1619)

Pricke, R., *A Very Godlie and Learned Sermon treating of Mans Mortalitie* (London, T. Creede, 1608)

Purchas, S., *Purchas his Pilgrimage* (London, W. Stansby, 1613)

Rich, B., *The true report of a late practise enterprised by a papist with a yong maiden in Wales* (London, J. Kingston, 1582)

Sampson, T., ed. & trans., *The Bible* [Geneva version] (London, R. Parker, 1599)

Sandys, E., *Sermons*, ed. J. Ayre (Cambridge, 1841)

Schroeder, H. J., *Canon and Decrees of the Council of Trent. Original Text with English Translation* (St Louis, 1941)

Scot, Reginald, *Discoverie of Witchcraft* (London, W. Brome, 1584)

Sehling, E., ed., *Die evangelischen Kirchenordnungen des XVI. Jahrhunderts* (Leipzig and Tübingen, 1902–77), 16 volumes

Smith, H., *Sermons* (London, T. Orwin, 1592)

Smith, Sydney, *Works* (London, 1848), 3 volumes

[Squire, Edward], *A lettre written out of England* (London, C. Barker, 1599)

Strode, G., *The Anatomie of Mortalitie* (London, W. Jones, 1632)

Stubbes, P., *Two wunderfull and rare examples of the undeferred judgement of God* (London, W. Wright, 1581)

Sutcliffe, M., *Adversus Roberti Bellarmini de Purgatorio Disputationem* (London, Bishop, Newberie & Barker, 1599)

Swinnerton, Thomas, *A mustre of scismatyke bysshoppes of Rome* (London, J. Byddell, 1534)

Szilágyi, Sándor, ed., *Monumenta Comitialia Regni Transylvaniae* (Budapest, 1975–98), 21 volumes

Taillepied, N., *A Treatise of Ghosts*, trans. M. Summers (London, 1934)

Thou, J.-A. de, *Histoire Universelle* (The Hague, n. pr., 1740), 11 volumes

Tinley, Robert, *Two Learned Sermons* (London, W. Halland and T. Adams, 1609)

Tyard, Pontus de, *Mantice ou Discours de la verité de Divination par Astrologie* (Lyon, J. de Tournes & G. Gazeau, 1558)

Ussher, James, *Ecclesiarum Britannicarum Antiquitates* (Dublin, n. pr., 1639)

Veress, Endre, ed., *Fontes Rerum Transylvanicarum. Epistolae et Acta Jesuitarum Transylvaniae (1571–1613)* (Budapest, 1911–13), 2 volumes

Véron, J., *The Huntyng of Purgatorye to Death* (London, J. Tysdale, 1561)

Videl, Laurens, *Declaration des abus, ignorances et seditions de Michel Nostradamus, de Salon de Craux en Provence oeuvre tresutile & profitable â un chacun* (Avignon, P. Roux & J. Tramblay, 1558)

Vignier, Nicolas, *Theatre de L'Antechrist* (Saumur, n. pr., 1610)

Viret, P., *The Christian Disputations*, trans. J. Brooke (London, J. Brooke, 1579)

Voragine, J. de, *The Golden Legend*, trans. W. Ryan (Princeton, 1993), 2 volumes

Waterworth, J., trans., *The Canons and Decrees of the Sacred and Oecumenical Council of Trent* (London, 1848)

Weyer, J., *De praestigiis daemonum*, in G. Mora and B. Kohl, eds., and J. Shea, trans., *Witches, Devils, and Doctors in the Renaissance* (Binghampton, NY, 1991)

White, T., *The Middle State of Souls* (London, n. pr., 1659)

Wier, J., *De praestigiis daemonum* (Basil, n. pr., 1677)

Willet, A., *Synopsis Papismi* (London, T. Orwin, 1592)

Wither, G., *A View of the Marginal Notes of the Popish Testament* (London, E. Bollifant, 1588)

Würfel, A., *Diptycha Cappellae B. Mariae* (Nuremberg, Roth, 1761)

Würfel, A., *Diptycha Ecclesiæ Laurentianæ* (Nuremberg, Roth, 1756)

Secondary sources

Abray, L. J., *The People's Reformation: Magistrates, Clergy, and Commons in Strasbourg, 1500–1598* (Cornell, 1985)

Alzati, Cesare, *Terra Romena tra Oriente e Occidente. Chiese ed etnie nel tardo '500* (Milan, 1981)

Andersson, C., 'Religiöse Bilder Cranachs im Dienste der Reformation', in L. W. Spitz, ed., *Humanismus und Reformation als kulturelle Kräfte in der deutschen Geschichte* (Berlin, 1980), 43–79

Anglo, S., 'Reginald Scot's *Discoverie of Witchcraft*: Scepticism and Sadduceeism', in S. Anglo, ed., *The Damned Art: Essays in the Literature of Witchcraft* (London, 1977), 106–39

Atkinson, James, *Martin Luther: Prophet of the Catholic Church* (Grand Rapids, 1983)

Bächtold, Hans Ulrich, 'Gegen den Hunger beten. Heinrich Bullinger, Zürich und die Einführung des Gemeinen Gebetes im Jahre 1571', in Hans Ulrich Bächtold, Rainer Henrich and Kurt Jakob Rüetschi, eds, *Vom Beten, vom Verketzern, vom Predigen. Beiträge zum Zeitalter Heinrich Bullingers und Rudolf Gwalthers* (Zürich, 1999), 9–44

Backus, Irena, *Les Sept Visions et la fin des temps: les commentaires genevois de l'Apocalypse entre 1539 et 1584* (Geneva, 1997)

Badrus, Andrei Kertesz, 'Aspecte privind tematica picturii transilvănene din secolul al 16-lea', *Studii și cercetări de istoria artei* 28 (1981), 135–40

Bagchi, David, *Luther's Earliest Opponents: Catholic Controversialists, 1518–1525*, (Minneapolis, 1991)

Barnes, Robin Bruce, *Prophecy and Gnosis. Apocalypticism in the Wake of the Lutheran Reformation* (Stanford, 1988)

Baron, H., 'Religion and Politics in the German Imperial Cities During the Reformation', *English Historical Review* 52 (1937), 405–27, 614–33

Bast, Robert, *Honor Your Fathers: Catechisms and the Emergence of a Patriarchal Ideology in Germany* (Leiden, 1997)

Baxter, Richard, *Autobiography* (London, 1974)

Behringer, W., *Witchcraft Persecutions in Bavaria* (Cambridge, 1997)

Belfield, J., 'Tarleton's News out of Purgatory (London, 1590): A Modern-Spelling Edition', unpublished Ph.D. thesis (University of Birmingham, 1978)

Beyer, Jürgen, 'A Lübeck Prophet in Local and Lutheran Context', in R. W. Scribner and Trevor Johnson, eds, *Popular Religion in Germany and Central Europe, 1400–1800* (London, 1996), 166–82, 264–72

Beyer, Jürgen, 'Lutheran Popular Prophets in the Sixteenth and Seventeenth Centuries. The Performance of Untrained Speakers', *ARV. Nordic Yearbook of Folklore* 51 (1995), 63–86

Beyer, Jürgen, 'Lutherische Propheten in Deutschland und Skandinavien im 16. und 17. Jahrhundert. Entstehung und Ausbreitung eines Kulturmusters zwischen Mündlichkeit und Schriftlichkeit', in Robert Bohn, ed., *Europa in Scandinavia. Kulturelle und soziale Dialoge in der frühen Neuzeit* (Frankfurt am Main, 1994), 35–55

Binder, Ludwig, *Grundlagen und Formen der Toleranz in Siebenbürgen bis zur mitte des 17 Jahrhunderts* (Vienna, 1976)

Bireley, Robert, *The Refashioning of Catholicism, 1450–1700* (London, 1999)

Bossy, John, 'The Character of Elizabethan Catholicism', *Past and Present* 21 (1962), 39–59

Bossy, John, *Christianity in the West, 1400–1700* (Oxford, 1985)

Bossy, John, 'The Counter-Reformation and the People of Catholic Europe', in David M. Luebke, ed., *The Counter-Reformation* (Oxford, 1999), 92–3

Boyes, Georgina, 'Cultural Survivals Theory and Traditional Customs', *Folk Life* (1987–8), 5–11

Bradford, E., and M. A., eds, *Encyclopedia of Superstitions* (London, 1961)

Briggs, K. M., *The Anatomy of Puck: An Examination of Fairy Beliefs among Shakespeare's Contemporaries* (London, 1959)

Brou, A., *Les Jésuites de la légende* (Paris, 1906), 2 volumes

Browe, Peter, *Die häufige Kommunion in Mittelalter* (Münster, 1938)

Brown, Catherine, *Pastor and Laity in the Theology of Jean Gerson* (Cambridge, 1987)

Brown, P. Hume, *John Knox: A Biography* (London, 1929), 2 volumes

Brownlow, F. W., *Shakespeare, Harnett, and the Devils of Denham* (London, 1993)

Bullinger, H., *The Decades: The Fourth Decade*, T. Harding, ed. (Cambridge, 1851)

Bynum, C. Walker, *Jesus as Mother: Studies in the Spirituality of the High Middle Ages* (London, 1984)

Caciola, N., 'Wraiths, Revenants and Ritual in Medieval Culture', *Past and Present* 152 (1996), 3–45

Calfhill, J., *An Answer to John Martiall's Treatise of the Cross*, R. Gibbings, ed. (Cambridge, 1846)

Cameron, Euan, 'Frankfurt and Geneva: The European Context of John Knox's Reformation', in Roger Mason, ed., *John Knox and the British Reformation* (Aldershot, 1998), 51–73

Cameron, Euan, 'For Reasoned Faith or Embattled Creed? Religion for the People in Early Modern Europe', *Transactions of the Royal Historical Society* (1988), 165–87

Capelli, Adriano, *Cronologia, cronografia e calendario perpetuo* (Milan, 1988)

Capern, Amanda L., 'The Caroline Church. James Ussher and the Irish Dimension', *Historical Journal* 39 (1996), 57–85

Capern, Amanda L., 'Slipperye Times and Dangerous Dayes. James Ussher and the Calvinist Reformation of Britain, 1560–1660', unpublished Ph.D. thesis (University of New South Wales, 1991)

Céard, Jean, *La Nature et les prodiges: l'insolite au XVIe siècle* (Geneva, 1996)

Chartier, R., *Cultural History: Between Practices and Representations*, Lydia G. Cochrane, trans. (Cambridge, 1988)

Chiniquy, C., *Fifty Years in the Church of Rome: The Thrilling Life Story of Pastor Chiniquy Who was for Twenty-Five Years a Priest in the Roman Church* (London, 1948)

Chomarat, Michel, 'De quelques dates clairement exprimées par Michel Nostradamus dans ses "Prophéties"', *Prophètes et prophéties au XVIe siècle*, Cahiers V. L. Saulnier 15 (1998), 83–93

Christensen, C., 'Iconoclasm and the Preservation of Ecclesiastical Art in Reformation Nuremberg', *Archiv für Reformationsgeschichte* 61 (1970), 205–21

Christian, William, *Local Religion in Sixteenth-Century Spain* (Princeton, 1981)

Clark, Stuart, 'King James's *Daemonologie*: Witchcraft and Kingship', in S. Anglo, ed., *The Damned Art: Essays in the Literature of Witchcraft* (London, 1977), 156–81

Clark, Stuart, *Thinking with Demons. The Idea of Witchcraft in Early Modern Europe* (Oxford, 1997)

Clarke, Aidan, 'Ireland and the General Crisis', *Past and Present* 48 (1970), 79–99

Cohen, M. R., *Under Crescent and Cross. The Jews in the Middle Ages* (Princeton, 1994)

Collinson, Patrick, *The Birthpangs of Protestant England. Religious and Cultural Change in the Sixteenth and Seventeenth Centuries* (London, 1988)

Crăciun, Maria, 'Superstition and Religious Difference in Sixteenth and Seventeenth Century Transylvania', in I. G. Tóth and E. Andor, eds, *Frontiers of Faith: Religious Exchange and the Constitution of Religious Identities 1400–1750* (Budapest, 2001), 213–31

Crăciun, Maria, 'The Use of the Vernacular in Catholic Propaganda during the Last Decades of the 16th Century', in Ambrus Miskolczy, ed., *Europa, Balcanica, Danubiana, Carpathica, 2A, Annales, Cultura, Historia, Philologia* (Budapest, 1995), 130–7

Cressy, David, *Bonfires and Bells. National Memory and the Protestant Calendar in Elizabethan and Stuart England* (London, 1989)

Cross, Claire, *Church and People, 1450–1660* (London, 1987)

Crouzet, Denis, *Les Guerriers de Dieu: la violence aux temps des troubles de religion, vers 1520–vers 1610* (Paris, 1990), 2 volumes

Cubbitt, G., *The Jesuit Myth: Conspiracy Theory and Politics in Nineteenth-Century France* (Oxford, 1993)

Cancu, Iuliana Fabritius, *Cetăți țărănești din Transilvania* (Sibiu, 1983)

Daniel, David P., 'Calvinism in Hungary: The Theological and Ecclesiastical Transition to the Reformed Faith', in A. Pettegree, A. Duke and G. Lewis, eds, *Calvinism in Europe 1540–1620* (Cambridge, 1994), 201–230

Daniel, David P., 'Hungary', in Andrew Pettegree, ed., *The Early Reformation in Europe* (Cambridge, 1992), 49–69

Daston, L., and Park, K., *Wonders and the Order of Nature, 1150–1750* (New York, 1998)

Davis, Natalie Zemon, 'Some Tasks and Themes in the Study of Popular Religion', in C. Trinkaus and H. O. Oberman, eds, *The Pursuit of Holiness in Late Medieval and Renaissance Religion* (Leiden, 1974), 333

Davis, Natalie Zemon, 'Towards Mixtures and Margins', *American Historical Review* 97 (1992), 1400–9

Dear, Peter, *Revolutionizing the Sciences: European Knowledge and its Ambitions, 1500–1700* (Houndsmill, 2001)

Della Porta, Giovanni Battista, *Magia Naturalis* (Lyon, P. Compagnon, 1650)

Delumeau, Jean, *Catholicism between Luther and Voltaire. A New View of the Counter Reformation* (London, 1977)

Devlin, C., 'Hamlet's Divinity', in *Hamlet's Divinity and Other Essays* (London, 1963)

Dictionary of National Biography (London, 1899), 63 volumes

Dixon, C. Scott, 'Popular Astrology and Lutheran Propaganda in Reformation Germany', *History* 84 (1999): 403–18

Dixon, C. Scott, *The Reformation and Rural Society: The Parishes of Brandenburg-Ansbach-Kulmbach, 1525–1603* (Cambridge, 1996)

Dobin, Howard, *Merlin's Disciples. Prophecy, Popetry, and Power in Renaissance England* (Stanford, SA, 1990)

Donaldson, Gordon, *The Scottish Reformation* (Cambridge, 1960)

Duffy, Eamon, *The Stripping of the Altars: Traditional Religion in England c.1400–c.1580* (New Haven, 1993)

Edwards, Mark U., Jr., *Luther and the False Brethren* (Stanford, 1975)

Ehrlich, E., *et al.*, eds, *Oxford American Dictionary* (Oxford, 1980)

Eire, Carlos, *From Madrid to Purgatory: The Art and Craft of Dying in Sixteenth-Century Spain* (Cambridge, 1995)

Elrington, Charles Richard, *The Life of the Most Rev. James Ussher, D.D.* (London, 1848)

Engammare, Max, 'Calvin: A Prophet without a Prophecy', *Church History* 67 (1998), 643–61

Evenett, Outram, *The Spirit of the Counter-Reformation* (South Bend, IN, 1970)

Fairfield, Leslie P., *John Bale. Mythmaker for the English Reformation* (West Lafayette, IN, 1976)

Fife, A. E., 'Birthmarks and Psychic Imprinting of Babies in Utah Folk Medicine', in W. D. Hand, ed., *American Folk Medicine, A Symposium* (Berkeley, 1976), 273–83

Finlayson, R. A., 'John Knox, His Theology', *The Bulwark* (1975), 1–11

Finucane, R., *Appearances of the Dead: A Cultural History of Ghosts* (London, 1982)

Firth, Katharine R., *The Apocalyptic Tradition in Reformation Britain 1530–1645* (Oxford, 1979)

Fleming, D. Hay, 'John Knox in the Hands of the Philistines', *The British Weekly* 33 (26 February 1903), 518

Flint, Valerie, *The Rise of Magic in Early Medieval Europe* (Princeton, 1991)

Ford, Alan, *The Protestant Reformation in Ireland, 1590–1641* (Dublin, 1997)

Fornhaber, Teuchs, *Urkundenbuch zur Geschichte Siebenbürgens* (Vienna, 1851)

Forster, Marc, *The Counter-Reformation in the Villages: Religion and Reform in the Bishopric of Speyer, 1560–1720* (Ithaca, 1992)

Franz, E., *Nürnberg, Kaiser und Reich: Studien zur Reichsstädtischen Aussenpolitik* (Munich, 1930)

Frazer, James, *The Golden Bough* (Basingstoke, 1914)

Friedrichs, Christopher, *Urban Society in an Age of War: Nördlingen, 1580–1720* (Princeton, 1979)

Friedrichsdorf, Joachim, *Umkehr. Prophetie und Bildung bei Johann Amos Comenius* (Idstein, 1995)

Frye, R. M., *The Renaissance Hamlet: Issues and Responses in 1600* (Princeton, 1984)

Gentilcore, David, *From Bishop to Witch. The System of the Sacred in Early Modern Terra d'Otranto* (Manchester, 1992)

Germanisches Nationalmuseum publication, *Veit Stoss in Nürnberg: Werke des Meisters und seiner Schule in Nürnberg und Umgebung* (Munich, 1983)

Gillespie, Raymond, *Devoted People. Belief and Religion in Early Modern Ireland* (Manchester, 1997)

Gillon, Robert Moffat, *John Davidson of Prestonpans* (London, 1936)

Gombrich, E. H., *Art and Illusion: A Study in the Psychology of Pictorial Representation* (London, 1960)

Graef, H., *Mary: A History of Doctrine and Devotion* (London, 1985), 2 volumes

Gray, John R., 'The Political Theory of John Knox', *Church History* 8 (1939), 132–47

Greaves, Richard L., 'The Nature of Authority in the Writings of John Knox', *Fides et Historia* 10 (1978), 4–24

Greaves, Richard L., *Theology and Revolution in the Scottish Reformation* (Grand Rapids, 1980)

Greenblatt, S., *Hamlet in Purgatory* (Princeton, 2001)

Greiner, Johannes, *Geschichte der Schule in Rottweil am Neckar* (Stuttgart, 1915)

Haag, Norbert, 'Frömmigkeit und sozialer Protest. Hans Keil, der Prophet von Gerlingen', *Zeitschift für Württembergische Landesgeschichte* 48 (1989), 127–41

Haigh, Christopher, 'The Continuity of Catholicism in the English Reformation', *Past and Present* 93 (1981), 37–69

Haller, William, *Foxe's Book of Martyrs and the Elect Nation* (London, 1963)

Hazlett, W. Ian O., 'The Scots Confession 1560: Context, Complexion and Critique', *Archiv für Reformationsgeschichte* 78 (1987), 287–320

Hecht, Winfried, 'Rottweils Magistrat kündigt den Pfarrer von Balgheim (1589)', *Rottweiler Heimatblätter*, 52/3 (1991), n. p.

Henderson, G. D., 'John Knox and the Bible', *Records of the Scottish Church History Society* 9 (1947), 97–110

Herold, M., *Alt-Nürnberg in seinen Gottesdiensten. Ein Beitrag zur Geschichte der Sitte und des Kultus* (Gütersloh, 1890)

Higman, Francis, 'The Origins of the Image of Geneva', in J. B. Roney and M. J. Klauber, eds, *The Identity of Geneva: The Christian Commonwealth 1564–1864* (London, 1998), 21–38

Hill, Christopher, *The World Turned Upside Down* (Middlesex, 1984)

Hirschmann, G., *Die Kirchenvisitation im Landgebiet der Reichstadt Nürnberg 1560 und 1561: Quellenedition* (Neustadt a. d. Aisch, 1994)

Hirschmann, G., 'The Second Nürnberg Church Visitation', in L. P. Buck and J. W. Zophy, eds, *The Social History of the Reformation* (Columbus, 1972), 355–80

Hsia, R. Po-chia, *Social Discipline in the Reformation: Central Europe 1550–1750*, (London, 1989)

Hufton, O., 'The Widow's Mite', *Transactions of the Royal Historical Society* 8 (1998), 117–37

Hutton, Ronald, 'The English Reformation and the Evidence of Folklore', *Past and Present* 148 (1995), 89–116

Hutton, Ronald, *The Rise and Fall of Merry England: The Ritual Year 1400–1700* (Oxford, 1994)

Jansen, Sharon L., *Political Protest and Prophecy under Henry VIII* (Woodbridge, 1991)

Jelsma, A., *Frontiers of the Reformation: Dissidence and Orthodoxy in Sixteenth-Century Europe* (Aldershot, 1998)

Johnston, George, 'Scripture in the Scottish Reformation', *Canadian Journal of Theology* 9 (1963), 40–9

Jones, N., 'Defining Superstitions: Treasonous Catholics and the Act against Witch-craft of 1563', in C. Carlton, R. L. Woods, M. L. Robertson and J. S. Black, eds, *State, Sovereigns and Society in Early Modern England* (Stroud, 1998), 187–204

Joseph, M., 'Discerning the Ghost in Hamlet', *Publications of the Modern Language Association of America* 76 (London, 1961), 493–502

Joutard, P., 'Protestantisme populaire et univers magique: le cas cévenol', *Religion populaire: le Monde alpin et rhodanien* 5 (1977)

Kagan, R. L., *Lucrecia's Dreams. Politics and Prophecy in 16th century Spain* (London, 1995)

Kamen, Henry, *The Phoenix and the Flame: Catalonia and the Counter-Reformation* (New Haven, 1993)

Kaplan, S. L., *Understanding Popular Culture. Europe from the Middle Ages to the Nineteenth Century* (New York, 1984)

Karant-Nunn, Susan C., *The Reformation of Ritual. An Interpretation of Early Modern Germany* (London, 1997)

Kieckhefer, R., *Magic in the Middle Ages* (Cambridge, 1989)

King, John N., *English Reformation Literature. The Tudor Origins of the Protestant Tradition* (Princeton, 1982)

Kittredge, G. L., *Witchcraft in Old and New England* (New York, 1929)

Klaniczay, Gabor, *The Uses of Supernatural Power* (Princeton, 1990)

Klaus, B., *Veit Dietrich. Leben und Werk* (Nuremberg, 1958)

Klingebiel, Thomas, 'Apokalyptik, Prodigienglaube und Prophetismus im Alten Reich. Einführung', in Hartmut Lehmann and Anne-Charlott Trepp, eds, *Im Zeichen der Krise. Religiosität in Europa des 17. Jahrhunderts* (Göttingen, 1999), 17–32

Knappen, M. M., *Tudor Puritanism: A Chapter in the History of Idealism* (Chicago, 1966)

Knox, R. Buick, *James Ussher, Archbishop of Armagh* (Cardiff, 1967)

Krusenstjern, Benigna von, 'Prodigienglaube und Dreißigjähriger Krieg', in Hartmut Lehmann and Anne-Charlott Trepp, eds, *Im Zeichen der Krise. Religiosität im Europa des 17. Jahrhunderts* (Göttingen, 1999), 53–78

Kvideland R., and Sehmsdorf, H. K., eds, *Scandinavian Folk Belief and Legend* (Oslo, 1991)

Kyle, Richard G., 'The Hermeneutical Patterns in John Knox's Use of Scripture', *Pacific Theological Review* 17: 3 (1984), 19–32

Kyle, Richard, 'John Knox and Apocalyptic Thought', *Sixteenth Century Journal* 15 (1984), 449–69

Kyle, Richard, 'John Knox's Concept of History: A Focus on the Providential and Apocalyptic Aspects of His Religious Faith', *Fides et Historia* 18 (1986), 5–19

Kyle, Richard, 'John Knox: The Main Themes of His Thought', *The Princeton Seminary Bulletin* 9 (1983), 102–4

Kyle, Richard, 'John Knox: A Man of the Old Testament', *Westminster Theological Journal*, 54 (Spring 1992), 65–78

Kyle, Richard, 'John Knox's Method of Biblical Interpretation: An Important Source of His Intellectual Radicalness', *Journal of Religious Studies* 12: 2 (1986), 57–70

Labrousse, E., *Conscience et conviction, études sur le XVIIe siècle* (Oxford, 1996)

Lake, P., 'Anti-popery: The Structure of a Prejudice', in R. Cust and A. Hughes, eds, *Conflict in Early Stuart England: Studies in Religion and Politics, 1603–1642* (London, 1989), 72–106

Lake, P., 'Deeds against Nature: Cheap Print, Protestantism and Murder in Early Seventeenth-Century England', in K. Sharpe and Lake, eds, *Culture and Politics in Early Stuart England* (Basingstoke, 1994)

Lambrecht, Karl, *Rottweiler Narren-Fibel* (Rottweil, 1988)

Lang, Andrew, *John Knox and the Reformation* (London, 1905).

Langstaff, Beth, 'A World without Wonders? Erasmus, Tyndale, and the Cessation of Miracles', an unpublished paper delivered at the *Sixteenth Century Studies Conference* (Toronto, 28 October 1994)

Little, Paul M., 'John Knox and the English Social Prophecy', *Presbyterian Historical Society of England* 14 (1970), 117–27

Lochner, G. W. K., *Die noch vorhandenen Abzeichen Nürnberger Häuser* (Nuremberg, 1855)

Lorimer, Peter, *John Knox and the Church of England* (London, 1895)

Lotz-Heumann, Ute, *Die doppelte Konfessionalisierung in Irland. Konflikt und Koexistenz im 16. und in der ersten Hälfte des 17. Jahrhunderts* (Tübingen, 2000), 310–11

MacDonald, M., *Mystical Bedlam: Madness, Anxiety, and Healing in Seventeenth-Century England* (Cambridge, 1981)

MacDonald, M., and Murphy, T., *Sleepless Souls: Suicide in Early Modern England* (Oxford, 1990)

MacGregor, Malcom B., *The Sources and Literature of Scottish Church History* (Glasgow, 1934)

MacIver, Martha Abele, 'Ian Paisely and the Reformed Tradition', *Political Studies* 35 (1987), 362–78

MacIver, Martha Abele, 'Militant Protestant Political Ideology: Ian Paisley and the Reformation Tradition', unpublished Ph.D. dissertation (University of Michigan, 1984)

Mack, Phyllis, 'Women as Prophets during the English Civil War', *Feminist Studies* 8: 1 (1982), 19–45

Mack, Phyllis, *Visionary Women. Ecstatic Prophecy in Seventeenth-Century England* (Berkeley, 1992)

Mândrescu, G., 'Altarul de la Guşteriţa', in *Ars Transilvaniae* 2 (1992), 73–6

Martin, A. Lynn, *The Jesuit Mind* (Ithaca, 1988)

Martin, A. Lynn, 'The Jesuit Mystique', *Sixteenth Century Journal* 4 (1973)

Martin, A. Lynn, *Plague? Jesuit Accounts of Epidemic Disease in the 16th Century* (Kirksville, MO, 1996)

Mason, Roger A., *John Knox on Rebellion* (Cambridge, 1993)

Maxwell-Stuart, P. G., *The Occult in Early Modern Europe: A Documentary History* (Basingstoke, 1999)

McGee, A., *The Elizabethan Hamlet* (New Haven, 1987)

McGoldrick, James Edward, *Luther's English Connection* (Milwaukee, 1979)

McKechnie, William S., 'Thomas Maitland', *Scottish Historical Review* 4 (1907), 274–93

M'Crie, Thomas, *The Life of John Knox* (Glasgow, 1976)

Megged, A., *Exporting the Catholic Reformation: Local Religion in Early-Colonial Mexico* (Leiden, 1996)

Melville, James, *The Autobiography and Diary of Mr. James Melville*, Robert Pitcairn, ed. (Edinburgh, 1842)

Meszlényi, Antal, *A Magyar jezsuitak a XV században* (Budapest, 1931)

Metropolitan Museum of Art and Germanisches Nationalmuseum publication, *Gothic and Renaissance Art in Nuremberg, 1300–1550* (New York, 1986)

Millet, Olivier, 'Feux croisés sur Nostradamus au XVIe siècle', *Divination et controverse religieuse en France au XVIe siècle*, Cahiers V. L. Saulnier 4 (1987)

Moeller, Bernd, 'Piety in Germany around 1500', in S. Ozment, ed., *The Reformation in Medieval Perspective* (Chicago, 1971), 50–75

Monter, E. William, *Ritual, Myth and Magic in Early Modern Europe* (Brighton, 1993)

Morris, Colin, *The Papal Monarchy, The Western Church from 1050 to 1250* (Oxford, 1989), 371–86

Mousnier, R., *L'Assassinat d'Henri IV* (Paris, 1964)

Mout, Nicolette, 'Chiliastic Prophecy and Revolt in the Habsburg Monarchy during the Seventeenth Century', in Michael Wilks, ed., *Prophecy and Eschatology* (Oxford, 1994), 93–109

Muchembled, R., *Popular and Elite Culture in France 1400–1750*, L. Cochrane, trans. (London, 1985)

Muir, Edwin, *John Knox: Portrait of a Calvinist* (London, 1929)

Müller, Hans-Joachim, 'Kriegserfahrung, Prophetie und Weltfriedenskonzepte während des Dreißigjährigen Krieges', in *Jahrbuch für Historische Friedensforschung* 6 (1997), 26–47

Murdock, Graeme, *Calvinism on the Frontier 1600–1660: International Calvinism and the Reformed Church in Hungary and Transylvania* (Oxford, 2000)

Myers, David, *'Poor, Sinning Folk': Confession and Conscience in Counter-Reformation Germany*, (Ithaca, 1996)

Niccoli, Ottavia, *Prophecy and People in Renaissance Italy* (Princeton, 1990)

Nischan, B., 'The Exorcism Controversy and Baptism in the Late Reformation', *Sixteenth Century Journal* 18 (1987): 31–51

Nye, Jason, 'Johannes Uhl on Penitence: Sermons of the Dean of Rottweil, 1579–1602', in Katharine Jackson Lualdi and Anne T. Thayer, eds, *Penitence in the Age of Reformations* (Aldershot, 2000), 152–68

Oestreich, B., and Koenigsberger, H. G., eds, *Neostoicism and the Early Modern State* (Cambridge, 1982)

Oestreich, Gerhard, 'Strukturprobleme des europäische Absolutismus', in G. Oestreich, ed., *Geist und Gestalt des frühmodernen Staates* (Berlin, 1969), 179–97

Owen, E., *Welsh Folk-Lore* (Oswestry and Wrexham, 1896)

Ozment, Steven, *The Reformation in the Cities* (New Haven, 1975)

Parker, K. L., and Carlson, E. J., *'Practical Divinity': The Works and Life of Revd Richard Greenham* (Aldershot, 1998)

Percy, Lord Eustace, *John Knox* (London, 1937)

Peter, Katalin, 'Hungary', in R. W. Scribner, R. Porter and M. Teich, eds, *The Reformation in National Context* (Cambridge, 1994), 135–167

Peters, Christine, 'Mural Paintings, Ethnicity and Religious Identity in Transylvania. The Context for Reformation', in M. Crăciun and O. Ghitta, eds, *Ethnicity and Religion in Central and Eastern Europe* (Cluj, 1995), 44–63

Pfeiffer, G., ed., *Quellen zur Nürnberger Reformationsgeschichte. Von der Duldung liturgischer Änderungen bis zur Ausübung des Kirchenregiments durch den Rat (Juni 1524–Juni 1525)* (Nuremberg, 1968)

Pohl, H., ed., *Willibald Imhoff, Enkel und Erbe Willibald Pirckheimers* (Nuremberg, 1992)

Pokoly, József, *Az erdély református egyház története* (Budapest, 1904), 5 volumes

Popkin, Richard H., 'Predicting, Prophecying, Divining and Foretelling from Nostradamus to Hume', *History of European Ideas* 5: 2 (1984), 117–35

Prosser, E., *Hamlet and Revenge* (Stanford, 1967)

Questier, M., '"Like Locusts over All the World": Conversion, Indoctrination and the Society of Jesus in late Elizabethan and Jacobean England', T. McCoog, ed., *The Reckoned Expense: Edmond Campion and the Early English Jesuits* (Woodbridge, 1996), 265–84

Racaut, Luc, *Hatred in Print: Catholic Propaganda and Protestant Identity during the French Wars of Religion* (Aldershot, 2002)

Racaut, Luc, 'Religious Polemic and the Protestant Self-Image', in R. Mentzer and A. Spicer, eds, *Society and Culture in the Huguenot World, 1559–1665* (Cambridge, 2002), 29–43

Reid, W. Stanford, 'French Influence on the First Scots Confession and Book of Discipline', *Westminster Theological Journal* 35 (1972–73), 1–14

Reid, W. Standford, 'Knox's Attitude to the English Reformation', *Westminster Theological Journal* 26 (1963), 1–32

Reid, W. Stanford, *Trumpeter of God* (New York, 1974)

Reinerth, K., *Die Grundung der Evangelischen Kirchen in Siebenbürgen* (Vienna, 1979)

Reinerth, K., 'Die Reformation der Siebenbürgische sächsischen Kirche', in *Schriften des Vereins für Reformationsgeschichte* I 73: 61 (Gutersloh, 1956), 43–47

Reinhard, Wolfgang, 'Reformation, Counter-Reformation, and the Early Modern State: A Reassessment', *The Catholic Historical Review*, 75 (1989), 383–404

Reinhard, Wolfgang, 'Zwang zur Konfessionalisierung? Prologemena zu einer Theorie des konfessionellen Zeitalters', *Zeitschrift für Historische Forschung*, 10 (1983), 257–77

Richardson, R., *Death, Dissection and the Destitute* (London, 1987)

Ridley, Jasper, *John Knox* (Oxford, 1968)

Roper, L., *The Holy Household: Women and Morals in Reformation Augsburg* (Oxford, 1991)

Roper, L., *Oedipus and the Devil: Witchcraft, Sexuality and Religion in Early Modern Europe* (London, 1994)

Roth, E., *Die Reformation in Siebenbürgen, ihr Verhältnis in Wittenberg und der Schweiz* (Cologne, 1962)

Roth, E., *Volkskultur in Franken. Band I: Kult und Kunst* (Bamberg and Würzburg, 1990)

Rubin, Miri, *Corpus Christi: The Eucharist in Late Medieval Culture* (Cambridge, 1991)

Rublack, Hans-Christoph, 'New Patterns of Christian Life', in T. A. Brady, H. A. Oberman and J. D. Tracy, eds, *Handbook of European History, 1400–1600: Late Middle Ages, Renaissance, and Reformation* (Leiden, 1994), 585–605

Rusu A. A., 'Bisericile româneşti din districtul Haţeg până la 1700', in *Ars Transilvaniae* 1 (1991), 129–42

Rusu, A. A., *Ctitori şi biserici din Ţara Haţegului până la 1700* (Satu Mare, 1997)

Rusu, A. A., 'A Glimpse at the Inner Life of a Transylvanian Monastery, The Dominican Monastery of Vinţu De Jos (Alba county)', in M. Crăciun and O. Ghitta, eds., *Church and Society in Central and Eastern Europe* (Cluj, 1998), 13–21

Sabean, David Warren, *Power in the Blood: Popular Culture and Village Discourse in Early Modern Germany* (Cambridge, 1984)

Sabean, David Warren, 'A Prophet in the Thirty Years' War. Penance as a Social Metaphor', in David Warren Sabean, *Power in the Blood. Popular Culture and Village Discourse in Early Modern Germany* (Cambridge, 1984), 61–93

Sands, K. R., 'The Doctrine of Transubstantiation and the English Protestant Dispossession of Demons', *History* 85 (2000), 447–8, 461

Scarisbrick, J. J., *The Reformation and the English People* (Oxford, 1984)

Schechner, Sara J., *Comets, Popular Culture and the Birth of Modern Cosmology* (Princeton, 1999)

Schiller, G., *Ikonographie der christlichen Kunst* (Gütersloh, 1966–90), 8 volumes

Schilling, Heinz, 'Confessionalisation in the Empire: Religious and Societal Change in Germany between 1555 and 1620,' in H. Schilling, ed., *Religion, Political Culture and the Emergence of Early Modern Society* (Leiden, 1992), 205–45

Schilling, Heinz, 'Die Konfessionalisierung von Kirche, Staat, und Gesellschaft', in Wolfgang Reinhard and Heinz Schilling, eds, *Die Katholische Konfessionalisierung*, in *Schriften des Vereins für Reformationsgeschichte*, 198 (Gütersloh, 1995), 1–49

Schilling, Heinz, 'Nationale Identität und Konfession in der europäischen Neuzeit', in B. Giesen, ed., *Nationale und kulturelle Identität. Studien zur Entwicklung des kollektiven Bewußtseins in der Neuzeit* (Frankfurt, 1991), 192–252

Schlemmer, K., *Gottesdienst und Frömmigkeit in der Reichsstadt Nürnberg am Vorabend der Reformation* (Würzburg, 1980)

Schmitt, J.-C., *Ghosts in the Middle Ages: the Living and the Dead in Medieval Society*, T. Fagan, trans. (London, 1998)

Schwemmer, W., 'Aus der Geschichte der Kunstsammlungen der Stadt Nürnberg', *Mitteilungen des Vereins für Geschichte der Stadt Nürnberg* 40 (1949), 97–133

Scribner, R. W., 'Cosmic Order and Daily Life', in Scribner, ed. *Popular Culture and Popular Movements in Reformation Germany* (London, 1987), 1–16

Scribner, R. W., 'Elements of Popular Belief', in T. A. Brady, H. Oberman and J. D. Tracey, eds, *Handbook of European History, 1400–1600: Late Middle Ages, Renais-*

sance, and Reformation (Leiden, 1994), 231–62

Scribner, R. W., *For the Sake of Simple Folk. Popular Propaganda for the German Reformation* (Cambridge, 1981; Oxford, 1994)

Scribner, R. W., 'The Impact of the Reformation on Daily Life', in Gerhard Jaritz, ed., *Mensch und Objekt in Mittelalter und in der fruhen Neuzeit. Leben, Alltag, Kultur* (Vienna, 1990)

Scribner, R. W., 'Incombustible Luther. The Image of the Reformer in Early Modern Germany', *Past and Present* 110 (1986), 38–68

Scribner, R. W., 'Introduction', in Scribner and Johnson, *Popular Religion* (Basingstoke, 1996)

Scribner, R. W., 'Luther Myth. A Popular Historiography of the Reformer', in Scribner, *Popular Culture*, 301–22

Scribner, R. W., *Popular Culture and Popular Movements in Reformation Germany* (London, 1987)

Scribner, R. W., 'Reformation, Carnival and the World Turned Upside-Down', in Scribner, *Popular Culture*, 71–102

Scribner, R. W., 'The Reformation and the "Disenchantment of the World"', in C. Scott Dixon, ed., *The German Reformation: The Essential Readings* (London, 1999), 262–79

Scribner, R. W., 'The Reformation, Popular Magic and the "Disenchantment of the World"', *Journal of Interdisciplinary History* 23 (1993), 475–94

Scribner, R. W., 'Ritual and Popular Religion in Catholic Germany at the Time of the Reformation', *Journal of Ecclesiastical History* 35: 1 (1984), 47–77

Scribner, R. W., 'Ritual and Popular Religion in Catholic Germany at the time of the Reformation', in Scribner, *Popular Culture*, 17–48

Scribner, R. W., 'Ritual and Reformation', in Scribner, *Popular Culture*, 103–23

Scribner, R. W., 'Ways of Seeing in the Age of Dürer', in D. Eichberger and C. Zike, eds, *Dürer and His Culture* (Cambridge, 1998), 93–117

Scribner, R. W., and Johnson, Trevor, eds, *Popular Religion in Germany and Central Europe 1400–1800* (Basingstoke, 1996)

Seebass, G., 'The Importance of the Imperial City of Nuremberg in the Reformation', in J. Kirk, ed., *Humanism and Reform: The Church in Europe, England, and Scotland 1400–1643. Essays in Honour of James K. Cameron* (Oxford, 1991), 113–27

Seebass, G., 'Mittelalterliche Kunstwerke in evangelisch gewordenen Kirchen Nürnbergs', in J. M. Fritz, ed., *Die bewahrende Kraft des Luthertums: mittelalterliche Kunstwerke in evangelischen Kirchen* (Regensburg, 1997), 34–53

Seebass, G., *Das reformatorische Werk des Andreas Osiander* (Nuremberg, 1967)

Seymour, St John D., *Irish Witchcraft and Demonology* (New York 1992)

Sharpe, Charles Kirkpatrick, *A Historical Account of the Belief in Witchcraft in Scotland* (New York, 1972)

Shaw, Duncan, ed., *John Knox: A Quartercentury Reappraisal* (Edinburgh, 1975)

Shibutani, T., *Improvised News: A Sociological Study of Rumor* (Indianapolis, 1966)

Skelton, John, *Maitland of Lethington and the Scotland of Mary Stuart, A History* (London, 1888)

Soergel, P., 'From Legends to Lies: Protestant Attacks on Catholic Miracles in Late
    Reformation Germany', *Fides et Historia* 21 (1989): 21–9
Soergel, P., *Wondrous in His Saints: Counter Reformation Propaganda in Bavaria* (Berkely
    and London, 1993)
Spottiswoode, John, *History of the Church of Scotland* (Edinburgh, 1851), 2 volumes
Stalker, James, *John Knox: His Ideas and Ideals* (London, 1904)
Strauss, Gerald, *Luther's House of Learning. Indoctrination of the Young in the German Refor-
    mation* (Baltimore, 1978)
Strauss, Gerald, *Nuremberg in the Sixteenth Century: City Politics and Life between Middle
    Ages and Modern Times* (London, 1976)
Strauss, Gerald, 'The reformation and its public in an age of orthodoxy', in R. Po-Chia
    Hsia, ed., *The German People and the Reformation* (Ithaca, 1988), 194–214
Strauss, Gerald, 'Success and Failure in the German Reformation', *Past and Present* 67
    (1975), 30–63
Strieder, P., *Tafelmalerei in Nürnberg 1350–1550* (Königstein im Taunus, 1993)
Styles, Philip, 'James Ussher and His Times', *Hermathena* 88 (1956), 12–33
Swanson, Robert, 'The Pre-Reformation Church', in A. Pettegree, ed., *The Reforma-
    tion World* (Routledge, 2000), 9–30
Sweetman, Leonard, Jr., 'The Gifts of the Spirit: A Study of Calvin's Comments on I
    Corinthians 12: 8–10, 28; Romans 12: 6–8; Ephesians 4: 11', in David E. Hol-
    werda, ed., *Exploring the Heritage of John Calvin: Essays in Honor of John Bratt*
    (Grand Rapids, 1976)
Székely, Sandor, *Az unitárius vallás története* (Budapest, 1949)
Talkenberger, Heike, *Sintflut. Prophetie und Zeitgeschehen in Texten und Holzschnitten
    astrologischer Flugschriften 1488–1528* (Tübingen, 1990)
Tanz, Sabine, and Werner, Ernst, *Spätmittelalterliche Laienmentalitäten im Spiegel von
    Visionen, Offenbarungen und Prophezeiungen* (Frankfurt am Main, 1993)
Theibault, John, 'Jeremiah in the Village. Prophecy, Preaching, Pamphlets, and
    Penance in the Thirty Years' War', *Central European History* 27 (1994), 441–60
Thomas, Keith, *Religion and the Decline of Magic. Studies in Popular Beliefs in Sixteenth and
    Seventeenth Century England* (London, 1971)
Thulin, O., *Cranach-Altäre der Reformation* (Berlin, 1955)
Trevor-Roper, Hugh, 'James Ussher, Archbishop of Armagh', in Hugh Trevor-Roper,
    Catholics, Anglicans, and Puritans. Seventeenth Century Essays (Chicago, 1988),
    120–65, 289–92
Tüchle, Hermann, 'Das Bistum Konstanz und das Konzil von Trient', in Georg Schreiber,
    ed., *Das Weltkonzil von Trient. Sein Werden und Wirken* (Freiburg, 1951), 191
Ungvary, Alexander, *The Hungarian Protestant Reformation in the 16th century under
    Ottoman Impact, Essays and Profiles* (Lewiston, 1989)
Vander Molen, Ronald J., 'Anglican against Puritan: Ideological Origins during the
    Marian Exiles', *Church History* 42 (1973), 45–57
Vander Molen, Ronald J., 'Providence as Mystery, Providence as Revelation: Puritan
    and Anglican Modifications of John Calvin's Doctrine of Providence', *Church
    History* 47 (1978), 27–47

Veress, Endre, *Izabella Királyne* (Budapest, 1901)

Walker, D. P., 'Demonic Possession Used as Propaganda in the later 16th Century', in P. Rossi, ed., *Scienze, Credenze Occulte, Livelli di Cultura* (Florence, 1982), 237–48

Walsh, Walter, 'The Jesuits', in C. Walsh, ed., *The Protestant Dictionary Containing Articles on the History, Doctrines and Practices of the Christian Church, New Edition* (London, 1933), 349

Walsham, Alexandra, '"Frantic Hackett": Prophecy, Sorcery, Insanity, and the Elizabethan Puritan Movement', *Historical Journal* 41: 1 (1998), 27–66

Walsham, Alexandra, '"Out of the Mouths of Babes and Sucklings": Prophecy, Puritanism and Childhood in Elizabethan Suffolk', *Studies in Church History* 31 (1994), 285–99

Walsham, Alexandra, *Providence in Early Modern England* (Oxford, 1999)

Walzer, Michael, *The Revolution of the Saints* (London, 1966)

Warr, C. L., *The Presbyterian Tradition* (London, 1933)

Watt, Diane, *Secretaries of God. Women Prophets in Late Medieval and Early Modern England* (Cambridge, 1997)

Watt, Hugh, *John Knox in Controversy* (New York, 1950)

Watt, Tessa, *Cheap Print and Popular Piety 1550–1640* (Cambridge, 1991)

Weber, Georg Renate, *Luther und Siebenbürgen* (Vienna, 1985)

Webster, Charles, *From Paracelsus to Newton. Magic and the Making of Modern Science* (Cambridge, 1982)

Weiner, C., 'The Beleaguered Isle. A study of Elizabethan and early Jacobean anti-Catholicism.', *Past and Present* 51 (1971), 27–62

West, R. H., *The Invisible World: A Study of Pneumatology in Elizabethan Drama* (New York, 1969)

West, R. H., *Shakespeare and the Outer Mystery* (Lexington, 1968)

Westerkamp, M. J., *Women and Religion in Early America, 1600–1850* (London, 1999)

Wilks, Michael, ed., *Prophecy and Eschatology* (Oxford, 1994)

Williamson, Arthur H., *Scottish National Consciousness in the Age of James VI: The Apocalypse, the Union and Shaping of Scotland's Public Culture* (Edinburgh, 1979)

Willock, R., *A Shetland Minister of the Eighteenth Century* (Kirkwall, 1897)

Wilson, J. Dover, *What Happens in Hamlet?* (Cambridge, 1951)

Wilson, Stephen, *The Magical Universe. Everyday Ritual and Magic in Pre-Modern Europe* (London, 2000)

Wunderli, Richard M., *Peasant Fires: the Drummer of Niklashausen* (Bloomington, 1992)

Zeeden, Ernst Walter, *Die Entstehung der Konfessionen. Grundlagen und Formen der Konfessionsbildung* (Munich, 1965)

Zeeden, Ernst Walter, *Katholische Überlieferungen in den lutherischen Kirchenordnungen des 16. Jahrhunderts* (Münster, 1959)

Zimmermann, G., 'Freiheit und Aberglaube in der Theologie des Genfer Reformators', *Zwingliana* 21 (1994), 59–81

Index

Note: page numbers in **bold** refer to main entries; page numbers in *italic* refer to illustrations.